S0-AHB-209

NETEZZA

TRANSFORMATION

Taming the dragon without
sorcery, alchemy or strange potions

DAVID C. BIRMINGHAM

Copyright © 2010 VMII - All rights reserved.

ISBN-13 is ISBN-13: 978-1453874059
ISBN-10: 1453874054

Safe harbor disclaimer: The authors and reviewers of this book make no claim nor guarantee as to the current or future applicability or viability of any technique or technology discussed herein.

I THANK THE MANY CLIENTS AND CUSTOMERS who have trusted me and my teams to provide large-scale data processing solutions. I have learned as much from them as they have hopefully received from us, for it is they that own the fertile soil and the enriched backdrop for the experiences that make a book like this possible.

I ALSO THANK THOSE who have encouraged me along the way, some of whom have already forgotten more than I'll ever know, and some who neither completely understand nor agree with all or part of the book's contents, and I'm okay with that. These include Kim Hall, Jody Mazolla, Dr. Craig Wood, Ben Gonzales, Chris Day, Bryan Hunter, Marguerite Birmingham, Tony Cinello, Bill Herman, Bob Luke, Neal Birmingham, John Neese, John Strong and the amazing leadership at Brightlight Consulting, including Mark Kettering, David Overcash and the entire Brightlight Leadership Council.

I ALSO ACKNOWLEDGE the many people at Netezza Corporation who have helped me (and many others) understand their technology and the vision behind it, in particular, Kim, Tim, Phil, Karina, Olga, Ray, Ralph, Rich, Martin, Mike L. Mike S. Mike M., Mike T., Paul G., Paul J., Peter, Rick, Courtney, and Jerry, who all *make it happen*.

THIS BOOK IS DEDICATED to my sweet and beautiful wife, who has helped me without measure in the production of this work. Also to my three wonderful children, who make my own life "massively parallel" with no additional effort on their part.

AND OF COURSE, to Enzees everywhere who have experienced the capabilities of the Netezza technology.

ALL SYSTEMS ARE GO FOR LAUNCH

A friend once told me that when he went back home to visit his birthplace, nothing had changed. Almost like he'd stepped through a time-portal into history. He couldn't get a signal on his phone and everyone was content with land-lines and snail mail. It was surreal.

When he chatted with his parents about his life and encounters in the Big City, they were both thrilled and alarmed. Trying to be good parents, they offered up the best advice they could muster to help him do well. But all of their ideas were stuck in the past.

Attending various conferences and podcasts, the "name brands" in data warehousing ideas and technological implementation are starting to sound a lot like this. Stuck in the past, unable to embrace the parallel-powered present, or the massively parallel-powered future. Unable to retread themselves to make their ideas more palatable to the next generation. Or is it that those ideas and approaches have themselves been supplanted by technological advance, and must now be challenged or set aside for this reason alone?

In the data warehousing landscape, ideas float around as the primary currency of the realm. Oddly, the scalable ideas and methods that fueled the "big iron" systems of "yesteryear" were set aside when the distributed processing revolution took hold. They weren't purely distributing the data onto client-server systems for set-based operations like reporting, but to increase *transactional* processing power. and to make computing more accessible to people with smaller budgets.

When the value of data warehousing and business intelligence was first realized, they had difficulty justifying their pervasive necessity or existence, much less the significant cash outlay for properly powered systems. So the idea-mongers put pen to paper and came up with clever ways to deploy warehouses on less expensive, *underpowered* systems. Whole methodologies and books, many of them best-sellers, were written to circumscribe how to deploy a warehouse on inexpensive hardware. Everyone was acutely aware of the problems of cost versus return-on-investment.

And now, the whole landscape is awash in methodologies, approaches and supporting tools and technologies that were born in the wake of the *underpowered yesterday.*

That, my friends is the chrysalis of the Enzee's *prior* existence. I technologist trapped in a shell that may one day offer the butterfly's promise to defy the gravity of their current environments, stretch new, bright, multi-colored wings and dance on the winds of change rather than being tossed about by them.

The IBM Netezza appliance has changed the game, forever transforming the data warehouse landscape. We now need those scalable methods back again. And where turnabout is fair play, all those ideas about data warehousing that were born in the more recent *underpowered yesterday*, we can feel free to challenge and even set aside.

Feel the rocket engines awaking from slumber just beneath our feet? Strap in.

CONTENTS

LAUNCH SEQUENCE 1

00:10

WELCOME BACK, and I trust your journeys have kept you well and you're ready for a another excursion. This time we'll dive a little deeper into the technology we know and love, and yes, we're gonna have some fun.

Since the first book came out in 2008, we've all been hit with a tsunami of new technical capabilities and features. Netezza rolled out the S-Blade Server version in 2009, knocking off our socks along with their competitors (and yes, I'll name names). People within our happy little ecosystem have raced to catch up or keep up and Netezza has added a wide range of new customers. Most significantly, Netezza is now an IBM company, and once again the game has changed.

Who this book is for: This work is partially technical and partially not. Some of the disconnect associated with Netezza is the belief that something so powerful must somehow also be very complex, but exactly the opposite is true. This often puzzles those who are steeped in their certifications or training in other complex database systems, because they expect an equivalent requirement of technical know-how for the Netezza platform. It's an *appliance*, and as a colleague has pointed out, we don't need to know the formula for freon in order to properly operate a refrigerator.

Like this book title suggests, the term "Transformation" has multivariant application and meaning. Transformation of our data, of the Netezza company itself, the products, how we use them, and of course, our own personal transformation. All of this change was borne on the wings of stress, and its influx has likewise created even more stress of a different kind. What kind of stress bore Netezza into these changes? Their driven nature for excellence, the competitor products nipping at their heels, the voracious demand of their users, the maturity and availability of better core technologies, and their relentless pursuit of producing the fastest machine on the planet.

Stress is a huge driver in the data warehousing community. The pressure to process data, to meet the needs of fire-breathing users, and perhaps even to keep a project moving, are all in play when our data processing machines run every night or on-demand. If we miss a processing deadline, we have more stress. If we have to upgrade the machines, stress arrives on the wings of expectation - of those paying for the upgrade and those desiring to see its effect. Stress leads decision makers to examine the marketplace and eventually purchase a machine. Once this happens, we can believe that everyone near it will be under stress to deploy it.

None of these forms of stress are particularly bad, unless of course we ignore them.

One source of stress is: What will happen to me when the smoke clears, Netezza is installed and all of our work is running in fractions of the time it used to? Won't this put people out of work? Won't I be on that list?

Uhh, not hardly. What most people don't realize is that even before the machine is installed, a backlog of functionality is already building (it cannot be implemented because their is no capacity). Don't imagine for a moment that when all that capacity opens up, there won't be opportunity to embrace even more processing, and even more activity that will fill the Netezza machine.

For an example of this kind of transformation, attend one of the Enzee Universe conferences and sit in on any of the sessions where users and principals share their adventures with leveraging the products. Sharing my personal experiences has some value, but some may sincerely object that these are simply limited windows of observation. No, it's the sweeping trend for the vast majority of the Netezza user base.

I mentioned in Underground that NASD presented their story at the '07 Enzee Universe, after my involvement in laying a foundation for this effort in '06. They went from a twenty-eight hour processing day down to less than three hours, half of which was getting data on-and-off the machine. So in net terms, twenty-eight hours was reduced to ninety minutes. This opened up so much capacity that they had the freedom to begin discussion about taking on more work. Not long after this, FINRA was born. This is not to say that Netezza was the prime mover, but face it, if the NASD group doesn't have the capacity to deal with their own data, what business do they have taking on more? The new capacity opened a window of opportunity that the prime movers could act on. FINRA now handles every stock trade in North America.

This is an example of upward-enablement of one (or more) corporations, a positive transformation borne on the wings of Netezza's applied power and the additional capacity it provides.

Does this sound like something that portends the conclusion of job opportunities by a company so-enabled? No - additional capacity means additional throughput, and that translates to additional opportunity for everyone involved.

And of course, in this book is a latent theme of space flight. It boils down to something very simple. Astronauts experience the raw power of machines with unimaginable capacity. It takes them to places few have been. Even in retirement, they join private space institutes for the opportunity to return. Perhaps not with the same power-factors, but let's face it, going into space is an irreversibly transforming experience. All the training in the world can only prepare one for embracing the voyage. But once the rockets fire, there's nothing stopping the journey.

In the data warehousing space, the countdown starts when we first experience Netezza's power. The transformation is on, and there's no turning back.

00:09

The technology we choose to implement will have a strong influence on how we conceptualize a problem. It will have an even stronger influence on the logical model and still stronger on the physical. Constrained by the weaknesses of certain technologies, our creativity is jailed inside a box. Whether we can conceptualize something loftier is immaterial. Just as gravity holds us firmly to the ground, we may conceptualize flight but will need a physical implementation that not only overcomes the effect of gravity, but like aerodynamics invokes a *different set of rules* altogether.

And of course, aerodynamics needs *power*, and lots of it.

Once that power is in our hands, will we think differently about the physical implementation, or will we remain lashed to the gravity of older thinking, weaker technology and underpowered hardware? Will we formulate stronger, more creative and effective logical constructs, or will we attempt to map them, perhaps shoe-horn them into logical constructs we're comfortable with? Likewise, can we dare to conceptualize "doing it a different way", or even "solving the same problem with a different approach". A "way" and "approach" that were never available to us in the underpowered systems. Can we mentally break free and transform our thinking?

If I have a two-slice toaster, I can support my wife and myself as a couple. But with three kids in the house, a four-slice toaster is the ticket. What if I had a *400*-slice toaster? My problem domain has now changed from the process of toasting bread to bread-*management*. How do I feed the toaster with bread and how do I deliver it once toasted? The four-slice toaster stunted our imagination. The 400-slice toaster will require our grandest creativity and forethought (if we intend to get anything out of it).

Perhaps our leaders just committed to the purchase of a Netezza machine, due to arrive any day now. We already have one (for the proof-of-concept) sitting across the hall. Everyone is impressed by its power, but this has set expectations very high. Our bosses are paying a lot of money for the machines. They've read the success stories and want to be *on that list*. Their expectation of return-on-investment might be a career changer for them. And if we don't pull it off, might be career-changer for us as well?

No pressure, right?

Stress comes in many forms, but what we want to do *right now* is embrace the incoming transformation and the additional stress following it. Netezza machines *are* change-agents. The environment around us *will* change. Resisting the change will not matter, and may even relegate us to the outer circle of influence. Failure to recognize the change will lull us into thinking the things happening around us are "just" the transient part of the "honeymoon" associated with any new purchase. Denying that the change is real, will ultimately leave us drowning in unfamiliar, open water, which is really the water covering our former existence, caused by a tsunami of change that we chose to ignore until now.

Sounds a bit ominous. Until we realize that this change-agent machine can transform *us*, and our environment, into something we not only like, but openly wonder why we ever settled for less. It is often impossible for an Enzee to characterize their current situation in terms of their prior existence, because they have long since set all that aside as something they never intend to return to. Some who leave their current Netezza environment head quickly for a Netezza-centric environment *again* because they know they cannot go back. More importantly, they *should* not go back.

Imagine leaving a small tribal village for the big city. Get involved in the high-traffic, high-technology life there, and then pay a visit back to the old town to see friends. Our wireless phones don't work, nobody understands anything about electronic communication and their latest technological advance is "running water". The difference between a "former" environment and a new, Netezza-centric environment exhibits the same disparity. Why go back to a time when our 2-minute reports ran in 2 days? Why settle for marginal analytics from an underpowered machine, when we can have globally game-changing analytics from Netezza's parallel power?

Back to conceptualization. Does the tribal villager conceptualize problems in a different way? Aren't those concepts already constrained by what they know and the power of technology available to them *where they are*? What of the butterfly (on the cover)? Does it see the world differently than it once did, and solve problems far differently in its new and wonderful, aerodynamically-*enabled* world - than its prior existence gravity-bound to the forest floor?

Just like putting our bodies into a training program is deliberately applied, controlled stress, it will make us stronger and more able. Conversely, if we don't deliberately face the stress bearing upon us even now, we become swept up in something that feels foreign. Engaging the transformation can be deliberate or passive, but transformation *is* coming.

At this point I could say, "I don't know about you, but I..." but that's not really true. I *do* know about you. I know that you wouldn't be here if it weren't important to you. I know lots of others like you too. We want to do it right and do it better. Let the others "go marginal". We'll muse about them later. Maybe.

I've met dozens of data architects and information analysts who have a common testimony – that working with the Netezza platform has changed them for the better. It has also in some ways spoiled them. After all, they would not be willing to leave their current job unless another one was waiting for them with Netezza on-deck for their data processing problem. In fact, I once switched horses, so to speak, when it was obvious that my current employer had no desire to pursue data warehousing projects, much less Netezza projects, and so it was time to find one that already did. Rather than look around for just another consulting firm, I looked for those that were working with Netezza as a focus and made a short list. Only one of those was a frontrunner, and the rest is history.

But how does it change a career inside the corporation where we currently work? Those who have already experienced the magic may have a rather sputtering explanation. They have experienced such radical change in their stature in their companies that it is difficult to initially articulate the before-and-after difference. They have been so immersed in their new existence that their former existence might be a wistful memory.

When asked, their answers are so matter-of-fact, like it should be obvious to an outsider. When the outsider hears oddities like billion-row-tables, no index structures, distributions, skew and the like, it's almost as though we're speaking different languages, certainly different wavelengths. Almost like a cult, but not quite. Call it the Cult of High Performance. The Cult of Big Data.

On second thought, don't do that. We're not a cult. Doing things right with the right equipment and right approach is a function of objectively pursuing science, and doesn't require any of us to shave our heads. If when talking to an outsider, we happen to experience this kind of dissonance, we can rest assured that our transformation is underway if not complete.

00:08

This is my chance to get a little creative, perhaps even artistic. My kids tell me I'm a great storyteller, and I take them to all kinds of imaginary places and adventures. We'll do some of that too, with a purpose, but I decided before accepting this challenge that this book would be different from the first.

Truth v4.2 - That was the tongue-in-cheek working title of all this, based on a funny conversation I had with a colleague at the 2010 Enzee Universe. He said very simply, "We now have one version of the truth, and it doesn't seem to bother anyone that our truth is under version control." With no disrespect to Bill Inmon, who coined "single version of the truth," we have to respect how people hear this and then apply it.

Ahh, well, we like to use these concepts and don't really expect anyone to take them *literally*, right? Oh, please, the simple fact is that the "truth" we promulgate to our data users is on an upward climb to maturity. It's better today than it's ever been, but we should not forget that it was worse a month ago, and worse still a year ago. Single-version-of-the-truth is a *concept*, not a literal reality. And that's my (2.0) version of the concept... Moving on....

A number of years ago we put our house on the market and the first realtor to show it gave us some simple advice. "You've been living here for ten years and have probably forgotten what originally turned you *off* about this house. If those things are still around, they will be turn-offs to the next buyer too. It looks like you've updated a number of things, but not others. If you don't update the minimum parts of the home's interior, you will limit the number of people who will want to buy it." This translated to something very significant, in that when we first built our data warehouse, we did it in a flurry of activity and smoke. We forgot about the things we tied off and sincerely *intended* to revisit. We just never did.

Now we're about to move from this environment into a Netezza machine. All those things we set aside or tied off - will rise from the mist like denizens of the ancient deep crawling from the slime to eat our flesh. And by the time we fully characterize how much of this stuff is running around in the basement, it can turn a simple migration project into a miry clay indeed.

"We're in the migration bizness, and cousin, bizness is a-boomin'," - Brad Pitt, *Inglourious Warehousing*

00:07

Okay so we'll chat (again) about migration projects because these are the bread-and-butter of new Netezza machines. I have seen only a few *new* (green field) projects, with no existing prior warehouse, launch into the future with jet propulsion. But these are not the typical reasons driving a purchase. Wish you all the best and all that, but *migration* projects are drivers in the Enzee Universe, and most of us rode the wave of a migration project to get here. As noted in Underground, some very specific and repeatable nuances await us with one of these efforts. I have specifically asked a number of colleagues to relate their war stories, scrubbed them for anonymity and will present them to the reader shortly. What we will find is that the migration itself is a form of significant stress that will strain and perhaps burst the plumbing of the existing environment, and likewise cinder-flash the temperaments of its weaker stakeholders.

Is our environment *ready* for the stress of the Big Black Box? Will it master our oceanic-scaled hydraulics? Will its installation alone begin the journey we so hoped for, or are we having to suit-up for a life-changing white-water raft ride that can make grown men cry, grown women jump from basement windows, and even cause young children to leap wildly in front of parked automobiles for no apparent reason? Coincidence? I think not.

When the machine is first under examination, the stress is already palpable. The engineers charged with propping up our current technology will, on one side, breath a sigh of relief that help is on the way. Once installed, they might be able to go home while it's still light outside. On the other side of the virtual camp, some will circle the wagons around the ensconced technology and its vendor. They will line up like birds on a wire, wearing logo'd vendor oxford shirts and matching baseball caps, and will disappear periodically as they go on job interviews. Whether they are champions for their favorite technology is about to become immaterial. Another champion is entering the arena and the tournament's outcome is strongly foreshadowed.

For they too, see that the Netezza machine, in its first round of testing, is blowing the socks off of their esteemed vendor's competitive offering. Rather than accept the stress of learning a new technology (and becoming more valuable in the marketplace) they would rather find a job doing, er, doing what they're doing *now*. Perhaps for more money, but the same job nonetheless. No matter, in the place where they are going, Netezza will darken that doorstep eventually. In point of fact, when scalability matters, there is no place to hide from such a powerful change-agent technology. And considering that this change-agent wants to make us better, stronger, faster - this is no different than our high school gym teacher hunting us down and putting us through a tendon-snapping, gluteus-busting, bone-bending workout in order to train us to be stronger.

Or we could settle for one of those *comparatively* lightweight, soda-pop workouts, like *P90X*.

So one of the first transformations we'll see is in how our current technology and user staff react or respond. Some will accept it, others will be dragged with heels-first, and others will simply cut the ropes and drift into the night. Our first mistake is in assuming that just because Netezza is in the house, *everyone* is excited about it. We're missing the evidence of a transformation already underway, and we need to be vigilant.

Truth be told, however, CEOs want *capacity*. Those who stand in their way, or settle for less, are exercising a form of disloyalty (from the senior management perspective). Ever heard of someone "not being on board"? Most of the time, those who are skeptical or even resistant will do so passively. It is wise to carefully consider one's situation before opening one's mouth. We did not hire unwise people did we? No, and so the folks that we hired will patiently wait as the transformation unfolds, will be transformed with it, and ultimately wonder why they ever resisted or doubted it in the first place. Other more foolish folk (we don't have any of those, because we don't hire foolish folk, right?) will dig in their heels to the very last drop of sanity, then update their resumes and hit the road. That's okay, because in the off-chance such foolish folk were once with us, they are no longer. And we would *rather* have those foolish folk working for our competitor, right? It's all good.

00:06

Flow-based thinking. Yes, I know it's hard. Sort of like going back to our sixth grade year to re-introduce our minds to the basics of physics. It must be done, and is a non-optional endeavor.

What does this look like? In a flow-based model, especially as it concerns punting data around inside the Netezza machine, we have to think in terms of what-happens-when. This is a non-trivial exercise. Here's an example: When we perform intake, we may need to execute a change-data-capture on the information *after* it is loaded into the machine, but *before* we do anything else with it. This after-and-before model is implicitly understood, but it gets better. What if we have to perform a de-duplication? Does this happen *before* the change-data-capture or *afterwards*? If before, our deduplication is slogging through data that it may not need to. If after, the deduplication may be superfluous since the change-data-capture already covered it. Likewise, what if some of the keys or other quantities need to be zapped or error-corrected? Or even the incoming row be taken of-fline because it's too dirty to load? Is this included in the change-data-capture? Which one happens first? What about data validation? Do we check-and-correct values like dates and integers, which could play into the change-data-capture, or do we wait until afterwards? Or not at all?

This after-and-before-and-after model can become mind-numbing in its permutations. The point is, none of this is possible without embracing the concept and implementation of *flow*. Without an objective and manageable flow model, these things can essentially happen at any time and any context. But clearly the timing and context are critical to both accuracy and the affect it has on downstream operations. And downstream *efficiency* (deduplication and change-data-capture radically reduce the volume of data, and thus the processing load of every subsequent process). In fact, when using the concepts of downstream we actually mean a subsequent operation, and upstream means a prior operation. But *upstream* and *downstream* are purely flow-based terms. Why is it that many technologists throw these terms around as if they know what they mean and how they apply, yet when inside the Netezza machine these concepts are forsaken, forgotten or just misapplied?

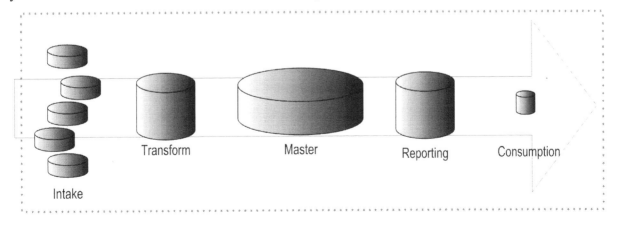

In the depiction (above) is a foreshortened version of the flow model mentioned in Under-ground. The significant conceptual takeaway here is that the databases are not endpoints, but *way-*

points. Data is on-the-move from the intake databases, through transformation into the master, ultimately transformed into the reporting database and exposed to consumers. The databases here are by no means endpoints. Yet this is how most people think of a database because of *ETL*-based thinking. For them, the database is the starting point or the end point, but not a *player* in the flow.

Netezza changes this. Through SQL-Transforms and a flow-modeled database layout, we can affect enormous functionality in fractions of time compared to any traditional approach. The databases are resting areas for data on its journey. We now have the option to keep the data moving, or as one global entity once said "Process the data as the world turns". They didn't have any options to set aside an evening for batch processing. Globalization is where many companies are moving and they need a warehouse/processing solution that will join them.

The above model has become oddly famous for its simplicity and ease-of-implementation. If we stay in the pragmatic, do-what-works zone, we will find that Netezza will meet us more than halfway. Netezza is ready to deal.

So let's deal.

00:05

For enterprise transformation, when we can show that we really have a handle on the data and the processes governing it, when we can show that the processes are borne on a scalable, maintainable substrate, when we can demonstrate the ability to embrace and respond to change – *watch* - as this capability transforms the company's decision-makers into people with vision. There's nothing worse than having a visionary in our midst who has been reduced in their effectiveness because we cannot feed their thinking engine with enough actionable data. Sort of like clipping an eagle's wings. Or a butterfly's wings. Ouch, there's a visual for ya'

"I like to think of myself as a peripheral visionary. I can see into the future, just way off to the side," - Stephen Wright, monologue.

And when the decision makers have processing power behind their decisions, things change, and often change in very big ways.

Yet another transformation happens when the proof-of-concept closes, the winners are chosen, and the champions of the defeated technology are forced to admit as much. Yeah, verily it was a valiant battle, forsooth, pass a flagon of mead and may all be well.

Ahh, but transformation-trouble's a brewin'. We may sincerely believe that this is like a high school football game, where everyone on the field and in the stands is consummately dedicated to the defeat of the opposing team. But when the final clock ticks to zero, and the score is etched in stone (or lights) for all eternity, the winners have been chosen and the losers have been designated. But the next day, everyone goes back to their lives and trains for the next battle on the gridiron. There will be one promptly at 8pm every Friday evening this Fall. We promise.

Not so with this proof-of-concept. Like a sinister movie bad guy with a long trenchcoat, ominous background music and a strange array of personal weaponry, the defeated foes will retreat into the mists to lick their wounds. But only for now. The battle is lost but the war is hardly over.

"They'll be back, and in greater number," JustWan CanShoMe, *Data Wars*

They are resisting the transformation now introduced by the mere presence of the data warehouse appliance. Forget for a moment that this is Netezza, the first name in appliance history, and imagine what's happening inside their heads. They have made a living by learning and mastering the technology we are about to replace. They may have certifications that they personally paid for, and handsomely at that. They may have written articles (or books!) on how to do this-or-that, and are now "out there" in the technological community. Changing horses is not just a difficult task, it is a real and very personal barrier that may as well be eight-hundred feet tall. While others cannot even see the wall, they are myopically mesmerized by it and cannot break their gaze.

As competitors go, I found myself in the midst of virtual duel with an employee of one of Netezza's competitors. He has his own blog site and essentially markets himself as an independent voice with the disclaimer "the views expressed by (name here) are not those of (vendor here)". Hey, anyone can disclaim it. That's so his employer won't come after him for saying something that his employer disagrees with (I know a little about how the "media disclaimer" game works, you see). But it says nothing about the quality of his *objectivity*. After all, I don't work for Netezza, I work *with* Netezza products. Just like you.

The troubling factor here is that he was hawking his employer's competitive product even in the light of glaring architectural flaws. At some point in the discussion, I finally had to call him on not having a true independent voice for his fab product. After all, if he really believes in it, he knows he can go independent and make a living using it. Unless, of course, he really *can't* make a living using it. All I asked for was *the* independent voice, the voice that had no ties or anything beholden (including a paycheck or the threat of removing same) that would taint the objectivity of the voice. Make no mistake, the independent voice is never a one-hundred-percent objective voice. There's always a reason for the voice, even if only to make a living by using the product. I have been an independent voice for a number of products, but eventually moved on when I saw that independent players could not particularly make a living using the product. People *intersecting* the product were wildly successful, but in order to make a living we need repeating intersections. For some products, this is not possible if the product's characteristics or the vendor's marketplace approach preclude this possibility.

The problem is, there are no industry success stories for *his* fab product. It's just a wannabee. Once some success stories rise, along with some independent voices, perhaps we can dialogue with *them*. Perhaps by that time, this guy will already be an independent voice. Most assuredly if he has enough crash-and-burn conversations like he had with me, his employer might actually accelerate his leap into independence. Ahh, the rush of cool, clear water. Maybe if that happened, he would turn and become a Netezza aficionado. Hey, there's plenty of room at the table. We don't deny anyone who is willing to enter and engage.

What does all this mean? *Industry* Transformation. With the acquisition of Netezza by IBM, it is clear that Netezza has made more than a splash in the marketplace. It has found a place in the solution domain and in my humble opinion, a place in the turning point of history. Whether IBM assimilates Netezza and its ecosystem, or preserves it for its unique value, is yet to be seen. Other products that IBM has purchased have not lost their marketplace identity. Enzees like the ecosystem the machine has created. Most of us would vote for its preservation if for no better reason than its uniqueness.

All that said, Netezza has transformed the industry and created an indelible mark. Even those who don't recognize Netezza as the best solution (those would be its competitors) are really no more than wannabees. With all due respect, imitation is the highest form of flattery. But one has to do more than imitate. Netezza is good because of the *architecture*. Cobbling together spare parts to simulate the same capabilities and functionalities does not an architectural synergy make. It's just another knock-off. Unlike other knock-offs, these cost as much or more than the real thing. What's up with that? Why buy the knock-off when we can have the *real* thing?

Immediate questions arise concerning scalability. How does the Netezza machine scale? All of the other database vendors suggest that the only viable means is through surgery on the patient with a transplant. Moving the entire operation from the smaller machine to the beefier one. This is often a stressful rollout. With the Netezza machine, no transplant is necessary. We only apply a simple outpatient operation, the "adaboxtomy". While we may occasionally need such operations for the Netezza machine, it's not as soon, often nor painful as the SMP-based transplants.

Industry transformation means that the whole of data warehousing is experiencing a shift in the direction toward the Netezza platform for so many facets of scalability, and those who are riding the wave today will be leaders in the industry tomorrow. Stay on the wave, baby.

00:04

The transforming architecture then has the power to transform *data* in mind-blowing proportions. What's that, not using the machine for SQL-Transforms, that is, data transformation inside the box? Oh for shame. That's not only a waste of perfectly good processing cycles, it's a missed opportunity altogether. A big part of the coming discussion will be on in-the-box transformations. How to build them harness them, deploy them, measure them - hey - we're not talking about tossing a SQL statement or two into the machine. But blasting instructions so hard and fast that it makes the machine's temperature rise a notch. We're not interested in boiling the ocean, but boiling our analyst's brainwaves - now *that's* a trick.

The hot buzz at both the 2010 and 2011 Netezza conferences was "ELT" (SQL-based transformation) in all its shapes and forms, and I must have been stopped to discuss this topic at least once an hour over the times I spent there. Everyone wants to know how to do it, but more importantly, they want to know what to avoid, how to sidestep the obvious stuff that is not-so-obvious, and generally how to do things in a way that cherishes a technologist's most hallowed principle, that of pattern-based reuse. Oh, we'll get to patterns, set and a few other meaty subjects, but transform the data, we can and we will.

Another subject area hides in the shadows of this discussion, and that is the desire for metadata capture of the transforms and their context. It seems the ETL tools have mastered the ability to per-form data lineage within their own structured-flow domains, but the SQL statement is still the out-cast. Always abbreviated, ever accommodated, but when attempting to capture for lineage, largely obviated. Some tools attempt to bridge the SQL statement into the metadata of the ETL tool. As we will see, ANSI SQL gives us infinite cosmic power over the data, so our SQL-transforms should never suffer under some artificial constraint requiring us to do it just-one-way so we can capture the ever-elusive metadata context. No, the database has the power to tell us what we need to know, so we should let it do so.

However, I am not so naive to suggest that metadata-lineage is an easy or even *desirable* func-tionality. The vast majority of people who want the data lineage, search high and low to get a tool that will perform it, then install it and see what kind of a daunting human exercise it is to main-tain said lineage model. They opt instead for something a bit more abbreviated. What they want, is what *works*. We can do that. So let's say we burst a few hundred transforms into the machine. What were the source tables, and the source-target columns? Can we apply a common source-to-target map, and if so, can we manage it once applied? Can we control the transforms in sequence, or even in branched-sequence, so that we can wrap as quickly as possible, burning the machine at high temperature? I mean, this is what we want, right, that the hardware is, as we say in Texas, a horse that is"rode hard and put away wet" - except maybe without the wet part. That could be messy. Chaining SQL transforms together in a flow operation, is a trick that the ETL tools have yet to embrace, because to the ETL tool, the SQL statement belongs elsewhere.

What of the other functionality we'll need in the flow? How about gateways, that serve as traf-fic cops and sync points, or the ability to define and leverage custom precalculated table content. How about cross-database replication, even across machines? Not of the entire database, but the surgical part we just changed?

Lots to think about that have very little to do with formulating a transform. So let's do this. Let's make the controlling processes the centerpiece and the transform along for the ride? How about setting up a templated rule format from which the insert, select and from-clauses are all outputs, as *artifacts* of the template, rather than hand-crafting each SQL statement, feeding it table scraps and tucking it into bed each night? Ah yes, now we're getting somewhere. A Netezza ma-chine only needs a SQL statement. We need something more.

00:03

When the machine arrives, hopes are high, and stress could not be higher. The people who just signed a check for the technology may have done so muttering epithets about the IT people. The people overseeing the installation and the first project on the machine, feel the pressure to produce. The folks about to receive the machine on the raised floor will install it with no fanfare, blissfully unaware of how it is about to utterly transform how they do things. From backup-and-restore to administrative maintenance, the sizes and speeds the machine will support will compel them to start each sentence with a common prefix. "What *the* ?"

But is the environment *really* ready to receive the machine? Is the environment ready to receive the work products about to come flying off the machine in one bashing wave after another? Are the people ready to *test* it? Is everyone prepared to drink from a fire hose both in knowledge transfer and in the Hawaii-Five-O-sized tidal wave of data and features that are about to arrive in all their unchecked and high-pressure glory?

Methinks not. Oh no, not by a long shot.

But it need not sound like, nor actually become, an unhealthy ride. Success is in our headlights and the future is lookin' good. Unless of course the basics are ignored and the assumptions with which the machine were built are foolishly set aside for another set of assumptions that the machine will utterly crush and pulverize into dust. Enter the fray with assumptions aligning with its horsepower and architecture, and we'll be one of those surfin' dudes riding the waves in slow-motion on cool Step-Into-Liquid-class surfing videos that the vendor shows at the Enzee Universe conferences. Likewise, enter the fray with the assumption borne on what we know, or think we know about data warehousing 101. That an SMP-based competitor can do just as well as Netezza.

And we would be mistaken.

As we look around the landscape of our environment, do we now see the things that are in the way of our success? Like the realtor told us, we've lived in the house so long we've chosen to accommodate its weaknesses and shortcomings, and have even built whole human-process infra-structures around guarding us and our end users from the fallout of underpowered or inadequate technologies. Few of those processes and procedures will serve us now. They are artificial props that the Netezza machine is about to turn a high-pressure hose against. Woe unto those artifacts that cannot withstand the pressure.

In short, the weaknesses of our environment that we have long since forgotten, are about to be stressed in unforeseen ways, eliciting unexpected and even unprofessional actions from the participants. But the benefit is that we will look forward to fewer sleepless nights. And we cannot really do anything about the unprofessional reactions. Netezza is like the drug that does not change a personality, but brings the real ones to the fore. If we don't learn anything from this exercise, we may definitely learn more about our coworkers and bosses than we ever wanted to know.

00:02

One of the questions that pervaded the 2009 and 2010 Enzee Universe conferences, was "how do we train newbies on the technology?" This resonated with many experienced Enzees because they understand that getting acclimated to how we solve problems in the machine requires something of a shift in thinking. I mentioned it briefly in Underground but it was a real hot-button in those conferences.

So transformation in this regard, applies directly to how we shepherd the minds of those new to Netezza, and those who want to know more about it. Or for that matter, those who know a lot but want to train others. Transformation of the *mind*, not of the data. Before the reader imagines that I'm starting a cult of some kind, get real. It is a recognized factor in technology development

(*Peopleware*, Demarco and Lister) that those first introduced to a technology take some time in becoming productive with it. Like any other technology, we have to roll up our sleeves and get our hands dirty. I will, however mention that we don't have to repeat the work of many who have come before us. Like any good scientific model, scalability-science, or perhaps information-scalability-science has working examples among the ranks who have proven the solutions. Trust their judgment. They know of whence they speak.

When attempting to grasp what the new future will look like, we may feel daunted by what we don't know. What we *do* know might be a liability, so it's important to take things systematically even if we cannot take them slowly. After all, our decision-makers have spent a pretty penny on this new platform and want to see turnaround "right quick" (a little Southern lingo there). But if we deliver quickly and sacrifice the Important for the Expedient, we really haven't done ourselves any favors. Applying a successful approach means we can tackle things with higher confidence without sacrificing time-to-delivery. Forsake the approach and it can get bumpy, nebulous and hard to explain. Simplicity is on our side now. As I have noted before, I am not a high-methodology person. But I've been at this long enough to know that hard problems (like large scale data) require a deliberate approach.

What happens if we *don't* embrace a deliberate approach? Haven't people been successful with Netezza just flying by the seat of their pants? Oh sure, *eventually* they achieve success. Our team would have to be seriously debilitated with nitrogen narcolepsy, drug abuse, potion-based enchantments or other mind-altering effects to utterly avoid success with a Netezza machine. Even the worst team with the worst approach will *eventually* achieve success. It's this "eventually" factor that bothers the folks at the top. Anyone can get there *eventually*. Success, or something close to it, is what they want *sooner* than later. They don't want their folks slogging through the swamps of known bad approaches or pitfalls.

The typical technologist approaches the Netezza machine with a bag of presuppositions. These will drive the initial form of the approach, for good or bad. The machine's power can always dig us out of a ditch, but it's a bit disconcerting to start out in the ditch or to keep driving into a ditch just because we're not privy to knowledge that will keep us on the road. Some are simple while some will have profound impact.

As a tactical example, I often have discussion on when to use BIGINT for a variable type. I am a big proponent of using integer types for join keys because they are so much more powerful than character types (100 times more, on any platform we choose). So if we can convert a varchar to an integer, this is a good thing. The SQL Toolkit gives us this capability with the hashN() functions, but here is where the doubts arise. Should I use a four-byte hash for the smaller tables to save space, or should I use the same 8-byte hash for all tables? The same question arises for sequence generators. Should we use smaller ones for smaller tables, and so forth.

But when we think about it, using BIGINT for all of them is portable and reduces or eliminates the likelihood of accidentally applying the wrong sequencer or hash algorithm. But another element, the saving-of-disk-space is a consideration. (Using smaller integers on smaller tables). But wait, we're saving space only on the *smaller* tables? But what if these smaller tables, over time or by chance, become much larger? The point here is: there's no value in saving some minor amount of disk space on *smaller* tables when we're trading off current portability and future scalability. Another factoid is in play here, that the Netezza machine allocates a minimum amount of space for each table anyhow, so those few bytes we thought we were saving aren't even available to us.

Important factors in a decision like this: The scalability of the table, the minimum space required for smaller tables, the compression factor for all tables and especially the BIGINT type, all make these kinds of decisions even more complicated (on any other platform). Then we introduce the notion that the key has to play on the larger tables, those tens-of-billion-rows tables, and now the picture is clearer. It's not about the smaller tables at all, is it?

So do we keep the BIGINT type for all, preserve portability and scalability, and clear our minds of any space-saving issues on the other end of the scale? Or do we carefully consider this decision? In times past, the only way to change a column type on a table was to rebuild the table. Now with 6.0, we can through several simple steps change a column type. So even if we choose BIGINT now, we're not stuck forever. BIGINT will get us *migrated* faster, so that's the ticket.

What's that, I just made a blanket, universally-applicable assertion based on the *consistency of the machine's architecture*? Uhh, get used to it. This is an example of how easy it is to navigate inside a machine that is covering-the-obvious and harnessing-the-complex so that we can get down to the business of solving functional issues. It's also doing something else: blowing away the chaff and cutting through the analysis-paralysis that besets such large-scale projects. Again, setting up a BIGINT isn't hard to do and we always have the option of moving the opposite direction. But if we really want portability and scalability, and there's no value in preserving this elusive, infinitesimally small, compressed-into-nonexistence and perhaps even unavailable disk space - good grief, why bother ourselves?

Another aspect is distribution, where we join larger tables to smaller ones, and we want the smaller tables (if they are not distributed on the same key as the larger) to broadcast into the larger table, not the other way around. But if the query is complex or the statistics are stale, we can sometimes see the larger table being broadcast into the smaller. The simplest way to avoid this is to use no distribution at all (random) on the smaller tables. The optimizer will make the easy choice to broadcast. The better outcome is that on Netezza, this table content is cached in memory for subsequent queries. But it's counter-intuitive to deliberately declare smaller tables as random right? Aren't *all* tables supposed to be distributed on *something*? Nope. And there we have yet another universally-applicable decision we can make based on the *consistency* of the machine.

The pitfalls, or the swerve-into-the-ditch factors are also predictable and knowable:

- Forsaking transactional thinking – this would be record-at-a-time thinking or even column-at-a-time thinking. We no longer have the luxury of thinking about a billion rows in terms of row-at-a-time.
- Embracing set-based thinking – that is approaching a problem from the set-only, as if this is the primary form of existence for a body of data. For example, if we make a given table the center-of-gravity for data, and swirl all of our activity around it, we miss an important opportunity to manage the data in other forms. Data sets are the final form of data for consumption, but they can take on many forms of existence prior to arrival.
- Embracing flow-based thinking – the approach that is the right balance between achieving

transactional-styled results using set-based operations. Seeing information moving along a continuum of *processing*, not just data-in-a-table.

00:01

Lastly, something I have been touching on through the prior countdown as I discussed the other subjects: Personal transformation is underway. Forget the fact that our bosses are breathing sighs of relief that a power-technology is about to fulfill their wish list and then some. Get on board with the idea that you, yes *you* have the power in your hands to be the one, the *one* that makes those wishes come true. Make no mistake about it, the Netezza machine is a game-changer and a change-agent, but it has a transforming effect on us, turning us into problem solvers that in number, are an unstoppable force. And individually, can make us an invaluable player in the eyes of those who count the most - decision-makers.

While some may not initially embrace the new machine with the intent of a personal paradigm shift, it happens a lot. It's usually not the epiphany-styled transformation, either. It takes the path of a continuum, such that we start out with slinging some SQL, then we move toward rapid productivity, then pushing mind-numbing amounts of data, then rise above it completely to build out control-based metadata, and upward we climb into the stratosphere, drawing energy from the machine to fuel ideas, solutions and applications. Think about it: innovation and creativity thrive with raw physical power. The lack of power is a form of mental slavery. People don't develop a creative edge in weakness, but in *strength*.

This realization arrives somewhere along the continuum. Either the machine allows us to do what we're already doing better, or it offers us something we never had before, the confidence to use the simplicity of raw power to solve hard problems. This is the difference between raw power and engineering. We only engineer because we require efficiency with what little power we have. But if the power is relatively unlimited, engineering takes an entirely different form.

So as one or more of the nay-saying technologists around us huff-and-puff, collect their desktop gear into a box and head for the elevator, we should do something for them as well. Hold the door and push the *down* button. It's where they're headed, and we should let them.

00:00

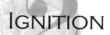

IGNITION

PROOF-OF-CONCEPT PROJECTS are delicate matters with the vendors. They know that a sale, perhaps a big one, hangs in the balance based on how well their product does in the so-called vendor derby on our site. The last thing they want to hear or see, is to be invited to the meeting where the chosen *consultant* firm will roll out *their* proof of concept results. This is a different matter if the vendor has chosen and commissioned the consulting firm, because they know the firm isn't going to show them in a bad light. For "independently minded" firms however, the vendor will work diligently to dismantle and discredit the consulting firm's results, sometime even if it is in their favor. Now why would they do that?

A colleague tells the tale of a proof-of-concept where all of the vendors showed up to display their wares, and were so utterly and summarily blown into-the-weeds by Netezza's performance, my colleague wondered why the competitors even showed up at all. "Didn't they know what they were up against? It made them look like a bunch of posers. Like a tournament of posers."

Tournament of Posers

If a potential sale (or license extension) hangs in the balance, the product competitors want to have their *own* product engineers overseeing the proof of concept so that they know the product is being shown in the best light. It's their baby, and they want it to shine. So don't be surprised if folks like me *strongly* suggest that the vendor be involved, especially on the application-development issues. It's very awkward for folks like us to render our honest assessment of "what we saw" when our observations could derail the sale of their product. The vendor would have liked to have been alongside us to help us if we hit a snag. After all, our conclusions will mean revenue, or lack thereof, for *them*. They have a vested interest in their product's success.

How does this transform the process at hand? Most folks want to oversee the POC, or have "their people" shepherd the POC specifically because they think the vendor is biased. Well, of *course* they're biased. But the danger here is that "their people" might not be as adept with the product as the vendor's product engineers. This is bad for the client and bad for the vendor. In such conditions, the client doesn't get to see all of the product's features (they see only the features their people are comfortable with). Even if these folks stumble into success like a drunken sailor, this still doesn't instill confidence into the onlookers. Also, the vendor does not get a chance to specifically answer questions that may represent go/no-go decision points.

If a client really wants objectivity, the client should focus on a particularly hard problem to solve. This way, the vendor is not given a kool-aid rendition of the problem and has to make their product step up to a much higher challenge. The eighty-twenty rule is in play here, where easy problems reign in the eighty-percent zone and hard problems dominate the twenty-percent. *Anyone* can be a hero in the eighty-percent zone. The atmosphere is thin in the twenty-percent zone. They are either equipped to deal, or not.

Case Study Short: A colleague relates that he laid out a contract that specifically called out the vendor's *required* involvement in application development on the POC, and specifically excluded his firms's *active* participation in the development process. No sooner was there ink on the page, than the client *insisted* that they had not understood this part of the contract, or why it was necessary, and then required his team to perform development activities with the product as part of the assessment.

When the smoke cleared and the assessment was completed, his firm reported their finding to the shock and alarm of both the client and the vendor. The client had thought that the product was so good that it would be a shoe-in, no-brainer kind of exercise. They had assured the vendor of this, even though the vendor had offered up resources to assist in the assessment and a strong objection to the evaluation approach. "No, they would have to remain at an arm's length," said the client, "for the sake of *objectivity*." When my colleague's firm rolled out the assessment, they had nothing but scathing comments about the product, and no way, no how would they ever recommend it to anyone they wanted to do business with. It was unstable, weak, hard to work with and the vendor support simply stank.

He told me that this was met with a long, awkward silence until the vendor finally said, "You are not qualified nor trained in the product, so how could you *possibly* speak with any kind of authority on this issue?" This reduced to a melee of spitting epithets between the client and the vendor, and here my friend was caught in the crosshairs of both. Just for being honest, right? No, just for being *sandbagged* by the client, and shanghai-style conscripted into doing the development work when they had already predicted this outcome, and had put it into the contract, but the client changed the rules.

What was the outcome? The client had to repeat the proof-of-concept with the vendor anyhow. This time they had to perform a bake-off between their favorite product and two other enterprise products, both of which outshined their favorite product and made it look even worse. This is the essence of where the marketplace is. None of them care what the client thinks on their own objectivity. If their thinking processes about product evaluation are already flawed, the outcome may as well be gibberish.

In the above case, my colleague had briefed them on what to expect, but had not briefed them on *why* to expect it. Even with verbal disclaimers strongly suggesting that this product was overrated and under-powered, the client seemed to have rose-colored glasses on, faithful that the *mere implementation* of the product would allay all doubts and set aside all fears. When in fact the opposite was true. It only fortified and solidified the claim that the product was not ready for prime-time and should be dismissed as a candidate entirely.

The client's naive approach to objective assessment failed to recognize that nobody is *truly* objective. That's a myth borne on the hope that folks will not be underhanded even if their job depends on it. It is not a consultant's role to execute evaluations of the products (that's the vendor's job), but to shepherd the evaluations as they are executed by the vendors. If the parameters of the test are sufficiently challenging, the vendor will have to meet the challenge or be excluded from the running. As with any tournament, we have judges (the client) the athletes (the various vendors and their products) and the referees (the consultant, if necessary). Referees simply make sure that the *process* is executed in a measurable way. I have written whole books (seriously) on the need to harness the development process because of the lack of objectivity of developers. After all, if developers were objective, they would all agree on the same rules. That this is a problem, means that developers are subjective in their work. If developers were objective, we would not need testers. It is the testers who enforce a common standard of quality, even if the developer has to be dragged to the table to discuss it.

"Why do we need the testers? They're just slowing us down," *a serious and sober sentiment from an older and* **very** *experienced development tech lead, who openly wanted all the testers working for him, so he could convert them to developers and fire those who did not want to cross over.*

In a proof-of-concept scenario, the best and most effective approach is to *assume the lack of objectivity* of all the players. This keeps any one player from being able to falsely claim high ground. Nobody showing up at the vendor tournament is going to say that the other products are better than their own. If they really believed that, then they are lying to us by trying to sell us a product they don't believe in. How's *that* for a reversal of logic?

So it's just naive to look over the landscape and presume objectivity. I offer this warning from an obviously non-objective platform (this book is hardly "objective" as it has an affinity toward one product). However, as an independent voice I can always walk away from the Netezza platform if another, better machine arrives on the scene (I can't *imagine*). I can do that without quitting my current employer or extraordinary personal sacrifice. Employees of the vendor (that is, *any* vendor) do not have the same independence. Later I'll share a humorous exchange with a vendor rep, which I heard through the grapevine had been watched and received with cheers in offices near Marlborough. I don't particularly mind throwing down on a vendor. It's their product. They *should* defend it. And not take it personally if I reject or challenge their defense.

Of technologies on the grill, so to speak, we have the Exadata platform, because two separate papers have been written on it, one from Netezza and one from Teradata. But we expect them to poo-poo their own competitors, right? Well, Exadata/Oracle can likewise poo-poo these assessments, but there's a simple truth here that bears review:

If someone openly lies about a product, the vendor can survive this over time, because their installed user base knows it's a lie. I spent several years on staff with Ab Initio Software Corp in Lexington, and I cannot count how many times we heard rumors and outright lies about the technology. In fact, I sat on the sidelines of a panel discussion watching one of the panelists self-immolate as he started repeating this "gossip" in the presence of those who knew better. Yes, the audience shouted him into silence. So a vendor *can* survive a lie.

But a vendor cannot survive the *truth*. And this is the most significant aspect of reviewing a vendor's wares. They can spin an assessment of their stuff, but if there's truth to it, this alerts the more savvy technologists who know how to directly verify it. Without refutation, the truth sticks on their lapel like an alligator-sized loogie. (Okay, that's a little gross, but it got your attention!)

This is why the Teradata and Netezza assessments have value, because the truth sticks, and no amount of spin can shake it off. I've watched vendor reps and other supporters spin themselves into a cinder trying to dispel the objections to Exadata's inherent weaknesses. And then one has to wonder, why does it matter so much to an independent voice like me? I don't have any affinity for Exadata and would not recommend it over Netezza or Teradata precisely because of its wannabee architecture. It would have to fully do an about face in its architectural philosophy in order to take my feet off the desk, so to speak.

The Exadata Platform

Some months ago on the LinkedIn boards, a conversation started about the Exadata machine. In one corner was an Oracle employee and in the other corner were defenders of a recent white paper promulgated by Netezza on the differences between the two technologies. Teradata has since come out with its own white paper and both of them are in harmony about one conclusion:

Exadata is a *poser*.

Dare I tread lightly here, in order not to offend someone or be more diplomatic? Another person on the LinkedIn boards asked me to do just that - try to be more diplomatic in the words I use about an inferior product. Well, it seems that any time I see a review of a movie, automobile or even a stock, there is no end to the people who will provide bare-knuckled commentary. So while this isn't exactly a fistfight, it is a competition.

This is large scale data warehousing. People migrated away from Oracle to Netezza for a reason: Oracle could not scale. This became a patently obvious marketplace truth that Oracle could not shake for love or money. Netezza was born in the wake of a frustrated marketplace that was tired of being held hostage by marginal technology.

Oracle RAC is "secondhand": At the 2007 Netezza conference in Boston, a representative of Business Objects said that they were officially recognizing that appliances were here to stay and had made a significant mark. As part of this, they were willing to promulgate a list of what they considered "secondhand" technologies. That is, technologies that had supported the warehousing industry for many years but were now considered placeholders in history, perhaps stepping stones to something larger. The first name on the screen was Oracle, eliciting a standing ovation from the crowd (most of them had migrated from an Oracle machine). He also noted that the leaders of Oracle had officially recognized the presence of appliances and that Oracle needed to have a response to it. This was the beginnings of the push for Exadata.

Now if I may be so bold as to make a simple observation here: Oracle itself was a core ingredient of data warehousing, particularly large data marts, for many, many years. It was (and is) a pervasive force in the industry. Relegating it to "secondhand" had to hurt. But think about what this means:

Oracle has more exposure to more warehouses than any other vendor.

Case Study Short: About ten years ago I helped roll out a system that included Oracle reporting and Oracle financials. By the time we were done, all of us had the same opinion: Oracle makes a great OLTP database, but all their other satellite products *bite*. And that's the most professional assessment we could offer at the time. This has been a running theme with the company's non-RDBMS offerings, almost as though they want to have marginal products in areas where they don't belong, and other, seasoned products were already established and doing very well. Could Exadata be "just another" of these satellite products?

Case Study Short: Many years ago a businessman in Orlando found himself a place among the leaders in the laser industry. As a physicist and a savvy business owner, he parlayed his knowledge of lasers and their applications into a multi-million dollar concern. He hammered into his sales people and product engineers: Examine how people are using the product, and more importantly, how they *wish* they could use the product. This second part is our growth industry. And so they grew, ever larger and more formidable but still by any estimation, a small company. Even the large laser manufacturers could not keep up with their agility and business acumen.

The point is, the owner drilled into his workforce the need to capture how people used their products, or how they wanted to use their products, and so spent significant resources improving their products toward the users' needs.

While that guy was founding his laser firm, Bill Gates was setting up a modest operation in Redmond with the same basic philosophy for product improvement. Their original offering of the Microsoft Foundation Class crashed and burned because it looked good to their technologists but had no real-world applicability. Embracing rapid, marketplace-facing maturation gave birth to the object-oriented, reusable nature of their products, and in the final analysis, gave birth to the CLR, .NET and the congealing of their many languages into a common substrate. The ongoing strategy: they would build things in a way that captured their own technical knowledge into the core. But for user-facing functionality, give them what they want, and more importantly, also build it into the core of the product line.

Oracle must have missed that memo.

Imagine, with the wide array of warehouses, marts and analytic databases, Oracle had a bursting cornucopia of information about what works - and what doesn't - in data warehousing. Could such knowledge be used to make their particular, target-marketed Exadata offering more capable or successful? Well, it *could* have, had it been actually applied. Or perhaps it wasn't applied because it wasn't available? We *assumed* that Oracle had all this time been keeping copious notes on their data warehouse encounters, congealing their (perhaps centuries worth of) collective warehousing exposure into a formidable offering.

What if the opposite were true? What if Oracle had not been keeping any notes at all, and had been treating each exposure of their product to data warehousing *as a necessary evil?* We know of one product in the marketplace that could not stand the fact that many people used it in manner outside of its original design. They spent millions of dollars trying to keep people from using-the-product-wrong before they finally got smart and started supporting and even marketing the product toward that user base. Oracle never seemed to embrace this philosophy until they *had to.*

In fact, just looking at the way the Exadata solution is constructed, and its operating philosophy, tells us that if Oracle has any data warehouse knowledge, it wasn't used, and if they have any data warehouse experts, they weren't consulted either. The end result is predictable, yet another marginal satellite Oracle offering, firmly ensconcing its OLTP engine, and now the Exadata machine, into the "secondhand technology" position for the foreseeable future.

Why am I so down on this technology here? I am disappointed more than anything else. Oracle had the opportunity to take the time and do it right. Many of us spent significant sweat equity in making their product successful for data warehousing, in many cases against-all-odds. We really thought they were listening to us, improving the product based on real-world feedback. How demoralizing must it be to fully realize that in all those help-desk sessions and punitive telephone interactions that they were really just trying to provide a spot-solution to *get us off the phone? All of us.* How were we to know that they had no intention of doing it right because they had no intention of *doing it at all?* Warehousing seems now to have been a latent *artifact* of the core product's capability.

The 2007 announcement that Oracle was "getting into an appliance mindset" was just another product division for them, something that would be a spin-off of their existing offerings but not an independent, focused effort to embrace and face a problem domain with gusto.

Just bust-o.

Anecdote: I travel, so I keep a lot of frequent-flyer program cards handy. Occasionally I found myself "stuck" in an upscale hotel. For any of you who don't know, most of these hotels are on a common frequent-stay program. Only once-or-twice-a-year did I get the chance to stay at one (not at my expense), but would whip out my member card each time because I knew, over time, I would earn some free nights. I earn them with other hotel chains and these are perfect for freebie anniversary getaways with my wife. One day I checked into a property, offered the card and the clerk told me that the card was no longer valid. In fact, the membership number was not found *at all.* He sheepishly offered me another sign-up card, but I went to the room in a funk. I found the logon credentials for the account and attempted to log on, but the system had never heard of me. I called the support line but they could offer nothing but consolation. All those nights and *all that time* had evaporated into nothing. And since I had turned in all of the hotel receipts over the course of years, the opportunity to attempt claiming those nights' stays from the receipts had long since expired. Now whenever I stay at one of those properties, they offer to sign me up with a new card and a new account. I decline. I still get offers from them. Into the trash can they go.

This is the same way a lot of data warehouse folks feel about the Exadata machine. *You mean all those conversations we had, all those interactions and all that time we spent, evaporated into nothing?* It feels a lot like betrayal, but there's a more professional concept for it:

Oracle doesn't *get* it. They weren't listening to the data warehouse arm of their customer base because they don't really believe it's the core implementation of their product line. The Exadata offering is tangible proof of it. I still get into deep conversations with Oracle colleagues who want *me* to understand where *they* are coming from. They want *me* to stop talking about the things the product doesn't do. I want *them* to fix the product so that we can actually *do* data warehousing with it. The conversation usually devolves into OLTP mumbo-jumbo. It's the only language they truly understand. They are clearly out of touch, and little can remediate this.

And this is the embarrassing part. If a contender chose to show up for a fight with Larry Holmes or Mike Tyson, and had not prepared themselves for fighting at this level, we would expect the champs to "knock 'em intuh tumorrah" as Mick would say to Rocky. Or for that matter, when one shows up to compete, one must be *ready* to compete. Showing up with a lack of readiness, or as some would say "phoning it in", means Exadata has not taken the competition seriously.

That said, when Oracle wants folks like me, and all the others who have migrated from their products into Netezza, to take them seriously, they first need to take our problem domain seriously. Right now, what we see is a level of naivete that's just downright shameful. Coming up are just a few of the issues that keep Exadata from being a power player. I would offer up all of the issues, but good grief, Oracle has virtually owned a huge market share of data warehousing for over a decade, and when they offer their own appliance *as though it is the fulcrum and focus* of all this knowledge base and experience rolled into an appliance, *and yet it is not*, this is more than just anticlimactic. We almost feel sorry for them. Almost.

A colleague relates: Exadata came knocking and we listened politely and sent them away. They kept calling, using relationship terms to describe their sales to us. We were only interested in product features. David, a number of years ago we had a group in-house that had control of every aspect of our technology. But something changed when we reached a certain level of data processing in both complexity and size that they could not resolve. We were patient with them, but eventually our struggles with them were so argumentative that we were just exasperated. We replaced them with some power-hitters and have been very happy since then. Now they come back on occasion, showing us resumes of power-hitter people they would like to deploy for us. They all look strong, but then we recall that when the going got tough, they chose to argue with us rather than find the right people. I see Oracle behaving the same way. Once we moved away from their technology, now they are back with Exadata, but we recall all of the struggles we originally had with Oracle and their generally dismissive attitude of coaching us on how to *live with it. It's a tradeoff* they kept telling us. *Some things you have to live with*. But we don't have to live with those things anymore, and it seems that Exadata didn't try to fix those things we hated most. Instead they seemed more interested in preserving their own software investment rather than embracing the large-scale nature of the problems.

Okay, so I know a few folks in the various echelons of Oracle and have interacted with them on occasion to pick their brains or just have a conversation. They know what I think of Exadata, and while their statements are guarded (they don't want to be quoted) they are also *hopeful*. Exadata isn't throwing in the towel any time soon, according to them. It's a long-haul gig. This bodes well for the *appliance*. Once again we have recognized evidence that the appliance approach is transforming the industry. Oracle won't give up on Exadata. I am interested in the outcome, and at the end of the chapter, I'll make a proposal of what Exadata needs to do to fix the product's shortcomings. I have no near-term expectation of their resolution.

But my colleague's comments struck a chord with me. The Exadata is about *preservation*, not competition. If we regard the machine in this light, things start to become very clear.

So out on the LinkedIn boards this conversation about Exadata heated up. Someone sent me an email to let me know that these folks were going toe-to-toe, and maybe I would want part of the action? Well, I didn't really have any reason to fight about it, but when I read some of the entries, posts and responses, I was appalled at the naivete and oversimplification of these very complex matters. One post after another not only missed the whole point of an appliance, but missed the whole point of data warehousing. I started responding and this elicited heat from some of the other posters.

Now, I've worked for product companies and was part owner of one not too long ago. Product companies have some rules around who talks about their products and when. As you may know, when I worked for Ab Initio some years ago, their word-of-mouth marketing model was something they protected (and still do) with the zeal of the Secret Service. They carefully controlled all words spoken about the product. Likewise with those companies that have a formal marketing arm. They spend millions, even billions of dollars over time to carefully shape the message of the product, what it can do, where it fits, all that stuff.

Does Netezza compensate me for anything? Of course not. Will IBM? I expect no more, because I really like having an independent voice. This book and Underground are published at my own expense and their revenues hardly line my pockets.

So why do I like talking about the Netezza product? It's not so much the product as the community it has created. After all, the Big Black Box cannot sit across from me at Starbucks and share its tales of derring-do. Only Enzees can do that.

"The people and product create a synergy that's like electric current. I love participating in this community and interacting with it..." - the author, upon acceptance of the Enzee Community Voice Award (Social Media Maven) at the Enzee Universe, June 2010.

And for this, the Enzee Community, we have a minimum threshold. Sort of like drawing a line in the sand where we say - if you want to play in Big Data, here's the minimum entry requirements. And by the way Oracle, most of us migrated from you, so we'll pay very careful attention to any claims you make about competing over here. Expect a slightly higher level of scrutiny, because when it comes to Big Data, you have a track record of "secondhand" and "marginality" we are already trying to escape. We really, *really* like it here and are committed to keeping it real.

Nobody gets a free pass in Big Data. The sizes and complexities are so massive that any chink in the armor represents such egregious risk that even approaching it has to be a carefully guarded activity. Some later discussions showcase the necessary rigor when larger, overarching stakes are high.

Exadata treats this aspect rather casually, almost dropping off a basket at the front door, ringing the doorbell and then running to hide in the bushes to see what happens when the door opens. So let's start from the failed philosophical framework, the well from which the product's ills seems to spring.

Oracle is a software company and its engineers and architects (apparently) think like software people should - to wit: that all power and might is found in software. Hardware supports the software, but the software contains the power and scalability. This is easily debunked on the surface, because we would not expect Oracle on a laptop to have the same processing power as Oracle in a 32-way SMP machine. Clearly hardware plays a role, but in the Oracle paradigm, it's not a lead role, just a supporting actor role.

How does this affect us? Data must be drawn from the disk drives and into the machine's memory where software can act on it. Only here can we apply filters, joins and the like, and all of them will be applied in *software*. We'll get some lift if we engineer our data model to take advantage of certain hardware benefits, like using integer join keys. But we'll get the same thing in other technologies so this isn't particular to Oracle. It's just a good approach to using it. If we need search power, we must draw on index structures, themselves entirely constructed and managed in memory, with software.

Now don't get me wrong, as an application programmer and OS engineer (yes, I've done software engineering at every imaginable level, including embedded systems on UVROM), I know that good programming practices lead to efficiency in *software* execution. But how do we measure such efficiencies? *Against how it uses the hardware.* But if the hardware itself is the wrong platform for scalability (an SMP machine), what hope does software have to remediate this? None.

Case Study Short: Many years ago I built an expert system for Value Health Sciences that used an in-memory database for all of its medical-code lookups. One evening we ran a batch of data against it and it ran unacceptably slow, in fact ten times slower than anything we had ever encountered. Doing some forensics, we discovered that the pain point was a mere handful of patients, but those patients had some interesting data anomalies that were exposing a latent inefficiency in the software. By fixing this inefficiency, all of the claims processing benefitted, but these particular claims sailed through as well.

As part of this investigation, we also profiled some of the lower level functions, namely the routines for performing a next/previous/first operation on the many in-memory lists. Since this software ran on a mainframe, we had to be cognizant of how the mainframe handled these kinds of programs. In that day, mainframes and object-oriented models did not get along, owing to the significant processing overhead of invoking a subroutine (one of the reasons why COBOL programs appeared so flat and lacking in deeply nested subroutines). These particular list-browsing routines were getting called *over a million times* for each patient (thank goodness for software profilers, in this case one from none other than IBM). On mainframes of course, for these little one-shot routines, we have the option of converting them to macros. This means they are compiled in-line and not called as a subroutine. They also have a propensity to bloat software size, but we noted that in our case the additional size was barely two percent. However, once we ran the program, we saw a *sixty percent boost* in speed. Patient claims that once ran in a minute now ran in twenty seconds or less. All owing to the efficiency of the *software*.

It is stories like these that give software types a false sense of security and perhaps even a heroic perspective on their own jobs. Keep in mind what we are talking about: If the program is already running in its *most* efficient form, heroic measures won't mean anything. At some point, tuning exercises become futile.

I offered an example of such an exercise in Underground, where the principals thought that a giant .NET engine could save the day, when what they really needed to do was toss the .NET and put all of the data "under air" - that is, .NET is not the domain to tackle set-based integration of tens of millions of rows in bulk. That's Netezza's job.

So as we examine the Exadata internals, we can be certain that the hardware system is tuned to its optimal speed, bandwidth and processing power, right? We should be able to pop the case, load the data, and get stellar performance without having to resort to heroics. We have come to expect such rollouts as normal affairs with Netezza, but not so much with Exadata.

A common scene at an Exadata proof of concept tournament is that the Exadata engineers turn out *en-masse* and swarm the machine. Across the raised floor, the relatively bored Netezza engineer is simply entering queries and hitting the return key. He gets lightning turnaround out of the box that the Exadata guys are still having to engineer and tune for. This does not bode well for fulfilling the desires for turnkey performance.

This dependency upon and direct faith in software as the source of all power is the primary flawed philosophy driving the engineering of Exadata's internals.

MISD/MIMD Processing, which I probably have beaten to death, but suffice to say that this processing model (Multiple-Instruction-Single-Data) (Multiple-Instruction-Multiple-Data) is why Exadata ultimately cannot compete. This model actually reserves the right to dissipate the machine's strength to the arbitrary whims of controlling software. Contrast this to the lockstep nature of the Netezza machines SIMD (Single Instruction Multiple Data) which focuses the machine's entire power frame on the completion of a single SQL operation, such that the instruction is dispatched within that focus, rather than having the machine's resources dissipated in an uncoordinated manner.

Exadata would say that their general purpose approach is a strength, but in point of fact, Netezza's purpose-built approach wins the day. And then one would ask the obvious - why Exadata would you *purport* to have produced a purpose-built machine, spending the time and effort to market and package it, and when all the smoke clears, you actually promulgate a *general*-purpose machine (in every imaginable way)? More importantly, it looks like Exadata's architects were deliberately sequestered from anyone who knows anything about data warehousing. And that's the real lost opportunity, because Oracle as a platform has been deployed for countless data warehouses, so we could only imagine that the lessons learned from all that would have - *should* have - formed a critical mass of invaluable knowledge. *None of which* is evident in the Exadata offering.

Contrast this (again starkly) to the wisdom boiled into the Netezza platform. It is clear that the engineers carved out and called out the specific, valuable and critical aspects of bulk data processing in general and data warehousing in particular, and produced a machine that harnesses the problem domain in a way that even the most casual observer can respond, "Yep, they *get* it."

First, a moment of ground-work. Disk drives are the slowest link in the chain. Anything we can do to mitigate or optimize our interaction with them will only yield bounty in the long run. However, if we simply plug disks into an array and hope for the best, we are no different than the cattle in the proverbial chute. And ask anyone who knows me, I hate being stuck in the cattle chute. Whether it's a line at the airport, a queue in traffic, or caught at the business end of a voice-mail labyrinth. Chutes are bad. Shared disks even more so.

Whenever we need to process data, we need to store it and retrieve it, and this simplest of needs is addressed quite simplistically by Exadata. It pushes data to the disk, pulls it from the disk, and does it the functionally-shared-nothing way, what could be simpler? Except that a disk drives are not shared-nothing at the hardware level. They are electromechanical device with a *finite perfor-mance profile.* So here is the first location, at the core of storage and retrieval, where the attendance to software efficiency leaves a glaring hole in the disk drive efficiency model. Not to be remedial (I am about to make a dramatic point) but in order for the software engine (in the CPUs) to do its work, it needs data. And data it will surely receive, pulled from the disk drives in a relatively arbi-trary fashion, and likewise pushed back down on the disk.

In the simplified graphic (right) we see the SMP's CPUs in one group and the shared drives in another. A pipe-line between them is how data is trans-ferred. Its size is immaterial, since the shared-disk, shared-CPU is the killer-flaw. Functionally shared-nothing. Ar-chitecturally, shared-*everything*.

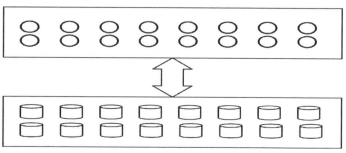

In stark contrast, the Netezza drives have two very special hardware-level power factors. The first is the disk drive itself. Data on the drive is not arbitrarily written to the disk. The circular plat-ter of the drive is divided into concentric circles of utility. At the center, this portion is used for RAID replication across drives. The next ring of activity holds system and temporary storage. And the outer rim of the disk hold user data. What does this mean? The user data is stored on the disk drive *where it is spinning fastest*, and the hardware power has the highest realization.

The second power factor is the FPGA, which controls a number of things, not the least of which is the capacity to ignore or capture data, filtering it at the hardware level. Unwanted data never sees the light of day. This is an aspect that some Netezza newbies fail to catch, but when they catch on it's like lightning bursts from their fingertips. The FPGA is doing a lot of work for us. If we but assist it in the mission of information delivery, our experience with Netezza technology will begin an upward, highly scalable climb. Failing to leverage the FPGA's power (through zone maps, filters and the like as discussed in Underground) won't yield a poor experience, just not an optimal one.

Next, in between the CPU and the disk drives is a significant bounty of RAM, where oft-requested data is cached, further reducing I/O. Recall the case study above where the most-often called software functions are usually the highest drag on performance. By pulling these into mem-ory, the highest pain point (disk I/O) is removed for the vast majority of queries.

At the next level up, all of the disk drives are acting in synergy, coordinated as an MPP fabric. But the drives are not shared in the same manner that Exadata shares them. Each CPU maintains ownership of its own drive. Every SQL statement sent to the machine is likewise received by each CPU and acted upon by the drive owned by that CPU.

Back to Exadata, where the CPUs don't "own" a disk drive. They are all shared in common. And for a shared-nothing *functional* architecture, sharing *everything* at the hardware level is a bad plan indeed. In fact, it's almost bipolar thinking.

Exadata's original inception had some sputters too. Hopes were very high for this product, which is why folks like me were scratching our heads. Doesn't Oracle have access to more data warehouses, and more warehousing requirements than practically *anyone* on the planet? Aren't they in touch with their user base? Well, the Exadata offering says they understand their OLTP model for data storage and retrieval, but the shortcomings of Oracle's model were something the aficionados lived with and tolerated until something better came along. Oracle on the other hand *seemed to think that everyone was happy with their approach.* Hadn't they listened to their user base in supporting star-schemas and index optimization for it? Hadn't they set up the installation process to optimize for either OLTP or a warehouse? Hadn't they gone the second mile to support all these things the users wanted?

Yes and no. Based on the Exadata architecture alone, it seems that Oracle either wasn't listening, wasn't paying attention, or translated the message to something their users weren't saying at all. Either way, Exadata may as well be a press release from Oracle with the message "We don't really understand warehousing, or why you people are so upset with us."

In the simplified depiction (right) the CPUs are dedicated to their disk drives and maintain complete control over their hardware-centric existence.

The role of software here, is to coordinate the CPU/drive workhorses, not to physically process data. All of the data processing happens close to the disk.

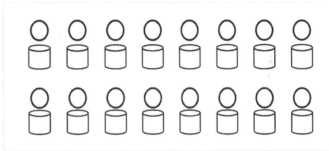

In a recent exchange on the LinkedIn boards, one new Exadata customer was ecstatic and hopeful that their recent selection of Exadata would fulfill their needs. Initially he made it sound like a fair-and-square proof-of-concept, but at the end of the conversation revealed that even though Exadata *wasn't* the best-in-show, Oracle cut a sweet financial deal with them. Hey, Netezza cuts deals and so does Teradata. They're a business, after all. But this discussion is not about the business purchase of the hardware, but whether the hardware itself is appropriate to solve the problem. I have seen more than one case of a company paying for this decision *five times.*

- The payout for the initial purchase of a hopeful solution
- The payout for the sweat equity and cost to roll it out, only to fail
- The payout for the purchase of another set of hardware to correct the first decision
- The payout for sweat equity and cost to roll it out, to succeed.
- The more intangible payout of the cost of the delay in time to market

Case Study Short: On site with a new Netezza customer, we proposed a short test-drive of our solution approach and brought some folks with us to roll it out. Time was short, the clock was ticking and we were on track for success. Ten days into the project, the manager took us aside and told us that they had decided not to use the Netezza machines, so our services would no longer be necessary. I learned from the Netezza sales folks that the vendor does not reverse a sale, so these two 10200 machines would now become bookends in the data center while someone *else* in the company decided what they intended to do with them. Why is this story important? It so happened that the site was one of the largest Oracle installations in North America, and Oracle had gotten wind of two things: one that Netezza was in the shop and two that my team was about to show a huge, quick win. A game-changing win.

Oracle had smelled a migration project brewing, and we were told that Oracle, in a flash of brilliance, made a licensing deal with our client such that Oracle would reduce licensing fees to effectively wash away the purchase of the Netezza machines, in return for promising not to use the machines or any consultants that would make it successful. The client did not have any issues whatsoever with this deal.

But again, it's a business. And I've heard more than once that if money *can* solve a problem, money *should* solve the problem. Rather than risk a hemorrhage in one of their largest installations, they invested to keep it intact.

Exadata is an *investment-in-preservation* mechanism more so than a serious data warehouse offering. Oracle's *investment* to keep the existing customers from bolting. Those who already love Oracle and sing its praises will assimilate Exadata without even regarding or reviewing Netezza, Teradata or any other product. It fits into their current environment, the RAC engine inside the Exadata machine is understood by their Oracle-ensconced IT user base, and more importantly, it preserves their loyalty. This is a matter of investing in loyalty by closing a differential, which is not always about the best choice, but the best overall *preservation* of investments on both sides.

Here's an example: We had a power-hitter data architect working for us at a customer site. Everything he touched turned to gold. Our company had invested in his education, training and certification in various technologies, and it was paying off. One day he came to the boss and asked for a raise. Another company had made him an offer, so he had inquired discreetly as to what his skill set would garner on the open market. When he came to us, he did not ask us to match the offer, but to meet the offer *halfway*. I thought this was an interesting approach, in that practically any of us could work hard to find a job with more money, but the higher the money, the higher the risk and all that goes with it. This employee did not want to leave his job. He liked working for us and the opportunities we could offer him. But he did not want to forego the money, either, and he clearly had evidence that we were paying him less than his market value. We worked something out.

We closed the gap by closing the differential. The other job might have been much better, and certainly better pay, but he was willing to settle for less of both because he had already made a significant investment in building his reputation inside our company, with our clients, which he would have to start over completely at his new employer. Likewise we had an investment in him and wanted to preserve it. It's just business. He preserved his investment. We preserved ours.

Another common tactic of retail stores is the loss-leader approach. A retail store will advertise large-scale items like major appliances at a price that will break-even or take a loss. But they know that in doing so, the majority of the purchasers will be repeat customers, recovering the loss into long-term profits because of brand/store loyalty. Oracle makes a lot of money on training, licensing and other products. It can sell its products for less if it can make it back over time.

I mentioned in Underground that one of our clients had been offered something similar with Sybase IQ. Licensing discounts and free consulting for the duration of the rollout. It is hard for

Netezza (or our firm) to compete with "free". While this sealed a place for IQ at the client, and an opportunity to roll out their product and show off their stuff, they took over a year. to deploy Sybase was willing to make this investment to seal the deal and preserve the client's loyalty. It did not last, because all the deals in the world don't make up for product failure. As of this writing, that same company has declared Netezza its "go to" technology.

And that's another transforming factor in all this. Oracle is willing to invest in its clients to preserve its footprint at the client's site. This is noble and wise investment. Likewise the clients have invested in training and certainly in Oracle-facing integration that would have to be undone (or redone) if they went with another technology. Exadata allows them to preserve this investment even if Exadata is not the best product. Exadata *could* be a better product, but it would require Oracle to give a nod to the notion that hardware, not software rules performance.

The author realizes that the above commentary may be received in some quarters, especially the back offices of Oracle, as a less than favorable commentary. Of course, the commentary is not entirely favorable since it points out the glaring weaknesses of the product and the loss-leader tactics used. It is better to find out about these weaknesses now rather than watching them rise from the ashes of a failed rollout, or watch the machine's touted capabilities buckle under the pressure of large-scale data warehousing, as Oracle's products simply do. But the folks at Oracle are big boys and can take some constructive criticism.

So if they're listening to that message, here's another. Improving the product means:

- Man-up that the RAC engine is a load-balancing mechanism and not a bulk data processing workhorse. It's a painless confession, because everyone already knows it.
- Preserve RAC *behavior* and its interfacing, but gut the internals and replace it with an engine that serves the large-scale purposes *by design*. This achieves the purpose of preserving the loyalty of the customer based on their investment in training and integration. In short, the interface behaves the same way superficially, but under the covers does something entirely different.
- While gutting the internals, also wrap-n-hide the table management mechanics. Stuff like table spaces and whatnot. We don't want to see it. It's your problem.
- While you're there, lose the create-ddl complexity. We want to see simple create statements without any additional overhead. Keep in mind that the reason your (former) users don't like you is that the create-ddl for a 20-column Netezza table requires exactly 22 lines of DDL, where the same table in Oracle RAC can and often does require thousands of lines. Simplify our lives, folks, table management is *your* problem.
- Before you're done, lose the rest of the complexity. It's an *appliance*, not Inspector Gadget. We want the product delivered with common default settings so we can break the plastic, plug it in and get to work. Exadata seems a far cry from this capability, so snap to it.
- Focus on hardware as the power-plant for performance, and wrap the new engine around it.
- Get away from commodity, horizontal SMPs. These are secondhand architectures for large-scale processing, and anything based on them stays firmly in the secondhand zone.
- Lose the shared disk approach, for goodness sake. Get a spine and use your new engine to

organize the disks for maximum power and I/O. Hanging a bunch of drives on a common I/O bus is just phoning-it-in.

- Get away from index structures. These are in the way, and we hate them. We have always hated them and all the things required to manage and maintain them. In conventional Oracle deployments they were necessary evils. It is stunning that they appear in a data warehouse *appliance.*

- Get away from anything that smells of transactional processing - it cannot happily coexist with report processing in the same system. It is why Netezza has been so successful in supporting transactional models, because with a Netezza machine the hardware does not support transactional processing *in any sense of the word.* We have to think about intraday models that will align with this aspect of Netezza. This means the "mini-batch" or "micro-batch" is how we solve it, and *we like it that way.* We don't want the Netezza machine to approach the data with anything less than full-bore, set-based operations. It's the *only* thing that scales.

- If you're only going to be a load-and-query machine, then you should advertise yourself as such. Sybase IQ, Vertica, Greenplum, these are your competitors since they are software products running on SMP machines, and only support load-and-query. This is not an ignoble class of folks to be associated with, since they are found all over the data warehousing landscape and people love them. But they are not appliances and do not *purport* to be.

- Price yourself according to your class of operation. If you are a load-and-query offering with some added hardware, so be it. But we need the budget dollars left over to purchase Informatica, Ab Initio or Datastage, and their attendant hardware, in order to support your care and feeding, and that's not something we want to find in the "fine print". Netezza doesn't need that stuff to thrive, so don't make the claim that "everyone does it this way" or that "nobody does it that way". We just know *you* don't do it that way.

- As a load-and-query offering, you don't do SQL-based transforms. This sets you aside from Netezza and Teradata and takes you out of their class completely. Don't come to the tournament strutting tailfeathers as though you are one of them, as this capability is incredibly powerful in its own right, and those of us who leverage it have a minimum ante for the tournament, and Exadata doesn't belong.

- Administration should be a part-time gig. The machine should be intelligent enough to make all of our administrative woes evaporate. It's an *appliance.* Make it so.

- Proof-of-concepts should include a single part-time product engineer, not a swarm of them. He/she should never appear overworked. Whatever level of effort *you* have to put into the machine to make it go, translates to the same level *we* will need to make it go. The point is, we cannot sustain a swarming model, so why present it to us that way?

- When at the proof of concept, show us your worst-case numbers, and do it within the hour of receiving the problems we present to you. The longer we have to wait for the answers, the more it means that you guys are engineering the solution at a human workload capacity we cannot sustain. If Netezza can turn it around with better numbers within the hour, so be it. But if it takes you days to even approach those levels, it does not bode well for us, since we'll have to do the same thing after the purchase. In short, a proof-of-concept has more facets than the scoreboard numbers.

The Teradata platform

Teradata has been a mainstay of data warehousing for over decade. As of this writing, a number of Netezza customers have co-located a Netezza platform with a Teradata system, but only one had embraced the task of migrating a complete solution away from Teradata and into Netezza, to forsake the Teradata machine as part of that solution's underpinning technology. By the time of publication of this book, more Netezza customers will have confidently embraced this path. This is no slight on Teradata, as it has a broad customer base and loyal following for many well-deserved reasons.

Earlier this year I was privy to the standard Teradata presentation. It is formidable product with a mature set of secondary offerings. I also observed that in the presentation they show a block with themselves in it, and another block with all-the-other-databases in it, including Netezza. Then the strangest notation at the top of the box: *OLTP Databases*. The presenter, a kind man of experience and years, went on to describe the Netezza machine as a *transactional database*. Now, we know this is not true in any sense of the word or concept. How strange that the Teradata sales rep had not done his homework on what he considers a competitor. I seriously doubt he described Netezza this way deliberately. But this is an interesting turn, in that the more times a presenter can claim that Netezza is only-as-good-as all those other SMP/transactional machines, it's not even in the same class of machine as the Teradata box, right?

Wrong-O. Netezza is not a transactional machine, it is an MPP that has stood toe-to-toe with Teradata, among others, and whipped them handily in proof-of-concept tournaments. This was not something that Teradata was accustomed to. Such outcomes have transformed them. This is what competition does, it increase the quality of the products. Nobody really cares if Teradata's 2550 appliance had a sputtering start. Now that it's gathering steam in the marketplace, it will be a contentious force and we're all looking forward to it. Because its presence will increase the quality of all the marketplace offerings, and all of us win.

We have often noted that by the time the data is nestled into a database system, there is no roadmap in place to remove it *in quantity*. No plan was ever made for a full data extraction from the warehouse (or transactional system) into another. When the Netezza machine arrives and starts these high-intensity extracts, people are very surprised at what they discover. Netezza is voracious when it comes to system resources for extraction. If we have a standard gigabit ethernet, we will find that upon using it for extraction into Netezza, that it's just *not* enough. Netezza can handle much more than this. Some extractions can literally hog the network bandwidth (if extracting machine-to-machine).

So people tend to extract from the source into a flat file, then allow Netezza to consume the flat file. This is very efficient for a lot of reasons, namely that the network bandwidth, if impacted at all, will be a one-time problem at the time of extraction. On the other hand, if we don't have enough file system space, offloading to flat files might not be an option. We should really make it a part of the plan, however, when first considering the endeavor, to allocate or even purchase enough file system space to support the extracts. Even if we only lease it, the time we save on this will be significant.

As an approach however, offloading the files and then gzip'ing them is a very efficient load tactic. The data will reside on the NAS disks in compressed form. When we read it into the gzip utility, it will stream from the NAS in compressed form, travel through any network or transports it must to arrive, ultimately joining the gzip utility in memory where it is first de-compressed for the nzload to receive it. This is a very efficient flow in that it radically reduces the I/O requirements for the load. The brunt of the data transportation hit is borne by the Teradata machine as it extracts into gzip and stores the results. Still, storing it in gzip'd form is very efficient and will make the disk-write time much shorter.

One particular note about Teradata that must be brought to the forefront, is that unlike other database systems, Teradata doesn't make it easy for us to extract data in large quantities for any other system but another Teradata system. As of this writing, the Teradata FastExport utility is by far the fastest way to extract data, but it embeds a lot of control characters inline to the data to support the downstream use of its own loading facilities like Multi-Load. The second Teradata utility, BTEQ, will perform a clean extraction of data but is *so much slower* than the FastExport that it behooves us to figure out a way to make the FastExport work for us.

As I browsed the Teradata support sites and interacted with experienced Teradata users, they kept coming back to a very consistent message. Perhaps this message has or will change since this writing, but as of today we have some constraints that provide significant challenges to plain text extract into a Netezza machine (or any other target machine that likes to see large quantities of plain ASCII text).

When performing the extract, we have to formulate a FastExport query. This query will determine the format of the data extracted. We're going to use a factory to manufacture this query for us, but in the meantime we need to carefully consider what we want the query to do. Here are some minimum constraints:

The variable-length, delimited record is fine for the column-level content, but the whole record will have to be wrapped and cast into a "char" datatype. Why is this? If we don't wrap the body of columns as a "char", the FastExport will automatically place control characters at the beginning of each record to support the "length" value of the overall varchar field. This is a binary value and can arbitrarily arrive as the same binary value as a newline character. In fact, the more records in the table, the higher the likelihood the latent newline will accidentally show up. This poses a problem for any downstream process, including nzload, that keys on a newline as an end-of-record.

The 6.0 version of Netezza's NPS has fixed-length loading capabilities, which will play into this discussion.

If we make the value a "char", that is cast the entire record as a "char", this eliminates the junk but effectively makes the entire record a fixed-length field. Well, that doesn't bode well for data extraction. We like delimited fields for a reason: it reduces the overall data transfer size between the machines. Also, on average most of the records will be significantly smaller than their potential maximum size. So if all of the records are fixed to the maximum size, we're pulling over a lot of dead space, aren't we? Good grief, this *is* the twenty-first century, right? The fix to this is more obvious than we realize. If we place a dummy column at the beginning of the record (by the extracting SQL) and then allow the nzload to receive all manner of bogus characters, this first dummy column will carry the leading control characters for the record. Now we're back to delimited length. Whew!

I will note here that even though BTEQ can pull clean ASCII data, it's still slower than the FastExport using fixed-length records/columns. So while it's tempting to use the BTEQ to overcome these functional issues, we won't be able to win against FastExport's performance. What we will win with BTEQ, is a clean data extract. If we do this in the background as a one-time extraction to a flat file, it won't matter how long BTEQ takes, and we won't have to deal with FastExport's introduction of these extraneous control characters.

But the use of BTEQ assumes the availability of flat file space. In our project, this was not available to us for the extraction process, so this led us down a rather painful road of using direct extracts from Teradata into the Netezza machine. This on-demand extract required us to forsake the idea of using BTEQ because it was so slow. Let's not forget also that the entire project was steeped in the sentiment of defying the existing Teradata fortress, so any requests for help from the Teradata staff was usually met with the sound of chirping crickets amidst the electronic smirks of the nay-sayers who wanted the experiment to fail. Several of the knowledge workers promulgated theoretical solutions to the problem, but when asked for working examples, the crickets appeared again.

As an aside, one proposal was to use a serialized Unix utility such as awk or sed to strip the extraneous FastExport characters from the stream as they arrived. This effectively enslaved the entire transfer to the lowest denominator (the utility). This too, was anathema to the data warehouse purist who does not see any efficiency in passing terabytes of information for character-level sifting through a utility like "awk". Not to dismiss it out of hand, however, because we have a tradeoff in play here also. Holistic performance flows are a balancing act.

To make matters even *worse*, the Teradata sources actually had unprintable characters embedded in their character fields. These ran the gamut from chr(0)-chr(31), and chr(128)-chr(255). That is, any and all unprintable characters, including newlines, were peppered throughout the data, making a simple extract-load impossible. We would have to fortify the extraction and the load with several more degrees of scrubbing.

Which brings us to the next challenge. If the Netezza nzload utility looks for newline characters for record delimiters, and likewise looks for delimiters between fields, how could we ever pick a delimiter that would work for all records in all cases? Would we have to choose a delimiter for one table that did not appear in the character-level junk, and could we rely on this condition forever? Hardly. We worked to find delimiters that would fit well with each table, and while the simple pipe "|" worked for the majority of them, we had to pick another in the upper range of characters for some of the tables. This worked fine until the source data was refreshed and this carefully chosen delimiter now appeared as part of the regular data. Funny thing about trash characters, they're just so random.

One direction was to use the Teradata oreplace() function to zap those delimiters at the time of extraction. Unfortunately, when some of the characters were newlines, we really needed the oreplace() to zap those instead. So in using the oreplace(), we applied it to all character fields and zapped the newline characters to an empty space. This solved the problem of the bogus newlines, but did not solve the problem of the spontaneous delimiters. Also, the oreplace() is very expensive on the extract. Embracing it tipped the flow-balancing point another direction.

Up until this point, we had been in a state of denial about the delimited data. We did not want to forsake the delimiters, even though the entire record was a fixed length, because we held out hope that the record-level fixed length might one day be eliminated. The more pressing issue, though, was that the spontaneous trash characters were masquerading as delimiters, inhibiting our ability to perform a simple intake of the data. So no matter what, we needed a fix in the here-and-now that we could live with for the foreseeable future.

So the solution was to continue leveraging oreplace() on the Teradata extract to zap all newline characters, but at the same time pull the extract into a Netezza table that was a single long varchar field, long enough to hold the entire record. Once inside the machine, we could use the MPP to scrub the data.

Of course, once inside the machine, we would no longer be privy to the nzload's ability to snip apart the incoming records based on delimiters. At this point we had to commit to using fixed-length *columns* for the extract, bringing us back to a fixed-length record size. We now had to manufacture two queries with the extract. One that would cast everything to fixed length and one that would unpack the fixed length with inline substring() calls. I could not have been more unhappy with this implementation.

To be specific, here is a simple example of each:

```
   select cast( cast(cdate as char(10)), cast(cname as char(30))      as char(40) ) from
extract_table;
   Select substring(record_body,1,10) as cdate, substring(record_body,11,30) as cname
from intake_table;
```

For each of the above queries, both are manufactured in-line at the time of the extraction, based on the catalog metadata for the designated table. If the algorithm to formulate these queries works for one table, they work for all of them. Can you imagine hand-crafting the SQL for each, when there could potentially be hundreds of them? Ahh, the factory-based approach means that all of the queries will operate and behave the same way.

And what of those pesky non-printable characters? Well, with fixed-length data snips, we are no longer beholden to delimiters or the false delimiters. So for the char/varchar fields all we really have to do is apply a scrubber like an overloaded translate() function (ore regexp_extract for those using the NZ SQL Toolkit). While this makes the overall query quite verbose and cumbersome, *we don't care* because we're using a factory to build it. The end result is clean, unadulterated character data.

Once we had all of this squared away, our Teradata cohorts cried foul. There shouldn't be *any* of these trash characters in those fields, they claimed. Well, of *course* there shouldn't, and we agreed with them because we scrubbed them out too! But on a stranger note, the client's project principals recoiled in horror that we had scrubbed these characters. Not because the characters were present, but because we had actually removed *information* from the source systems without asking permission! Now, this seemed a little odd when we first heard it, because our efforts had made the data better. But, asked the principals, what if those characters were there for a reason?

I raised an eyebrow at this suggestion, but then trotted down to the reporting gurus and asked them some simple questions. Are you performing plain, straight queries against the source data in the Teradata machine, or do your queries have a lot of extra wrapping to avoid data anomalies? Their answer was very interesting, in that there sure were a lot of junk characters in the information content! Some of it even impeded joining the data on character keys. Once the core content was scrubbed, all of their reports worked. Armed with this information, and the statements from the data owners that "there shouldn't be any junk data like that in the source tables" we pronounced victory and pressed forward. Not so fast, claimed the principals, we need a write-up on all of the data that was removed from the sources and the algorithm used to perform it.

Okay, while this sounded a bit oblique, it makes sense in a highly-scrutinized system. If we removed data from the source, we need to define what was removed and why. If the users agreed with the action, they would simply approve it. However, this wasn't a highly-scrutinized system, nor was it even a high-risk, high visibility platform. Methinks the pride of ownership, and the realization that the data wasn't as clean as they though it was, had a bitter aftertaste for them.

So true to form, the principals kept hammering on our team to find out what other information we had removed from the sources, and this terminology became a very interesting fulcrum for making decisions. *Junk, unprintable characters are not information.* They are **noise**. Scrubbing noise from the data is something that happens deep in the systems all the time. Applying a few rules to scrub it some more, where's the beef? So the running mantra for the remainder of this exercise soon became, that we are not and have not removed any *information* from the sources. If the testers should find that information is missing, we will address it. Now that's a kick in the pants, because the testers weren't prepared to test for *missing unprintable* characters in character data.

Anecdote: A military wife, after having relocated repeatedly with her husband for over twenty years, was in attendance at her husband's honor dinner for his promotion to Colonel, and a station in Washington DC. She mentioned to a dinner guest that she had finally thrown out all the junk they had accumulated over the years before moving to DC. Her husband overheard this comment and asked her, *What did you throw out?* To which she responded, *Tell me what you're missing, and I'll tell you if we still have it.*

When dealing with trash characters in the data, we will likely encounter a full range of them, including a spontaneous new-line character. Since the nzload expects a newline for a record separator, this can create a significant issue in data intake, because an embedded newline character will prematurely create a new row. We have two options to fix this.

The first option is to perform an inline-replace of newline characters on the data as it leaves the source, like a database. But if the data is already extracted to a file, or is presented to the nzloader as a file, we don't have the option of prescrubbing the data on extraction. Now we have to deal with it in the file. If perchance the file is being produced by an upstream source and is arriving with embedded newlines, *we have every reason* to reject the file as corrupt and invalid. Don't forget that some *process* has to create the file, and if the file is not within this minimum specification, it is not a valid file. It doesn't remove the newlines, but it means we don't load it either.

Is it that simple? We can load the file but it won't be complete. We then have the issue of having not one, but *two* bad records (because one good record is split into two). If we attempt to load either record, one of them is a shortened record, and one of them is misaligned completely. It is possible however (and this has happened) that both records will load into the target. Now we have two corrupt records instead of one good record, and we have this combination for each and every place where there is an embedded newline. If we have multiple newlines in a record, this only makes it worse. Here are the scenarios we'll deal with and their resolution:

- The file is delivered with this problem. It is technically corrupt. We don't have to accept it because it doesn't meet the file specification, no different that if a column header was in the wrong place. Some problems are not ours to fix.
- The file is extracted under our control. In the extraction SQL, include the scrubbers at the column-level, usually with character-keys only. Teradata has an "unauthorized" inline function called "oreplace()" that will replace one and only one character for each column. Used wisely, this function can zap the newlines, because we can deal with all the others later. We submit the extract SQL with the embedded oreplace() and the newlines will be filtered as the data exits the machine.
- The file was extracted under the control of another utility, but we can influence the SQL that it uses, or we can specify that the newlines are omitted before transmission.
- We can do a fixed-length load. If we're using Teradata's fastexport, we would have to do this anyhow. With a fixed-length load, there is no need for a newline character anyhow. If present in the data, we would account for it like the rest of the information, assigning a single-byte column to the data definition to hold the newline character. This option is only available in the 6.0 version of the NPS.
- If the newlines or un-printables have to remain in the data, do something that one of my colleagues did. In the extraction of the data, they used a SQL statement that called for the record identifier at the front of the record, the end of the record, and before each known offending character field, along with additional identifying metadata. Once the data was loaded into Netezza, the nzloader would dutifully break the bad row apart into multiple rows, but it could be reassembled by using the record identifiers to put the Humpty-Dumpty record back together again. All this, because the owners of the data refused to acknowledge or scrub the characters that everyone knew should not be there in the first place.

When I asked the reader to "hold that thought" concerning the use of a serialized awk script, the final analysis for the newline characters resolution leveraged one. Examine for a moment all the hoops we were jumping through (experimentally of course) and having to deal with the trade-off of fixed-length records and fixed-length fields. Could the use of an awk script allow us to compress all this back down to a delimited data format? In this case, even though the awk script could perform a row-level scrub of the newline and effectively repair the information (and keep the newline in the data per the odd wishes of the principals), it still added some processing time to the stream. In the trade-off however, the additional time for the awk script was far less than the time eaten up in using fixed-length data. And it was *still* far less time than using oreplace() on the extraction. Recall that holistic performance tuning looks at all components of the flow not just a small section. In this case we could reduce functional complexity (keep delimited data) with only a small penalty.

I have to take a pause here, because the typical Teradata instance is on the far, far end of a host of data processing that is already guarding against junk in every possible way before it ever even loads data into the machine. The likelihood that the average Teradata instance is anything less than pristine, is vanishingly small. So take the advice above with a bit of adaptation. If the data is clean, load it and move on. Life is too short to over-code for something that is not daunting us.

More importantly, the migration of data from the Teradata machine to the Netezza machine is not an operational problem, but a one-time migration problem. It may be that if we find any errors in the information, we literally have to perform a one-time manual fix on the source or the target to affect our fate. As a migration problem, it's a one-time load, requiring one-time permission to do one-time things. We're not asking for ongoing permission for all this, just something to wrap the migration. As we will see in a later chapter, the migration project is a special, one-time animal that requires care and feeding not required by other projects.

In recent years, Teradata has recognized the threat of appliances to their business model. If a customer could get the right level of functionality and scalable power for the right price, they would bolt for Netezza. Oracle experienced the same stress. However, that Teradata recognized the threat meant that the penetration of appliances is real and the industry is transforming towards it. The complaint of many Teradata customers was that they were paying for things they weren't using and would never use. Couldn't Teradata offer up a "lite" version of the machine? In fact, the complaints weren't coming from the IT staff. They loved the machine. The complaints were coming from the office of the CFO, the people who were writing checks for the technology but weren't seeing the return on their investment. Teradata ignored such complaints and sentiments until Netezza answered them without Teradata's permission to do so. Time to take off the gloves and enter the fray with a loaded weapon.

The first Teradata appliance was a scaled down version of their entry-level big machine. A valiant attempt, but it had issues. They corrected these and continued to aggressively market the machine. In part they knew many of their customers would opt for it as a means to scale horizontally when scaling vertically was not financially feasible. Teradata would rather their customers scale horizontally using their equipment and not someone else's, so it seemed that to put the brakes on this impending and rather looming problem, they needed to get on the stick and have their own answer to the appliance question. It is a formidable one, to be sure, and has the capability to go toe-to-toe with Netezza in a number of areas. What it has going for it, is that folks who already have a Teradata machine will not have to retool anything. It functionally works like the big machine, only smaller. What is doesn't have going for it, is that the smaller machine doesn't compete well with the Netezza appliance. Perhaps this isn't entirely Teradata's fault, since their appliance was born in the wake of the Netezza Mustang series. How were they to know that in 2009 Netezza would roll out a platform that quite literally left the competition's head spinning in place?

I've been an armchair participant, directly on the project or just on an after-action assessment when Teradata was on the short list for a competitive proof-of-concept with Netezza, among other players. In Teradata's earlier offerings, queries that took Netezza single-digit minutes would require Teradata much longer. In another form of test, a potential customer gave Netezza and Teradata a list of queries to execute to see how long it would take them to return back. Not the queries, mind you, but the *consultants*. This was a way of testing the productivity/turnaround time to get an answer. The Netezza folks came back after a couple of hours, where the Teradata folks came back in a couple of *days*, again with Netezza's queries multiple-X faster. I mentioned in Underground that even if we post Netezza's worst case number, it still makes the machine look good because we can achieve those numbers without days of engineering. It is a natural product of a good architecture.

So Teradata scrambled to keep up, and this was a new experience for them. Notice that in this chapter's discussion, I laid out some of the challenges we experienced in migrating to a Netezza machine, because the migration *is* happening and it's *real*.

Notice also that Teradata is scrambling to compete and not throwing in the towel.

What does this mean? That the industry transformation is on, Teradata recognizes it and is throwing millions of dollars and countless hours into their investment in the future-that-is-already-here. Where will it lead? Hey, more work for folks like me, that's for sure. Our company is a Teradata partner. But it will lead to higher quality products for all of us, our customers and clients included. Competition always increases quality, and to see a company like Teradata going into it full bore is a sign that the appliance marketplace is hot, the solutions will be even hotter, and all the players are looking for the next big thing.

In short, it's a wave, a really big one, and my suggestion is that *you get on it*.

Now it may occur to someone at Teradata that I have provided here an assessment of their technology that is somewhat less than favorable, but this isn't so. The purpose of this section was to highlight some of the issues we would experience when migrating from a Teradata machine, and that those things are expected and even healthy for a company that wants to protect its product from being mothballed. However, I suspect that as the confidence in Teradata's appliance increases, we will see more Netezza and Teradata machines living in harmony side-by-side. I would not expect the Teradata appliance to eclipse Netezza, especially now that it's owned by IBM, but I would expect data-center-variety to increase if for no better reason than Netezza will be part of the IBM family and flow into the existing IBM marketplace footprint, one that eclipses Teradata's by orders of magnitude.

The conclusion is, with the relationship management in the bag, perhaps we'll see these technologies go toe-to-toe in a tournament that doesn't regard the softer skills, but rather requires the contenders to shoot the arrow as close to the target's center as possible? Of course, I am not that naive. What we'll likely see is IBM and Teradata existing along parallel continuums that rarely meet, and when they do, professional discourse rather than proof-of-concept will determine the direction, the client will quietly sign agreements with no fanfare, and the technologists will continue to solve the world's problems before bedtime.

Java again?

For now, I will direct my spyglass across the way to another product which quite frankly betrayed me on a mission-critical project. In this regard, I should have known better. So rather than call the product out specifically by name, I will simply describe what our team saw, and the reader can connect the dots more objectively. This is not about whether I may invite a lawsuit or other backlash, clearly Exadata is larger than this product by far. But this will be instructive and will, of course, drive the vendor mad as I describe why they have failed.

It's an Open Source ETL product. I'm a member of several open-source forums and interact with open source environments on a regular basis. I appreciate the collaboration that it offers, but would be the first to note that we would never install and run open-source products "as is". We would first apply our own acumen in the problem domain and value-add the offering. I don't mind pumping the value-add back into the open-source as long as nobody interrupts my already abbreviate project deadlines to stop and explain what I've done, or why I did it. All that aside, we have two primary issues with open source that cannot be ignored. (One) is that there is no direct accountability for the contents and (two) that they usually center on feature points and not *performance*.

ETL tools require performance, period. Nobody cares about their features if the lethargy of its processing model impedes aggressive, high-volume intake. It's hard enough to pull off high-volume data processing with the products that *do* scale. Why would we embrace one that does not, and more importantly, *does not even promise it?*

What are the hottest ETL tools that have the highest performance and most robust feature sets? Only a handful can *scale*, and the others can just take a back seat or find a home in lower-scale implementations. They will find a happy, profitable home there, so I by no means disparage their existence or viability. But they cannot *scale* for a simple reason: it takes a dedicated architectural approach by a few people who really know what they are doing and are well-paid for it, not an open-source gaggle with no accountability. Solving large-scale problems is hard work. It's worth lots of money. It requires higher, more objective accountability. Open-source ETL doesn't play in this arena.

But come on, this is a book about the most scalable technology on the planet, so only the scalable tools need apply. And scalability comes in more forms than just volume and performance. Can it scale to multiple developers, sites, multivariant applications and venues, so just how scalable and adaptable is it? Open source software is not privy to a brain-trust that understands *scale*. This is not something to be trivialized. Scalability has brutal, uncompromising and rigid requirements that cannot be ignored. What's that? Never heard the word "brutal" associated with the rather passive open-source approach? How about "uncompromising", or even "rigid". Uh, no you have not and there's a reason for it. Open source is all about flexibility and collaboration, and is not the place we would expect to find people fighting for the *best* way to get *highest* performance, even though they do fight for the best way to get functionality.

In this particular product, the lack of attention to performance is painfully obvious.

ETL performance is not really about functionality more than *capability*. It does not face the users or developers, but the systems and hardware. It introduces the developers to the systems without compromising performance, but will never trade off a user feature for performance. The contrast between the two is significant, because capability is borne on the ability to smoke-test the performance in a controlled environment. Open-source, in the *bazarre*, has no regular access to such machinery. Capability faces *systems*, where functionality faces *users*. This is why we find advocates talking about open source from the *user community,* not the system community. And note, I am not disparaging open source, but I am disparaging the naivete of open source proponents who actually *believe* that they can compete with the likes of Ab Initio or other high-performance data processing products *on user-centric features alone.*

For this particular product, I asked some direct questions about largest, most complex implementations and all that, and all I received were kool-aid answers or anecdotes that could not be verified. They knew what I was asking, but could not objectively prove it. In fact, they offered me up the standard guy-with-vacuous-eyes speech about how easy the product was to navigate, with plenteous drop-downs and user helps, all the stuff that helps me understand their product, but doesn't *solve the problem.* When the guy-with-the-vacuous-eyes was finished talking, his cohort guy-with-the-manchu-mustache chimed in about how all their developers and users *loved* the product. What problems had they solved with it? Where is it installed in production? Where is it processing billions of rows? Chirping crickets ensued.

Java is the product's core language. This part of the ETL tool really bothered me. Java is notorious for being a non-player in bulk processing. I recall an encounter with a group that was trying to deploy Microsoft BizTalk at their site, and the principal integrators were building a custom set of props around it to so that it could bypass BizTalk's inherent weaknesses with bulk processing. The problem was, they didn't have a flawed architecture, they had a flawed *approach*. All of their props would be written in Java, and once completed, the application actually ran slower on its giant machine than BizTalk did on its little one.

The point - Java is a *general purpose* language. When we need scale, the phrase *general purpose* falls by the wayside and *purpose-built* comes to the fore. Some might object here, claiming that this could apply to any language at all. But no, Java doesn't boil itself down to efficient, machine-facing code. It provides functionality at the sacrifice of efficiency. Java is utterly inefficient in how it leverages the system. Using it for performance tuning is no different than pouring sand down the oil chamber of a high-performance vehicle. Or perhaps swapping out the high-viscosity oil for maple syrup. Are these analogies absurd? *So is using Java for bulk processing.* It is anathema to the mission. It relegates the offering to worse than a laughable joke. It's a joke that just isn't funny. At all.

Case Study Short: Working for a former employer, I was asked openly about a certain technology that I had never heard of. The complaint was that even though it had solved a lot of problems for a large customer base, it's current implementation was *just so slow*. I asked basic questions about the tool until we got to Java. "Stop there," said another person in the room, a Java guru, and proceeded to offer up a litany of reasons why Java should never be used for bulk processing. Others chimed in when they heard the different technical aspects and heartily agreed. If Java really does that aspect poorly, or this aspect badly etc, then it's a no-brainer. Java is the wrong choice for an ETL tool. The Java aficionado finished his review with "Everybody knows that." But by this time the person who had originally asked the question was quietly staring at his screen, seemingly catatonic with grief. I asked him why he had wanted to know, and he told me that our company now owned the product, because we had just purchased and assimilated the consulting firm that had created it.

I would also accept that a consulting firm can create solid, reusable and packageable offerings. One would just have to be careful as to the nature of that offering. If Java doesn't play, the offering doesn't either.

However, I could see Java playing a role in the ability to process *metadata* in a framework/rules-driven fashion, as a means to control the Netezza machine's heavy-lifting. But not as a means to actually *process* data. Nothing should be responsible for touching the data but the Netezza machine. (That said, if we wanted a true metadata-processing language, would we choose Java for this either?)

As would be expected with a product designed-by-committee, the thing was wholly unstable. The running joke soon became: *It's easy to install, and after installing it about twenty times, I guess that's a good thing.* So one of my colleagues rolled out a proof-of-concept with this product and could not stop laughing every time it crashed, went offline, or just spontaneously combusted. The developers using the tool had long since been immersed in real ETL tools, so when trying to map their understanding of flow-based concepts into a product that didn't "get it", the disconnects were palpable. It was as if this product was invented and shepherded by a group of programmers who did not have a clue about the capabilities and features necessary to support the simplest flow-based model.

The evaluation above is offered in part to show those particular products as good examples of bad examples, but more importantly to highlight a pattern that we need to master if we intend to please the decision-makers. We need to put more information in their hands so that we are not personally saddled with rolling out bad products and the accepting the risk. After all, if we *recommend* a product we already know is bad, we'll be asked to *deploy* it, and accept the heat for the failure.

Exactly this has happened more than once to colleagues and coworkers, and in every case, because I had already been exposed to high-performance systems in the earliest part of my career, I could tell them where the pitfalls were. Some listened, some did not. Those who did not, suffered for it when they didn't have to.

It's all in the presentation (layer)?

Now let's take a look at the scene from the presentation layer. I did some congenial verbal sparring with a friend on the difference between Business Intelligence and Data Warehousing. He whipped out a printed marketing slick that showed all of the front-end and back-end activities normally associated with both. His point was that this was a depiction of a Business Intelligence solution. It rolled all data warehousing activities together with reporting activities and called it Business Intelligence. So we can set aside the term data warehouse, he claimed, because Business Intelligence now describes both. Ironically, the slick he was displaying had the phrase Data Warehousing/Business Intelligence at the top of the page. Not sure how he missed it, but I pointed it out anyhow. He said, well, it *should* describe both. We don't need two terms for it.

And yet we *have* two terms for it.

So as I ribbed him a little more, he's a good sport and all, he really wanted me to accept that we could start *marketing* the two concepts as one, to which I responded, Well, the marketplace decides those definitions, not us, and most companies deliberately segregate data warehousing from business intelligence, one being the back-end and the other being the front-end. He continued to make a case, and it was valiant indeed. Later in the day he boldly asserted that Microsoft Excel was the most popular and pervasive Business Intelligence tool on the planet. To which I asked him, tongue in cheek, so Excel does all the ETL, back-end integration and all that? To which he responded, somewhat irritated that I already knew the answer, "No", and then I noted, so Business Intelligence and Data Warehousing really *are* different disciplines? Like I said, he was a good sport about it.

But the only reason I was prepared to address the question was because I had already addressed it in multiple white papers many years prior.

Business Intelligence is the name we affectionately apply to the *presentation* layer. We have two kinds of these products. I will loosely bucket them so nobody is offended.

The first kind is rich in screen functionality and has the right level of due diligence between the user and the Netezza system. The second kind purports to integrate data all the way from the depths of the back end, *on demand*, and present it to the user. This second kind is missing two very important aspects of data warehousing - and those are (a) synchronizing data from multiple sources that are only available in disparate time frames, and (b) scrubbing dirt (*once*, not on demand) so that the presentation layer is buffered from repeated work that will bog down its performance.

We are seeing a few more products in this second group. The first group is actually more expensive, but is *extensive* in its reporting capabilities. The second group is usually marginal in reporting, because all of its strength and knowledge-ware is found in attacking and tackling data from the back end. I don't particularly disparage such products unless we're talking about scalability (and we are) so these don't scale. They can functionally scale, and in many ways harness a lot of complexity and front-end disparity, but because they don't synchronize or scrub, even an average enterprise would be remiss in just knee-jerking the purchase to get it underway. However, if the enterprise simply wanted the support for disparate front-ends, one such tool can push displays to PDAs, cell phones, smartphones and the like. The other tools don't support the front-end like this, but are more expensive. Seems like a balancing act would to use the second-group product to support a lot of disparate front-ends but forego any assumption that it could perform scalable integration. Leave that part to a back-end product and everybody wins.

For the presentation-strength tools, even they have some challenges when it comes to the Netezza machine, because they don't really know how to intuitively address the database. I offered up one example last year on the Gather 'Round the Grill blog on the Netezza Community site. It showed how a simple and subtle rollup can be enormously inefficient just because the tool does not know how to properly characterize and formulate the queries. In fact, the tool was behaving as we would expect it to - if facing Oracle or another relational database. But because it's facing Netezza, the best and most scalable path to the answer was exactly *reverse* of what the tool generated.

Ahh, well we cannot expect all vendors to just jump at the chance to conform to Netezza, but nothing requires us to buy their products either. Keep in mind that we are now scaled into a rare atmosphere. It is beyond the scope of the average product to survive much less thrive in such a rarefied environment.

All that said, we must choose, and choose wisely.

One of my colleagues was called to a shop to perform an "objective" proof of concept that essentially violated every principle above, and then some. To make matters worse, the client all but required him to *recommend* the marginal products. Why is that? Budgets were tight and the vendor had already established an enterprise license, so this guy's team would be able to use the product on someone else's nickel. However, in the truest sense of "you get what you pay for", they have not entered production operations even as of this writing, and last I heard, still won't for the next six months. And they thought the licensing was free! It cost them over a year's time to wrangle with and deploy this relatively new product.

See, nothing is for free. Not *completely* free.

Case Study Short: In the late nineties, a major retailer wanted to see a warehouse solution installed along with a customer campaign management environment. Our consulting firm was partners with *Epiphany*, and the current CEO of Epiphany was the former CEO of our firm, so there was a lot of "partnering" going on. Those of us in the trenches had the odious duty of rolling out the solution, and watched mesmerized as their product engineers swarmed on the product to make it work. I don't have a particular problem with architectural involvement in the solution, provided that the solution is being promoted in this context, The fact that they had presented it as a product, and an expensive one, came at the higher price of explaining why the product would not execute in its basic functional form, and why it would not scale. We found out far too late that the product architects had opted to make all of their warehouse keys varchar() data types. This bloated the size of the warehouse, since things that could normally be integers were now characters. It also debilitated performance since integer keys can join one-hundred times faster than their character equivalent. In fact, such performance compromises existed all over the architecture. I'm all for using relaxed data types to get data *into* the machine, as long as they don't stay that way. Seems like everyone who touched the product could not stop complaining about it. They matured as products do, but it's interesting that all of their scalability features, without exception, now face the system and harness hardware, without dependence on software for success. It's a common outcome for those that survive and eventually become scalable.

The marketplace is now replete with workbenches, toolkits, toasters, blenders, juicers, WHEW! It's software appliance fu!

And every time I turn around, another one is on the marketplace. Invariably I am asked to review one of them and then we start down the path of an awkward conversation. Perhaps some people on site worked with it in a prior career and have a "pretty good idea" of what they need now, and this toolkit purports to solve things. Can we get one, huh-huh, can we get one, pleeeeze, oh please -

Oh, *please*. It's important to know where the limitations are.

Recently we had to coach someone off the ledge in their approach to a reporting tool. They had opted for a "second group" technology that "only has to be pointed to the sources." The problem is, now we're dealing with some real scale, like tens of billions of rows in a Netezza machine (a common implementation). They wanted to perform a bake-off between the reporting tool's capability (hey, they said they were scalable) and what the Netezza machine could do. In the middle of this, the reporting tool's engineers were smirking-on-the-inside because they just *knew* we'd have to make a special request for a transformation tool (e.g. Informatica) to make the transforms work. We departed the arena to prepare for the tournament, and when we returned the next day, the reporting engineers were nowhere to be found.

We, however demonstrated simply how to intake data, transform it and prep it for reporting. Average turnaround time for a query: several seconds.

The reason they hadn't yet shown up for the tournament: something about ten billion rows had crushed their solution into the floor. In fact, they couldn't even get data off the source machines within an *hour*, much less in time to integrate it, scrub it, all that stuff. So they made an appeal to cache the results so that only the *first* query would take the hit, and all other queries would experience speed. This wish granted, they took another couple of days to return before - alas - throwing in the towel. Seems that the cache they would need required eight *terabytes* of space. Reports still returned in tens of minutes, but not at the turnaround demanded by the users.

This elicited the most obvious question, that eight terabytes was better hosted in the Netezza machine, and if so, *what do we need your product for?*

The warehouse-in-a-box products seem like a good idea. My simple suggestion would be to do a proof-of-concept like the scalable products do. Take the client's hardest problem, not a softball problem, and solve it with the product. If we have any doubts about what questions to ask, then ask for professional assistance. But don't just show the solution, but the *process* for solving the problem. After all, if a product has to jump through a lot of untenable hoops to make the solution work, it will feel like the solution is out of control, or at the very best, like a solution that is too brittle to trust with the pressing weight of our enterprise.

Getting the Story Straight

Every novel has a storyline and this one is no different. The what-happens-when and what-do-I-do-now questions pop up a lot. Here's a basic roadmap of how to set up our new Netezza environment, and we'll loosely use it as a guide in this book. These may not appear in the order listed, but we'll touch on each one in context.

- **To Migrate old, or establish new?** - Are we setting up a completely new environment, migrating an existing environment into it, or something in between?
- **Establish Data flow** - Data models, source to target map - Now it may sound strange that the data models are part of flow, but if we really intend to embrace data processing inside the machine, the databases are just utility-waypoints to another outcome, not the end-game. This again is a different way to think about databases.
- **Define the Environment** - Install stuff, define the database layout, install the databases. We'll need to get things underway. Like companion servers, installation of client software, setting up directories and file services, things that are normal in data warehousing but might be news to an application developer
- **Activate Models** - produce DDL, install tables, install exception rules - we'll want to us an

active data model, not a passive one. This means the model drives the production of other supporting assets rather than just something that arrives in the database catalog

- **Establish Intake** - acquisition paths, static data files, exercise intake - the first part of a thing is the most tenuous, so goes our intake requirements. Will the data be presented by another tool, or will we have to fetch it? Acquiring data is one thing, but then we have to assimilate it into the machine and make it consumption-ready.
- **Establish Behaviors** - Flow Control, Transform Control, SQL-Transforms - If the plan is to make Netezza a load-and-query server on the farthest end of an ETL flow, hey I can understand that. But if the plan is to use it for larger-scale data processing, then flow is happening inside the machine and we need to get a handle on it.
- **Configure Operations** - Integrate the scheduler, orchestration, notification and of course, release management and version control
- **Deploy Operations** - logging, metadata control, replication, housekeeping - okay the usual stuff, but now we need to provide the operators/admins with a window to the health of a processing machine, not just a passive warehouse.

We have ignition. Now let's step on the accelerator.

FULL THRUST 3

LET'S TAKE A BRIEF STROLL through the anatomy of a system's lifecycle. Stay with me, because we're chasing down an important artifact: The role of the SQL-Transform, the core data processing workhorse inside the Netezza appliance.

When a transactional system is first developed and deployed, often little or no consideration is given to long-term reporting needs. At least, not *scalable* reporting needs. The delivered reports typically plumb the depths of the operational model and provide useful information. For a while. Then they reach a saturation point. Every time a report runs, it starts to affect transactional response time. Throttles are put in place to avoid this effect, but then reporting users complain about slow reports.

Without having fully and formally embraced the mechanics and infrastructure of a reporting system, often the first step taken is to carve the data into structures that are specifically geared to support reporting. This is an introduction of "ELT" into the environment in the form of database-centric **E**xtract (from the operational tables), then **L**oad (into the reporting tables) and **T**ransform (as a part of the SQL statements used) to affect this data movement within the database.

Now for more clarity, the *Extract* in this operation really isn't a system-level extract, but more like a complicated *Select* statement. Likewise the *Load* in this operation is typically not a system-level load, but an *Insert* statement. It's a SQL-Transform, the "T" in "ELT", but not a *formal* "ELT". Formal "ELT" - Extract-Load-Transform, describes something much larger: *Extract*-From-Source-System, *Load*-To-Target-System, *Transform*-Data-Once-Inside (as a SQL-Transform).

So as we are already inside the database with no intention of exit, and the data is actually being SQL-Transformed from the operational tables to the reporting tables, this style of operation isn't really "ELT" (the data isn't outside the system) but firmly in the zone of SQL-Transforms, or what one conference guru once alluded to as SQL-T. I'm not trying to officially transform this thinking or nomenclature, but for the following discussion, SQL-Transform is where we will spend the most time, experience the most lift and solve the most problems. In Underground I described an Intake architecture that serves as a model for the "Extract-Load" portion of the ELT. We'll focus on the "T" portion of the ELT.

Back to the story, when the engineers must begin carving the data via SQL-Transforms, several unacceptable aspects appear as de-facto artifacts that will raise concerns from its inception to its eventual remediation. One of these is the violation of [1]Rule #10 – "Never perform bulk data processing inside an SMP-based Relational Database Management System". Another of these is the use of hand-coded SQL statements rather than utility-generated SQL statements. The first of these affects performance. The second of these affects maintenance and the effectiveness of the IT and operations staff. Trust me when I say, they *hate* hand-coded SQL-Transforms. And since these transforms in Netezza directly affect and shape performance, we need to get a stronger handle on their construction. Automated, rule-based generation is the key.

But if our first foray into SQL-Transforms is in hand-coded form, it will leave a sour taste in our mouths and we won't want to keep it around. We'll likely jump at the chance to use something more maintainable.

Case Study Short: One environment centered on SQLServer-based SSIS implementation for more than just a simple insert-select scenario. They wanted full-bore flow. Unfortunately, however, invoking SSIS against SQLServer for this purpose is a direct violation of Rule#10. Once down this path, the systems predictably started to run out of power trying to support it. Operators hated it because the flow was a black-box of dozens of SQL-Transforms. Developers hated it because it was always a thorny implementation to maintain.

But note the consistent continuum. We build/deploy a transactional environment. We need reports so eventually move into a solution with SQL-Transforms. We then realize that the database-hosted reporting solution is voracious in its processing needs, and eventually eclipses the transaction-centric RDBMS in its capacity requirements.

The next step then is to add more horsepower to the server, which works for a time. We ultimately realize that these two systems are like dogs fighting in a cage. The larger, hungrier dog (the reporting system) wins all fights. So we put these in separate cages, so to speak, by standing up separate servers and copying the data between them. This is the first foray into *ETL*, that is Extract (from the transactional server), Transform (the data along the way, in the transportation tool) and Load (the data into the reporting server, ready for consumption upon its arrival). In this case, the bulk data processing is now handled in the ETL tool, between the databases, not inside the database. We are no longer in violation of Rule #10 and the IT staff can more easily maintain the business logic in the ETL tool.

For many installations, the above progression is predictable, so some will rightly recognize that they are inevitable and will purchase/apply the appropriate technologies right away instead of suffering through the progression and its attendant risks. Others may have directly experienced the progression (as I have described it here) and sidestep the issue entirely with a formal processing environment.

Since SQL-Transform is in the first part of this progression, replaced in-total without revisiting it, often the first knee-jerk reaction to SQL-Transform is that it won't work, for a number of perfectly valid objections. These objections are being challenged now by appliances such as Netezza, causing the community to revisit and even apply SQL-Transforms as a viable bulk processing solution. Below are some of the objections and the reasons to reconsider.

- *It violates Rule #10, never do bulk processing inside the database.* - With Netezza, we are no longer constrained by the SMP-based relational database issues. It is a massively parallel (MPP) machine that is purpose-*built* for bulk processing on the inside. No indexes, no constraints, and the ability to build and throw away tables without any intervention from a DBA.

- *Requires hand-coded SQL* - well, it requires *customized* SQL, but we would never suggest hand-coding it. This is just how people first encounter it, so object to it now on the same grounds. If the SQL had been generated for them, this would be a non-issue. It is in fact a non-issue with Netezza, because it provides such easy-access to its catalog and the ability to build and teardown intermediate structures with no penalty. We can easily craft SQL generators that remove this burden.

- *Is not supported by common ETL tools* - It is functionally supported, but not *practically* supported, as we will see in the following discussions. ETL tools are not predisposed to delegate their hard-won performance capabilities to another higher-powered technology.

- *Creates black-boxed, unmanageable, long-running processes* - Always true with an SMP-based relational database because of its constraints. Never necessary with Netezza. This is entirely avoidable and shouldn't stand in our way.

- *Difficult to harness and maintain* - All flow-based processes require controlling capability. The industry has stepped up to the challenge with certain third-party accelerators while the common industry ETL tool vendors come up to speed with new capabilities.

So until the enterprise embraces and assimilates Netezza or an equivalent (I can't imagine) then they are stuck with the common [1]Jurassic Park Model. That is, extract data, crunch the daylights out of it and present it load-ready and consumption-ready to the target database's back door.

When discussing these two models, it superficially appears that we have only transposed the position of the *T* as a matter of semantics. One does T, the Transform, in the *middle* of the flow, where the other does T, the Transform at the *end*. However, there is more to this than a simple transposition of letters.

Inside a business data processing model, we have [1]two levels of "transform", one is the row-level transforms that scrub columns and data types. Another is the heavy-lifting transforms used for joining, rollup, aggregation, integration, enrichment and ordering of the information - *in scale*. This second "T", the heavy lifting, is the one that is of most interest, since it requires the most capacity and is voracious in its processing needs.

Any time an ETL environment starts to run out of power, we may look no further than how it's processing the heavy-lifting transforms. Is it joining, aggregating or enriching the data with lookups? These will over time become significant sources of stress, and will be the focus of tuning exercises for the duration of the solution's (remaining) existence. We can certainly take some pressure off the heavy lifting by performing some row-level pre-calculations, but eventually the model will reach its saturation point, where every tuning exercise only delivers a few percentage points of additional lift. Even upgrading the hardware does not significantly improve the situation, as it does not provide orders-of-magnitude of boost, but simply additional percentage points of boost.

The heavy-lifting operations have a common characteristic, in that they are *set-based*. If our database target is an SMP-based machine, our best option is to perform set-based operations in the ETL domain, even if it means pulling data from the SMP engine, processing it and putting it back (lift-and-shift).

However, with a Netezza platform in the house, there is another, highly viable option. We can now perform the smaller, row-level operations in the ETL tool, taking the heavy-lifting pressure off the ETL environment. We then defer the heavy-lifting for after the data arrives in the Netezza machine, where set-based operations rule and massively parallel power is the machine's architectural purpose.

This shift in purpose is something that the ETL tool vendors do not embrace because it relegates their role to that of a [1]data transportation mechanism. Once in this position, the owners of the environment openly question the value of the ETL tool, primarily because the typical tool licensing model includes performance as part of the licensing footprint, driving its *price*. If the customer is no longer using it for the heavy-lifting role, the customer begins to see the tool as a *high-priced data transport mechanism* and may actively look toward retiring the ETL tool for something that only does data transport, or does basic data transport and ELT in all in one package.

This inevitable outcome is why the ETL tool vendors are reluctant to embrace full-bore SQL-Transform models. It would require them to install a SQL-generation capability, embrace the database as part of the flow, and abdicate their role as power-player.

This is of course an obvious invitation for them to follow in Teradata and Exadata's footsteps and act in *preservation*. That is, offer up a lighter, less expensive form of the tool that focuses only on low-level transformation and no heavy lifting. One such product, WisdomForce, has embraced its role as a provider of high-speed data transport. I would recommend this product based on its track record alone, but its role in the SQL-Transform paradigm is intriguing. It finds its place as a powerhouse data broker and (of late) is priced to push out any incumbent ETL tools that would fill the same role at a higher price.

ETL Tools Reviewed against SQL-Transforms

The ETL technology offerings on the marketplace have been through a veritable use-case crucible so have functionally matured into interface-driven environments with common nomenclature, concepts and tasks that developers understand and like to work with. With high-productivity offerings, generating many assets the developer would normally have to manually produce, they provide ease-of-integration to an existing operational model.

However, some drawbacks are notable also. The ETL tool expects all processing to take place within its domain, and the database(s) involved are simply *book-ends*. Lift-and-shift can provide some processing power at first, then slow down as the data sizes and complexities grow, stress and ultimately overpower the systems, primarily the network. This may lead to hardware upgrade or wholesale re-architecture of the deployed solution. ETL tools also don't solve the most pressing database-facing problems, discussed in Underground, most significant of which is the inability to provide context to multiple shared-nothing database operations. The customer must also find and hire people who know how to work with the tool. The more rarefied the tool in the marketplace, the more expensive and harder-to-find are its practitioners, especially those who use it well (or even conceptually understand its application). If a product should fall out of market favor, the practitioners are even harder to find, and grow more expensive as they become more rare.

SQL-Transforms, specifically in Netezza, do not suffer the same disadvantages of the ETL tools. They leverage the power of the hosting database machine, so are directly and intimately integrated to the database. As a scalable AMPP platform, Netezza's power eclipses the available power in any ETL tool we might choose. It is simple to deploy and understand, requiring less uptake for a new technologist using it.

This makes it easier to staff, since core requirements are fewer - we need someone with data warehousing experience, SQL-skills and shell script, but not specific tool knowledge. Also that SQL-generation utilities are easy to craft and maintain, so that we're not in the business of hand-crafted SQL construction or maintenance. But in using SQL, we have a powerful language base at our fingertips, one that is understood outside of the language-base of the typical ETL tool. With Netezza's power and metadata-driven utilities, SQL-Transforms are more adaptable to the changing nature of the processing environment. With all this, the data never leaves the machine, so we get the additional security along with the additional boost.

Truth be told, however, any discussion of SQL-Transforms needs to be out-in-the-open with disadvantages also. So let's be realistic, in that *SQL-Transforms are not scalable on an SMP platform. Period.*

Case-Study Short: A large retailer of rental materials did not have the immediate funds to purchase a Netezza machine, but knew what they wanted in the way of infrastructure. They requested that our team put together a model that assumed the Netezza machine would be the final target, but for now go ahead and point it to that Oracle machine over there. We tried to warn them off, but they were insistent, even adamant.

This was a disaster. The SMP database cannot simulate a Netezza machine. Unwitting developers built many of the parts of the implementation on top of the Oracle system with the assumption of transactional capability. After all, what did the developers know about Netezza's requirements in this regard? By the time they could connect it up to a proof-of-concept Netezza machine, they realized that they had built huge sections of the solution completely wrong.

SQL-Transforms are not scalable on an SMP platform (see Rule #10), where most people tend to encounter them first. Likewise their (appropriate) use is not pervasive enough for vendors to see patterns on the best ways to use them. Apart from SSIS, which I would still argue is not ready for prime-time for SQL-Transforms either, none of the vendors see it as an important capability. This invites the question, as to whether the ETL vendors don't see any need for it, or if they do, don't want to find themselves relegated to a lesser role just because they did not think-through the offering's impact. Metadata capture is problematic with SQL-Transforms also, but this is simply a reason to embrace utility-based SQL-generation over its hand-coded form, so we can capture its essence at design time. Lastly, ETL tools may support "a few good SQL statements" but not the hundreds-at-a-time required for adequate SQL-Transform deployment.

Some ETL tools have recently embraced "push down optimization" or other support for database-side execution of SQL statements. While this is a step in the right direction, it has yet to embrace the simplicity necessary for practical application. Such environments as Oracle Data Integrator (formerly Sunopsis) and Microsoft's SSIS environment attempt to provide a flow-based development and execution platform for SQL-based transformations. However, we still see that an enormous amount of complexity is required to affect seemingly simple operations. These *seem* functionally complete at the time of initial implementation, but do not functionally scale and quickly become impractical for operation and maintenance. Often they reduce to black-boxed implementations that leave operators and administrators very nervous as to their run-time state when they cannot peek inside to check on them after an hour, or *two*, has passed in their execution.

Such capabilities are impractical because even the simplest SQL-Transform solution will invariably face every table in the target model. Fifty tables means at least fifty SQL-Transform operations. As functionality grows (and its attendant table count) the implementation tends toward functional brittleness rather than maintain its original feel of adaptive scale. We need to *know* that it can already scale into the hundreds or even thousands of SQL-Transform operations without loss of operational or data lineage control. In addition, once the deployment is complete we need a way to update the many SQL-Transforms we have deployed. This would include the ability to merge data model changes into the SQL-Transforms, or at least tell us which ones are affected by a change in the target database. Using ETL tools, this kind of metadata-merge with the database catalog (for SQL-Transform support) is not possible. ETL tools have not matured to this point, nor do we expect them to in the foreseeable future.

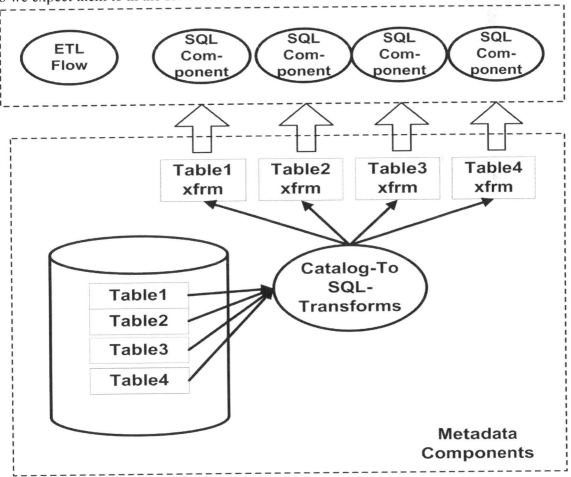

We do have an interim "bridge" compromise however. In ETL tools (depicted above), they all have the capability to consume a preformulated SQL statement. If we can set up a catalog-aware set of components (e.g. the approach I commonly use will glean the catalog and produce actionable SQL statements as artifacts). If we then expose these artifacts to the ETL tool's consuming components, the ETL tool can then behave as an orchestrator of these statements. This allows us to leverage catalog-aware SQL statements, a mature ETL tool to orchestrate them, and minimizes the impact on both. A number of install-bases have successfully deployed this approach with the DataStage product, although the concepts are portable to any ETL tool. Keep in mind that this is not an integrated capability, but an approach toward integration.

Another critical factor is the testability of the work products, both in the data content and the processing they are borne on. This doesn't mean the ability of testers to peek into the operational flow, per se. But their ability to develop test cases against a database. This presumes the availability of a metadata-driven testing capability. To keep up, testers will need this support (discussed later) and a lot more.

One aspect of SQL-Transforms that is absolutely necessary for successful deployment is the concept and implementation of SQL components, or rather, componentized SQL. In this approach, we are able to define certain parts of the SQL statements as components, and based upon dynamic conditions the proper, final SQL statement is assembled and executed. Currently ETL tools cannot achieve this because they require a fully-formed actionable SQL statement to be installed at design time. There is little opportunity to define parameterized portions of it in context of the flow section where it must run. Other tools may support this superficially, but require the SQL statement to be ready and finalized at startup, rather than how we actually need it, responding to data and metadata cues and conditions as they appear dynamically in the flow. In fact, Ab Initio application configurations do not respond to data in the flow at all. We cannot turn-on/turn-off components or functionality after the flow commences.

Another drawback of the ETL tool is its inability manage the SQL-Transforms as successive, flow-based operations. Each SQL statement is considered a standalone, shared-nothing operation with no prior dependency and no dependent downstream. In an ETL tool, recall, we can put together flows within the tool and they will automatically and naturally progress from component to component in controlled succession. But once we get to the SQL-Transform support, each operation stands alone with no operational transition from one to the next. There is no concept of a flow between SQL statements that is built-in to the tool. We have to rig it to behave this way, and the rigging has attendant risks. The rigging you see, must be installed as part of the ETL tool's *implementation*, not its underpinning architectural layer. So if we get an application running with cool database controls, we need to hold on to our hats because if this is an application-level implementation, it is likely a one-trick pony as well.

I've even had people object to this assertion with "Wait a second, we could boil up a loader utility that could handle all this." That's right, and it would continue to treat the database as an endpoint, not a waypoint.

Shared-nothing Operation Problem

Each SQL statement is by definition a shared-nothing, independently executed operation. SQL-Transform is not about moving data from one location to another, but moving data in context, under control, through multiple locations to multiple destinations. Data is *flowing*, and we need objective, deterministic control of the outcome as well as each individual process. ETL tools can execute the process and manage its *independent* outcome, but have no concept of flow from one SQL statement to the next.

As noted above, in an ETL flow model, metadata describing the flowing data is passed from component to component through propagated interface definitions. Such that the input definition for one component can be driven by the output definition of a preceding component. Developers then define rules within the component that will determine how data moves from the component's input port to its output port. While this seems obvious and simplistic, the ETL Tool's SQL-Transform *component* needs to do the same thing, except that the rules will be reduced to parts in a SQL statement's "select" clause. Additionally the input ports of the component are real, physical tables on the database, and the output port is likewise a real physical table on the database. In SQL-Transform, data leap-frogs from one table to the next.

This leap-frogging effect is required by SQL-Transform, and consummately efficient in a platform like Netezza. But it is shunned by ETL tools that specifically adjure the developer to keep the data *off* the I/O. The ETL equivalent, on the ETL server, would be to put an intermediate file between each component, which would simply kill the flow's performance as it leap-frogged on and off the disk. In an SMP shared-disk arrangement like that used by Oracle RAC (and incidentally, by Oracle Exadata) this leap-frogging is *supremely* inefficient. But in a Netezza system the leap-frogging is more incidental than wholesale bulk, since we can copy data from one table to another without the data ever even entering the Netezza host. All the work is done on the hardware. This powerfully shifts the performance metrics from the software (where the ETL tool or Oracle would do the work) into hardware (where Netezza will do the work).

The SMP-based RDBMS has no choice but to perform all of its operations, and derive all of its transformation power, from *software*. Netezza changes this game by pushing the performance deep into the hardware. This is what makes SQL-Transform viable on the Netezza platform.

Back to the shared-nothing capture. If we have a process control model that shepherds each SQL-Transform and maintains a flow-based harness for controlled succession, we then have the power to connect the SQL-Transforms with dependencies on the upstream operations, and provide results for dependent downstream operations. This is a controlled flow model that can be maintained, enhanced, branched, shared and otherwise experience all the benefits of the desired visualized flow model. But today, no such visualized model exists (even in ETL tools).

Shared-nothing insert

Like the above shared-nothing transforms, the final operation to actually push the data into the target database is also a share-nothing gig. In an ETL tool these also appear as standalone components. For example, if we are trying to push data into say, ten separate tables as part of a contextually complete operation (e.g. nine dimensions and one fact table, all integrated in context of the current flow), what do we do if all the dimensions load correctly but the fact table fails? Now the database is in an unknown state. Do we attempt to reload the fact table from a checkpoint? Do we rollback all the dimensions?

More importantly, what will we do if, several days after a successful operation, a user asserts that the data is corrupted and we need to rollback the entire load, and only *that* load? With independent shared-nothing inserts, the ETL tool has no inherent or intrinsic means to affect this necessary activity, so cannot help us. We have adjured database modelers to leverage "operational columns" that can be used to support such activities, but even if we do this, the ETL tool is not aware of them. We would have to engineer, rig or otherwise bolster the ETL application, not the ETL tool itself, to affect this on a per-application basis.

However, with a flow-based approach that deliberately harnesses this aspect, again using simple utility-based flow controls we can easily harness the SQL-Transforms, including the ones that will be used to affect the final target. Configuring these control mechanisms to automatically recognize the operational column likewise enables automatic behaviors as a substrate to all applications, not just one.

Componentized or Conditional SQL

Common ETL tools require us to put a fully mature SQL statement into place, complete with insert/select/from clauses. They don't allow for *parts* of these clauses to be parameterized, especially heavily parameterized, so that we can share and reuse SQL logic, conditionally affecting the use of this logic through changes in operational context. By disallowing or disregarding *dynamic* SQL parameterization, this leads to a great deal of cut-and-paste, manual hand-coding and embraces all the things people dislike about SQL-Transforms.

Because a typical SQL-Transform environment is controlled with structured script rather than a formal tool, opportunities for surgical control of the data, in massive set-based form, also provide us with the ability to component-ize the SQL itself. We will see insert-clause components, select-clause components, and snap-together join/where/group etc clauses based upon conditions discovered in the data, the metadata, the environment and the current processing state, among other contexts. Such far-reaching contextual control is not possible in the limited context of an ETL tool.

What people love about Netezza-based SQL-Transform, is the ability to take reusable SQL templates and snap-together the remainder as part of a SQL generation protocol. This preserves the investment in SQL and drives toward an object-oriented transformation model. SQL rules, filters, transformations and the like, become part of a reusable component library, not a singleton problem-solved-in-one-place.

Metadata Capture

If the transforms in the SQL-Transform flow are captured in their original sequence and logged, this becomes a rich repository for lineage information. Imagine a business analyst performing a simple "grep" on this file to locate a particular column that has produced questionable information in the database. Typically this will yield a lot of information about the column's traversion through the flows. But if it begins in the middle of the flow, the analyst can then zoom in on the transform that first produced it (by line number in the log), then can check for source columns feeding it, and source tables owning those columns etc. The process to browse the transform log is actually faster and more information-rich than most visual interfaces with less functionality.

In the final analysis, BAs rarely perform any sort of regular, deep data lineage analysis, and the need is so sparse that no software company will step up to the plate to produce the capability. Those that do, require the customer to buy into their other offerings, such as ETL tools and controls, to support the lineage metadata. That there is a periodic need for such lineage analysis is undeniable, so supporting the periodic need with an enriched, sequenced log is often just the right level of information the analysts require, no more often than they require it.

In short, the general objection that transform metadata capture is not supported is not valid. A simple linear transform log can and does support the vast majority of tasks required of an analyst, and does not have the formal overhead of metadata management. Why is this of benefit? SQL-based flows can be represented in any flexible, arbitrary form, unlike the rigid, structured, compliance-driven interfaces of an ETL tool. But as the ETL tool does not have the capacity to arbitrarily expand its functional capabilities, we have the additional benefit (in SQL) of unlimited functional expansion. With this however, comes the caveat that no metadata capture tool will be sufficient to catch up and keep up with the ever-expanding creative edge of the SQL-based solution. This is why a simple transform log can capture all the activity and context and never loses track of anything.

Multi-threaded, parallel operations

Whenever an ETL tool interfaces to a database, it will typically do so facing a dedicated interface table that it will load and commit information into. If it doesn't use an interface table, it will load the data directly into the table that will be consumed by the users. This requires the ETL tool to produce load-ready and consumption-ready data prior to the load.

This also means that the risk rises if the ETL tool must run multiple simultaneous operations, or operations that could commence before the prior operation completes (intraday models). To affect a multi-threaded load, this often requires some extraordinary engineering or configuration in the ETL tool, artificially increasing the complexity of the implementation in order to support a core processing need.

A simpler approach is to allow the ETL to simply drop-off the data in flat files, using a controlled model to perform the multi-threaded intake, bypassing the need to push this programming into the ETL tool where it has to be rigged for operation. Even shell-script and other programmable control mechanisms are simple to set up and maintain, compared to the relatively high tool-rigging required in the ETL tool.

Loops

Some may express concern over the need for loops in a data processing paradigm. Of course, we eschew the common transactional "cursor" loop because this embraces a transaction-based (Multiple-Instruction, Single Data) model that is not scalable. The most common example of the difference is as follows:

[1]One financial services provider had a nightly batch process, running on the database in SQL-Transform, that would process 3400 counter-parties inside a stored procedure. It would put the counterparties into a cursor, pull them one at a time, pass them through four business rules and put them back. Average time for each entity was around thirty seconds. This process could run for over ten hours.

When applied in Netezza, we "stand on it's side" the rules for the process, so that the first rule is applied to all 3400 records. As many know, a system like Netezza or Teradata can make short work of 3400 records for a single operation. Likewise the second rule and so forth using intermediate tables to store the results. This process completed in less than a minute, grand total. It arrived at the same answer, but used a set-based path to get there.

So this is the common "loop" path that is converted inside a Netezza-facing SQL-Transform solution. The other forms of loops are (as noted in the section above) using parameterized, component-SQL inside a loop that is controlling the values of the parameters. If this is performed in simple shell script, the parameters are $ variables and the loop is a simple for-loop. But each SQL statement must itself affect the data at the table-level, not the row-at-a-time level. It is important not to over-complicate the problem we are trying to solve. We'll look at more examples later.

Problematic for Insert/Update/Delete

A typical ETL tool has difficulty in managing a combination of updates, inserts and deletes. The de-facto standard is to put all of them in one flow and then transactionally apply them in a single component. A more robust method is to pull all the keys from the target table, use this to divide the flow into updates/deletes and inserts, then allow specialized components to deal with each. Note that this requires the database keys for the target table in order to be successful.

In a SQL-Transform model, we have direct access to the target table so can easily, in set-based form, winnow the updates from the flow and apply the same logic as above, but without needing to pull information off-the-box. Primary and foreign keys are at our fingertips.

In fact, referential control and management is far simpler inside the machine, provided we have a machine like Netezza that offers the set-based power to put it to work. More examples later.

Housekeeping

The ETL tools provide their own internal housekeeping for the assets they create. But if the ETL tool needs to create assets on the target database, such as intermediate tables to support SQL-Transform operations, does it also take responsibility for their cleanup? No, the ETL tool is not aware of such assets. They are part of the *application's* implementation. If we want to take advantage of them in the next application, we will have to forklift this, copy-and-paste style. Transparently reusing it is problematic.

We cannot set aside nor diminish the significant administrative overhead of these assets. If a common SQL-Transform job creates dozens of them, if left behind without cleanup these rapidly accumulate into hundreds or thousands. Housekeeping is a non-optional aspect of SQL-Transform processing, and it must be deliberate, aggressive and *automatic*.

However, with an integrated framework approach, using simple utilities, housekeeping can track assets as they are created, and provide multiple levels for their cleanup, all transparent to the SQL-Transform applications and automatically reusable by all applications as part of the substrate of the framework. For example, let's say we want to throw away the intermediate assets at the end of each run. We need a way to execute this in immediate context. We may, however, want to keep the assets in place for troubleshooting or support, but we don't want them to remain forever. We need yet another means to capture their presence so that they can be automatically or manually housekept later. So we have a run-time housekeeping and a deferred housekeeping. We will need it for temporary files as well as intermediate tables or views.

ETL tools do not supply the necessary housekeeping to support the above, but we know that this activity is necessary and non-optional. They are simple to implement in an integrated form, provided we have the right controlling mechanism.

Troubleshooting

Data type mismatch checking is something that ETL tools do well, inside their *own* domains. But what if we have an SQL-Transform that the ETL tool will run for us, and the types on the sources are mismatched on the target? Of course, obvious mismatches will cause the SQL statement to fail, but what about too-large to too-small transfers, truncated varchars, integers, numeric precision and the like? This are like a black hole of problems that are difficult to characterize much less locate.

In addition, what about detecting the compatability between source and target distribution? If the distribution is mismatched, performance will not be optimum. Likewise, what if the distribution is matched but the keys are not referenced in the join-clause? We can set up simple utilities to help us with this, but the ETL tool will not step up.

A properly configured database-facing SQL-Transform control utility has direct access to the catalog and can provide these side-by-side reports as warnings to developers, invaluable to the initial troubleshooting and testing mission but also critical for enhancements and maintenance. If a column was correct once-upon-a time and then was recharacterized later, plain SQL statements will not always detect the discrepancy. We need something that will do it for us aggressively, deliberately and *automatically*.

Conclusions

In a secondhand data warehouse technology such as Oracle, Sybase or SQLServer, the function of SQL-Transform is a transient implementation leg of an ongoing journey toward a more powerful Jurassic Park-Model data warehouse. Once we embrace an MPP platform like Netezza, not only does SQL-Transform become viable, it actually invites us to shake off the Jurassic Park model and move toward something more self-contained and independent. It invites us to embrace

Netezza's internal power for scalable *data processing.*

Common ETL tools are still firmly ensconced in support of the Jurassic Park model, and are likewise unwilling or even unable to embrace the significant challenges of SQL-Transform in the core substrate of their tool offerings.

For those who have forsaken SQL-Transform for traditional reasons, they should reconsider and embrace it for machines like Netezza that not only actively support it, but are very efficient and scalable in a SQL-Transform context. More so than any other traditional database engine can provide, and eclipsing the power of common ETL tools.

Add to this the power of the UDX through such tools as nzLua, and we have a more-than-formidable means to affect data at every level with high scalability.

LIFTOFF
4

THE PRODUCT IS CHOSEN, Netezza is on the way or in the house, and now it's time to activate our purchasing decision into more than just an action item. As with any new purchase, the excitement is high and the expectations are higher. If Netezza was compared to something else, then everyone is just coming down from the Tournament of Posers and the *Real* Data Processing Appliance is now standing up.

We are now walking in a living stream of water that is rapidly growing in width, depth, and strength. This water represents the current of transformation. We cannot get to the water's edge without leaving the company altogether. If we stay, we need to figure out a way to manage our existence. We cannot deny that the current exists nor can we ignore its growing strength. Just like in a space shuttle liftoff, the astronauts are strapped in. The opportunity to step away from the launch pad has passed.

Of course, we might be one of those chaps (or know one of those chaps) who will spend all of his strength swimming to shore. He had been certain that his favorite champion would win the Tournament, but alas, it was not so. The Netezza appliance is on the way and he either needs to knuckle-down and double-down, or he needs to move along. Or as the old adage goes, there is only one thing worse than quitting and leaving, and that's quitting and staying. The last thing we need on our hands are folks that will make the upcoming months a hassle or even painful for us. In short, when we hit bumps in the road (and we will, however minor), who needs a naysayer? Especially one that reminds us he is a naysayer while chanting "I told you so." It's just bad form.

So depending on the nature of the Tournament, and whether the techs around us really got passionate about maintaining their status quo, or got passionate about the new direction, we need to take a pulse. Liftoff is upon us, the next phase of operation is already underway, and we may have people who are onboard the craft but mentally checked-out of the process, or worse, are doing Doctor Smith number behind our backs and are spending more time watching our backs (to get a good target for the knife) than we are. In this situation, we'd rather not be watching our backs, but what's ahead of us. I seriously doubt that any astronaut at the time of liftoff, is concerned about how rapidly the Earth is disappearing behind them. Rather, they are focused on frontier they are about to enter.

And this time, it won't be on a Mustang.

It behooves the leaders of our organization to attend the next open conference on Netezza technology. Whether this is a local users group meeting or the main conclave, they will have access to other users and their tales of success and challenge. We learn most from the tales of challenge.

NETEZZA TRANSFORMATION

At the San Francisco '09 conference one of the customer leads went through an explanation of a series of roadblocks and challenges within the industry and her company. She overcame and did well. Tales like these help strengthen our resolve, because in many cases it's not really about the technology, it's about the *change.*

Case Study Short: A consulting colleague tells me that upon his arrival to a client site, the principal architect let him know that he hated consultants. He had is own ideas about the solution and didn't need any smarty-pants in khakis telling him how to do his business.

Ooookay, well this was off to a smashing start. Over the next weeks, my colleague won the principal's confidence, but unbeknownst to my colleague, the principal was setting him up for a fall. He did not like consultants, but he really didn't like the fact that he had architected a completely different solution (that had been rejected at the top of the company in favor of Netezza) and he was sort of stewing in his own juice. If he could make this consultant fail, and likewise make Netezza fail, he could swoop in and save the day with his architecture.

Of course, true to form, Netezza has so much power that one would have to be stumbling in the dark to miss an opportunity with it. What the principal found was just that - not only did the Netezza machine help them solve problems faster, it also simplified the overall solution. His architecture, after all, would have been wildly complex if compared to a simple appliance.

The point is, none of the other project bosses knew of his hidden agenda to derail the project. The signs should have been obvious. He had proposed another solution and it had been dismissed, but the project bosses thought he had gotten over it. Well, he never got over it. Many years went by and he still wasn't over it.

Author's note: The project bosses need to know even at project liftoff: who is with them and who is against them. One of the most significant tasks that we as consultants have, is in assessing this landscape as quickly as possible. One of the most significant tasks that the project boss' ensconced consulting firm has before them, is to hide their animus until the time is right.

Case Study Short: With the appliance on the way, several internal managed services groups bid for the work. The project boss did not see any strength among them and had not expected to. Buying into Netezza meant (in their minds) accepting some risk of using a niche market of consultants, and while those consultants came at a (slightly) higher price, the risk of not using them (over a novice) seemed so much higher.

So the boss brought the niche consultants into the shop, showed them around and got them started. All the while the internal managed services crew were plotting their overthrow. In local papers, they advertised for Netezza skills. In national forums they went after people who were at least trainable in Netezza, so they could onboard them to the project and get trained by the niche consultants. Their objective in no uncertain terms, was to supplant these niche operatives at the first available opportunity.

In the meantime, the managed services crew found chinks in the armor of the niche players, and exploited them. They were small and unable to provide the same strengths as the larger firms. This was played against them and slowly gained an audience. The niche firm's agility seemed to be no match for the managed services firm's size and resources.

Then one day a management principal saw a memo from the managed services firm containing their "agenda" toward the niche firm. He performed his own private investigation to determine if the activities of the larger firm were in keeping with the memo. They were in fact attempting to drum out the smaller firm. The management principal took this state of affairs to his managers, who then took it to a review board, and before the end of the month the managed services firm went on probation and all of their personnel were required to leave the project.

Now that they were on probation, more memos surfaced. Before the next thirty days expired, the managed services firm had been completely black-listed from the IT division. No word on if they survived in the remainder of the company.

The point of these machinations is this: It is never business-as-usual once the Netezza machine is in play. Liftoff has happened and people need to be on board with making the entire mission successful. Those that want to play political games cannot be stopped, of course, because gamesmen are ever-present. It may however, change the stakes of the game, something that the gamesman is not prepared for.

In this regard, the landscape underwent more than just transformation. It experienced upheaval. The Netezza machine was deployed with no additional fanfare and is quietly solving that firm's business problems with the expected aplomb. What of the niche firm's folks? Some of them are still on site, managing the Netezza experience. Interestingly, none of them even knew about the powerplays that had created such a maelstrom around them. They simply executed their work and stayed clear of the fray.

But the question is - what *caused* the fray? Territorialism? Market share? A managed services firm with such aggressive, or vindictive sales folk that they just could not stand to lose?

It doesn't matter. The *transformation* happened anyhow.

Answer honestly...

Are *we* ready for this transition?
Is everyone *else* ready for this transition?
Is the *infrastructure* ready for this transition?

And the envelope please: we will *never* be ready for this transition. Netezza is a game-changer and a change-agent rolled into one. Attempting to prepare for its arrival, instantiation and leveraging it to full potential is no different than any of the following scenarios:

- We receive a phone call that our high school chum, now a sports superstar, is coming over to our house and will arrive in fifteen minutes with a camera crew. They are interviewing old acquaintances for a color story on the athlete. How much time do we *need* to prepare? It doesn't matter. We have fifteen minutes or less.
- An IRS agent shows up at the doorstep of our fledgling business and claims to require our undivided attention for several days of audit. How much time do we need to prepare? What does it matter?
- Our son/daughter has just called and is about to introduce us to the person they intend to

spend the rest of their lives with, and can we meet them at the most upscale restaurant in town, in half an hour, and bring our credit card? Can we ask for more time in this? Would more time really matter?

We can see from these, that the transforming event is upon us, it is a *one-time/first-time* event, and we are either fully prepared "as is" to embrace and run with it, or we are not. Accepting that we are *prepared* to embrace, and the *act* of embracing, are two different things. Accepting that we are prepared to engage this event, however transforming and life-changing it may be, for good or bad, is much different than saying we actually *are* prepared for the engagement *itself*.

To illustrate this difference, many people purchase technology with the intention of using it to its fullest value and power. They would not buy it otherwise. They are prepared to *start* using it, but they are not necessarily prepared to *fully* use it. Several years ago I purchased a piece of technology that I fully intended to put to work. But when I brought it home, it was incomplete. It needed this part, or that part. It required this or that download. Where I was prepared to use it, I couldn't quite use it yet.

Each day I am thoroughly amazed at the number of apps available for the iPhone. I received an iPhone from my employer but I probably would not have purchased one myself. I had been warned that the battery runs down easily, I cannot receive a meeting request and have it added to my iPhone calendar unless other technologies are in play. Meeting request issues were fixed in a new iPhone software version, and the battery thing was fixed, I'm told, with the iPhone 4.

We conclude here that as a person executing in a high-speed *business* world, the iPhone wasn't ready to join me. Other devices, like the Blackberry, had already proven their mettle and I was very happy with them. But switching to the iPhone was a step down. Some may wonder why the complaint, because they would love to have one. Sure, I can understand that sentiment. I like the iPhone for those same reasons. But those are using personal, non-critical communications. However, as a business asset, it falls short, to wit: Nothing is worse than being in a business conference call and getting the dreaded "switch to battery power" message when I'm standing in a location that offers no such option. I will lose the call, I will not be able to re-engage without a secondary battery or recharge, and this could lead to loss. Of revenue, of engagements, of reputation, all for the sake of liking the personal benefits of the device. I never had these issues with the Blackberry. As a note, Apple has spent millions of dollars and significant thought labor on improving their products for business users. This "desire to improve" will be a theme we'll notice among the appliance competitors. If a competitor has a desire to improve, it means that the marketplace opportunity is real.

Back to the issue: was the iPhone *ready* to be used as a business phone? Clearly not. Is it marketed or engineered to be a business phone? Clearly not. So why am I trying to use it outside the zone of operation for which it was constructed and sold?

Why *indeed?*

Why this dramatic lead-in? For this reason, not to be trivialized:

Our current environment is no more configured or ready to receive a Netezza machine, from the process/infrastructure to the systems to the people. It is important that we not assume that any of these areas are even remotely ready for what's about to happen to them.

All of them will have to change. It is a necessary and positive transformation, but it is being caused and pressed by the assimilation of the Netezza machine. It is considered by some to resemble a violating act, at least of someone's career sensibilities (you know, the nay-sayers). But it is no more this than it would be to take a plow to the field, to turn it under and prepare it for planting. What some don't understand, is that one or more of these areas, infrastructure, people and systems, are about to be hit with the plowshare blade, turning their world askance, perhaps even upside down. We don't care about what the "soil" thinks concerning this action, but we *must* care what our people think, and we must care about the environmental impact because it will affect everything we are about to do. From day one, we need to set expectations around them.

People are involved, we must be judicious.

For those who have already experienced these effects, for some the process of Netezza induction was a series of non-events. The machine and its capabilities were assimilated in the same manner as any other new or even strangely aligned technologies, because one or more of them had pioneered the process already. Well and good. For others, Netezza was/is the pioneer, we are in uncharted territory and are wondering what to expect.

Sometime back on the ITToolbox *Ab Initio Underground* blog, I posted an article that was a spinoff from another Data Warehouse Journal article entitled There Be Dragons. It started out with the allusion to ancient maps of uncharted territories. In these would be the notation "There be dragons" as a warning to anyone who dared enter. Nobody's been here before, we don't know what to expect, you're on your own. And all that.

Mentioned here was the simple situation that many data warehouse "gurus" approach the Dragon the wrong way. They see the Dragon as something to kill with swords and staves, or something to take apart, or even destroy in a blaze of glory. What they miss is that the dragon is immortal, and the only way to deal with it is to put it in a controlled environment, and then put it to work. Make it earn its keep, so to speak. I received so much hilarious (and some dark) anecdotal feedback from that article that I could not resist referencing it in part of this book's subtitle.

The fact remains that we are about to embark on a journey that will include moving the Dragon from it comfortable quarters into a new digs, the Netezza machine, and make no mistake about it. That Dragon is *comfortable*. He knows the guards and the warden. He is happy with the feeding schedule. The dank smell has become familiar, and even the nightly sounds are part of his regular habitat. And now we intend to move him to another location? Take him from his quiet contentment, where even though he has suffered the humiliation of having his freedom removed, at least he is useful. He hears that the new location is a bigger dungeon with more powerful locks. And all this time he had just been biding his time for when the current locks would rust out, the door would rot and the dungeon could no longer contain him.

He's immortal after all. Time is on his side.

But with this news, now he knows that the dungeon-masters have cleverly protracted his stay. He will need more patience. But don't think for a moment that he intends to trot right out into his new accommodations and be happy about it. No, he will curl up into a ball and make everyone work very hard for what they want. Dragons are big and hard to move. We get that.

When we first consider data migration, the first hurdle we will encounter is that the data is behind several layers of protection. Not just security, but functional layers. As noted in Underground, nobody ever intended for the data to leave in quantity, so it was never configured to support such a thing. Now we want data delivered in quantity, extracted to move it to another home. No, it's curled up in a ball and won't leave without a fight. In this fight, where we actually believe that those who shepherd and care for the dragon are planning to help us, we might find it a bit daunting when they don't. Or in some cases *won't.* They worked very hard to stand up the current environment. Asking them to dismantle it because of the ingress of new uppity technology, feels (to some) like a backhand. For those of us who know better, it's actually a breath of air, and the sooner we get it up and running, the sooner we can go back to normal lifestyles. More on that later.

For now, we have the pending issue of the actual migration process, and what it might hold for us. I noted also in Underground that the functional priority should be to take what we want to keep and leave the rest behind. People have taken this quite seriously and that's a good thing. What was missing from that discussion (for lack of space more than lack of content) was the business process of the migration and how it will affect, and radically transform, the processes and people around us.

For those who want to maintain the status quo, brace yourself. Once the Netezza machine wrapped the proof-of-concept, we entered what some call the whitewater phase, or in this case the Liftoff.

At EPCOT Center in DisneyWorld Orlando, one of the experiences is *Mission Space,* hosted by Gary Sinise (no doubt chosen because of his work in *Apollo 13*). In Mission Space, this is a high-speed virtual reality experience where the riders are gravitationally and inertially manipulated into thinking they are actually launching into space. The effect of being pulled into the chair, and the skin on the face being drawn back toward one's ears, and the blood in one's head gathering to the rear of the skull, is very hard to describe in words. The rider is on a giant spinning gimbal, so the inertia is real. Also at MGM Studios in DisneyWorld Orlando, the Rockin' RollerCoaster uses a linear motor to launch the cars (think, *rail-gun*). We experience horizontally what Mission Space simulates vertically. But the rush is no different.

The phase directly after the proof-of-concept feels just like this Liftoff experience, mentally, emotionally and just short of physically. It's no simulation and it's not a thrill ride. On either of those, the experience will end and we'll exit the thrill-chamber to flit off to the next one. Not this time. It's sustained, intense, stressful and the frankly most fun we'll ever have on an IT project without filling the entire room with laughing gas and closing the door.

The train leaves the station, with or without us. If we happen to jump onto the train's last car, it doesn't matter, we're still on the train. If it's someone like me, however, the client has to hire a chopper pilot to fly us close enough to alight on the roof and hope the wind speed doesn't knock us off. Some analogies are tortured. This one seems to fit every time we engage.

And like a speeding locomotive, it gathers strength and speed with every passing moment. We need assurance of one thing at this point: that we are on the right track. We still have time to switch to the right track later, but there is a point of commitment, where we reach certain speeds that will require us to slow down if we want to change tracks. This is often not a bad thing, because slowing down so that we can later move many times faster, has a payoff in the long run.

But just how *long* is this "long run", and how long are our stakeholders willing to wait? "Long runs" have to start producing traction, you see. If the stakeholders see traction, they are more confident in measuring the length of the "long run". But if the project is sitting in the water, or worse, regressing against the schedule, expect alarms to go off. Don't take it personally. They want results, and don't think *some* progress is too much to ask.

Case Study Short: A particular project brought in some hired guns and they got to work. The objective was to stand up, inside a Netezza machine, a fully functional operational model, plus a fully functional reporting model. Both targets had hundreds of tables. Each would require hundreds of specific transform operations. They also had hundreds of source tables that would require specific mappings, since the column names and table names did not match. Add to this the need to perform change-data-capture, and that very few people really understood the new data model all that well, and the heroic team of six-shooters had their work cut out for them.

True to form, within two weeks the intake model was filling the Netezza machine's intake tables. Within another four weeks, the operational model was populated and testable while the reporting model was already consuming major parts of the operational data. Within eight weeks of project inception, both models were testable. Within another four weeks, the entire infrastructure, including scheduling and exception processing was fully operational and ready for testing.

This had, for all practical purposes broken several land speed records for all these areas, and then some. Yet in this final push, something arose concerning scope. It seems that there were over one-hundred intake tables missing from the sources, things the client-side modelers had simply overlooked or had forgotten about. This would take time to correct, but no harm done. The six-shooters rolled up their sleeves to make it happen. Just give us four weeks and we'll square it away.

Four weeks, for this kind of refactoring, seems unheard of, right? All that work and retrofitting and they could make it all happen in only four weeks? Or as some would say, "I'll believe that when I see it!" Or perhaps, "Prove it!"

But this was not the reaction received by the team. Rather than hearing sighs of relief that it would only take a mere four more weeks, the principals in charge rather became alarmed and unraveled.

Whose fault was this oversight? Why didn't the six-shooters recognize they were missing data? Or a better question was, why didn't the testers recognize it, considering they had given the entire model a big thumb's up? Or considering that the source-to-target map was already so poor, and that the six-shooters had been hired for their technical skills, where did the answer lie? The simple response to this: It's not anyone's *fault*. It's the *natural* progression of a migration project. Responses like the principal's reaction speak a thousand words, starting with "We've never done this before" because only an amateur would ask such questions, or react this way in the face of such an already scintillating success story. Recall the case study in Underground where I asserted that we can easily discern a person's skill level or experience by the questions they ask? Or even by the ones they *don't?* Hmmm.

The next step of the above tale was even more absurd. The principals pulled the plug. Then, after months of attempting to re-assemble another, this time far-less-skilled team, they stumbled through the project and finally had something up and running at the end of *nine more months*. The project principal telling me this story lamented, "If we had just swallowed the need for four more weeks instead of going on a witch hunt..." Yes, totally agreed. Four more weeks would have cost them, well, *four* more weeks. The witch hunt and the aftermath cost them nine times this, and that was just to get reset to *where they had been before,* not with the same momentum, not with the same skills and, more unfortunately, with a lethargic inertia that would eventually put them into production with all the speed and swiftness of a Galapagos turtle on anti-depressants.

"Inertia - an object in motion tends to remain in motion, an object at rest tends to remain at rest," Sir Isaac Newton.

"For every action, there is an equal and opposite reaction," Sir Isaac Newton.

Over-reaction. Under-reaction. *Any* reaction. Newton's law kicked in here when the principals failed to get *behind* the team, but rather pushed back on the team. Inertia and the laws of motion apply to more than just physics. Push back on a project team and we're not only inviting an equal and opposite reaction, we are embracing the *false idea* that the friction, not lubrication, will make the project go faster. I would point out the obvious parallels here, but it's more than analogy. *It's how things work.*

Migration projects are a continuum of discovery. There is no time or place for reaction, only *response*, refactor and movement, maintaining the inertia of the project in the form of motion, not rest. Or as famous someone succinctly put it:

"We keep moving *forward*..." excerpt from Walt Disney's quotes, emphasis mine, soon to be yours.

Forward momentum, shaking off the old and embracing the new. Onward and upward. All that stuff. We don't want to get stuck in a rut. For that matter, we don't want to gather a head of steam, ready to take on the next big challenge, only to be told stop-and-wait.

"I didn't come this far to listen to a two-bit carny hypnotist," Robert Redford. *The Natural Key.*

Okay, I'll get out of your head. For now. I'll come back later when it's not so full (of ideas). Let's press on and look at the more operational aspects of data migration that may well supersede the success of technical/functional migration. All of our tables are noted, sources mapped to targets and we're ready to rock. But something is in the way. Hmm. Something quite unexpected.

We're ready to go, but nobody else is ready to go with us. How weird is that? If we made the mistake of signing up to migrate the old-to-new on a fixed price while everyone around us is working on a time-and-materials basis, or just plain old salary, every appeal to urgency and forward momentum will be met with a blank stare. Moving forward is doable, but not on a schedule. Especially not a tight one.

Many years ago my wife and I lived near one of the largest theme parks in the world. As local folk, we could get deep discounts on tickets. Whenever people visited us, the deal was that we would use our local discount if someone would pay for our ticket. Or at least one of us. After all, discounts aside, it's still pricey to get inside the park. For the value, especially with a family, get four-day unlimited-access tickets. They are worth every penny and if we don't use them, they are still good - forever. The point is, when we have an non-expiring ticket, we are not on a fixed-price outing with a finite time frame. We feel like we are on a time-and-materials outing and if we miss something, we can always pick it up when we come back. It's still a "not to exceed" model but with some significant benefits.

What's the difference, one may ask? I'm glad one asked.

When visting the park, we saw an interesting effect at the end of the day, largely from families that had bought single-day passes. The closing hours approached, there were tons of things left to do, and the family members realize that time had run out. Loving families are suddenly shouting at each other. Moms and Dads saying things to each other and their children that could go unsaid forever. All because the clock is running down, the fixed-price gig is about to close, and they're not done.

Connect the dots.

In case the dots remain in solo mode, let's just cut to the chase. Doing a migration project on a fixed price, seriously expecting it to work out in our favor, is a lot like this family outing. It starts out in a wonderland-honeymoon for the vast majority of the work. Then something happens, or several somethings that affect the timeline. The clock is ticking down. Is it about to get ugly or can we convert the ticket?

Look, in a migration project, so many unknowns are in play that to even attempt to put a fixed price on it is tantamount to a leap of faith in the most critically dire circumstances. My wife is an architectural interior specialist for large-scale facilities like nursing homes and the like. Her job is to outfit the facility with the best stuff for the best price, and bring it all up to code at the same time. Invariably, when calling in contractors to rip out walls or floorings, they receive a surprise. It could be termites, or dry rot, or something larger. Either way, the problem has to be corrected before proceeding. More time, more waiting, usually more money.

In the virtual world, migration minefields like this are lying around all over the place. No matter how savvy our client contacts purport to be, they have missed something, and a *lot* of little somethings. We will encounter those, if we're lucky, on day one of the project. If we're really unlucky, on day thirty, or *sixty*. Yikes. We'll get partly into it and discover something and they will all look around to each other and say, "Ohhhhh, yeaaaahh." Yeah, that's the sound of fixed-price breaking.

So if we want to do it fixed price, there needs to be a higher objective than money alone. After all, Wal-Mart sells certain items at a loss because they know it will draw us to the store to buy other things and make up the difference. The objective is to get us into the store. If we ain't in the store, we ain't spendin' money. Some consultant folks launch projects in places that are "hard to get into", so that once inside, they can penetrate and radiate and all that, and start making money on follow-on projects that never would have happened without getting into the door in the first place They see the fixed price project as the price for entry. But again, we should be careful what we wish for, because two can play that game.

Case Study Short: One consultant project manager told me that his entire team was ecstatic to win the bid, and sold it *as a loss to get inside*. All the managers at the consulting shop were hopeful that it would pan out for more follow-on projects. A number of opportunities presented themselves, but the sales folk were asleep at the switch. The project foundered, money wise, into a ditch that required revisiting the contract for more money. This was a clear warning sign to the sales folk to get in there and close some deals. But too much time had passed and the only thing anyone *now* recognized or knew about their firm, was that the project was behind. Some unexpected scope issues arose (they always do) and this had protracted the time frame. Stuff like this happens, but without the sales folk tending the farm, so to speak, weeds of neglect crept in and this was all the client could see.

Later we will look at one of the immutable truths of migration projects, that is, *the timeline will slip*. It is important for the sales team to get inside and close deals before this juncture arrives.

Case Study Short - one project manager relates that during the course of the project, more functionality kept popping out of the woodwork, mostly from quarters that had not been examined in the design review. Some thought that the client had deliberately withheld these aspects in order to elicit a lower bid. When the aspects were realized, the project manager claimed that these "extraordinary extras" were out of scope. What he may have meant to say was that these represented an extraordinary *change* in scope. Either way, it had not been accounted for.

The draconian in all of us wants to say "tough noogies", but when the information was actually withheld, with the clear knowledge of all involved that the withholding was to garner a lower price, this is the type of skullduggery that makes for bad client relationships.

All because it was *originally* set up as a fixed price and both sides thought they had something to gain. For our first case study above, the project manager related that when the effort started to hemorrhage, the consulting leaders on his side conveniently forgot that they had signed up for a loss. A loss no less, for the higher goal of gaining and keeping a foothold in a particularly tough client site. When the loss was fully realized, and the news was that the sales folk had never even bothered to stop by, the message was clear: fixed price for a migration project has to have a larger game plan, so that when the cost goes up and the functionality rises with it, we are not taken aback or by surprise. *And everyone has to play the game.*

It was all part of the plan anyhow. Of course, if this is something the leaders stumbled into without a plan, then they join the ranks of those who made bad business decisions and suffered for it. This goes a long way back, folks. Millennia even.

So perhaps this horse is dead and certainly doesn't deserve another beating, but beat it we will, as the story goes, because for whatever reason, people don't realize the unintended and unexpected scope involved in a migration project. This unstable scope represents a risk of delay for all involved, and if on a fixed priced, represents a loss of revenue and even being stuck in an upside-down project.

Is that scary enough? Hey, liftoff is meant to take our breath away. We just expect it to come back sometime soon, before we red-out.

The anatomy of a new technology installation (in this case Netezza, but it applies to all technologies) sometimes has a protracted cycle. It often starts when a manager with moxy decides that enough-is-enough with the current reporting or warehousing environment. He or she initiates the process of replacing it. At this point the proponents of the ensconced vendor come out of the woodwork (and the flooring even) and make a pitch to upgrade. Already having heard (or even acted on) this song, the manager looks elsewhere, initiating a vendor candidate selection, a bake-off between candidates and a final selection. That's a lot of activity over the course of many months, and it is starting to build excitement, a lot like how an electrical storm builds energy around a radio tower, or perhaps how a comet develops a giant coma as it approaches the Sun. Hearts and minds are being affected, and then, the choice is made.

Netezza is on the way.

But it's really already here, isn't it? People are taking action, reading up on the technology, finding out what they can from the vendor, perhaps attending training. They are preparing for the transition, and because of the numbers Netezza put on the scoreboard, they are *pumped* about it.

So look at what's happening here. By choosing a new technology, people have started to change. They might have a spring in their step, or they might have a resume' in hand. Not everyone is on board with the choice of vendor, and we can count on that. In any tournament there are winners and losers, and the losers really hate to lose. Especially because they have something to lose. Netezza is the new player in the shop and has no footprint or stronghold. But toppling the stronghold of another is often downright personal.

People will start to prepare for the machine's arrival in strange ways. They will call upon their experience in their chosen technology or realm of operation, but it doesn't quite fit. Or perhaps it does, then it doesn't, then it does. This knowledge-transfer phase can be like a rollercoaster, or a white-water ride, or we can just do like Katherine Hepburn did in African Queen, and ride it out because it fills our lungs with emotional oxygen. This is one of those one-time, first time experiences we will want to remember. Oh yes we will.

So the buzz is on, the people are excited and the new machine can't get here any sooner. Oddly though, when it finally arrives and gets situated, the buzz comes to a standstill as the principals say to themselves *Now what?*

It's not a bad thing of course, but for some this is an issue of pride. It's almost like a person who has been bragging about their ability to drive a sports car, yet nobody has ever seen him drive anything but the standard economy car. One day someone puts him in front of the sports car and there is a feeling of dread welling up inside him. He knows everything there is to *know* about driving and operating one of these things, but never one with this kind of power, or that drives quite like it. He asks himself: What if I make even a single mistake? They will bury me in their derision. I must therefore keep quiet, under the radar until I have mastered every nuance.

And then there's the other guy, who cracks open the manual and starts working with the machine because it's in front of him, he has things to learn, and we're burnin' daylight. Oddly enough, many times both of these people arrive to the point of "master" at the same time, even though they take different paths at different speeds. The point is, dig in, but we should pace ourselves. Drinking from a fire hose doesn't mean we will quench our thirst any faster.

Apart from all this, our people will run up to us with a million new ideas. Where were all those ideas when we were on the *old* system? Those ideas didn't have a power-plant. There wasn't enough spare time to plan anything (they were always fire-fighting) and not enough power to buy back some time. What good are new ideas if we can't even make the old ones work, or at least, not work in time to use them?

We will find that some of our folks have a *lot* of pent-up anxiety, but also a lot of pent-up anger. The kind of anger that comes from the inability to please their own managers because there's not enough time in the day to get reports out of an oatmeal-powered machine, or even a high-powered machine that is overwhelmed, or a well-powered machine that has been improperly implemented. Another thing they fear: *What if this is an indictment of my technical prowess? After all, I designed the prior system that they are replacing. Surely this is not a vote of confidence!*

Bingo. Even if the machine's ingress does not replace us outright, it will so change the way we do business that we may as well re-learn the data quality environment. Those who cannot re-learn and re-tool, might be left behind. Or at least, they *fear* this, misplaced though it is. Those who have been exposed to a Netezza machine and experienced the transition, see the Netezza machine as a valuable asset, a career-builder and for many, a career-changer, at least to the extent that they have been freed from the malaise of an underpowered system and have accelerated their exposure to large-scale data and massively parallel data processing.

It seems the lost opportunity *here*, would be to walk away. Alas.

One way or another, we are witnessing people under stress. People do interesting things under stress. Sometime they shine, sometimes they burn out, but for certain, they will transform.

Other things are under stress too, and it's building.

In the movie series *The Matrix*, the main character Neo has these odd abilities to affect his virtual-physical environment. In the first movie, after realizing his avatar-ness, he flexes his body and the dripping-number walls around him bend and warp. In the second movie, he would squat in anticipation of flight, and the ground around him would ripple like a pond. At the end of this show, we see him flying through the virtual city with a trail of debris (and automobiles?) whirling in his virtual wake.

A Netezza appliance, in all respects but the immediate physical world, has a tendency to bend and warp the environment around it. I joke sometimes about "gravity-bending" power, but if the customer's infrastructure is the virtual world of dripping numbers we are about to push the appliance into, rest assured that those numbers will warp into another shape. Depending on the infrastructure's immediate ability to adapt, stress ensues.

Case Study Short: The appliances showed up *en-masse* at the customer data center. *Sixteen* of them in various strengths. The data center managers were ready to receive them, so placed them in their designated locations on the raised floor. Popping the tiles to access power, they then learned that the techs who had installed the power supplies, did so in the wrong place. They had been installed fifteen feet away. Unable to run power to the machines, they called for the power-installer guys to come back and fix the location. They would arrive in the morning and move the power supplies accordingly. In the meantime, several entrepreneurial chaps called Netezza and asked them to come over and move the machines closer to the power supplies. Netezza did so that evening. The following morning the power guys dutifully moved the power supplies, but put them over where the appliances used to be, not where they were now. In twenty-four hours, two teams scrambled to get the machines squared away, and both of them failed.

Once the power was finally on, they discovered that they had the wrong network cables to connect them into the network grid. This would take over a week to order the correct ones. (Keep in mind that the Netezza installers provide a punch list with all of this information in infinitesimal detail, so it's not like they could claim ignorance).

In the final analysis, the data center took over eight weeks to get the machines in place and running. Why so long? The people working in the data center were used to standing up machines by a certain protocol. The power cables are in that drawer over there, and the network cables are on that shelf over there. The process of standing up a new machine has become so routine and mundane,

And yet when the Netezza machines showed up, it's installation was outside-of-routine.

Once installed and connected, we want to start moving data. We find that the networks are configured for transactional loads, not bulk loads. The machines are in different network clusters, and moving data between them is problematic. We want the max throughput of the network between the machines, but alas, a single point in the pipeline between source and target will rapidly become a source of stress and conflict.

"The new machines are here! The machines are here! Look! The contract in print! Now we're really *somebody*!" - Steve Martin, *Data Jerk*

Upon the machines' arrival however, we have another opportunity at hand. I will cover this in more detail later, but what I'm about to suggest will simply send shiver up the spine of a policy-minded person, regardless of how perfectly reasonable it sounds! I first wrote about this back in '09 on the Gather 'Round The Grill blog on the Netezza Community, called *First Bubble Blues*.

Even before we purchased the machine, we had a backlog of work (this is normal) or we plan to migrate an existing environment into it. One way or another, we have a huge bubble of work before us that is a one-time/first-time condition around the machine's ingress.

So we have a Skimmer, a P6, a p12 and a p24 rolled out on the dance floor. The common wisdom is to take the Skimmer and the P6, put them over in the Development / Test zone, and then the P12/P24 go over into the production center, inside the enclosure, behind smoked glass.

Then we get to work. Our principals tell us that we have a lot of projects underway, and all of them will be developed on the Skimmer. Not to put too fine a point on it, but the Skimmer and even the P6 are development machines for single teams. It is important not to dogpile lots of teams onto these machines. But that's not entirely the point.

In this first-time/one-time monster Bubble of work we are attempting to squeeze all of it into and through the Skimmer. It's a lot of workload to be pushing through a machine this small. In terms of a pipeline of work, think about how much power it would take to empty a swimming pool. Should we use a garden hose or a bilge pump?

Or rather, *how much time do you want to spend on the project?*

Now some of us may not have the Skimmer, so think this doesn't apply to us, but wait. It applies in the sense that whatever proportion of work we intend to do for the Bubble, there is no doubt a much larger, more powerful, production-designated machine sitting on the raised floor, behind smoked glass, humming, and doing nothing. Absolutely nothing.

Oh, but wait, it's doing *something*. It's mocking us. As we struggle to roll out this monster, one-time/first-time bubble of functionality and squeeze it through a machine that represents only a fraction of the power of its designated home, it mocks our efforts. The proportion of the *effort* is what we're looking at now.

In working with a Mustang system, one group was given a 10100 (108 SPUs) to perform all their development work. Five different development teams and one functional testing team dog-piled onto the 10100, essentially swamping it with work. In the meantime, significant deadlines were looming on all the teams. One of the primary tests for end-to-end processing ran in forty minutes on the 10100, but ran in only five minutes on the 10400 (432 SPUs) in the other room, behind the smoked glass. If we extrapolate this into a timeline, it means that the 10400 is eight times more powerful (for this application) than the 10100. It also means that whatever time it takes to roll out on the 10100, would largely be cut down to one/eighth the time on the 10100. Why is this?

The majority of work in a migration project, or new data warehouse project, is not in the development. It is in the **testing**.

If we don't have the power to test the environment, we will either have to take longer to test, or we will have to forego testing in order to meet the project timeline. Since testing is all about running through a series of set-based queries and comparing their results in automated form, the entire process is usually automated. *It just takes time.*

It will take eight times longer (for this application) on the 10100 than on the 10400. This same equation translates directly to the Blade-based Netezza appliance, because it's scalability profile is much more linear and objective than the Mustangs. We can get pretty close to predicting how long a project will take based on the available power of the machines.

But here's the kicker: We claimed we could pull off the project in two months, but that was with the assumption that we would have access to *at least eight times* more power than we were actually given. Would this translate into sixteen months of work instead of just two? No, but it did translate into a brutal climb to get it closed within five months, and this was unnecessary.

And for that five months, the 10400 sat idle behind the smoked glass, mocking us.

For the past ten years I've written or spoken on this aspect of first-time/one time Bubble (the First Bubble Blues) and others have openly noticed it and complained about it, but few have done anything about it. The fear I suppose is that once a machine is deployed for a certain purpose it cannot be scratched and redeployed. It's *policy*, you see.

But the average data warehouse folk know of whence I speak, because for the last decade or two this has been a consistent state of affairs. This is true for both warehousing and common app-dev projects. Large, muscled machines are rolled out for production environment and sit idle for months while the Dev and QA teams struggle on underpowered hardware.

What is the real value in this exercise? We have high-priced developers and testers burning the midnight oil, and if they are contractors are costing us much more tangible dollars, yet we have hamstrung their efforts by under-powering their work environment. It's costing us the time-to-market, and it's costing us far more in labor dollars than the value in protecting the larger machine, especially when it isn't doing anything.

I wrote an article many years ago as a lead application developer, noting the overall downtime of the junior application developers when the main database machine started to run out of power. I watched as a developer would open a screen and wait. Then drill to the next screen and wait. And to the next and wait. I ran a simple calculation that for all the developers on the project, in the time lost waiting between key-clicks, that an upgrade to the main database server would save us over five months of project time, just because it would boost the productivity of the developers by giving them faster turnaround *on unit testing alone.*

So the suggestion here is to place the order for the machines necessary to take the solution into production, but make them *all* available for development and testing until the project is past the First Bubble.

And avoid those First Bubble Blues.

Infrastructure

If no spare appliance was purchased for disaster recovery, might want to check into that. In addition, backups are generally easier if we have a spare machine to back things into. The overall load of a Netezza machine, once populated, can crush the average unsuspecting backup host.

But the nzbackup and nzrestore utilities will use compressed files for their work, basically a 16x or better on the 6.0 host. So run don't walk to this scenario. Use nzbackup to roll data to a compressed flat file, then backup this flat file with a regular backup scenario, Reverse it for restoration. Overall, our data backup admins won't have a heart attack the first time we broach the subject.

Next, in order to affect the backup we'll need to mount some file space to the NPS host. We want this for two reasons: backup and replication. There is an nzmigrate utility that will move data between machines. An upcoming chapter talks about our options. But to make things a bit more operationally palatable, that is a change-data-capture, incremental replication that is simple to implement and manage- we will need this file mount. It will have to be visible to all the NPS hosts we plan to replicate data between.

Finally, if we're using a Linux server as an operational companion server for the Netezza machine, we need to investigate the network componentry on the device. If it has dual network cards on it, plan to set up a special connectivity scenario. Set up one of the network cards to be fully dedicated facing the Netezza appliance. Setup the second network card to face the outside world. Of course, make sure that neither of the cards shares the same router. The objective is to make our data flow between the source and the Netezza appliance, to be *unidirectional* as it passes through the Linux server. Why do this?

If the Linux server shares the same network with the source and target machines, when we begin an intake/load process it will start to pull from the source even as it is writing to the appliance Sharing the network means that the normal 100+ megabytes-per-second we would experience on a read-operation will now be *halved* as we simultaneously use the same network for the write-operation. The data is essentially meeting itself coming and going at the same time. This means an average throughput of around forty megabytes per second, sometimes less, sometimes as high as fifty megabytes per second, but this will only be occasionally high.

Keep in mind that the appliance can inhale data at the rate of over a terabyte an hour. That's four times (or more) faster than this paltry throughput we've saddled our system with. So apart from installing special 10-gig-ethernet infrastructure, which many sites cannot easily assimilate overnight, this unidirectional model is easy to implement and will serve until the whole thing can be optimized.

But by the way, if we want the appliance to run at highest capacity, there's 10gigE in our future. By the time this book is published, I suspect that 10gig Ethernet might be "so-yesterday" - so take the advice in the right spirit. Jack up the network bandwidth to match the appliance. Make that investment count.

System Layout

For the most part, the new math is that most admins and sites will roll out the appliance as a separately administered machine, and will roll out a companion Linux server with it. The spirit of this book assumes this configuration is in play, primarily because the vendor strongly suggests to avoid running anything on the Netezza host besides the host itself.

But this opens up an opportunity in that the Linux server will now be the HQ so to speak, or the operational hub for all of our activities. We can now load database clients on it (do that now) and mount file systems on it (do that now) as well as put the Netezza utilities and such on the machine (nzload, nzsql etc) and oh yes, (do that now!).

Once these are in place, get one of the user admin gurus to lay out the user groups. In this particular case, we will need a special user group called the "XFR" or "PROC" user group. This will be the group that has the power to perform data processing operations on the Linux machine coupled with a user id on the Netezza database(s) that has the power to perform the necessary SQL-transform operations (e.g. add and drop tables etc.).

We will put users in groups and manage groups, not users

We typically follow a generalized granting structure that allows the user groups certain powers based on pre-defined settings. These include:

RO	Read Only
ROT	Read-Only, with Temp Tables (like to support Microstrategy)
RW	Read/Write, the permission for a user doing SQL-transforms
NO	Specifically denied permission

These translate to the following grant strings. I have provide the parameterization notation so if the reader wants to drop this into a parameterized shell script, it's good to go.

Here, DBNAME is the database name and DBGROUP is the specific group. Note that the NO option is missing, because by default all of the databases offer no access.

```
RW="
```

```
grant    create function, create procedure, create aggregate,
create library, create table, create external table, create view, create sequence,
create synonym,create materialized view, create temp table
to group $DBGROUP;

grant abort, execute, alter, drop, genstats, insert,
list, select, truncate,  update
on $DBNAME to group $DBGROUP ;
grant execute, alter, drop, list on function to group $DBGROUP;
"


RO="
grant abort, list, select on $DBNAME to group $DBGROUP ;
"


ROT="
grant create temp table to group $DBGROUP;
grant abort, list, select on $DBNAME to group $DBGROUP ;
"
```

Once we get users set up and the databases in play, we now have options to do all kinds of other stuff. As noted, the reason the above is mentioned separately is because at most sites the admins may well allow us to install all kinds of stuff on the development machines, but they will want automated processes to assist in administration on the Test and Prod machines. We do ourselves an enormous favor by prescribing their experience because it will also preempt unnecessary headaches down the line.

STAGE SEPARATION - OPERATIONAL TRANSFORMATION

SO NOW IT'S TIME to lay down a little lingo that seems to be rising to the surface in the transformational buzz. Everyone wants to put their mark on the industry, and the author is no different. Since I have your attention, let's walk through some concepts and terms to describe them, and of course may the marketplace let them fall where they will. We need a common language to chat about these things, so we need to start somewhere.

Firstly, let's go back in time to the first time we may have encountered "ELT". That is, in-the-database bulk-data processing, or *SQL-transform*. Once upon a time, we had a case where a transactional system needed a bit of reporting functionality, so we added that. Then people wanted more reports so we added those. Usually just by forming views or queries against the operational tables. After a while, it was apparent that we needed to pre-calculate some of the reporting content because the operational tables weren't enough. Perhaps we bought into a reporting tool that would pre-cache this for us, but one way or another we were running database-side bulk processing operations.

If we had SQLServer, we probably invoked SSIS, or Analysis Services, to use that bulk-SQL to build out our content. Maybe we just used a plain vanilla stored procedure. But one way or another we ran into the problem of [1]Rule #10, never do bulk processing in an SMP-based RDBMS. We saw back then that we needed to move away from that solution.

Now we are many years down the road, and many more iterations of functionality, but it sounds like folks are expecting us to go back to what we forsook as unworkable and unscalable. Is it suddenly workable and scalable *now?* What gives?

No, not *suddenly* workable and scalable. I seriously doubt that the folks at Netezza would say there is anything "sudden" about the arrival of the Netezza products. They were introduced and matured over time and now here we are. Perhaps this is a "sudden" realization for the person who has never been exposed to Netezza. But rest assured it is most definitely workable and scalable, and now needs to be revisited. However, we'll not revisit SQL-based transforms in the form with which we were first exposed to it (hand-crafted SQL) and take a look at how to make it better, stronger, faster so that we don't spend a lot of time hand-crafting SQL!

In Underground I offered up some transformation notions that I must rehash here, so forgive the repetition but it's necessary, and I'll make it short. The SQL-transform paradigm places the Netezza machine at the center of the universe, where the ETL paradigm places the Netezza machine at the end of a flow, or a terminus if you will. In SQL-transform, Netezza is the prime mover and owner of the processing domain, but not so with ETL. This is why ETL tools don't particularly do SQL-transforms all that well, because in SQL-transforms the machine must be the center of the universe when the ETL tools thinks that all roads lead to its domain. It's a source of stress and tension rather than synergy and integration.

So in ETL space the database is a terminus. This doesn't work for us if each intermediate step starts and stops in the database (using intermediate tables). In the ETL tool, each operational step becomes a standalone application, of sorts, and this is not the way we want to manage it.

In flow-based operation, we divide the machine's internals into multiple databases that are logical groupings of data rather than the predefined terminus for a flow of operation. They can still be formal source-of-record databases where information is checkpointed and synchronized, but we have to see the data as on-the-move. A repository is a place of storage but also carries the connotation of a "depot", that is, data that is dropped off with the expectation that it will be picked up again. The most applicable context is a software repository. Nobody expects software to be dropped off never to be seen again. Before we get ahead of ourselves, let's start from the left hand side of the flow and move to the right.

As Netezza is at the core an input-process-output device, we have to start as data arrives into the machine. We have several terms we can use for this. One is a staging database, or perhaps a landing database, But these are from the perspective of the ETL tool, outside-looking-in. The ETL tool will stage the data, or land the data. If we want a particular Netezza-centric moniker, we need to call it an [1]Intake database. This allows us to regard the intake processes in their proper light, that of pulling the data into the machine so *that we can do more with it.* If we call it a landing or staging zone, we are essentially defining it as an end-point, when it's actually a starting point.

From here we need a way to control data as it arrives, when it arrives and what happens to it during a *continuum of arrival.* The ETL tool only cares about inserting the data and moving on. There is no continuum of activity associated with the insert. In our Intake scenario, we have need for a number of different activities that shepherd the data into the machine. After all, if we want to do all of the data processing, it means we need to accept responsibility that some dirt or malformed data will show up. We need a plan for that stuff if we want to take over the role of the ETL platform entirely.

Manifest - think in terms of a ship's manifest with the vessels' cargo inventory, or a software installation's list of components in its manifest. The manifest file, in plain terms, carries a description of the cargo (file streams) and the holds (tables) where the cargo will be stored. In physical warehousing terms, a truck would pull up to a loading dock, hand off its manifest to the foreman and then worker would empty the truck and dispatch its contents to the appropriate warehouse bins. Not meaning to be remedial here, so bear with me.

In terms of the Netezza machine, we'll need a *virtual* loading dock. The presentation of the manifest (by an external process) constitutes a trigger. It is also the virtual truck containing URL/Filenames or paths to database extraction tables, along with corresponding locations (tables) to dispatch the data.

Now a manifest is not something we'll find in the Netezza manuals either. It is a simple means to represent an otherwise highly complex context of work. I described the manifest in more detail in Underground, but let me note here that the manifest file concept has only gathered strength since then and has become a faithful and invaluable companion to the Intake process.

To recap, the manifest file contains instructions and notations that depict an I/O relationship. In terms of a framework, these behave as *mnemonics* such that when presented in context, initiate a body of processing activities. For example:

```
url/filename1.dat        table1
url/filename2.dat        table2
...
```

We can list as many urls and filenames as we want, and we could essentially repeat the table names if necessary. It's an insert-only operation after all. What we would expect to see is an external publisher of information drop flat files for intake into a visible location, record those locations and their corresponding target tables in the manifest, then present the manifest to us. It is now simple enough for us to wrap some logic around formulating an intake table (from the designated table name), executing an nzload using the file url/name as the source, and voila, data is now inside the box.

The manifest concept has all kinds of creative uses, but the bottom line is that it describes parameters for getting data into the machine and it is simple enough for external publishers to create as part of their publication protocol. If everyone provides a manifest, or we simply wrap a non-player's data with one of our own, all data arrives on our virtual loading dock the same way.

Intake Table- Of course, getting the data into the machine is number-one priority. We will intake the data into a loosely-typed varchar-only table that we'll call an Intake table. This guarantees that no data will be left behind for reasons of malformed or "bad" data, because all varchars are welcome, 24x7.

We will also reserve the right to draw data into a "long varchar" that holds the entire record, for purposes of aggregate scrubbing activities or the like. The chapter on Teradata provides some more insight.

Masking - Especially necessary in some financial services quarters, the need to leave data behind or mask it to a default value. This has to happen as a first-order-of-operation to placate the fear than the data is being persisted in unmasked form. If this is on a database we're extracting, then the mask needs to be applied on the extraction SQL, otherwise applied as the first operation. Still, if no rule exists for this, we have nothing to do, so move on.

Validation - Filled with varchars, we still know the target data types for the individual columns, so we need to validate each of the columns against the target. What of those that do not pass muster? We have to take a predefined action. But hey, if no rule exists for this one either, just move on.

Exceptions - We'll now capture all of the exceptions (e.g. validation violations above) or other malformed or null information. We don't necessarily have to report the exception if we have a rule that can fire with a default to apply. If the rule fires with no default, we have to suppress the data if its current form actually keeps it from entering the database. In one case we had a standard numeric column but one row in eighteen billion rows contained a numeric with a minus sign embedded in the number like so: 1234-5678. We had no rule to apply and the database would not allow us to write the row to a numeric column. The exception rule fired and the exception was recorded, and the record suppressed. Later the users gave us a rule for this malformed information, and we applied it. Now when the rule fired, it would apply the default, suppress the reporting of the exception, and continue on as if all was good. This kind of exception handling is very easy to pull off with rules in set-based form (discussed in a later chapter) but also follows a repeatable pattern we will want to apply to all of our intake operations. Can *our* ETL tool do this? In scale? *Not like Netezza!*

Transformations - where we'll want to do type-level scrubbing, for example simple things like upper-casing the primary keys of lookup tables (if necessary) or re-formatting a time stamp so that Netezza will accept it, or transforming null values to defaults for the data type, or based on a transform rule for that column. Or how about zapping non-printable characters? When it's rules-based, we can handle exceptions or the whole enchilada. Here we are pulling data from the Intake table and into the Target (so it's moving anyhow). This is where we move from varchar-based columns to formal Netezza data types. The prior operations cleared the deck for this one so that it won't fail.

Hash keys - These are particularly handy for unique identification of multi-part keys, and we need to apply them as the first order of business after the transformation. There's no better place to apply them because if we plan to use them, it will be in the first transforms right out of the Intake gate.

Change-data-capture - Then comes the change-data-capture scenario, where we want to find records that have already arrived in a prior intake. Rules here will point us to a Repository target for key-comparisons or perhaps a local snapshot table that contains a running accumulation of the data in question, keys-only of course. We apply the pattern, strip it of extraneous data and now every downstream operation will be more efficient.

Deduplication - A good use for the hash keys of course, but as long as it's key-based, we can apply a rule to it. I've seen a lot of SQL-transform statements have to harden themselves or pre-boil the data for duplicates before they could use them. This only resulted in clutter in the SQL-transformations, but they all followed a common pattern. Here we get to apply the pattern as a rule, where it counts most, and perhaps even trim out a lot of the data we don't intend to use anyhow.

The change-data-capture will often strip out the vast majority of data, and we should apply it before we apply any deduplication, primarily because if the same data really is arriving day-after-day, duplicates are already in there anyhow, right? So which is better, to rip out all the data we know we don't need and then dedupe, or to dedupe against the majority of the data and then rip out the stuff we didn't need anyhow?

The school of thought on the two, is that they should be either/or but also be able to swap their position, on demand, based on the rules of the intake. Nobody likes to be wired into a corner, and nothing about these two complex functionalities dictates that their ordering shall-always-be. *Again, can our ETL tool hot-swap like this?*

Clearly we need to skinny-down the data size and volume to the workable portion that matters, and not carry baggage with us just because it happened to arrive on the front door. This follows the operational protocol of squeezing the data into smaller chunks horizontally (with change-data-capture and dedupe) and vertically (by trimming unnecessary columns).

And only just now we're ready to present the final results to the next stage of the flow, the operations that will perform business transforms from Intake into the first target database(s).

Target Databases

So what do we call those target database(s). Are there more than one? Surely, we will see a need for multiple targets coming from intake and will probably want to accommodate them with more than one database. Actually one database can serve for all three, but some purists like to divide them up, and as I noted, the database in Netezza is a means to logically group the data. It does not have a more formal meaning when using it for data processing.

Operational Store - only as an endpoint, not a waypoint. We never want to pass data into an operational store and pass it out again to the next downstream database. [1]The ODS is a terminus.

Repository - the business-facing or business-formed data store, with entities that best represent how the business works, always contains most recent activity and history as well. Some say 3NF, others say "make it look like the business." Some now ask, "Is there a *difference?*"

Reference - We know of one site with over fourteen hundred lookup tables. Many enterprises have a wide swath of references sources that when added to a common Repository become unwieldy and cluttered. This may require us to logically and physically separate them for better management. But since many reference sources behave as lookups and can take on a truncate-load flavor for their maintenance, it is easy to set up regular operational activities that maintain this database separately from the application flows, and likewise allow reports to access it independently of the Repository.

Reporting - Typically the next step in the flow after the Repository, but it doesn't have to be. Many sites manufacture their reporting stores from all of the above as sources, including Intake. We may see one or more reporting databases, or even tables that have been replicated from the Repository to the Reporting database for purposes of changing the distribution to better support user queries.

Consumption-point - this is a separate database filled with views and user-facing tables. We put the specific user-facing tables here so they don't clutter the Report or Repository. But the views can point to practically any source behind-the-scenes.

Replicated store - This is also a separate database but can be onboard the machine (as a replicated archive for intake support), or for replicating any of the other databases to another location. Also includes (via compressed data transfer) targets that are not on the machine.

Transformation - When transforming data toward the target, in this case we'll just use the Repository as the first stop, we need a simple means to define the transform operation between the Intake source and the target. When all is said and done, we may well have at least one SQL-transform for each target table and may likely have many more supporting or intermediate results for them. This can translate to hundreds of SQL-transform operations.

As noted elsewhere in this book, this portent leads some to believe that they need a specifically called out operational application to watch over this activity because they honestly believe it will take hours to accomplish, when in fact it will complete in mere *minutes*. Why embrace the largesse of harnessing this veritable sprint of activity when it will be over almost before we know it's running?

Case Study Short: An environment running SQLServer had several overnight operations running in a SQL-transform model. When we asked the operators about the processes, they had nothing but complaints. They reported that the entire thing runs as a black box for over two hours. One night a particular table wasn't loaded, causing the first joins to be empty, cascading into one empty table after another. It ran for two hours with no errors, because the joins didn't fail, they just didn't produce any data. At the end of the run, all of the result tables were empty. There was no checkpoint to restart from, since the error occurred so early in the flow. It never comes up for air, lamented one, so at least we could know where it is in the process, or even if we should kill it and not waste all that time.

Situations like the above elicit fond memories of late nights babysitting a warm CPU by the light of the LEDs, don't they? Nobody wants to repeat that, so when folks start talking about processing data inside the machine again, all this wash of malaise overtakes them and they start out each question with *What The*?

But these fears are easily placated when we start talking about putting scalable numbers on the board that make *sense*. If we were to tell them that a handful of queries would take hours, why *wouldn't* they balk? But this invites an even more interesting question:

If their technologists believed that it would take hours (owing to the high walls of infrastructure they are preparing to embrace) why *didn't* they balk? Good grief, there's no value at all in moving toward a SQL-transform model unless it can utterly blow the living daylights out of every other processing model in the room.

So now we get to the next term:

Leg - this is the rather short but sometimes meaty and hardworking set of SQL-transform operations that deliver data from one database to another (e.g. Intake to Repository) in a fashion that embraces formal integration and transformation. This is the core of what we would call SQL-based transformation. What happens in a Leg?

Any arbitrary SQL operation(s), from manufacturing lookups, to special intermediate working tables, to actual target-facing transforms. Basically any business logic we choose. And with the Netezza SQL Toolkit, UDFs and Stored Procedures, we have nothing holding us back from highly scalable success. Just keep in mind that a Leg can consist of one or more queries, in fact hundreds of transform operations, but in the end, even for large and complex intraday operations will complete in minutes and not hours.

We call this a "Leg" in part to define it as a short sprint of a larger journey. After all, if we were taking multiple planes, trains and automobiles across country or the Great Atlantic Pond, we would describe our trip in legs. In transportation logistics, we would see the managers of a package watch it as it completed legs of its journey whether on rail, van or ship.

But we don't want to call it an application, or anything that resembles something standalone or stovepiped, silo'd or any of that. Inside the Netezza machine, every leg is part of an integrated flow of work. If we arbitrarily separate them on artificial boundaries, we haven't bought ourselves anything but trouble.

Case Study Short: One group practically begged us to separate the legs as distinct applications, so deep were they steeped in the ETL-database-is-terminus mindset. We could not shake them from this myopia no matter what we said or did. To our surprise, they made this distinct-application-model part of the project's exit criteria! Not only were they committed to it, they were planning to withhold payment until they got what they wanted. Well, we rigged the show to make this work, but the people receiving it thought it was ridiculous that the flow had been broken apart in to five-minute apps. In fact, this became a running joke within their four walls, that what we had originally termed a "leg" had been transformed into a "five minute app". It didn't matter that most of the apps ran in two minutes or less. The name seemed to stick. More unfortunately, the processing environment centered on exactly four of these. One of them dealt with a flow of data from the Intake to the Repository at 2am, while another did the same at 4am. Two more handled their transition from the Repository to reporting. All that overhead and infrastructure to support *four* "five-minute apps", when they could have run the entire operation as a single flow of work.

Another aspect of "leg" nomenclature is that it removes us from ETL-tool terminology After all, a series of transforms in an ETL tool is an *application*. ETL tools harness flows in terms of *pipes* (multiple end-to-end components in a flow) and *branches*, that is multiple pipes. But in the ETL tools, the pipes use the databases for a terminus, while our legs will use the database as *workspace*. We will now use the term Flow to depict multiple legs, and whether those legs exist independently or not is a matter for the application holding the flow. There may (and will) come a time when we want all these legs, and ultimately multiple flows, under the same application umbrella.

Transforms in the Working Database - which we will nickname the XFORM database. This is a distinctly Netezza-centric approach[1] and simply mandates that no transforms will take place inside the target databases. We will always perform transform operations in the XFORM database, never, ever, never-*infinity* perform them in the target. Perhaps I should repeat that. Oh well, the reason we don't do this is if a job should fail or be interrupted, it does not leave the database in an unknown state, and likewise does not leave intermediate table clutter in the target. Why is this important? Because administrators will need to perform housekeeping on the databases, and we don't want them performing any operation that even remotely looks like a "drop table" while connected to a target database! Let all the intermediate tables exist in the XFORM database, and the admin can clean those out with reckless abandon anytime it's necessary or desired.

Replica vs Local Table - So as we commit to performing SQL-transform in another (XFORM) database, what is the proper method for this? Firstly, we need a way to create local tables. A local table is one that sits as a resource in the XFORM database to serve our immediate purposes, because when the flow finishes, the local table evaporates with it. We should be able to make any arbitrary local table and fill it with whatever we want. It's a resource for upcoming SQL-transform operations.

A *replica* table, on the other hand, is one that looks identical (at least) to a table in our target. We can always add some working columns to it to support SQL-transforms, but it will have the same columns and datatypes as the target table its data is destined for.

So how does this work? We form the replica table with a simple CTAS. We then use local resources, perhaps other replica tables and almost certainly one or more Intake tables to put data into the replica *just as though* the table is the actual target table.

We can create as many replica tables as we have tables in the target, but we won't make more than one of each. We'll then fill these replicas one by one with the data we intend for them to transport into their target table counterpart. Actually, in development mode we might fill them one-by-one to gain visibility, but in the actual production zone we'll cut them loose to run in parallel streams. One way or another, all of this activity will finally simmer down and stop.

Now we check for errors. We allowed all those operations to burst forth as the thundering herd on the machine's virtual plain, but now we want to know if any of them had a problem. Notice that we don't check along the way and then attempt to kill the job if one of the transforms has a problem. It's just faster and easier to let them all get to a stopping point and then check the error or master log for any reported errors. If errors exist, we may use an error threshold to determine what to do. If no errors exist, we move on to the next stop.

Notice how the above flow of work and data is intended to keep things moving at their highest possible speed. Nowhere are we trying to slow down the processes but rather help them run as quickly as possible with positive handoffs, parallel operation and objective, non-invasive error control. Notice also how we are not wasting the operator's time with superfluous messages when all is well. It's slowing down a short run, offering no value whatsoever.

Finalization - Not sure if anyone out there has ever burned a CD or a DVD, but the concept here is the same. We would use the CD burner software to select-and-drag music into the burner's canvas window. We would then organize the songs as we wanted them to play. At this point, we've done a lot of work that are all shared-nothing operations. We can add more songs, delete others without affecting the remaining songs or the CD. But when we want to burn the songs onto the media, we *finalize* the content. This takes each and every selected song and burns it onto the CD. Once completed, we have committed the songs to the CD. All of this *should* look very familiar.

This is exactly how we will put our replica tables into the target. If we kept track of each replica that we built, now we can just run a finalization procedure and it will take care of business. It will copy the contents of each replica table into its target, and can also do this one-by-one or in parallel, because now it doesn't matter in what order they arrive. Once completed, we will record the table, the row count and the AUDIT_ID of each copy operation in our local Load Log. This allows us to go back and find the data if need be (e.g. for a rollback).

Gateways - are flow decision points that can be an application-variant means for flows to synchronize with certain conditions, or with other flows. For example, if a data store normally arrives in intake at 2am and the follow-on work kicks off at 3am but is dependent on the 2am arrival, the 3am flow could use a Gateway to either check for the existence of the data or pend for a certain timeout to wait for its arrival. When it detects arrival, it proceeds with its normal activity. If the 2am data never shows up, the Gateway times out and stops, dutifully notifies someone, but does not proceed with the flow if data is missing.

Consumption Point - (a whole chapter on this later) but this is a facade or proxy database that is configured solely with views to support a particular user base. They enter the system in this database and what-they-see-is-what-they-get (and no more). This way we don't expose the consumers to tables that are immaterial to their consumption experience. We also have the option of installing local tables that support the consumption experience, primarily to avoid putting things in the underpinning databases (like the Reporting or Repository) that apply to only one consumption point (Microstrategy write-back tables come to mind).

Reporting Adaptation - the tactical use of a view, UDF, stored proc or other mechanism to support a reporting tool's lack of ability to properly form the most optimized queries. We may find that the BI tool formulates an answer by boiling up three or four intermediate queries, and upon examination find that these are very inefficient. We may spend many hours trying to get the BI tool to generate more efficient SQL, or we might just craft it ourselves, put it into a view or stored procedure, implementing it with the hope that someday the BI tool will support what we want to do.

Checkpoint - okay that's a lot of stuff to wiggle into the terminology dictionary of SQL-transform, but it is useful terminology for operational reasons. What is the flow doing now? Where did it stop? Where did it fail? What assets was it using? etc etc. If the above terms or concepts seem apropos, run with them. If you attempt to reprint them you'll need to reference this book, but otherwise feel free to leverage them in your everyday work. I did not publish them to keep them to myself, and if I were to show up at your site, these terms or concepts would likely end up somewhere in our deliverable documentation.

But we have to note that the concepts necessary for SQL-transform are not the same as for ETL, nor for any other form of data processing. So if we're going to take it seriously, let's talk the same language instead of talkin' trash (hey, we can talk trash to the Exadata guys, they're used to it.)

And while we're at a checkpoint, and the concept of checkpointing is also an operational issue, let's treat it separately.

Checkpointing

ETL Tools perform their own checkpointing, a way to save their current workflow so that in case of failure the flow can restart from a known point. In a common ETL tool, the database is not part of this intermediate flow model because to the ETL tool, the database extract and load are *themselves* checkpoints. Once the data is transmitted the database, it is out of the ETL tool's hands.

So in a SQL-transform model, the database tables are also potential checkpoints, and in many quarters, the sentiment is that we should be able to restart the job from any point where the data was placed into an intermediate table. However, this is not the *spirit* of a checkpoint. Arbitrarily stopping and starting at any intermediate table operation is an inaccurate view of the role of checkpoints.

The checkpoint's sole duty is to safeguard against breaching the pre-allocated time window within which the job must execute to error-free completion.

For example, if the upstream data source is available for processing by 2am, and our users expect the data to be available consumption by 6am, then our window is 4 hours. Where a checkpoint comes into play is simply this: If a particular job will take longer than half of eighty percent of the total available time, it is in danger of breaching the window if start-to-finish re-execution is necessary. What is eighty percent of four hours? About 192 minutes, so we'll cut that in half, for about 96 minutes. This means that our executable must complete within 96 minutes or there may not be enough time to recover in case of failure (should the job restart from scratch). So let's say we have a job that runs for three hours. If the job fails late in its execution, there's no way that we can restart the job from scratch without breaching the window.

So now we introduce checkpoints, each of which becomes a potential restart point as the flow proceeds. So that if the job should die in the middle, we restart in the middle and not from the beginning. This sounds remedial, but it's offered as a reminder and as a caution.

In (Netezza-based especially) SQL-transform we may see hundreds of queries execute in a matter of *minutes*. Whole legs of the data flow may complete in such a short time frame that the need for a checkpoint becomes meaningless. After all, if we have 96 minutes to get done, and the flow only takes 3 minutes from start to finish, we could restart the job from scratch *over thirty times* in the spare overhead provided by the Netezza machine.

This does not obviate checkpoints in the transform process, but we don't place them on *every* transform and intermediate table because there's no operational value in it. In fact, the overhead for doing so would actually compromise the speed of the operation. Imagine three hundred transforms taking place in three minutes or less. Now imagine carefully cataloguing each so that in case of failure, we can restart. If it takes only half-a-second to perform such an operation, we've added one-hundred-fifty seconds (two and one half minutes) to a flow that only requires three minutes already. That's almost *doubling* the duration of the flow, and what did it buy us? There is no danger of an SLA breach so there is no need for checkpoints. What would checkpoints do for us? Nothing, they would only slow down an otherwise optimized flow. There is no value in the intermediate checkpoints. This is something of a departure for those who see checkpoints as necessary in the nth degree of detail.

Checkpoints in a SQL-transform paradigm have value in the following forms:

- Intake – once data arrives in the machine, it has usually undergone a significant transition time and series of flow operations that we won't want to revisit. If the intake fails, we restart from scratch (generally) because most intake operations happen so fast, or we can throttle them to happen fast.

- SQL-Transform Target(s) – Once data arrives in target database, such as a repository, reference or reporting store, we would want to checkpoint this operation since it may be the basis for a rollback (below) or may be the basis of the next downstream operation. It is generally the product of a managed multi-part series of shared-nothing operations, and as such carries context we would like to keep, even if the overall duration is minor. Therefore it is important to checkpoint the flow so that the next downstream will have *traceable* information and not a data store that is in flux.

- Replication – once data arrives in a target, we may have need to copy all or part of it to another database or another server. Replication is also a checkpointed process because it bases its workload on all the checkpointed workload that has come before it. If that workload is still in flux, the replication will not be accurate.

Case Study Short: We had set up an assessment and quality review protocol for an Ab Initio installation. In this protocol, we would follow a simple punch-list of review items. The punch-list was open and available to all Ab Initio developers on the site, wasn't particularly draconian or hard to follow, but had elements in it that the client principals had decided beforehand were non-optional and required a post-development review.

In one particular review we encountered a graph (that's an Ab Initio application) that contained a large number of checkpoints. In fact, the total count of checkpoints almost rivaled the total count of components in the application itself. When we inquired of this application, we learned that its total execution time never exceeded fifteen minutes, even with the checkpoints in place. Considering that the total available window for its execution was over an hour, this raised some significant questions.

We required the developer to go back and remove all the checkpoints, as they were superfluous. We thought he understood our reasoning. At the follow-on review the next day, we discovered that he had replaced all the checkpoints with intermediate files! We asked him why, and he said it was because the intermediate files were "necessary", but could not explain a reason for their existence. In the end, the files only existed in case the job failed, so that he could troubleshoot the graph. I noted to him that said troubleshooting would never be performed by him anyhow. Not only that, but the graphical environment was reserved for developers, not operators. They would never have the option to pop open the application and check out the intermediate file contents, and nobody would let a developer do it either.

His response: *Oh.*

Case Study Short: Upon arrival at a client site, several of their technologists had painstakingly designed and laid out the database tables for an operational control environment. Not only would it track every transform operation, it would do so through Autosys, their designated job scheduler. What would this mean? The installation of over *five hundred* Autosys jobs, not including the launcher jobs that would hold sub-jobs. As I attempted to talk them out of this, they became even more adamant that it was necessary. Whence comes such overkill?

It seems that one of their techs had been part of a SQL-transform rollout in a prior workplace and they had used an ETL tool to manage the SQL queries fired over to the database machine (in this case, not a Netezza machine, so each one of them took an egregiously protracted duration). In that implementation, multiple transform operations continued without coming up for air, meaning that half a dozen of them could take over an hour without reporting any status at all. This was an unacceptably long time to wait for feedback, so rather than simply accept that the same queries in Netezza would take mere seconds and handily deliver them from such malaise, they rather overcompensated with this overkill form of process control that would provide even less value.

Why is this? They wanted us to implement the Autosys jobs by launching master jobs with transform subjobs (we already have a framework that does just this without Autosys, so why invent a new one?). It became immediately clear that we would be embracing two major pieces of functionality to test - one the application and one this job scheduling setup. And if we experienced hiccups along the way, we'd have to first figure out which one was having a problem. Considering that the job scheduling setup would itself eclipse the complexity of the application, it also became clear that the lines would blur as to what sort of implementation we were addressing: business flows or operational control. Because when it was all said and done, the vast majority of hours would have been spent in developing, debugging and testing the operational control, not the business application.

Apart from all this, what happens when we need to add or subtract a transform operation from the mix? When developing SQL-transforms, the operations come and go like flowing water. Sometimes we need to retrofit, divide or combine. We would then have to revisit the Autosys installation and install or remove Autosys jobs in order to support the transform flows at a granular level. I don't particularly disagree with this approach if the flow is running against an SMP/RDBMS, because if that's the case we're already in violation of Rule #10 and no good can come of anything we do to fix it. But when inside the Netezza MPP, this is a level of micro-management that will stall out the development process.

Is this *really* what we want? Methinks not.

So this became another case of talking the client off the ledge and convincing them that such a model had no value.

Undaunted, these same technologists had also convinced the client principals that even if we didn't need this overkill process controller, we *definitely* needed control at the flow level. I'm a big proponent of installing multiple databases to achieve a flow-based model[1]. But what they wanted was to divide the flow into legs and then treat those legs like full-blown, independent applications rather than legs in a much larger application. Why does this matter?

It means we would have a leg for intake, one from intake to the master repository, one from the repository to the reporting tables, and perhaps one from the reporting tables to one or more replicated servers, like dedicated reporting servers or disaster recovery servers. Considering that while each leg may be comprised of hundreds of operations, they are still destined to complete their mission in a matter of minutes.

It behooves us therefore to think about the efficiency of the overall flow. Do we want independent jobs that last only a few minutes, cascading them off each other using Autosys or some other scheduler? Or does it make sense to treat them as smaller parts of a larger application flow? With each one lasting only minutes, we lose time in the job start/stop latency. Once a job closes, this status would rise into the Autosys scheduler where it would make choices and launch the next leg.

Of course, in doing so we completely lose the context between the legs. In the flow-based operation, the context of the entire flow is very valuable. Arbitrarily throwing it out for the sake of process control is unwise.

Once again, however, this whole paranoia about leg-level controls was founded on a prior encounter with the wrong-way-to-do-it. But these folks had a pretty-good-idea of what was necessary at least. Flow control and all that. Just the wrong level at which to monitor the work. In their prior misadventure, their "legs" had taken many hours to complete. Breaking it apart by leg seemed as natural as the springtime rain. But as with all things Netezza, the sheer power and speed of completion when inside-the-machine forces us to think about things differently. We might expect it to transform our data, but in fact it's transforming *us* and how we think.

I mentioned in Underground the nature of the *Towers of Hanoi* game. We pick up one disk and place it on another post, where no larger disk can be on top of a smaller, and the objective is to move all of the disks from one post to another with the fewest possible moves. Without the artificial rules, we would just pick up the entire stack and drop it on another. However, in underpowered systems these are not artificial rules. We don't have the raw power to pick up the disks and drop them. Think about how we would solve the problem if each disk weighed about twenty pounds, then it wouldn't be an option to move them all at once unless we had some kind power-crane or like equipment. Underpowered systems look a lot like this, with operations taking too long, having to take their turn because they cannot run side-by-side etc. Once we're inside *power-central*, the Netezza MPP, more things are possible in less time with less effort.

In the above scenario, I asked the techs if they could make the Autosys-controlled leg run in parallel. That is, many of the flow jobs really are shared-nothing operations and unless one is feeding from the intermediate table created by another, it can run in its own thread of activity. We see this sort of thing all the time with backfills, operational tables and the like. Some of the tables are tied to each other. Other legs create intermediate work tables that the others consume. But once created, it doesn't matter what order the remaining work actually executes in, and they aren't sharing any other resource, so let them run in parallel themselves. Converge their results downstream.

Of course, their answer was that this would be too complex to control, which is why *our* flow control implementation could and should handle just that, in a much more simplified manner, without any intervention from the scheduler. In fact, if we have a whole gaggle of independent queries, usually they complete far faster than we can possibly feed the machine. So why not feed the machine in quantity, kicking off multiples of these, or just pushin' the queries into the machine as fast as we can. It will queue the ones it cannot get to, and will do smart things like short-query optimization and the like. We can now leverage the built-in aspects of the machine to get even more work done instead of just waiting for a boring end-to-end flow to complete its mission.

How does this work? Each transform operation in the flow that constitutes a dependency is given a Node Name. Others that are dependent on it will simply PEND on the completion of the given Node Name. Since these transform nodes can be chained together, it means that a lot of the nodes will have no dependency at all, while some of them may only have a dependency on a first few (like an transform that fills up a local lookup or resource table). From there, the transforms run at their own speed rather than being shepherded by a flow controller. Does this look a little scary to debug? Only because it really *is* scary to debug. That's why we'd like our flow controller to manage the transforms in an end-to-end fashion for development and troubleshooting, but forego this artificiality when in actual production. Otherwise what we'll see is that the Netezza machine, during one of these transform flows, even the most complex and intense forms, is barely breaking a sweat. No, we want the machine working *hard*, so we'll cut those queries loose in quantity and square up the results when the smoke clears.

This is also why we want to execute certain "global" services only when the smoke clears, and some of the more important ones include change-data-capture, upserts, global transformations like lookup resets or even a slowly-changing-dimension implementation. Let's get the initial transformations out of the way,because the next wave of set-based operations will need some of that time to further cook the data.

Inter-Machine Replication

Once our environment is mature (or as a matter of core architecture) we will have a need to replicate data both inside and across machines. Copying data within the machine is a nit compared to across the machines.

In a safe-harbour declaration in 2011 in Charlotte, a Netezza spokesperson mentioned their plans to build out a special machine with the role of "replication server". This is probably a breath of fresh air for folks who want to reliably replicate their data across machines, or across the world and don't want to stand up one-off architectures for this. Until that time, however, the general *nzmigrate* utility will have to serve as a default for this functionality. This section discusses something a bit more flexible.

Now, I know what one might think, why not just use *nzmigrate*? For those unfamiliar with this little utility, it will migrate one table from one machine to another. However, it takes the whole table unless we apply some filtration. More unfortunately, nzmigrate must execute on-board the Netezza platform's host. It cannot be initiated externally like the other client-side utilities (e.g. nzload, nzsql). The primary reason being, it needs to be able to declare a pipe that can be shared by the external table and nzload. The constraint here is the external table. It needs to have a place to unload its data, and it must be visible to the unloading machine. A pipe works fine if we are running on board the machine itself. It requires no space or overhead,

Except for the fact that in most installations, only an administrator has access to run anything on board the Netezza host.

Not to worry, as this is a mere logistical bump in the road, unless our system admins have heartburn to mounting an external file system to the Netezza's host. Well, considering that this little exercise is for the specific purpose of exporting data to another Netezza machine, perhaps we will get a reprieve from the policy-meisters if the application calls for replication. Not trying to be facetious or anything, but I've been in places that had requirements for moving data between machines and then promptly threw very high walls in place between the machines, including the requirement of kerberos authentication, just to make sure the connection was accounted for. I'm all for security and locking down the average soul's ability to do mayhem, accidental or otherwise. But this is an operational problem, under operator control, not some ad-hoc hacker. Either way, just be aware that asking someone to open up a file system hook to the Netezza host might be met with resistance. It is, however, the only means to affect replication between Netezza machines without using an nzmigrate. If the policy is that such operations as nzmigrate simply may not execute under application control, then we have to pursue getting an external file system mount.

More importantly, this is not something we want to do with plain ASCII data, or even binary data between the machines. No, the best way to pull this off is to use Netezza-*compressed* data. That's right - just like the *nzmigrate* we will export data in compressed form and deliver it in compressed form, relieving our network of the rather significant overhead of doing it otherwise. How much time will this save? Trust me, you don't want to do this any other way but in a compressed transfer. So lobby heavily for the file-system mount. It will save seventy-to-ninety percent of time required to perform the inter-machine copy with non-compressed data. We could of course do a bake-off between the to methods (e.g. a plain straight export of data and then into an nzload). Perhaps this will put our nay-sayers at bay in case they want the metrics (and some of them will, so just be prepared).

So the basic configuration is that the source system will export the data using an EXTERNAL TABLE and this will have for its target a temporary file on the mounted file system. Then on our Linux scripting/flow host we will launch a common external table instance on the target Netezza machine, referencing the common file on the file mount. Again, this looks a lot like nzmigrate, but there are some fundamental differences that we will be able to automatically exploit.

In our application, recall that we are loading data into tables as an insert-only model, or at least a model that has identifiable actions taken on the target database. We will also stamp every record associated with this action using the AUDIT_ID of the job that affected the table. We will also record this activity in our LOAD_LOG for the database, that is the table affected, the AUDIT_ID affecting it, and the total records affected, among other operational quantities. This in hand, we know at any given point the activities taken on the database, because no actions outside of this protocol will be allowed to affect the database. Any operations that do so, such as maintenance and the like, need to be brought under this umbrella so that everything is traceable. For example, if we should perform an update on a table, we should also use the AUDIT_ID of the current job and add that operation to the LOAD_LOG.

Now when we want to replicate, our primary goal will be to *reconcile* the LOAD_LOGs of the source and target. This will be the most objective way to know if any operations are affecting the database without being part of the common LOAD_LOG/AUDIT_ID protocol, and is the simplest way to achieve objective change-data-capture.

Our first step is to capture the AUDIT_IDs from the target. The objective is to make the target whole, so we need to know what this will take. The first question then is, what does the target already have? We don't need to capture all of the records from the Load Log, just the unique Audit_ids. I'll use variables for the host and target databases.

```
filevar-$(date_time_stamp)    #make a unique stamp for the file variable
EXTRACT_FILE=$MOUNT_POINT/extract_$filevar    #make a unique file
```

These resource in play, let's pull the unique Audit_ids:

```
nzsql -q -h $TGT_HOST -d $TGT_DB -o $EXTRACT_FILE -A -t <<!  &
select distinct AUDIT_ID from T_LOAD_LOG a where a.tgt_tab is not null and trim(a.
tgt_tab) <> '' ;
  !
```

The next step is to get these into the local source database so that we can form a delta. We will need two intermediate tables. One to receive the Audit Ids and one to form the working delta. We'll set them both up for housekeeping, so we don't need to mess with them after they are built.

```
LOAD_LOG_TEMP=TEMP_T_LOAD_LOG_$AUDIT_ID
mret=$( nz_table_housekeep $LOAD_LOG_TEMP $TARGET_XFR )
```

```
LOAD_LOG_REPLICATE=TEMP_T_LOAD_LOG_REPL_$AUDIT_ID
mret=$( nz_table_housekeep $LOAD_LOG_REPLICATE $TARGET_XFR )
```

Use the mighty CTAS to create an empty table in our working (Transform) database, depicted here with the TARGET_XFR variable.

```
#echo "Making Temp Table ${TARGET_XFR}..${LOAD_LOG_TEMP}"
nzsql -q -h $SRC_HOST -d $TARGET_XFR  <<!
create table $LOAD_LOG_TEMP as select AUDIT_ID from ${SRC_DB}..T_LOAD_LOG
limit 0;
!
```

Here we would simply use nzload to pull the $EXTRACT_FILE into the $LOAD_LOG_TEMP

```
nzload -host ${SRC_HOST} -db ${SRC_DB} -lf ${NZLOG_FILE} -bf $NZBAD_FILE -maxErrors
100 -delim $NZ_FILE_DELIM -df ${EXTRACT_FILE} -t $LOAD_LOG_TEMP
 -skipRows 0 -fillRecord > /dev/null
```

Note that the above can easily be converted into a reusable function call, but I've blown it out here for the sake of clarity.

Now let's fill the delta table with the information we will need to perform the replication.

```
nzsql -q -d $TARGET_XFR -h $SRC_HOST  <<!
create table $LOAD_LOG_REPLICATE as
select audit_id, tgt_tab, records_written
 from ${SRC_DB}..T_LOAD_LOG limit 0;
insert into $LOAD_LOG_REPLICATE
select audit_id, tgt_tab, records_written from ${SRC_DB}..T_LOAD_LOG a
  where
  a.records_written > 0 and
  a.tgt_tab is not null and trim(a.tgt_tab) <> '' and
  not exists
(select b.AUDIT_ID from $LOAD_LOG_TEMP b where a.AUDIT_ID = b.AUDIT_ID )
 ;
!
```

This provides us with the audit_id, table name and the records written. Of course, we need the table name to access the local and remote tables to transfer information between them. We need the audit Id to determine what portion of the table to extract and load. And we need the records-written to determine whether we need to copy any data at all. After all, if this value is zero, then it may mean that some automatic function just put a placeholder in the load log and we can ignore it. More importantly however, we will want to use this number to compare it to the total records that arrived on the target system as a means to validate the replication.

However, this means I want to perform a more surgical, cursor-styled operation and I don't want to do this kind of thing on the Netezza machine. So we'll now extract this result as "candidate list" of tables, and perform our replication on them surgically.

```
CANDIDATE_FILE=$(create_temp_file)

nzsql -q -host $SRC_HOST -d $SRC_DB -o $ CANDIDATE_FILE -A -t ${EXTRACT_SEPARATOR}
<<!
set nz_encoding=latin9;
select a.* from $LOAD_LOG_REPLICATE order by tgt_tab
!
```

Now let's use this local file as a cursor-style operation:

```
while read line
do
replicate_table "$line"
done < $CANDIDATE_FILE
```

So now in our replicate_table() function, we will have some very simple operations, but now at least we're down to the compressed file transfer. We also have the option, since the above cursor-style operation is self-contained for each table operation, to execute the above in parallel form. That is, multiple extract-load operations happening at once. To do this, we would need to leverage a throttle that keeps the total count of in-flight transfers to a threshold, otherwise we will bump up against the maximum allowable transfer count and could lose some data.

replicate_table function will consist of:

```
replicate_line=$1     #copy the incoming line parameter
LOC_AUDIT_ID=$(s_get_word_delim 1 "$S_PIPE" "${replicate_line}" )
LOC_TAB_NAME=$(s_get_word_delim 2 "$S_PIPE" "${replicate_line}" )
LOC_REC_CNT=$(s_get_word_delim 3 "$S_PIPE" "${replicate_line}" )
```

If the LOC_REC_CNT is equal to zero, we can bail out now. Nothing to replicate. Otherwise we need to initiate the extract_load. The following operations will extract the required data from the source table and load it to the target table.

Recall that we need a mount point visible to the Netezza host, not just our local Linux host. We'll call it REPLICATION_WORK_DIR.

```
timevar-$(date_time_stamp)    #make a unique stamp for the file variable
MFILE= $REPLICATION_WORK_DIR/EXT_FILE_$timevar

nzsql -host $SRC_HOST -d $SRC_DB -A -t <<!
create external table '$MFILE' using
( LOGDIR '${REPLICATION_WORK_DIR}' COMPRESS true FORMAT 'internal'  )
as select a.* from  $LOC_TAB_NAME a where audit_id = $ LOC_AUDIT_ID
;
!
```

Notice that the above doesn't actually create a table. This is a *transient* external table. It will exist only for the operation, and creates a compressed file for output. Not so for the following notation, where we have to build an external table to perform the operation.

```
EXT_TAB= ${LOC_TAB_NAME}_$timevar
nzsql -q -d $TGT_DB -h $TGT_HOST -A -t  <<!
create external table $EXT_TAB sameas $LOC_TAB_NAME
using (dataobject('$MFILE') COMPRESS true FORMAT 'internal' );

insert into $LOC_TAB_NAME select a.* from $EXT_TAB a ;

drop table $EXT_TAB;
!
```

Note that immediately after creating the external table, we perform the insert/select and drop the table, all inside one transaction. While this seems neat and clean, we will likely want to break these up into several operations for purposes of troubleshooting. Not to be overkill on hardening such a simple solution, but in some cases the additional overhead might make sense.

Now lets truncate the compressed file. We don't want to leave it around cluttering up the place, but we may want forensic evidence of what happened when. We'll do this with one more transient external table:

```
nzsql -q -host $SRC_HOST -d $SRC_DB -A -t <<!
create external table '$MFILE' using
( LOGDIR '${REPLICATION_WORK_DIR}' COMPRESS true FORMAT 'internal'  )
as select 1 limit 1 ;
!
```

Which brings us back to the LOAD_LOG. While we've just moved all the data from point A to point B, the load-log is not as significant a move. It will always be a lightweight push compared to the actual data content. For this, we would use a common extract-to-pipe and load-to-target. Essentially this means an nzsql statement with its output to a pipe, pushed to background, followed by an nzload reading from the same pipe. Enzees know how to do this in their sleep, and plenty of examples exist on the Netezza Community boards so I won't rehash here.

However, re-examine the steps in the above discussion and understand this: these are *exactly* the steps taken by the nz-migrate utility except that they can run on an external Linux host (provided that the disk space has been mounted to both source and target machines). The alternative to the above would be to use an nzload in place of the second external table read, and then run the whole thing on board the Netezza host.

But as I have noted in Underground, it is not advisable to run any (regular automated) data processing operations on board the Netezza host, rather let an external Linux server take the heat for this part and let the Netezza host do what it does best: manage the Netezza machine's assets.

Regarding Operators

Operators need visibility to what's-going-on and really hate black-boxed operations. They also hate having to touch code, script or any other aspect of the delivery. This means we need some coded controls, wrappers etc to make it a fairly lights-out experience for them. In fact, the box should be humming all the time, and only need their intervention when there is a *system* failure. For some, this seems obvious. For others, it's treated like a necessary evil. But as I have noted, the operators *are one of the most significant users of our work products*. Many regard the data, the information promulgated to the reporting users as the sole work product, with all other aspects a means-to-an-end. This is patently false. Operators, admins, troubleshooters and maintenance developers all receive our work products and will have an opinion on their quality.

Whenever we deliver the application, certain "sticky" files are integrated that contain environment-specific information. For example, in the DEV environment we may have access to certain URLs or databases (by name) that are different in the SIT or UAT environments. We have configuration files that capture these values for DEV and have corresponding placeholders for the others. When the application first arrives, we help them set up for their environment.

But when we have to re-deliver the application, this file will get over-written or replaced with the DEV version, which does not contain their changes. We provide for a persistent "sticky" location where these configuration files can be written and preserved, and the application will look in the sticky location first before looking in the other standard location. Occasionally we need to enrich the sticky file, so on installation the installer will find the sticky file, dovetail the new information into the file without modifying the old, and the update is complete. This usually means that we have defined a new variable or other element that needs to be added to the sticky file, which is easy enough to affect. The point is, we want to help the operator preserve the local environmental configuration across new installations or patches. It is time consuming and error-prone to have them manually re-apply these things upon each installation. However, this does not alleviate the need to be as comprehensive and anticipatory as possible when we first deliver. If we can collect the environmental differences ahead of time, this is that much less the operator has to change, and minimizes the need for a sticky location at all.

Notification

We will also need to support several notification protocols. Like the above sticky location, some of our notification destinations, such as email addresses, may be different across environments, so we provide a means to manage this in sticky files also. Otherwise an admin might set everything up only to have it overwritten by a new installation of code.

In the Appendix, I provide a detailed way to send a message body along with an attachment using the *sendmail* utility, which only supports this kind of message with a nuanced notation. The *mailx* utility is a lot more powerful, but it's also so straightforward I don't need to make any special notes on it.

I have mentioned elsewhere in the book that we use a concept called Flow Templates, where each of the actions in the template is a standalone operation that has a lot of lights-out infrastructure around it. With this template we can define multiple complex transform stages. At the end of the flow template, we typically execute the notification protocol by default. But there is another option. Each action in the template can also generate a notification. This allows operators to know which stage of the flow is complete. After all, if a nightly run of incremental data only takes half an hour or less, why does the operator need high-frequency messages at the end of each stage of work when they only last a few minutes each? Rather, tie these intermediate notifications to longer running jobs, so the operator can track them more easily.

Case Study Short - Our client's team was accustomed to long-running data flows through their ETL tool. They wanted us to post a message after the completion of each transform query. Considering that some of the queries ran in seconds, we would likely be spending more time delivering messages than doing actual work. But one of the databases had over two hundred tables, requiring over two-hundred and sixty transformation queries. Do you think the operator wanted to see this many messages come over? How about this: that the entire transformation workflow took less than ten minutes. Do you think an operator would have any appreciation for receiving over two hundred and sixty messages in ten minutes? What is the real value?

Operators want alerts when things go south. For things that are chugging along, they don't tap a keyboard to get minute-by-minute status. Alerts will let them know when something completes, because they were expecting it, and when something goes wrong, because they need to take action.

Verbose logging - is handy for the troubleshooter but is useless to the operator. The operator can email the verbose log to a troubleshooter, but they probably won't have any use for it otherwise. So it's a bad protocol to hand over a verbose log at the end of a job run and say, "It's in there". Rather we should have some summary operations that deliver to the operator all he cares about anyhow. Errors and failures. What we do in our applications is shoot everything to the run-time log. If a component reports an error, we reshape that error into the log and prefix it with "ERROR_STAT:" This allows us to capture and later glean the information from the log. Likewise Netezza utilities will automatically emit the keyword "ERROR:" along with a message.

At the end of a run, we perform a simple "grep" on the major keywords we care about, and summarize these into a short text file. This is packaged into a message, the original log file attached to it, and all this sent out to members of the predefined notification list.

Operators also like to know when individual queries have gone south. For example if an application has a runaway query, it could mean an application error or a system failure, but it's outside the normal envelope of activity so they want to know. In our environment, we have the Observation Deck, which runs on periodic boundaries and proactively analyzes the application queries, not just the machine's health. In this regard, we have visibility to how efficiently the application is using the machine, like queries with bad SPU distribution, singleton operations, collisions with updates / deletes, and monitoring candidates for table reclaim. Along with this, more advanced aspects include application processing exception statistics, data exception statistics (like referential violations) and aspects that would otherwise be buried under the covers. All of this and much more can be automated, performed in set-based, scalable fashion, and leveraging the machine's architecture in the most efficient manner.

Regarding Administrators

The Netezza admins already have a part-time job so we don't want to encroach on that with a bunch of full-time activities. Like operator, they want alerts, but these are more at the system level. Netezza provides those as part of the package, so I covered them (in the shortest chapter) in

Underground.

What the administrator really wants, though, is to have a lot of the application maintenance off his hands. This comes in the form of ease of use and automation of mundane, rote processes. A few of those follow:

Releases and patched releases: The administrator wants a clean way to hit a button, get a release, and know that the release "took" and is underway. Not much simpler than that. The admin doesn't want to know about version control systems, tagging or high-maintenance models of code. Like any admin, he wants to receive a "build" like a self-contained "tar" file. We deliver the "tar" file, he puts it into a controlled location, executes the extract and the install, and he's done. In some cases, I've seen people completely bundle the tar and installation as a single delivery. Execute the file and it does the work with no additional fuss. The admin doesn't need anything more than a success/fail message, because there's not really anything he can do if it fails, and if it succeeds, he doesn't care either. He has other work to do. On the installation side, we can put alerts into the installation process that notify us when the installation is completed. So he doesn't have to lift a finger.

Along with the release, recall that we have "sticky" directories for the application overseers, and we also maintain some sticky files for the admin. One of these is the external database configuration file. This file maintains an inventory of all the external databases to which the application will attempt to connect and pull information. It has either clear-text or encrypted passwords, but allows the admin to put in database names for say SIT, UAT and PRD environments which may be widely different across regions. Once configured, he can put this into a sticky directory and it won't get over-written on subsequent installations.

I've already mentioned some of the database maintenance stuff we manufacture from the catalog. The admin will also find these useful in helping build out database suites and performing general maintenance. Which brings us to housekeeping.

Since the database install utility can know which tables it installed, it can also know which ones it can truncate (as a whole), reclaim or teardown. Truncation and teardown are invaluable for initial development of the environment. Reclaim is handy for ongoing maintenance of the tables. In the Mustang series, reclaim is a necessary evil to keep the tables healthy. In the 6.0 NPS, the groom utility is far less in overhead and does not lock the table from access. Still, we need a clean way to manage the groom / reclaim activity. Both are expensive operations and do high-intensity cleanup on the given table. We only want to execute it on the tables that need it.

Case Study Short: The client wanted to keep all of the constraints produced by ERStudio and push them into the Netezza catalog. We had already set up special processes for table installation, so all we needed was the DDL. This worked great until some general changes were required a few weeks into the project. We would have to teardown the constraints, shuffle some tables and columns, then re-apply the constraints. Unfortunately, we could not re-apply the constraints in the same order as they had originally arrived. When primary/foreign key constraints exist, we have to tear them down in a certain order. So we captured the DDL for this and used some simple manipulation scripts to churn this as metadata into an install script and a teardown script. These worked flawlessly and we've not heard a peep out of them in a very long time.

Across the fruited plain, I've seen people with various models of this kind of maintenance, but the most pervasive is the once-a-month, all-at-once, reclaim-every-table-in-the-database kind of model. It is the easiest to implement, guarantees that all tables will eventually be reclaimed, but is also the least efficient.

There is a way to examine the tables to find reclaim/groom candidates and zoom in on them. If we have an efficient model already, using insert-only methods and the like, our tables will be healthy most of the time. Arbitrary reclaim/groom is overkill. Even if we have a messy implementation with lots of dead space, arbitrary reclaim/groom is still very inefficient. However, I will say that a messy implementation can be masked by the sheer power of the machine. Inefficient models eat up a machine's power and can lead to premature upgrade. By this I mean, our machine could probably last a bit longer without an expensive upgrade if we're using it efficiently. Otherwise the only way to get additional power really is to upgrade, but this will only mask the problem.

Here is a rework of an excerpt I posted out on the Gather 'Round The Grill blog on the Netezza Community site.

```
#Get a list of tables
TABLES=$(nzsql -q -d DATABASE_NAME -A -t  -c"select tablename from _v_table;" )

MAX_PCT=20

for table in $TABLES
do
mret=$( nz_reclaim_candidate DATABASE_NAME $table $MAX_PCT )
if [ $mret -eq 1 ]`
then
nz_reclaim DATABASE_NAME $table
fi
done

#===================================
nz_reclaim_candidate()
#===================================
{
exec >&2
DBNAME=$1
TABNAME=$2
MAX_PCT=$3
if [ "x${MAX_PCT}" = "x" ] ; then MAX_PCT=20 ; fi

MDEL=$(nzsql -q -d $DBNAME -A -t -c "set show_deleted_records=true;select count(*)
from $TABNAME where deletexid <> 0;" )
  echo "delete count=$MDEL"
  if [ $MDEL -eq 0 ] ; then return 0 ; fi

MCNT=$(nzsql -q -d $DBNAME -A -t -c "select count(*) from $TABNAME ;" )
  echo "table count=$MCNT"
  if [ $MCNT -lt $MDEL ] ; then return 1 ; fi

MPCT=$(nzsql -q -d $DBNAME -A -t -c "select (${MDEL}*100)::bigint / ${MCNT}::bigint
; " )
```

```
echo "percentage deleted=$MPCT "
if [ $MPCT -ge $MAX_PCT ] ; then return 1 ; fi

return 0

}
```

The key of the solution is the "show_deleted_records" switch. This will show us which of the rows have been deleted (they are non-zero in their deletexid value). We get a count of visible records in the table, then the deleted records. If the deleted-count exceeds the threshold, then reclaim it. If we have aggressive delete/update activity, twenty percent is the sweet-spot threshold. If we have an efficient, insert-only model, then it is geared to expect a lower delete-count by design, so set the threshold a little lower. I know of a site that set the threshold at ten percent, and the total times they have run nz_reclaim, on all tables and all databases, is for only ten of their most active tables, twice each in one year. Their largest table, with over 100 billion rows, has only been reclaimed once in three years time. This is the most efficient way to leverage reclaim and maintain the health of the machine and the application besides.

Housekeeping

Our housekeeping issue is twofold - temporary work files (in the framework's execution) and intermediate / transient tables used by the transform flows. While the temporary files are something of a nit, there is a nuance here that applies to both tables and files, and that is the timing and scope of housekeeping.

Whenever a job runs, we leverage two housekeeping files for monitoring temporary files. One is the run-time housekeeping that will be executed at the very end of the job. Every temporary file that is created, is logged into this file with the "rm -f path/file" specification, so that at the end of the run, the framework just executes the housekeeping file and it dispatches all of the temporary assets. The second file we maintain is practically identical in function to the first, with a longer fuse on the files. Each time we make a file, we log it into both places. This way, if the job fails, we still have a track of the created files. They will be housekept later. For example, the primary run log is not housekept by the job's housekeeping log, but by the external long-term housekeeping log. This allows the primary run log to persist after the job is done (so operators and such can review it), but it is still under housekeeping control. Thus an admin has a one-stop-shop to housekeep both temporary files and the run logs, all in one place. We could also apply an expiration hook that looks for a daily threshold, say twenty days. Housekeeping archives any older than this, it automatically executes without the admin's intervention. It also deletes itself, so nothing remains behind.

Another side benefit of this is the creation of intermediate data files. If we perform an extract of data from the database into files, we may load those files up immediately, or we may defer the load. If we load them immediately, we might want to housekeep them right away. Or not, if the extract took a long time. We can keep them around a bit longer, wrapped with a manifest file for loading, and this takes the burden off the intake to constantly reproduce the data. Very handy for building regression data sets.

For tables, whenever a job runs, we leverage two housekeeping files for monitoring intermediate tables. When the table is first named, we throw its full name and path into a self-contained "drop" statement similar to the following:

```
nzsql -q -d DATABASENAME -c "drop table TABLENAME;"
```

Such that when the job run completes, this housekeeping file is also executed to drop all of the tables created during the run. Like the file housekeeping scenario, we also put this same drop command into a secondary file, so that if the job should die before housekeeping runs, we won't lose track of the tables. These are landed in a similarly named housekeeping file, but prefixed with the database name so that they are not all jumbled into one file. Why do this?

While at one site we had all of this housekeeping in a common file for both temporary files and tables, and it worked swimmingly. One day the operators decided it was time to perform a complete history pull from the source database, and they intended to layer this data into the intake database using segmented/threaded tables. This would allow them to divide the data into suites of information spanning dozens of tables. For example, all of the data for a given day's run would be put into all the tables, but these would be intermediate tables that were replicas of the original, all suffixed with the YYYYMMDD notation of the data they contained. With over three years of data, they decided to bundle these up a few days at a time, but we still ended up with thousands of tables of information. Still, we could systematically select any day of the year and immediately process the data, so it was pretty cool stuff.

Then one day the 20-day limit arrived for housekeeping, and the housekeeping control file dutifully executed, removing all temporary files and intermediate tables created that were older than 20 days, and it included these many thousands of tables that had been painstakingly crafted into existence. We recovered from this by reproducing the tables again, and taking them out of scope of the daily housekeeping, but it was a painful lesson on automated housekeeping and the need to delineate what is in scope for automation.

Now with the database housekeeping files prefixed with the database name, the admins have the visibility to execute housekeeping for say, the transform databases where intermediate tables rule. But not necessarily the intake databases where intermediate tables may be serving a more permanent purpose.

Another aspect of this is that we never manufacture intermediate tables in a target database (e.g. the REP , RPT etc). This is because, if the job fails in the middle of the run, it will leave all that trash behind in the target database. Rather, intermediate resources are built out in a transform database and the final results *finalized* or copied into the target when all processing is completed with no errors or failures. This approach gives the admin permission to drop tables in the transform database if they are stale or the housekeeping protocol somehow missed them or the housekeeping file was accidentally deleted before execution. Either way, a given transform run can produce hundreds upon hundreds of intermediate tables on each and every run of the flow. It is incumbent upon the framework creating this to also housekeep it. The alternative, that the admin should do it by hand, is abusive and should be avoided.

Be kind to your local admin.

6 STRATOSPHERIC

IF OUR SINCERE OBJECTIVE is to leave the gravitational attraction of the existing environment, we need some tools and practices to help us reach escape velocity. Recall from 6th grade science that escape velocity is the speed required to escape the gravitational attraction of a larger body. For our purposes, this larger body might be an existing warehouse, or an existing set of processes and protocols that are asphyxiating the information and anyone who touches it. Maybe we want a fresh start with a new technology, but don't really want to leave behind the hard-won knowledge of our current existence. Perhaps we're trying to escape past failures, lost loves or the ghosts on the virtual playground. For the Three Amigos, *El Guapo* became a metaphor for a personal or a common adversary, a hurdle to overcome, a situation to exit, or a habit to break, etc.

"For some people, Oracle might be our El Guapo. For others, a bad implementation might be our El Guapo. For still others, engineered complexity might be our El Guapo. And of course, for many, a El Guapo is a really ugly guy with pistols. For wherever there is poor performance, obfuscated logic, or fire-breathing users, we'll be there to help." - Martin ShortInt, *The Three Warehouse Amigos*

Let's take a look at *Four* Amigos, what some have called the Four Horsemen, but the whole equestrian analogy is already etched in stone so it's hard to add another Horseman. But if we want to add another Amigo, hey, plenty of room for as many Amigos as we need. In the 2009 Roadshow where the new S-Blade appliance was originally rolled out, I was invited to host the best practices sessions and upon introducing the three panelists at each session, said they would "affectionately be called the Three Amigos". I received more feedback from that rather casual off-the-cuff statement than one might imagine, with the additional note that it made the powerhitters on the panel "feel more like one of us". Without the Singing Bush.

The spirit of the Enzee Universe is just that. Sure, we have competitors and combatants among the ranks, but the general spirit is that of an Amigo, or Amiga, as the case may be.

For our purposes, to transform a Netezza machine into a data processing hub, The Four Amigos in no particular order are:

Intake - We gotta get the data into the machine. The word "intake" is preferred over the term "staging", "loading" or "landing" because we're looking at things from the inside-out. If Netezza is the center of the universe, then all of the data we want is outside of that universe. Getting the data inside is an Intake operation. If our ETL tool or other environment is the center of the processing universe, then loading, staging or other term might be appropriate - for *them*.

Flows - Inside the machine we will want to execute SQL-Transforms within a context. The transforms themselves carry very little context. In a flow-based operation, we'll harness a progression of these transforms to meet a conclusion and business outcome. Without a flow model, the transforms are just out-in-the-open and no different than executing the transform from the command line.

Replication - Once all the SQL-Transform smoke clears, we will have consumption-ready data. One school of thought says to replicate the data into another database, or even another machine. This is great for archival too. Replication has 1001 uses and is a painless way to move data toward a consumer no matter where they are.

Consumption Points - The best, most flexible and adaptive way to present data to the users. Or perhaps more appropriately, to introduce the user to the data.

We drive these larger, thematic modules with a configured set of tools, and perhaps these are the horses we're looking for. The Amigos have a ranch, you see, and on that ranch are lots of horses. Some of them are thoroughbreds, some plow the fields, others help work the ranch, we have a lot of equestrianisms at this level. I won't bother fleshing out the ranch analogy, but anyone from Texas can imagine the temptation to do so.

Utilities - Install and maintain the flow's supporting structures. We want the utilities to use a common set of configuration rules.

Processes - Activate and control the flows and their internal parts, synchronize flows and maintain contextual integrity.

Metadata - Prescribe the flow with rules. Such constructs as flow-templates, transform-templates and other controlling metadata are handy and simple to implement.

SQL Transforms - Now that the data is inside the machine, everything we do with it will be a SQL-Transform insert/select operation. Put these together and we have a flow. Put flows together and we have an application

Factories - When mentioned will conjure up notions of abstract concepts. But wait, we already use factories in everyday life. We may not call them that, but the original Fab Four designated the Design Pattern of the Factory for what I am about to describe in our local context. For example, do we want to use hand-crafted SQL or a SQL generator? The generator is a type of factory. Do we want to manually install and configure each database, or will we use a database generator for this? The generator is a type of factory. Even if we aren't formally calling it a factory, it still fits the pattern. And in true design-pattern form, will appear as merely a latent, non-reusable artifact if we don't deliberately embrace, harness and leverage them.

Active Data Model - is a form of using the common tools of ErWin, ERStudio or even Visio in concert with integrated tools that extract their contents and manufacture all kinds of useful artifacts. Once the model is physically ensconced into the database, Netezza will have standardized it into its own catalog. We will then extract this more enriched form to perform all kinds of useful things. Keep in mind that it's easier to manage metadata than data. We can't shoot sixty billion rows through a shell script. But we can use shell script to shape SQL statements and formulate supporting Netezza assets. Let the SQL harness the data, because that's its job.

In this regard, once the model is first published, we activate it by deriving our application assets from it. If the tables and columns are the substrate through which all data passes, then they will only pass this way through SQL statements. We must get the developer out of the SQL-statement-crafting business and into the business-rule-crafting business. It's the only way to scale.

With an Active Data Model, we get the structure out of its cloistered existence and literally put it to work. Many of us are already doing this in one way or another. An example might be that we hit the catalog for a table definition in order to perform some operation on the table. But this is exactly what we want - the use of the catalog, which is derived from the model itself, as a means to generate SQL and useful utilities that will aid us along the way. Some of the general-purpose stuff we'll need in the arsenal includes:

The ability to install the data model without the benefit of the modeling tool. What does this mean? We have a utility (that is simple to build, and we may already have one) that requires only the create-statement DDL file produced by the modeling tool. From this, it will create a series of actual create-statements that are wrapped with additional functionality. When done, we have a way to install and re-install the database in a consistent manner. But when first developing and deploying a database, we have needs that eclipse the database administration capacity of most environments, because we are not treating databases as cloistered hubs, nor tables as managed assets. We are treating them respectively like directories and files (because Netezza manages everything else under the covers) This is a luxury not found in most other technologies, where even instantiating a table is a major affair. It creates a significant challenge for a development team if the DBAs have a policy that every table and structure must be carefully catalogued. Here we get the best of both worlds and the acceleration to go with it.

Case in point: The Netezza 6.0 host now allows us to modify a table by adding a column. For some, this seems like a good thing when we want to extend a tabie's assets . But it's also a good thing when we want to change the table's internal structure. For example, we can't use alter/modify to change a smallint to a bigint, nor can we use it to change the precision of a numeric, or any other data type conversion. But with the ability to add a column, think about the following:

```
#assumes B1 is a smallint
TIME_VAR=$(date '+%Y%m%d%H%M%S%5N' )
alter table mytable rename column B1 to B1_$TIME_VAR ;
alter table mytable add column (B1 integer) ;
update table mytable set B1 = B1_$TIME_VAR ;
alter table mytable drop column B1_$TIME_VAR  restricted ;
```

In the above scenario, we simply changed the name of the existing column, added a new one of the desired type, copied the old values to the new and dropped the old. Now imagine this: What if we have the table already in place and we want to apply a delta, that is, a new table definition that modifies the current one, or for that matter modifies multiple tables? Here are the steps in pseudo-code:

- Build the NEW_TABLE as the Original Table name plus the TIME_VAR
- Pull all of the columns in the new table
- Pull all the columns in the current table
- Compare column names and data types
- Missing columns we drop
- Changed data types we apply through the above protocol
- New columns we simply add
- Groom the table

Now we have a metadata-driven means to affect changes to the tables even after they have been deployed. We don't have to rebuild with a CTAS (egregious for billion-row-tables) and we don't have to deal with nz_reclaim any more. Update the table to reset values, groom it and we're done.

Some utility roles may include:

Create - a package that we can hand off to a DBA or admin and they can pop the hood, so to speak, clearly see what the function does and tailor it to their needs (or we can work with them to tailor it in the handoff). DBAs rarely like for us to create whole databases on-the-fly, but in a SQL-transform model we will have multiple databases (like multiple directory folders) and we will know what these databases are early-on. They will appear as an "application suite" and can consist of a dozen or more databases for a single application. Once we add multiple development zones, testing zones and even sandboxes for users, the databases start multiplying like rabbits and this brings anxiety to our DBAs. Not to worry, with utilities to manage them, name them and track them, we can handle this no differently than we manage multiple directory folders on a NAS device.

Init - which is probably my favorite because it instantiates operational framework tables and assets onto each database, causing them to share a common, object-oriented means to trace data as it flows from one database to the next, and one table to the next. Imagine if we had a bunch of database silos and the only way we could track anything between them was to glean the query histories in the catalog for any queries executed in one that cross-accessed the other? But with a common set of infrastructure tables, the databases operationally cross-talk and behave as a cohesive whole. We can also easily identify a database that is not "framework initialized". These common-interface tables are what make the databases "polymorphic" to our growing framework and to each other.

Conversion - to convert the ERStudio/ERWin - produced DDL into actionable assets that support a wide range of automatic table, column and constraint management. In addition, pre-scrub utilities that convert "raw" Teradata, SQLServer or Oracle DDL into a form that is consumable by this converter.

Install - to install all of the tables in a database and stand it up very quickly with a repeatable, manageable executable. As noted above, the ability to re-install the data tables without destroying data. In addition, once the tables are installed, we want to be able to update their structure without drop-and-replace. With NPS 6.0, we now have the ability to alter-table and add a column. Our utility installer needs to recognize this and merge the new columns onto the original table.

Install-data - to manufacture installable data and store them in consistently-named data files, so that when we execute this function for a given database, it simply finds the files and loads them correctly, even if the table may have changed or expanded. It expects the data file of course to use a file column header. But this kind of facility is very handy all the way through implementation and beyond to set up or rebuild certain lookup tables and the like.

It also promotes the best practice of packaging and version-controlling this kind of data so that it arrives with the installation rather than as a separately managed entity.

Truncate - Since we already know what tables we created, we likewise know which ones can be truncated for a given application. When building and rebuilding the warehouse, especially at the outset of the project, the ability to zero-out the entire database is very useful and powerful to turnaround a data processing flow stream.

Teardown - Since we can track what tables we created, we likewise know which ones to rip out of the database (for a given application). Tables, columns and constraints, especially those that have to be removed in a particular order (like referential constraints). So now we can execute a targeted teardown and essentially "undo" the installation. Again this is for warehouse inception and the early stages of migration when the target structures are in flux.

Replicate - which is a lot like the nz_migrate utility with the exception that it uses the afore-mentioned infrastructure tables to move data around. So it has the capacity to functionally replicate (that is surgically move data incrementally from one table to another, or one machine to another) faithfully copying the new-and-changed information as though it had been just-processed locally. And doing it only for all the tables touched by the most recent operations. Two flavors we will need to support - the flavor that copies the tables by column name whether the source and target are structurally sync'd or not, and the flavor that uses compression, requiring the source and target tables to be identically in structure.

Reclaim - an important aspect of maintenance is to make sure the database tables are in proper health. Since it is aware of which tables belong to an application, it can browse the table, determine if their unused table space is over an acceptable threshold, and reclaim as necessary. Threshold-based reclaim gives us the efficiency we need to keep all the tables healthy, reclaiming them as necessary rather than doing it in blanket, scatter-shot or (gulp) by manual execution. Of course, the appliance's *groom* utility mitigates the need for a high-ceremony nz_reclaim, but we still need to be diligent about how often we invoke it.

SQL-Transform Template Factory - We also have the ability to make the template itself smart enough to be table-aware. How useless is it to have a fire-and-forget template that is disconnected from its original source? No, what we want is to have a way to sync and re-sync the template to its original source in an objective way. Perform a diff, or even a merge, of the new/changed/deleted columns on the table into the template without an ounce of manual intervention on our part. Can an ETL tool do this? None of them do and I seriously doubt any of them have this on their enhancement-radar for the near future. I will be happy to be wrong about this, of course.

First off, let's recall that transforms in the Netezza machine ultimately reduce to insert/select SQL statement (SQL-Transforms). We could allow our developers to craft these statements "in the raw" or we can craft the statements in a more formalized manner. What we need is a way to assist the developer in the crafting SQL statements by generating the statement from a factory. Statements then become *artifacts* of process, not the centerpiece.

Think about the mechanics of crafting even one of these statements. We have to account for the target table and all its columns. We have to account for the source tables and their columns. We have to formulate rules between the source and target columns, and we have to formulate a filter/join to connect source tables. What if on each of these iterations, we have to plumb the catalog for the various assets and generally make it tedious beyond comprehension? Folk who do it this way want to get away from it and I cannot blame them one bit.

The major ETL tools don't do this. They merely pull from the catalog and present the developer with structured I/O points for data to enter or leave the ETL tool's domain. If we want to direct the Netezza machine to do something else, this requires a crafted SQL statement and we're back to square one (I'll talk about push-down in a later section).

We can likewise formulate structured I/O templates derived directly from the catalog, but manufactured automatically into a holding area for the developers to pull from and fill out like a form. This structured form is then submitted to the framework controls where all of the implicit assets are manufactured around it. This is a secondary factory, or Transform Factory that uses the template as its primary source of instructions. So there is no confusion, here are the steps:

The Template Factory - executed only when the catalog changes, so that the templates remain stable. The developer configures the template(s) with rules and instructions that will ultimately be used to generate a SQL-Transform. *Templates are therefore design-time.* In addition, because they are manufactured from the catalog, they are catalog-aware. Changes to the catalog can therefore be merged into the templates even after they are deployed. Since they are the basis for SQL-Transform generation, we have a direct linkage between the catalog and the SQL-Transforms.

The Transform Factory - at run-time this factory consumes the template(s) and manufactures a SQL-transform from it. Each SQL-transform is submitted to the Netezza machine and their results logged in a Transform Log (SQL statement, records affected, start/end times, template file name etc). This log keeps the running, sequential context of the transforms so that we don't have to reconstruct them from query histories. *This factory is run-time.*

This kind of template approach accelerates development and testing, and better constrains the developers into a compliant harness for each and every SQL statement. Thus no SQL statements are submitted "in the raw" by an errant developer. They are either in compliance in the harness or they don't work. Shaping them into compliance *at design time* is much easier than remediating an entire flow of in-the-raw SQL statements.

Some may suggest that this approach is a drawback to the overall lifecycle. That an ETL tool could harness all of this stuff equally well. Perhaps so in some cases. But the ETL tools still require us to manufacture and install a complete, fully crafted SQL statement into their SQL harness. They also have far less options to use advanced constructs like loops, trees, lists and the like. In fact, we can't get very creative at all in the ETL tool. All we can do is fire a fairly canned and rigid SQL statement over the wall. We also don't have the metadata-transform capture we would like, and we don't have any flow capability unless we want to use the ETL tool to string these complex SQL statements together. Likewise when updates to the database model are applied, we will have to go back to the ETL tool and *manually* apply each. This of itself will discourage developers from doing-the-right-thing required for Netezza-centric SQL-transforms, and that is breaking up larger queries into smaller ones to accelerate the whole. Invariably when I visit sites using ETL tools to affect the Netezza machine, they have boiled the functionality into a handful of very complex, Oracle-styled operations. They only do this because breaking apart the statement creates too much *maintenance* overhead. Just keep in mind that in the ETL tool, it expects us to bring the SQL statement to the tool, because the tool won't help us manufacture it on the fly.

So look at the simple sacrifice here: If we stay inside the ETL tool, its metadata will be our substrate between components. One component's output port describes the next component's input port. Changing one is automatically detected by the tool's analysis capabilities. But what of a SQL statement? If the table on the database changes, will it let us know this? The SQL harness of a common ETL tool is not catalog-aware. We have to stamp out bugs and anomalies at run time (whack-a-mole) and not design time.

Run-time-configuration generation - We have a couple of options with run-time configuration. One is the simple on-off switch that will drive behavior. I covered this in detail in Underground, but this is ubiquitous in app-dev and configuration management circles so probably doesn't need rehash here.

The *generated* form of this aspect is more interesting. For example, if the presence of a switch or configuration rule drives a common pattern of behavior, and that behavior has a common interface specification, it makes sense to compile these things out to overloaded function calls just for this purpose. That's a little abstract, so later I offer up an example in the *function_exec* protocol the Set-Based Stuff chapter. The primary reason for this protocol is that attempting to manage the overhead in the wildly disparate run-time configurations across projects and applications, can inadvertently drive application functionality into our core software architecture. There it will become a source of irritation as the application permutations make it quite unwieldy To avoid pain and injury, if for no better reason that avoiding the juggling of sharp objects, we can pre-compile these into dedicated function calls. This gives us the agility and stability we need without hardwiring the rules or the code into a rigid model.

Think of it in these terms: I could apply a parsing algorithm that will, at run time, derive the correct behavior for a disparate number of arbitrary applications. Or I could provide the core capabilities of the pattern and then introduce the algorithm *from* the application, generated in context of the rules that fit the pattern. As an example, let's say the Intake pattern needs to perform a deduplication of the data. This will be table-centric, so we need the following parameters for the operation: the Table, the Columns and the Function. We will place these rules in a file associated with the given database, These will drive the generation of rules:

```
Table=<mytable> Columns=<key1,key2,key3> etc Function=<filtration function here>
```

Ultimately we will generate a callable interface that overloads the database and table. The Intake operation will use function_exec() to find the generated interface and execute it.

```
databasename_tablename_deduplication( $Replica Table Name )
```

Note the use of the replica table name. Even though we know the name of the 'seed' table from which the table's metadata has been derived (via CTAS), this may have (and likely did) spawn the generation of a threaded-form of this table. We will want to call this function in that context. Note also that according to the rules of *function_exec* (which will be used to invoke the above) if the function was never generated (no rule provided) then the Intake pattern calling it will not bomb off, it will simply keep moving. This means all of these rules-driven sub-patterns are both optional and customizable. Exactly the qualities we want for the highest adaptability of the Intake pattern.

After all, what we really want the Intake pattern to cover are the complexities of the Intake operation. It cannot always complete the mission, however, because of localized application dependencies or malformed data. We don't want to embed those conversions into the Intake as this will only make it rigid (and therefore brittle) over time.

So with the above *function_exec* protocol, we can now burst out a shell-script file filled with these pre-defined functions and their content. For deduplication, change_data_capture, validation etc that were mentioned earlier in the chapter as workhorses. The file then behaves as a self-contained object, part of an intake class. When we load the file, we instantiate the object. A common intake component simply consumes its interface.

The most important aspect of the above utilities, is that they share a common substrate of structural and configuration metadata. That is the database definition and naming convention, the security and user groups, DDL for tables and views and a lot more. All of it falls out of a plan to start harnessing Netezza as an application and data processing workhorse. With common configuration metadata, adding tables to a database is easy, adding databases to a suite is easy, and managing the contents of these assets becomes a utility-based exercise.

Can we imagine the converse? What if we wanted to deduplicate a wide number of intake tables. Do we specifically code a SQL-transform to support each? It is virtually guaranteed that they will all follow a common operational pattern. What if we want to truncate the tables in our warehouse to reload them? Do we tediously bring up the admin GUI and click on "truncate" for each one, for *hundreds* of tables? What about cleaning out a database without dropping it? I'll follow up with some simple examples of how this kind of structure and the attendant utilities dovetail into it. Building our own (which I always encourage) will help us appreciate and embrace the Netezza machine as a data processing workhorse. Without them, building out a new database and managing it will be a source of tedium and potential pain when we want to scale all of our data processing applications, and I'm all over pain reduction.

Metadata-driven modeling and deployment - If we intend to use the data model as the source of all wisdom, this means we need a strong, configurable modeling approach and a means to rapidly deploy it.

One of the most pernicious issues in data model deployment is in the propensity of such installations to blow away our testing data and testbeds. The next most pernicious issue is that data modelers surgically add and subtract columns (we want them to, don't we?) and this creates havoc in the SQL layer. Could we even imagine the impact of a 200-table database with 400 supporting SQL transforms, and then the modelers publish a new model? Do we have to *manually* merge the model with the transforms? This alone is a full time job to implement, much less test. With a metadata-driven model, the SQL is generated from templates which are in turn generated from the catalog. So if the catalog changes, the templates change, and this will bring about the SQL that we need anyhow. (In the metaphor, the utilities and the metadata are our horses)

If we remanufacture and re-install the model, we will destroy the *data* in it. Some of the data may require additional time to remanufacture from a flow. Imagine losing the data in hundreds of tables that may cost hours to rebuild. In a metadata-driven model, we take the plain-vanilla CRE-ATE TABLE statements, wrap them with a framework-level function call, and then place them all into a callable utility. This utility is then invoked and the tables are created in context of some rules. If the rule is to preserve the table contents, the existing tables will be renamed. If this rule is not on, the existing tables will be truncated or even dropped.

The difference in these steps is dramatic. For one application prior to 6.0, we added the no-truncation switch and removed an enormous thorn in our side. The client was wont to change several critical but very large tables. Our process would rename the table with a timestamped name, make the new table and then copy the columns from the existing table into the new one. This guaranteed table content preservation, and kept the heat off while we were trying to move really fast.

View factories - more on these in the Consumption Point chapter. We also want to be out of the business of constructing hand-crafted views, especially the high-risk kind. What kind is that? The *nested* kind. Manufacturing a view's logic, even if just to validate that no views are nested within it, is an excellent means of shepherding a view into the reporting database. It also guards against accidental performance degradation and provides a means to scan the view in context of all other views and tables. The nested view, for multi-billion-row tables, is a danger we need to avoid, and doing so means we need to take views more seriously, not treat them as "simple" objects.

Stored Proc Factories - In keeping with the factory theme, guess how many stored procedures look practically identical to each other in how they are configured and installed? Isn't there a pattern in their interior construction also? Of course there is, and we should bottle this lightning too, so that the developer simply concentrates on the mechanics of the intended application, not the overhead for instantiating the procedure itself. Drop our logic into the factory and the stored procedure should pop out of the other end. Is it really that simple? Hmm, yes and no. But the factory gets us as close as we need to be for the majority of stuff we want to do. We can always accommodate and eventually assimilate the exceptional cases.

UDX Factories - Oh, yeah, there's a factory for these too. I watched the rollout of the nz Lua capability at the 2010 Enzee Universe and walked away stoked. Here we have a structured and safe means to instantiate UDX functionality that just begs to be wrapped up in a factory. After all, the overhead for putting together a UDX and deploying it are, like the stored procedure and the view, a repeatable pattern. We want to exploit the pattern so that we can focus on the logic and the implementation, not the tedium of installing the UDX itself. This will allow us to hand off a task to a junior developer to go manufacture the necessary run-time logic for the UDX without having to engage the uptake on UDX mechanics. They will learn the UDX mechanics from what we have provided for them, but once again the factory model itself becomes the basis for active knowledge transfer. There's no better kind.

Recapping Some Terms

I thought it best to recap some core terms that I have carried over from Underground, which will make things simpler on the reader than just providing a reference. These are more like glossary entries here. For full explanation and examples, Underground has the stuff.

Jurassic Park Model: Named more for the movie than the timeframe, although some may wonder. In the movie, technologists crunched hundreds of hours of video, computer graphics and such to produce a relatively few seconds of movie magic. Standard warehouses use a cruncher like an ETL tool to process data and present it to the database in load-ready/consumption-ready form. Once loaded, the user gets a crisp, high-performance experience, just like in the movies. The contrast is a Netezza SQL-transform model, where data arrives to the machine raw, is loaded raw and then crunched after it's inside. This obviates the role of an ETL tool and thus the Jurassic Park model evaporates (somewhat). We'll still need crunching, but not so significantly.

Scalable: That is, millions or billions of rows. Loading them, crunching them, presenting them. Scalability has as much to do with loading/processing billions of rows once, as it does multiple times, and in parallel processing threads. It has to scale for developers, testers and final users. Plenty of scalability concerns in the mix. Multi-threaded, on-demand processing is rapidly becoming the standard modus operandi of the global data warehouse.

We bought the Netezza platform on the direct promise of scalability. Why is it that some users surround the Netezza platform with products or solutions with limited scalability. This is like tying a bald eagle to a tether. It will never soar as high as possible, only as high as the tether allows.

Adaptable: The data warehouse (or BI environment) must exist with the expectation of change. Anything built without this explicit and pervasive theme is already dead-on-arrival. No sooner will the first rollout occur than the users will hammer the delivery folks with more requirements. The test of adaptability is not in rollout number one, or even number two. But the ability to perform rollouts in the hundreds with no loss of momentum. A adaptable model is practically fluid in how it operates. We'll look later at how metadata helps us get as close as possible to this goal.

Stability: Latent flaws in the architecture will result in hampered or stalled adaptability, and as such directly affect scalability. An unstable solution can neither adapt nor scale. It is better to take a few steps back and refactor the architecture itself rather than attempting to bolt-on additional instabilities. One very popular enterprise tool was originally a core of integrated features. The product's software company bought another software company and attempted to integrate the two tools. Then another and another until the whole thing was an unstable patchwork quilt. The product continues to sputter in the marketplace because the holes in the integration remain. It would have been better for the software company to revamp the architecture rather than continue to present these products as an integrated whole. They are not, and it's obvious to anyone who uses them for the first time.

Metadata: This word has been hacked to death in the marketplace. In this book, we'll drive in a very specific way on a well-defined path as to what metadata can do for us and what its limitations are. We have a cafeteria to choose from – structural, behavioral, administrative, operational, descriptive, configuration, component – whew! We'll use all those and more to achieve a means to guide our application logic from a reusable platform. Embracing metadata is the means to achieve stratospheric lift in our applications. It's the best way to guarantee that a pattern used by one application will behave the same as another. We can fix a bug and have it apply to all places, or for that matter, trace a bug's effect in one application and discover the root.

Metadata is the essence of reusability. In fact, when we look at the core underpinnings of object-oriented languages and design, we see that the primary *reuse* aspects of these environments are driven by metadata constructs. This is nothing new to those folks who once-upon-a-time had to program objects in non-object languages like assembly language or C-language. The very impetus for the creation of C++ was the propensity for people to use C-language in an object-relational form *by discipline* rather than by language-based enforcement. Those folks who have been down that path recognize the role of metadata to lash together structures and processes into a common object-oriented model.

That's all we're talking about here, but we're applying it to large-scale data processing, not screen widgets, database access components or all that presentation firepower normally associated with objects. For us, the objects are databases, tables and columns. But these are just metadata-based labels for the underpinning data they represent. This is why metadata is the essence of our object-modeled experience and why manipulating metadata is a major key to harnessing the data itself, and ultimately harnessing the machine where it's stored.

Metadata-Driven - In Underground, one of the "10 Rules" presented was to embrace The Expectation of Change. We cannot afford to put a hard shell around the solution. As-yet unknown requirements are already on their way to us. Sort of like a FedEx package that the marketplace has already put in the mail, and it will arrive at a time-certain. We don't know what's in the package, but we can be sure this, and many other packages will arrive and present significant, sometimes daunting challenges to what we're trying to accomplish. These packages can often arrive as simple new requirements that dovetail into what we're already doing. They can be high-drama inflection points that require a large project initiative.

What they should not include, is a forklift, rework, migrate or other such like. Such an eventuality means that the solution started out as functionally hardened, then moved to brittleness, then finally to something so functionally dense that it frightened people to approach it. Workarounds ensued, until someone at the top said Enough! The solution had apparently not been built with the expectation of change, but with the directive to lockdown and protect it from change. A high wall was built around it. People wanted changes. They were told to wait six months. This is not a solution that embraces change.

Which brings us back to "meta". This word means "abstraction", or "above" – but it also means "change or changing". In fact, looking around at the different uses of "meta" tells us that what it purports to describe can stay the same or it can change, but the meta-description is what actually determines its nature and identity. While all of that may sound very abstract, think for a moment about how people regard "metadata". They usually regard it as the structural description of data. While this is important, it is limited. But now that we're here, what other forms does this take?

The most obvious is table/column/data type definitions in a database. But we also have file-system directory structures (locations of inbound/outbound files). Likewise the descriptions of those files contents. We also have files that themselves contain metadata, like the trigger files arriving from a distant system that provide the description of the data files just landed by some other enterprise process. But suffice to say that these structural quantities have many forms and permutations. We need to regard all of them. Can we set up an extractor that is able, through metadata cues, to select the correct extraction technology/client, configure it, pull-and-present the data to our front door? We likewise cannot assume that we can arrive on site and tell the file management folks that they have to drop all their data files into a very specific, prescribed location or our framework cannot see it.

No, they will object and say that to copy the file from its original landing zone to another one doubles the required file-space. And when we consider <Billions of rows here> we just don't have the luxury of the additional hop, nor can we make a plea to the administrators to provide soft-links to directories that are often manufactured on-the-fly to support their source consumption needs. They will say, we'll send you the URL. That's all you need to fetch the file anyhow, right? Nor is it easy to tell someone who has data on the mainframe (or other disparate technology) that they have to perform all the heavy lifting to get the data into our hands when it is easy enough (seriously) to set up a metadata-based specification to fetch the files ourselves. Such metadata is a mainstay in many data processing environments, forgive me if this is old-hat to you. For some, I assure, it is not.

Why are these things important? For one, we don't want to hard-code the descriptions of tables and columns into our application if we can avoid it. We'll do some of that in the application layer (likely) but not the layer that is brokering data and commanding the machine. Even the application layer will enjoy some degree of abstraction from knowing specific data structures and data types. We can control all of that with metadata-based controls.

Oh, David, you mean you want us to *code* all that metadata manipulation? The funny thing is, most of you already are without even realizing it. Or perhaps you do realize it and want more control over it. A major opportunity is passing by like standing on a bridge and watching the churning river pass below. Yep, that flow is under control. But we are not braced for change.

Here's a simple analogy to test our wits. We set up a plain database intake, then perform some transformations on the data (using SQL) and then push the data to the target tables. This is a pretty standard transform model. Some folks deploy this by performing all the transforms directly in the intake database prior to forwarding it to the target. Some send it straight to the target with no fuss at all. Others set up a transformation database, pulling the staged information into this work area, manipulating the data and then push it to the target. Yet others do all the work in the target database in "shadow" tables and when the data Is ready to present, the shadow tables are copied (or swapped) with their active counterparts and off we go.

Each of these styles of solution has its attendant drawbacks and advantages. What we don't want to embrace, are the drawbacks that will literally draw us back to the drawing board in order to fix a flaw. It doesn't mean "overbuilding" the environment, but there are happy mediums that we can embrace in order to avoid the less obvious put pending pitfalls.

Case in point – the Intake database should be dedicated to intake, its associated processes (deduplication etc) and nothing more. This is simply a choice of using a component architecture versus one where the lines are not so easily discerned. Why is this? At one site we put up an intake database to face their primary source and ran the whole operation with intake-level metadata. Six months later they announced a new source database that we would extract in addition to the original. And one month later they told us about a web service they needed to plumb to capture some "street" data. Our intake module had already been braced for change, so adding these new sources was largely a matter of cookie-cutter configuration rather than wholesale reprogramming. In fact, the adaptability of the intake framework became renown in its own right. No longer did they fear a conversation concerning the intake of data. As a metadata-driven intake model, it simply wrapped around the catalog metadata without making any assumptions about the source. So metadata decouples and isolates us.

This is a critical asset for many reasons, not the least of which is this: Pulling data from a source and landing it "raw" into the Netezza machine is nothing more than a matter of metadata-driven control. We stand up the utilities, configure them with simple run-time scripts, connect their I/O points and *voila*, the data is moving. The control-factor here is the job/utility instructions and these are very easy to circumscribe with simple metadata processing. The operant factor is that we are physically manipulating metadata, not data. We are getting the data into the machine, and will command the machine to process the data. This allows us to scale without a formal data processing tool.

Oops, did I let the cat out of the bag? Not really – I relegated ETL tools to the role of data transport mechanisms in Underground. And if the ETL tool is nothing more than a glorified data transport device, can't we do that with simple utilities? Ironically, the ETL tools also do it with the utilities (database clients, ftp, curl, etc.) Take a look under the covers and realize that the ETL tools are elaborate (and perhaps expensive) wrappers for those extraction utilities. They aren't really providing any additional value, or at least value that we could not find in the simple utilities themselves.

For example, standard FTP utilities can download EBCDIC data from a mainframe, convert it to ASCII and present it to a file stream. The IBM DB2 client utility for that same mainframe machine can likewise provide database extraction and present it in structured ASCII. For both of those utilities, it is literally child's play to write a simple metadata factory that will provide the parameters and script instructions. Suddenly we are pulling data from a mainframe, converting it to ASCII and it's ready to process. All without the expensive ETL tool to do the same thing. Even if the ETL engine is specifically coded (in its engine) to do this without the utility, the overlap of functionality does not justify purchasing an ETL tool to perform the same function as the utilities. This is not a dissertation on throwing the client / Unix utilities into a big pile. It is rather an assertion that we can define specific patterns of behavior, employ utilities to support the effect we want, and circumscribe all of it as a reusable component.

However, let's not go completely overboard with utilities here. We want the utilities that provide a high level of function that we cannot find inside the Netezza machine either. In that context, I cannot count how many places I've seen folks using Serialized Unix Utilities (SUU) to perform actual data processing. Like sed/awk and gawk, or just plain script-driven parsing. On the *data*. About now some are scratching their heads as to why I object to this, so I guess it's them I might be talkin' to.

Here's the deal: **Billions of rows.**

Okay, that's it in a nutshell. We cannot use Serialized Unix Utilities to physically touch and examine the stream of billions-of-rows-data as it passes into the machine. Nor can we pull the data from the machine, process it with such utilities and put it back. This practice enslaves the scalability of the entire solution to the very limited power of Unix utilities, and effectively dishonors the power of the Netezza machine. About now I could brush the back of my fingernails against my neck in Marlon Brando style, offer up my best Godfather impression and say "Don't dishonor the machine." Ahh, well, I'm not a Mafioso.

But Unix utilities are a perfect platform for manipulating *metadata*. We can pull the catalog definition of a table, parse out the column names and data types, manufacture SQL statements or functional intermediate data structures on-the-fly and do all kinds of useful things to the metadata.

With the full intention to present the metadata back to the machine, as generated SQL, to let it do the heavy lifting.

Structural Layout

In Underground, I presented a structural layout of the internal Netezza databases that at the time I had successfully and painlessly rolled out at a number of sites. I have repeated this success numerous times and now people ask me questions in context of doing-it-this-way. The main thrust of the layout, simple though it is, was to use the databases in functional roles, such as intake, transform, repository and reporting etc, then flow data through them as waypoints to a final destination.

The reason why this took hold in Enzee idea-space, was that the ETL tools merely treated these databases as endpoints. The ETL tool controlled the flow, after all, and as an extract-transform-load scenario, the databases were book-ends, or perhaps parenthesis, but not assets that were directly involved in the flow of data.

One aficionado who had put together a rather sophisticated data loading paradigm, first commented on this approach with a dismissive tenor. In his estimation, we didn't need to do anything more than get the data into the machine. Each load thread could be treated as standalone. Keep it simple and all that.

Then one day he encountered a group that was loading multiple tables into the intake zone (the daily transactional feed carrying the point-of-sale data as well as new-and-changed reference information). All of it was arriving in context and had to be processed in-context. If the reference data could not be applied to the dimensions, the fact table would also have a bumpy ride. This changed the scope of the intake from one of single-source-single-target into one of single-source-multiple-targets or even multiple-source-multiple-targets. Of course, ETL tools still treat all of these as standalone, shared-nothing operations, so there's no additional help on that front. If these streams are arriving in context, they share that context and need to be processed completely in that context, even to the point of arrival in their final targets.

The simplified structural layout is easy enough to note even without doing any graphics. We can white-board this and talk about it on the back of napkins, if necessary.,

Intake->Transform->Repository->Transform->Reporting->Consumption->Replication

See the Four Amigos standing tall? We don't need much explanation here because everyone understands the role of each of these data stores. Note the "arrow" between each. This is not an artifact. At this point, we need to take a checkpoint on what the databases mean versus how we mentally map them.

In an ETL tool, each database is regarded as an *endpoint*. But in a SQL-Transform enabled flow, processing data inside the machine, each database is a *waypoint*. The difference in the two is dramatic. If the database is merely an endpoint, data will remain there until externally queried, whenever that may be. If however the database is a *waypoint*, data is placed there on the assumption that it will be leveraged soon if not immediately. It the difference between an active model and a passive one. Technologists who are ETL-centric thinkers will have difficulty with these concepts. They will say "I understand what you are talking about" but will behave *as if they do not*. They will fall back to antiquated comfort-zones, stovepipe models, and require the building-out of each database as a standalone, stovepipe functionality. They will declare that each "leg" between the databases is a standalone application, not an integrated flow model. They will require waterfall-style development and testing. Each of these is not only "so yesterday" for development and testing purposes, they are so antiquated that they no longer have a place.

What else we might not see in all this, is that the Transform database is shared for the Repository and Reporting roles, but the Intake is a transform database unto itself. Why is this? The Repository and Reporting databases are "protected" forms of data that our transforms will shepherd data *into*. But the data in the Intake arrives raw and unfettered, with no particular organization or context (generally) so we need more flexibility here. In the Intake, we are not shepherding the data into another database, but into the *machine itself*. We need some transformation power. In addition, the data is not *officially* in the machine and published to the downstream until it makes it *past* the Intake gauntlet, so we have many degrees of freedom to shakedown the data without instantiating additional database resource to support it.

With this structural layout however, we also see opportunities for replication in other directions, for example to copy data off the machine into a standalone reporting Netezza machine. Or replication into DR servers, etc. The replication can be invoked any time the data is stable (enough) in the given Intake, Repository, Reporting etc zone. As noted, it is easy to automate and manage this kind of replication, and if Netezza can proffer the replication services as they have discussed, it will change how we view the entire flow.

For example, what if we flow the data into a primary hub machine, crunch it for reporting and then flow it to yet another machine, where we repeat some or all of these transform cycles (with downstream logic). Then flow it to more machines where yet more cycles change or enrich it. We are effectively flowing the data from sources to multiple targets in a seamless information stream that still maintains a decoupled identity from the whole. We can't do this with hand-crafted SQL-transforms. ETL tools would choke on it.

As for naming conventions, we've seen one in particular that works very well, and it goes like this:

Application_Region_Role

For example, the application might be a Brightlight Jump Start database, so we would use BL_JS for this section. Then we have options for DEV1, DEV2, UAT1, PRD1 etc. as necessity dictates. Then lets say we have a Repository, and perhaps an intake database facing our customer master (CUSTMAS) database.

```
BL_JS_DEV1_REP
BL_JS_DEV1_INTK_CUSTMAS
BL_JS_DEV1_XFORM
BL_JS_DEV1_RPT
```

As we roll out the database suites (that is groups of databases that are all part of the BL_JS application) we will see the structural themes in the naming convention.

This also allows us to develop rule tags that are portable for the databases. For example, the portable database name REP can be used in metadata rules, because under the covers we will blow it out to the complete value depending on the underpinning configuration. The version above, for example in the UAT1 environment, would appear as:

```
BL_JS_UAT1_REP
BL_JS_UAT1_INTK_CUSTMAS
BL_JS_UAT1_XFORM
BL_JS_UAT1_RPT
```

This in mind, now we can construct simple flow templates that are portable as our application is migrated from Dev to Prod and all stages in between. We want this kind of configurable adaptability.

In our processing paradigm, we will need a way to manage the overarching flows between our internal databases. After all, if the databases are like file folders, and the tables are like files, we need a way to component-ize the ability to move data from one folder/file to another. This is in essence the place where we say which of the four horsemen will run, and whether they will run serially, side-by-side and all that. Think for a moment about the following mnemonics:

```
FLOW SRC_DB=INTK_CUSTMAS TGT_DB=REP XFORM=filename.sh
```

What if the above describes everything we need to know, at a flow level, about what's happening? A Transform is underway, it has a primary source and target database, and the filename.sh contains specific instructions governing the transform.

In essence, the filename.sh where we apply our implementation wizardry, but it is invoked in the context of a *specific* source and target. More importantly, let's say we have three databases, that we want to flow data through.

```
FLOW SRC_DB=INTK_CUSTMAS TGT_DB=REP  XFORM=rep.intk_custmas.sh
FLOW SRC_DB=REP TGT_DB=RPT  XFORM=rpt.rep.sh
```

In the above scenario, one flow leg deals with the logic flowing from target A to target B. The `rep.intk_custmas.sh` in this case is now a real working script. It is a Transform Flow (next section). The notations are simple and easy to understand, but more importantly are programmable. We can set up a flow template to do practically anything. Each of the operations can be harnessed and checkpointed, along with a host of other framework-level automation that will be common to each section. It's stuff we have to do anyhow, so let's just formalize it and make it available to all of them. Frameworks promote high reusability, after all.

Notice how the filename has the target database as the first part of the name. This is a matter of convention, of course, that all transform assets are owned by the target, so are prefixed with the target's name. If this is uncomfortable, think in terms of the opposite. If these files are in a file system, with a simple "ls" command, everything destined for target B will collate together. Do we really care which ones were sourced from target A? Perhaps, and we can always shape the "ls" to find them. But in a practical sense, the target owns the logic in the transforms facing it, so why not name it for the target?

Note also that the names of the databases are the portable names without the configuration regions applied. The flow template is then portable from region-to-region, application-to-application.

Now let's say we have a series of business transforms from multiple sources into the target, and I want them to run independently. All I really need are additional instructions on the flow template entry, such as

```
FLOW THREAD=ASYNC<other parms here>
```

Now these notations cue the flow controller to launch the transform as an independent thread. We will want to synchronize this thread to the flow when it completes, but when first launched it is largely fire-and-forget. Note that the flow controller is a simple bash parsing utility that looks for these simplified keywords and launches the appropriate context. No need to rehash the code for something this simple. The Flow Template is intended to be a place where we configure the environment prior to invoking a given Amigo such as Intake or Transform. Sort of like giving the Amigo his work orders.

So in the above we now have a means to capture any number of unlimited command line key-value pairs. This is not a new concept in Unix/Linux at all, so forgive me if it sounds remedial. I am simply pushing the value of named parameters because I see so many positional/ command-line-intelligent implementations that the command line itself has fomented a sort of rigidity that we cannot easily escape without changing the command line implementation. With named pairs, we only need keep an inventory of the possible command line named parameters, and now it won't matter a bit if we get them out of order, or if they are missing completely. We can always set up defaults at the beginning of the flow template.

This style of notation comes in particularly handy when we take a look at the inter-machine replication. It is common to copy data from one master database to another machine. What will we need for this notation? A minor extension. We still need the source database, the final target database on the other machine, and then an intake database in case we need to replicate data into the other machine and land it to an intermediate database first. What's that? Why not just copy it to the machine? Take a look at the chapter on Intake in the Underground tome. Lots of snares exist when we want to move between machines. Just because it's the same technology, doesn't mean we won't pass through a lot of *other* technology to get there. If anything should fail in this transfer (network, disk drives, etc), we don't want to have a partially loaded target. Especially if it's an intraday model, and most especially if users are simultaneously accessing the same tables. We have the luxury of power at our fingertips. We don't have to do it the old fashioned way.

Back to the flow template notations. We might have other necessary options, but this three-database-in-one operation is definitely a departure from the other form, and can we begin to imagine how to use positional parameters to pull this off? The ensuing confusion would have us racing to named parameters very quickly, so why not just embrace them now? Again, the objective of standing up a framework is not to cut corners, but to drive high-reuse into the *core* so that leveraging it on the *edges* becomes a very consistent experience.

As we piece notations together, however, each of the FLOW segments will create assets. For example, one of them may create a working table that holds customer data. Another may leverage this same table to read incoming data in context, or may want to add more stuff to the table prior to finalization. Either way, each operation's work products are available to the next downstream operation. Our next challenge becomes whether we can link all this together into a data lineage map. Hold on to your hats, 'cause we're goin' there soon.

Transform Flow - As noted in the above Flow Template, the flow controller will call this module to affect one or more transforms. It will contain more specific instructions that are executed and harnessed in context of this portion of the flow. The Transform Flows can run asynchronously and in parallel. So we need to be mindful in the transform of what our purpose and mission is. After all, if the transform is a housekeeping function, we would not expect it to execute until the end of the flow template. However, if it performs destructive operations, such as cleaning up intermediate tables or files, we must guarantee that it will not run while transform operations are still underway. This is in part the responsibility of the Flow Template and in part the responsibility of the Transform Flow at hand. Each Transform Flow should "play nice" inside the framework.

```
Flow-Controller->
Intake->Transform->Repository
        ->Transform Flow -> One or more transforms
        ->Transform Flow -> One or more transforms
```

Transformation Pattern - As the book's title suggests, this is a radical extension of the concepts I covered in Netezza Underground. There, the box itself was characterized as an Input/Process/Output asset in an effort to get mental juices flowing in the direction of using Netezza for more than just a simple (or rather common) store-and-query device like all of the other wannabee technologies nipping at its heels. This was also prior to the advent of the S-blade configuration, which itself accelerated the possibilities of SQL-transforms into the hyper-mach zone.

So now imagine that the machine itself is not only an input/process/output asset, but that we can use this conceptual pattern to define programmable, configurable components that *themselves* perform as input-process-output assets, and then we formally link these together to create an application.

Does this sound familiar? Ahh, well it may sound a lot like the common string-of-pearls applications that are so deleterious in ETL tools. For example, let's say we take a product like DataStage, Ab Initio or Informatica, and we define a lot of little "toy" applications that basically leverage one or more of the environment's components. In Ab Initio, we would call these "toy graphs" where one toy is a join, the next is a sort, the next is a rollup etc. all as self-contained applications. They read data off disk, process it and land it back to disk for the next toy in the chain. String a bunch of these together and you have an application, and perhaps one of the most inefficient and ugly implementations on the planet (called a string-of-pearls). Apart from being downright product-abuse, it requires the data to "porpoise" or leap-frog on-and-off the disk as it muscles its way through the components. A lot like a salmon swimming upstream. This debilitates the application's performance. The most efficient way to solve this is to eliminate all the intermediate files, pull everything into a common graph application and keep it there (snuggled next to the CPUs) for as long as possible.

Okay, so we don't have that option in Netezza. But we don't *need* it. The data is down on a massively parallel platform, *already* snuggled next to the CPUs. In fact, pulling data out of its environment removes it from the power source, so we want to keep it as close as possible. This means using a lot of intermediate tables to affect an application flow.

Now the obvious question here is that if a string-of-pearls application is so *bad* in an ETL platform, why is it a *best* practice in the MPP? The primary reason is that in an ETL platform the data is serialized on the disk drives as far away from the CPUs as technically possible. Even if we can make the data stream go parallel (as in Ab Initio) we still have the problem of the NAS device or SAN device failing to fully parallelize the data as it goes to disk. In fact, I would have no expectation that the SAN would offer this kind of parallel performance in anywhere near the same scale as a Netezza machine, if it offered this at all.

The MPP on the other hand, the data is serialized to disk *as close to the CPUs* as possible. This configuration is the source of Netezza's incredible power, but is somehow overlooked by Netezza's competitors, especially the software-centric ones. In the appliance, we have something more dramatic than simple hardware between the CPU and the Disk, we have RAM, and lots of it. This means that when a table comes off the disk, it can potentially be cached in memory for reuse, boosting the machine's power to a completely new level.

Our most significant charge therefore, is to use the MPP as our core processing asset with heavy use of intermediate tables. We'll talk later about the overhead and housekeeping of these tables that can be easily automated in their construction and teardown. We'll even dive into some of the more non-functional aspects of this construct, like tracking transform metadata, data lineage and the like.

So in building out transformations, the objective is to provide a means for our developers to plug into a framework and be able to install the transform elements without any guesswork. For this to have the most efficient effect, we need to back up a bit into our catalog assets and then sling-shot forward again into how they apply to transforms. In short, we have structural metadata and then we have behavioral metadata. The behavioral stuff is what our developers will wrap around what is, for them, predefined structure. Since this structure is ultimately delivered to the Netezza catalog through one method or another, we need a way to capture and package it for use in behavioral metadata.

Metadata ETL

In the scheme of things, we will be heavily reliant on metadata ETL, that is the practice of pulling, parsing and transforming catalog information into useful assets and structures.

Okay, that's a lot of concept, so let's put some flesh on those conceptual bones with some practical stuff. Let's say we have just installed some complement of Netezza tables into the database, of varying size and purpose. Now we can perform a one-time metadata extraction of all this, fetching the tables, columns and data types from the catalog. We end up with a lot of flat text that doesn't have any particular meaning until we breathe some life into it. We'll start with our customer table, which for our example will have a minimum amount of columns just to show the functional direction.

```
Customer_name              varchar(100),
Customer_address           varchar(100),
Customer_id                bigint,
Customer_location_id       bigint,
Customer_zip_code          integer
Distribute on (Customer_ID);
```

When performing a transform, we need to define the target columns, and likewise a means to populate those columns. Below is a simple script construct that can be fully formulated in an automated way by examining the table's metadata and laying out this construct:

```
[TARGET COLUMNS]
[Customer_name]            a.customer_name
[Customer_address]         a.customer_address
[Customer_id]              a.customer_id
[Customer_location_id]     a.customer_location_id
[Customer_zip_code]        a.customer_zip_code
[ FILTER CLAUSE ]
From tables, where clause, join expressions, filters etc
```

Now let's say we put some meat in the FILTER CLAUSE such as:

```
from $customer_table a where a.customer_id is not null
```

In the above example, all our developers have to do is "fill out a form" in two locations. One location is in the FILTER CLAUSE to determine the tables that will play in the join, and the second is in the actual column assignments. Basically just type the given rule into the white space. No mess, no fuss.

We can now:

- Derive the insert-clause from the target columns
- Derive the select-clause from the notations alongside the target columns
- Add the filter clause to the above
- When the template is first built, put default pass-thrus in all the columns, because we know that *a big percentage of* SQL-transform logic is just pass-through anyhow, and this saves us time.

And *voila*, we have generated a SQL statement on-the-fly.

If this looks over-simplified, it's actually not. By requiring the developers to fill out the form in this manner, with pass-thrus for the defaults, it guarantees that all of the columns are accounted for with some form of data.

A subtle aspect of this notation is that we can now, for the developers, turn on some interesting functionalities that are not available in the ETL tools *at all*.

- **Data type checking** - In our manufactured select-clause, we will alias the source column's rule to the target column, aligning the portions of the select clause *by name* with their target table counterparts Then by performing a simple CTAS of the "select" portion of the generated statement (with the limit 0 option) we can manufacture a temporary table. This table will likewise contain the columns, aligned in order and by name to the target table. But with one subtle difference, each of these columns will carry the derived data type from the *source*. We can then pull the catalog-form of this table, and the catalog-form of the target table, compare the data types side-by-side and give the developer a data-type-check report. This is invaluable for finding errors in type conversions, moving data from large-to-small fields, truncations of strings or numeric precision etc. These aspects are otherwise invisible in SQL-transform logic but are a pernicious source of errors.
- **Distribution checking** - once the CTAS is complete, the temp table will also have a distribution, whether we overrode or accepted the default. Now we have in-hand the (a) distribution of the source, (b) distribution of the target and (c) the FILTER CLAUSE that should mention and leverage both. Many SQL-transform statements run slow for two reasons - (1) the distribution of the source and target are misaligned or (2) the distributions are aligned but are not mentioned in Join logic. Our distribution check can now validate the presence and usage of both and provide information to the developer at run time. This aids in quickly driving out the performance issues around mismatched or misapplied distributions in SQL-transform logic.

Case Study Short: In a quick assessment of an environment, it was clear that the distribution had been applied for all the tables. We noted however that the join-phrases were not using the distribution columns at all. This meant that even though the tables were distributed on the same value, and could experience the lift of a co-located join, they weren't experiencing the lift because they weren't *using* them. Leverage of the distribution is not automatic. It has to be mentioned in the join-phrase of the query or Netezza won't use it. We also noted however, that a particular column that wasn't the distribution was ubiquitous in all the transforms. Rather than rework all of the transforms to use the currently designated distribution key, we performed a quick check to see if this other column would make a good distribution key. It did in fact distribute the data with minimal skew, so we redistributed the tables on this column and ran the transforms again. A forty-five-minute series of transforms now ran in less than five minutes. *No SQL changes at all*. The moral to this story is twofold. (a) if we declare a distribution, we should use it and (b) if we *can* distribute on a heavily-joined column, we *should* do so rather than arbitrarily selecting another.

There's something else not obvious about this notation however, so here's another benefit. Let's say that this select-clause is feeding an insert-statement. In a plain-vanilla implementation, the complete insert-into-select would look like this:

```
    Insert into customer ( customer_name , customer_address  ,  customer_id  , custom-
er_location_id  , customer_zip_code   )
    Select a.customer_name , a.customer_address  ,  a.customer_id  , a.customer_loca-
tion_id  , a.customer_zip_code   from mycustomertable a where a.customer_id is not null
```

Which seems easy to manage, until we get into typical denormalized data warehouse tables with 200 columns or more. Then the above notation is completely impractical, so the developer resorts to this:

```
Insert into customer (
customer_name ,
customer_address  ,
customer_id   ,
customer_location_id  ,
customer_zip_code
)
Select
a.customer_name ,
a.customer_address  ,
a.customer_id   ,
a.customer_location_id  ,
a.customer_zip_code
  from mycustomertable a where a.customer_id is not null
```

And this provides some relief, but not much because it does not scale *for development* because it gets painfully unwieldy the more columns we add to it. For example, let's say the table width is more realistically 200 columns wide. If we need to remove a column from the list, and this column happens to be the 145th column, we will need to carefully remove it from the top (insert) clause and from the bottom (select) clause, hoping that we did not accidentally misalign the columns when we did so. If we want to add a column, it's even worse, so we would always have to add to the bottom of both lists for fear of misaligning all of them. This only increases the overhead for developers and troubleshooters to debug and create new constructs. It is also a bane of SQL-transform development, and something developers simply loathe. I am one of them, so I know of whence I speak.

The proposed construct, however relieves them of this burden. The columns are only noted once in the left-hand side. If we add or delete, it applies to a single line, so we don't have to fret with misalignment. In fact, we could allow for a simple "#" character to disable a line and achieve the same effect.

So now that we have a structured means to build the actual SQL-transform statements, this leads us into another even more powerful capability – that of capturing the transforms as metadata so that we can use them for impact analysis or data lineage. Since this is a fairly lengthy discussion, we'll defer it for later.

Cache is King

Thought I'd try a pithy phrase to make a point. The machine now has memory between the CPU and the storage drive, meaning that oft-used tables "stick" in memory and further boost the query firepower. This is especially important for reference lookups and the like, such as the ones that can sometimes initiate a table scan. Hey, if it's all in memory, what do we care?

But in the SQL-transformation model, the caching principle can work wonders for our performance, only this time we're caching *metadata* products on disk (and not using Netezza memory, just capitalizing on the principle here). A number of SQL-transform-facing products out there will use the database catalog as a transactional database (e.g. Oracle Data Integrator). While this isn't particularly egregious, a lot of catalog hits will only slow us down. Considering that we'll use that metadata to manufacture other assets, such as SQL statements and automated transform activities, we'll likely want to reconstruct that stuff just once, and then cache it for later. The principle is the same, in that we don't do the same work twice.

For example, in the above transform discussion, we had an intake component. The intake, if facing a database, will require a SQL statement to select the extract from the source, a DDL statement to manufacture an intake table, another SQL statement to transform the data from the Intake table to the final target table, etc. All of these assets require some time to construct, but hardly any time to consume. So when we create them, we should cache them, and provide the option to cache them so that the caching does not frustrate a developer trying to debug them.

Case in point, the aforementioned SQL statement has certain aspects that are canned, straight from the catalog. We preconstruct a skeletal form of the SQL statement that divides the static (catalog parts) from the dynamic (where-clause or filter construction) and cache it. At run time we pull up the cache and then snap these back together just before executing the statement. Many of you are doing this already so this suggestion might seem remedial.

The reason it's important, is that in many sites I visit there is a strong catalog-facing metadata engine that makes configuration-and-development life so much simpler for everyone. But it runs slow. In some cases, so slow that operations people openly wonder why they are using it at all. They may spend a bunch of time trying to optimize their catalog queries, or try to cache the catalog itself. None of these solutions is particularly workable because the problem cannot be solved by optimizing the catalog queries. It can only be solved by caching the catalog query *results*, and caching the collateral derived from it. BI tools do this all the time, by facing the catalog, drawing out all of its metadata into the BI Tool's own metadata repository, then never touching the catalog again unless it has more changes to assimilate. After this, it is the BI Tool's problem to optimize its own metadata repository.

Since we are working with SQL-transformation scenarios we need to optimize the assets we use for it and not keep going-back-to-the-well so to speak. I was onsite for an evaluation of the Oracle Data Integrator product and how it deals with transform-related solutions. Basically that it formulates a SQL statement and sends it to the Netezza machine and can do this successively within what appears to be an application harness. However, in this case a subtle problem remained in that the product was very slow in its own operation because it relied heavily on the Netezza catalog *as a database*. Rather than caching and reusing the metadata from the catalog, it kept fetching and reproducing the assets created from it. Interestingly, if the tech staff performed a catalog re-index of the Netezza catalog, the problem would go away for a day or two, and then bog down again. This is just as symptom of depending on the catalog as a database rather than a one-time initialization resource for other assets. Said assets we intend to cache so that we don't have to reconstruct them and certainly don't have to go back to the database catalog.

All that said, as in the intake model we'll want to manufacture even more stuff from the table definition, like queries, extractions, transforms etc that we'll want to manufacture once and reuse often. Going back to the catalog each time, just for the basic metadata definition, means we have already foregone the need to cache all of the rather static products built (and rebuilt) from it.

This gets especially interesting when it comes to performing things like a CTAS, which uses the catalog to reproduce another table. This is more efficient than a blind CREATE because the assets are already on the catalog, so it only needs to photocopy and not parse the CREATE. The various BI Tools use CTAS to manufacture temporary assets in fulfilling a query, so individual CTAS operations are very fast. But in transforms, we might have dozens or hundreds of these in a flow. At one site, over twenty thousand of them were executed by the SQL-transform environment every day. If each one is doing a catalog hit, *plus hits along with all the other secondary assets it will need,* then in the aggregate we may see performance drag. But is this a bad thing? The balancing act here is that a CTAS is more efficient than a common CREATE TABLE command. For a CTAS, the assets to manufacture a table are already prescribed and ensconced in the Netezza catalog and only have to be copied and renamed. Where a CREATE TABLE statement has to be parsed and all of the assets created from scratch. To test this, perform a CREATE TABLE with a plain-vanilla table description of say, 100 columns. Once created, perform a CTAS to create a clone. The difference is obvious. So where it may seem like there is catalog-query drag for a lot of CTAS operations, this should not be the focus of attention. Rather focus on the types of catalog queries that produce other assets, especially the insert/select SQL statements that are bread-and-butter for database-centric processing. Caching those can take pressure off the flow and therefore drag on the execution time.

So there are some things we want to deliberately cache, and some things that the catalog will do for us far more efficiently than caching might.

What does caching look like? We need a file naming convention and a place to put the assets so that they don't get stomped on. I like to keep an application /tmp directory to contain assets like this. They are generously and obviously named so that a DBA is not tempted to delete them. But even so, if missing they will be reproduced on the next execution. If they are accidentally deleted, we never really lose the asset because they will be reconstructed automatically on the next run.

Metadata Considerations

I've pointed out that metadata has a number of different faces, and here are a few in no particular order:

- **Structural**: Describes data by type, physical location and configuration etc.
- **Behavioral**: Describes what happens to the data as it moves from one structural form to another
- **Administrative**: Various artifacts of processing that assist administrators in their duties
- **Operational**: Various artifacts of processing that support operators in their duties
- **Statistical**: Various artifacts of processing that provide summary information to one or more user groups. In many cases, a star schema and its fact tables are forms of statistical metadata, because they are statistical recastings of the original information.

Of the above, it seems that "all-the-rage" is the *behavioral* metadata. This is because if we can get a handle on the behavioral metadata, we can effectively form a data *lineage* stream from source-structure-to-target-structure. In a Netezza machine, this is a SQL-transform statement that appears in the form of "insert into target /select from source(s)". This of course can take the form of any arbitrary SQL statement, so is something to be feared by a common SQL parser. We could simplify the construction of the SQL transform statement itself, but is this realistic? In many ways it is, because it will require us to break apart complex SQL statements into smaller ones, which will leverage Netezza's architecture more efficiently. The problem then becomes, can we track data through these intermediate steps?

I asked some direct questions to a metadata tool vendor:

Question: "I have a need to track data lineage from a source to target"
Vendor: "No problem, if you can define it, we can track it."
Question: "Well, I have a need to track it through SQL statements."
Vendor (short silence): "We can do that, within limits."
Question: "What kind of limits?"
Vendor: "A SQL statement between two tables, we can track that."
Question: "Why did you hesitate at first? This is exactly what I want to do."
Vendor: "Well, a lot of people think it means any table to any table, when it doesn't."
Question: "You make a distinction between tables?"
Vendor: "Of course. Like a temp table. It evaporates and we can't tell what the structure was."
Question: "Okay, I can see that. What about an intermediate table? One that is not a temp table but is created to support the transform?"

Vendor: "Is it thrown away after the runtime quits?"

Question: "Yes."

Vendor: "What's the difference? We cannot go to the catalog to resolve the table structure, so it's like the table never existed at all."

Question: "So you *don't* support SQL-based transforms, that is, making dozens of these intermediate tables to process information in a logical flow?"

Vendor (after a longer pause): "Well no. That's like the domain of an ETL tool. We don't support that kind of thing."

Question: "So do you support tracking data lineage through the ETL tools? What vendors are those?"

Vendor: "Now hold on a second, those tools have their own controls and reporting."

Question: "But I want an integrated view."

The conversation unravels and we hang up.

The Push-Down Pandorum

Yet another solution is the *push-down* technology that some ETL vendors offer to support setting up a transform in their tool that is, under-the-covers, converted to a SQL statement and executed on the host. This is problematic in that the ETL tools still have not provided a seamless means to integrate this as part the tool's flow model. The actual work is executed over *there*, in the Netezza machine, not over *here* in the ETL tool. What if I need *hundreds* of these? Pushdown gets pushed-down, so to speak, and we're back to square one.

However, that some ETL tool vendors are *pursuing* push-down is itself evidence of their viability in the new appliance-centric-warehouse world. I have no doubt that if these tool vendors take the problem seriously, they will harness the best way to pull this off. Until that time, shared-nothing SQL-Transforms *without* a harness is a complete lack of control. Why is this?

Think about this scenario: We have an ETL tool that is processing data in several branches of work. When it completes, it is ready to load data to the database tables it is about to affect. Each database-facing component is shared-nothing. It has no context whatsoever to the other flows and is about to throw its data across the processing wall to the other technology, a database. Each of the others is about to do the same. Let's say that one of them fails (for whatever reason). Now we have a situation where four of the flows have loaded data into the database but one has not, effectively corrupting all five target tables because they all have to be loaded together.

Now we either correct the one that failed, or rollback the ones that succeeded. The ETL tool's components to load the data don't know anything about each other. They are all standalone, shared-nothing processes. The ETL tool therefore, cannot perform an automatic recovery of anything on the database. It is a fire-and-forget operation. Some external process has to pull this off, but only if the data itself was configured for this sort of operation, and the ETL tool faithfully applied it. So now we already have two processing scenarios in place. One in the ETL tool and one in Netezza, and the ETL tool has yet to fully harness the Netezza machine's power.

Close your eyes and think about the most complex Business-Intelligence SQL statement you've ever seen. Perhaps pages and pages of notations with countless permutations. Now imagine driving this structure into the database as metadata, to the extent that we could accurately (and easily) discern data lineage from a source table and column, the rules used to modify that column, the target table and column, and the participating tables and columns in the filter (where-join-etc) clause. Oh, and by the way, we have to regard the *aliases* used in the filter clause and map them to their respective columns in the select-clause. Oh, tish-tosh, this is the easy part! The next step is to map multiples of these sequences together in a form that allows us to trace *through* the SQL statements, all the way back to the first one, or at least the point where the data first entered the machine.

This is a *non-trivial exercise*, but the Netezza machine is all-over the non-trivial. And considering that such models can only be persisted to a database in object-relational form, and the Netezza machine is bread-and-butter on object-relational models, it appears that we not only have the framework to capture the transforms, we have the perfect hardware platform to store them in their simplest form for easy extraction.

Okay so when I first vetted this chapter with a few tech types, their eyes went wide and their eyebrows went up. It did not seem that the solution was simple as much as simplistic, or rather that I had over-simplified something that already contained countless permutations. However, being the kinda guy I am (having done this enough times) I embraced the tried-and-true notions of patterns and simply addressed the SQL-statement-as-transform in a manner that allows us to radically reduce the total permutations and be fairly quick about such an implementation. The key here, and it cannot be over-emphasized, is the structured Transform metadata that we produce as part of the transform flow. If the developers follow the aforementioned template, the output is automatically structured in a precision, predictable manner. The more stricture (and structure) we put around the SQL transform templates, the more they will be in compliance "as deployed" rather than attempting to retrofit them later. In short, it follows the pattern of stewardship – make it better for the next downstream operation. In this case, the next downstream operation is an operational transform metadata capture-and-store. Once stored, it should provide us with a fairly automatic means to distill into reportable metadata.

Now let's take a quick breather. Data lineage is what we're after. Not a perfectly interconnected table-to-table flow that flawlessly catalogues each and every nuance and subtle meandering of the data flow. Nor do we care about the creative cross-hatching of rules, formulas, filter-hijinks and the like. We can store the raw SQL statement and the analyst can get the detailed context from all that as necessary.

What they are asking for is data *lineage*. This means, in no uncertain terms, the ability to form a line between a target column and a source column/table. What does one of these animals look like? If we break down complex SQL statements into multiple simpler ones (the best way to use a Netezza machine anyhow) the SQL statements themselves tell the tale. We have all the clues we need. First are the source columns, or rather the source quantities, since they can be computations of columns, values and so forth. Keep in mind we have potentially more than one source column involved in populating a single target column. Then we have the target columns. This seems to be straightforward since they are all headed toward an existing table. But are they? No, they are headed toward an *intermediate* table that was derived *from* an existing table. So we need to track that relationship too. So then we have source tables, which are part of the join/filter/where-clause section. Important here is that all of the tables are aliased, and those aliases appear in the aforementioned source quantities. We'll have to tie them together too.

What did I leave out? Oh that all this stuff is happening across whole databases, so we need to avoid getting lost. Also that since some of these tables will evaporate when the run-time completes, we need to capture as much as possible about their transient structure. Enough at least, so that it's reproducible as a metadata flow. Do we need to track the data types of each column? Yes and no. Mercifully since we will base every table on an existing one, (via the transform) we will not have to track spontaneous data types. With a less-disciplined or more free-form approach in the transform, yes, we would have to track the data types as well. We see here that tracking and tying all this together really does require a lot of forethought. Netezza can harness it if we can get our arms around it.

Trust me when I say, the average data lineage dude will ask tough questions, and the more we can put at his fingertips (with no holes) the better off we are. The challenge here of course is in setting their expectations. Lineage cannot conquer the world and cannot be made to track *all* things. Something will always be hidden, like the programmatic rule that fetches a unique key and parameterizes it into the SQL statement (appearing we recall, like a magic quantity). Over time we can find ways to inject this relationship into the metadata. In the meantime, expect to mature the model. And don't take the feedback of the data lineage types as being personal. (At least, not right away!) Sheath those scimitars and listen to the constituency. It is the foundation of building something way cooler than what the guys down the hall are doing.

Facets of Transformation

So as our craft enters orbit, we can now circumscribe the planet and watch as it transforms before us, dark to light, in a cycle it engages frequently and often. We're now part of that cycle, so we can see more than the fifty-thousand-foot view, because in orbit, we're far enough above the stratosphere to see there are no lines, no boundaries and nothing hidden from view.

Transform business - For the business model that the potential customer wants to engage, they need power, and lots of it. The leaders don't just want to beat the competitors, they want to accelerate past them, leave them in dust, and quench their fires forever. This means a nitrous-oxide booster and really good drivers, because the competitors, if they are lucky, have not opted for a performance engine quite yet. There's still time to get ahead.

But when this engine is engaged and the blood rushes to the backs of their skulls, it will affect the entire organization. If they are any good at the business they're in, they will also impact their own industry, transforming it in their wake.

Transform methods - Once the time required to produce results is foreshortened, so the methods for producing those results must be tightened up. This is true both for producing reports on the front end, and producing capabilities on the back end. Rapid turnaround will crush antiquated methods, once propped up by the stovepipe, waterfall scenarios so necessary with underpowered technology. They are sandblasted from memory and replaced with protocols and processes that are akin to a whitewater raft ride.

Transform operations - When the operator punches the button, or watches the Autosys job kick off, he bites into his Apple, puts his feet on the desk and allows his mind to drift to anywhere-but-here. He knows that the underpowered technology will crunch-and-munch for hours before he has anything else to do, besides start his own internet business or channel-surf for the latest 1-800 purchases. But now, even before the first Magic Juicer commercial can hit the screen, he has a light beckoning for his attention. The job has completed with no errors. The next job kicks off and has dispatched its workload before the 3am re-run of the Munsters can get through the opening credits. With two more jobs in the queue, they'll be done in time for him to clock out, hit 24-hour fitness and have breakfast before the Today show hits the airwaves. This is good for his personal budget too, since he didn't really have any time to surf the 1-800 channel for midnight purchases of interesting-items-his-wife-will-hate.

Every night, every week, every month, the machine hums and churns He can very nearly set his watch by the lockstep consistency. Operations become more efficient, activities become more visible and correctable (like they'll need it, pshaw!) and people begin to measure the machine in terms of its idle time, not its remaining capacity. Time to start giving it more work. By this time of course, our hero has lost weight and his first son is in college, but no matter...

Transform people - Those who can handle the new pace will find themselves in the groove. Those who cannot will have to go into a mental exercise program, so to speak, to work off the mental fat and career largesse. We know of one fat-cat who had data warehouse oozing from his pores, and a giant budget to produce so little results. One day that giant budget was redirected to newer technology and he could no longer hide in his office tapping out slow reports. Once the users knew the technology could produce their stuff almost as fast as they could think it, he was overwhelmed with work. In times gone by, users would make a request and it was anybody's guess how long it would take to return. They used all the waiting time (for reports to return) to take coffee breaks, play cards, channel surf or download and organize their iTunes (apart from balancing their checkbooks and running another business on the side). Power changes these things, too.

Inefficient people will essentially enter a fitness program, both in workload and mental acuity. Many will survive and thrive in this upgraded existence. Others will catch up. We subscribe to the principle of No Technologist Left Behind.

Transform approaches - All the ways we think about solving problems are either accelerating into the stratosphere or are summarily *kaput*. Very little middle ground here. It either scales or it doesn't. It can keep up or it can't. It can tackle the problem or wrangle with it. We have the power to avoid wrangling. Did Indiana Jones wrangle with the big scary guy with the scimitar? No, he did not. Bad approaches get the execution-style poppa-cappa, and the good approaches sprout wings. We'll know them when we see them, and some have been around us all this time, suffocated in their chrysalis until now.

Transform data - And of course, the ability and capacity to transform data in Libraries-of-Congress-at-a-time, with speeds that would make Vin Diesel blush. The pent-up pile of questions, we go through like old socks, dispatch and are ready for more. This kind of throughput changes things.

Rather than look at a problem from a transactional point-of-view, we will always now regard the problems from a set-based point-of-view. Our peers will wonder about us, that our minds are somehow on a different wavelength. Yes, the Netezza machine talks on a different frequency than the other machines. We call that frequency the Turnaround Channel. We will not be allowed to conform the machine to our precocious wiles.

One day a University of Texas Student and a Texas A&M student were out fishing. The UT student caught a fish, then suddenly gripped it on both sides and stared deeply into its eyes. In moments, the fish took on the countenance of the student, and the A&M student was stunned. "How do you do that?" he asked. "My mind is stronger than his," said the other. Presently the A&M student caught a fish and tried the same experiment. After a few moments, the A&M student started sucking in his cheeks, his face starting to look like a fish....

Later in the day, after they had caught their limit, the UT student said, "This was a really good fishing spot. Why don't you mark it?" The A&M student agreed, but after they got to shore, the UT student noticed a big white X on the side of the boat. Upon inquiry, the A&M student responded, "You said mark the spot." The UT student muttered some epithets under his breath and stalked away. The A&M student scratched his head and said, "Come to think of it, how will we know we would get the same boat next time?" - from *Compendium of Aggie Jokes*, 1989.

In keeping with the fish tale, we're fooling ourselves if we think the Netezza machine can be harnessed into a stall and be happy in this existence. The Mustang did not exhibit this spirit (no Mustang does) and the Netezza appliance embodies this spirit of freedom over the power of *overwhelming oceanic hydraulics*.

No, the machine will assimilate *us*.

"Resistance is useless," - scary alien guy, *Hitchhiker's Guide to Warehousing*.

Transformation Shock

Some aspects of the transformation are a shock to the system. Whether its our personal preferences, work habits, career choices - or even the workplace itself (in the infrastructure, the methods and approaches, etc.) Introduction of the Netezza appliance produces the kind of stress that demands and even initiates the transforming process whether we agree with it, or participate in it. This feeling, that of somehow having lost control, is only an illusion.

What's really happening is that as we pass into the outer atmosphere, into the most rarefied air in the world (the air breathed by very-large-scale-database-aficionados) we are starting to feel weightless. The crushing burden of our prior system's gravity is being slowly peeled away. Only now, as the lack of gravity fully takes over, we find that we need to get around another way. We cannot walk around inside the spacecraft. We have to push off a wall and land on another one. We have to drink from a straw and do other things in terms of a weightless state. Our situation has changed. We must do things differently. We must *think* differently. Whether we *act* differently is another matter.

Capacity for Transformation - What does the CEO need to have in-the-bag when attempting to close a deal? Capacity. What does a consulting firm need in order to capture a backlog of consulting gigs? Capacity. What does Donkey *lack* in Shrek-2 when he claims that he has the right to remain silent? The capacity to do so.

Without capacity, transformation stalls out. The chrysalis remains intact.

In speaking with IT professionals, they have a priority to shrink the batch window so that they can "meet their service-level-agreement (SLA)". Ahh, the SLA, with all its ability to make us look stellar or just the opposite. It is a line in the sand. If we have enough capacity, we can confidently rest in the notion that the SLA is not in jeopardy.

But the CEO doesn't care about the SLA. He cares about *capacity*. I've noted elsewhere that one firm was able to merge with another once they finally realized "capacity". After all, if they could not meet their own daily processing deadlines, how could they hope to assimilate more workload? Meeting-the-SLA does not tell the CEO that he has the necessary capacity to add more customers. It won't stop him from doing so, but if he knows that the environment's capacity is in jeopardy, he can take proactive steps to resolve it before the new customers go online.

Case Study Short: One financial services firm had people running around on roller skates putting out fires as a regular part of the business day. Seems there was no end to their operational woes. Three new and very large customers had been added since the first of the year, and the processing requirements for the three completely eclipsed all the other customers combined. The shop was out of power with the old customer base, but these three new customers would crush it.

The principals called in a consulting team to help and assist with the growing issues around these new clients, because they weren't having a good client experience. At least one of them threatened to bolt if something didn't change fast. In essence, the consulting firm had to provide a stopgap answer for-the-time-being and work hard to resolve issues long-term.

In this case, the principals rightly perceived that their systems were running out of power and their in-house talent lacked the capacity (experience or otherwise) to implement anything new. Indeed, transformation was under way - the company was passively transforming into an unreliable, inconsistent and evasive firm to deal with. The customer service reps could not call customers to upsell their products. Because the base products were so unstable, the customer would give the rep such an earful of complaints that the rep did not have any traction to initiate a sales opportunity. Within that month, auditors arrived to review their systems and information content, and could not have arrived at a worse time. When the auditors asked for information, they expected it to be provided by the end of the day. But the questions they were asking required special queries that would not return with an answer even after many hours. The answers to their questions finally arrived three days after they asked them, eliciting accusations of evasiveness until one of the business analysts, fed up with their frustration, asked them to watch while she execute the queries that the auditors had asked for. After forty-five minutes of waiting one of them finally asked, "Is it ever going to return?" to which she said "Eventually."

To which the analyst quipped, "How is it you guys are still in business?"

How indeed.

Modeling the Transformation - Perhaps the most important aspect we need to reshape along the path, is how we choose to model the information in the machine. Keep in mind that both the rigidly normalized model and the dimensional model are both *artifacts* of the constraints of an SMP-hosted machine. I know that's a little controversial, because both models dominate thought. Their architectural constraints are boiled into every conversation or touchpoint we have about the subject of warehousing. Should we normalize? Should we denormalize? Should we dimensionalize? None of these really have more than a *conceptual* context inside Netezza.

We *can* use any of these - or none of these. Modeling tools and techniques will require us to have an affinity toward one or the other, but they remain artificial in this sense: Normalized models are typically used to capture business-entity information into a form that aligns with the *hosting technology's ability to represent it* (in this case, the defacto is an SMP-based RDBMS). What if this model does not translate to what we *actually* want to do? Do we shoe-horn the model into the machine and force it to work for us?

Case Study Short: I just left a where a group wanted to apply specialized structures that are foreign to ERStudio. It's clear what they want to do with them. It's innovative, creative and very leading edge, things we would expect of Enzees stretching their wings. But it's not normalization, object-relational, dimensional or anything resembling common modeling concepts. About the only identifiable characteristic is row/column storage. And this is a *simple* example of what we see in the field on the leading edges of data storage, analytics and high speed processing.

Similarly, a dimensional model is aligned with *indexing* constraints of the SMP-based RDBMS. But we don't *have* index structures inside Netezza, so what good is the dimensional model except (again) to align with the expectations of a BI tool that more easily understands dimensions than anything else? On site with a customer in 2009, one colleague claimed that the BI folks kept whining about how "MicroStrategy works best with a snowflake schema" so why can't we have one inside the Netezza machine? Because a snowflake is driven by a *heavily-indexed* model that does not exist (nor needs to) in its new home. All they are saying, without actually saying it, is that the BI tool expects and honors traditional SMP-based RDBMS concepts and constructs. Without these artificial props, the tool cannot be successful. I disagree, since MicroStrategy has been very successful with Netezza deployments. This "lament of the snowflake" is not valid.

Again, what if these concepts are *themselves* artifacts of an underpowered RDBMS implementation? We would be remiss in shoe-horning into a Netezza database a model that was borne on the constraints of a weaker system.

What we're really talking about now is the best-fit to integrate concepts and technologies, not necessarily what *works best* in the machine. While it is true that Netezza does not require us to think of data in oblique and unfamiliar terms, it also does not require us align with canned forms or techniques. I can make a case that a dimensional model is superfluous and even architecturally unsound for a Netezza machine. I can make the same case against the normalized model. Why is this? Because both the dimensional and normalized models are aligned to work with an SMP-based model. We have simply forgotten this, and forgotten that the common modeling tools mask this reality because it is expedient to do so.

This point of view, of course, is highly controversial, provocative, counter-intuitive and all that. But so are many things about the infinite-cosmic-power models we can formulate inside the appliance. Truth be told, many times we lament the fact that one of Netezza's competitors told us that we could take our existing model and drop it right inside the box with no changes. The dirty little secret they're not sharing: Their hardware can make even the worst model look stellar, but given enough time its inefficiency will show and it will be too late to do anything else but buy more hardware to dig ourselves out of the pit. Make no mistake, they are counting on this.

Netezza on the other hand may suggest that we put the data into the box "as is", but this is not the rest-of-the-story. The objective of such an exercise is to profile the data. As a means to discover the right-sized model and the most appropriate balance of normalization and performance. Where better to profile billions of records but inside the machine itself?

In a traditional SMP-based RDBMS, our modelers will place their master-stroke on their model-of-choice. It *represents*, they will claim in gangsta-lingo. They may have applied their favorite warehousing-guru's approaches and are very happy with the functionality they expect to receive. They have thought-it-through.

Another analyst asks them to add a special kind of object-relational structure to support their reports. It's very strange one of them notes, and we can't model that.

The data starts to grow. The model's weaknesses are not apparent at first. Business user-demands start to fluctuate, requiring changes in the structures and perhaps even the addition of that oddball structure they asked for long ago.

Performance starts to slide, so engineers step in to shore up the system. They chop apart the core sections of the model to re-optimize them into something *else* we can't model. Anyone can put together an elegant model in the cool air conditioning of the break room. But when the heat rises and the elegance starts to look ugly, they will toss the model purism in favor of expedience or pragmatism. This continues until the system really does run out of gas and they have no choice but to refactor the reporting environment entirely.

Will they refactor it into another "elegant" model that is normalized for how they intend to use it (even though it already metastasized into something they could use but could not model)?

Once again, the physical plant's lack of power is the undoing of the logical model. Is the logical model invalid? Or is it so aligned with common RDBMS constraints that we really can't tell where the modeling tool's "modeling" ends and it starts making assumptions about the platform where it will land?

Let's say we have a bunch of users in the aforementioned case of pushing for a snowflake model to support Microstrategy. Would we acquiesce and apply the snowflake (*uber*-normalized data) into the Netezza machine? Or would we go the other direction, align with the machine's physics and denormalize the data? We can always formulate adaptations so that Microstrategy doesn't know the difference. But should the tail wag the dog?

Case Study Short: The fact table contained one-hundred-fifty billion rows and was set up as a dimensional model against a constellation of dimensions. It had grown into this size (in a year's time) from an original volume of fifty billion records. Only now, the model seemed to be slowing down for the queries touching this table. Of course, we don't buy into the competitor-promulgated mythology that "the more data you add to Netezza, the slower it gets". No, it was clear that in the inception of their rollout, they had simply forgotten or foregone some scalability factor that now, once applied, would get them back into good stead with the users.

Zone maps helped, along with making all of their onesy-twosy lookups randomly distributed (this clarifies for the optimizer that the miniature lookup should always be broadcasted when a larger table is involved). With the smaller lookups consistently held in memory (Netezza does it) we saw significant boosts with no additional effort.

However, upon further profiling we also found a number of "high-traffic columns" that appeared repeatedly in over ninety-five percent of the queries. These ten or so columns were peppered all over the dimensions. By bringing these several columns onto the fact table, this eliminated the joins to the dimension. This one action provided another several-order-of-magnitude boost in performance that was over-and-above the initial optimization.

It would seem obvious that we want to organize the data into the path that the user walks the most. But the conversation around this "high-traffic migration" first reduced to "how do we *model* that?" and concluded with "Why do we *have* to?"

A normalized model is handy for organizing data (we have to start somewhere), but if we cannot get it into an optimized distribution model, our Netezza experience will likely be stunted (compared to what it could be without the artificial normalization constraint). Same for the dimensional model. If by placing the master-stroke on the facts and dimensions we still have not aligned them on a common distribution, our design will not appropriately leverage Netezza's power. So which is it - stay inside industry norms or align with the machine's architecture? I say run don't walk to the architecture. In the final analysis, in the dead of night when the wolves are howling, the bats are chittering, the ghouls of warehousing are coming out of their virtual graves to haunt us - the *machine's* architecture alone will be our escape from certain doom. We can count on this.

Need for Transformation - A decision-maker surveys the landscape all around and draws a conclusion, that things cannot continue the way they are if the company, or perhaps the manager personally, wants to be successful. The manager sees either inefficiency or largesse, or other things that make the environment unpalatable, and regards the under-powered technology as the center-of-woes. Does the manager need to blow the dust off the top of the existing systems, shake off the cobwebs and all that? Or is it that the systems are not particularly old, or lacking in functionality. They just aren't getting it done. Reports don't arrive on time. Users are upset and want their answers. The manager wonders, Do they think I'm incompetent?

The situation is untenable and unacceptable. Consultants are called. They assess. They propose. The internal grapevine starts to buzz. People jockey for position to get their ideas in front. The manager cannot tell the difference between idea and agenda, between loyalty or self-serving. Normal is no longer normal. The environment is no longer ruled by "normal", but by exception. The exceptions have become the norm, and everyone has forgotten what normal used to be.

This must change. For the sake of personal sanity, or for no better reason than not being able to fall asleep at night. The manager forms a plan. It's a bold plan, but a *necessary* plan.

Justification for Transformation - A gaggle of technologists runs past, heading for the server room. Another runs past, heading for the call center floor. Yet another runs past, on a beeline for the developers' bullpen. The manager can tell by the direction of the flow what problem is currently under scrutiny. He would buy them roller skates, but fears that he would start a roller-skate cult like at his last employer.

Appealing to his boss, he asks for funding. The boss wonders why. Things seem to be working fine for him. He doesn't see it. Going over his head won't help the cause. The manager has the choice of waiting it out or moving on. The problem with justification is that it requires common eyes and hearts, and a common vision, all the way up the decision chain. Money is at stake, and nobody releases it for free, or easily.

What justifies change? Critical mass and an inflection point. The *critical mass* arrives upon, and maintains the condition that nobody, or at least very few, are willing to *defend* the current implementation. It has to be more than just "everyone is disgruntled." Mainly because nobody considers any solution picture-perfect. If even one of our respected technologists will champion it, the dragon will remain alive, unfettered and unassailable.

The *inflection point* is the recognition that something is amiss, alarming and affecting decision makers. It may arrive slowly over a continuum, or may be a sudden realization. It often happens when the dragon steps on the toe of a decision maker in a manner that calls that decision maker from their managerial sleep-state. It crosses a line. Violates a sensibility or arrives on the heels of mass terminations. For one company, this was realized in the Summer of '07 when the stock market activity reached a crushing transactional level and took all their systems to their knees. This was a wakeup call. The company recovered, but the stress of the event lit a fire of movement, funding and action toward fixing the problem rather than denying its presence.

For another company, an inflection event was when they irreversibly lost a major marketing bid because they lacked the capacity to fulfill it. They realized that they would never be able to meet their processing goals without a change in orders-of-magnitude over their present nibble-the-edge efforts.

For still another company, the CIO announced that they had finally won a major bid, sealing the marketing database management for one of the world's largest hotel chains, eliciting the immediate resignation of three of his four chief technologists within the following three days. Their stated reason for their exit? The systems were already crushed into powder from trying to keep up with capacity a fraction of the size of what he'd just signed up for, and none of them wanted the impending failure hung around their necks.

It's one thing to win the business, finally signing up dream-customers, but quite another to have our principals secretly sigh "Oh *no*."

Process of Transformation - An acquaintance is a triathlete. He and his wife travel to various meets, 10ks-runs and outings with other triathletes. It's sort of an exclusive club. He's raced in Ironman competitions for every year that I have known him, but has never finished even close to first. Still, he's usually a solid middle-of-the-pack participant and never caught straggling or struggling.

Some may well ask, why bother? I mean, if we can never win, and we *know* we can never win, why race at all? But to read the prior paragraph, the emphasis is on the word *finished*. I know what's involved in the Ironman competition. That he *finished* it is an accomplishment unto itself.

He will confess that the training cycle is at least as grueling as the event (I can only imagine). Like Mick said to Rocky, "For a 45 minute fight, you gotta train for 45 *thousand* minutes". The process of transformation, during the training period and well beyond the afterglow of the event, is a continuum of challenges and successes that are part of a lifestyle-committment.

The process of transformation in our IT and business environments is no different. We might think that the transformation is a one-time thing when in fact, we are signing up for - a drum roll please - an environment that exists with the expectation of change, not the fear of it.

That's right. *Ironman Data Warehousing*. With virtual data warehouse tats and everything.

"You don't qualify for the official big-data tattoo until you've mastered fifty billion records," - *overheard at a conference, with a sketch of the "tat" - an offset "B" and "D" with a lightning-bolt diagonally through them.*

Speed of Transformation - So how fast can we make all this happen? One of my colleagues was asked. The inquiry was serious and the need very urgent. But wait, some objects are in our path that we might not expect, including this little Newtonian thing called inertia. As we will note later, objects at rest (that is, our data folk who have become accustomed to waiting on the under-powered systems) don't seem all that busy. Not all the time anyhow. They have bursts of frenetic activity, but overall seem to have some extra capacity. Or perhaps its the other way around, that they are all busy fighting fires, forming fire-fighting teams, roasting marshmallows by the fire and occasionally enjoying the season of respite in the dragon's shadow, before it belches another fireball.

Either way, we need to assess the capacity of the people we're about to leverage before we can truly determine the pace of change. If our Smartest People are constantly fighting fires, when will they have time for this new deployment? One suspects that they would rather gnaw their arm off at the shoulder to get away from their current malaise, even if just to start something new.

But it's more than just the people. We will need documentation. Knowledge transfer. Team-work across multiple subject areas. Coordination. Time set aside to think about the problems, not just the solution-*du-jour*. These are things that only immediately affect our speed of transforma-tion, and should not daunt us as we embrace and fulfill them. Like a locomotive leaving the station, it doesn't start out at top speed. But we need to make sure it starts out on the right *track*. Changing tracks later is messy business.

Try to think of the process as just that, gathering a head of steam. Don't be afraid to slow down, refactor and move forward again. Many times this carries a slingshot-effect, that our speed out of the gate is much faster than it was before. Plan to refactor. It's a healthy thing.

Promise of Transformation - This comes from two directions. First that the transformation has been promised to us and is underway, and second that we have hope in the transformation's effect. Unfortunately, many people get so immersed in deploying stuff with the machine (it's fun, no?) that they forget to come up for air more often. One would think that in this model of immersion-and-emergence, we would more easily see some disparity in how-things-were versus how-things-are. But this is not a Rip-Van-Winkle effect we're talking about. Our immersion cycles are like microsleep. We thought we were deep in it for a longer period of time, but so was everyone else. Time went by but everything else stood still. Rather than Newtonian inertia, we're now experiencing Einsteinian time-warp.

Rather that suggest taking a before-and-after photograph of the team and the environment (for such is the drama of weight-loss commercials) why not take a checkpoint at the most strategic intervals? Is the team growing? Getting stronger? Are we seeing the return-on-investment or do we find ourselves avoiding the conversation because our hope is deferred for other reasons entirely?

More importantly, have *we* changed? Do we find that the machine is coming under our control or are we still struggling with basics? Do we fear jumping into the more advanced aspects of the technology? Have we become bored with what we are doing, but inertia is keeping us from the next step?

Part of the promise of transformation is in keeping it, to ourselves. Exposure to the Netezza machine is a sought-after opportunity that we should embrace with gusto. Even if we spend a little more time learning a little-bit-more, the payoff later is huge.

Path of Transformation - Every person, line-of-business, company, department and project will follow a different path but it will look strangely the same. Some may take the road of discovery and adoption before assimilation. Others may take the path of jump-in-with-both-feet-because-the-pain's-too-high. Still others may be more deliberate, while another may have already adopted and assimilated similar solutions or technologies, and now Netezza will be in their arsenal as well. The path of the transformation will invariably take a turn or two we did not expect and we will encounter methods, approaches and people that seem odd and oblique, think of problems in different ways, and do not particularly shrink from a challenge. It's good to be on the path with folks like that.

Why do we need to consider the path? Because taking the first step is something that Netezza's doubters and frankly our own intuition may be advising us against. It is a counter-intuitive approach to data processing. Nay-sayers have a comfort zone and vested interest in the status-quo. The path is not for the faint of heart, nor for those who don't like the challenge. It's not for quitters either. Every step we take on the path, we feel the wind at our back and the sunshine in our face, walking into the light and leaving the darkness of doubt and fear. This is itself a transition.

In Underground I noted that the whole *notion* of an Underground is partly tongue-in-cheek and partly not. At the time, few sources existed to learn about and get comfortable with the technology and what it could mean for us. After all, salespeople are always stoked about their own product, and how do we get an objective opinion from the marketplace otherwise? People like me can offer one, but even this has limits that we need to explore further. Getting the information out of the darkness of ignorance and into the light of day is the primary mission of the Underground. There's no intention to keep secrets, but get things into the open (hence the tongue-in-cheek).

But the person who wants to walk this path must leave certain things at the entry gate. Baggage of their transactional knowledge, antiquated lifecycle methods, non-scalable testing protocols,

136

rigid project protocols and hand-crafted logic. We must embrace components, both technical and abstract, that accelerate and *scale*, not debilitate and sputter.

The machine awaiting us demands no less.

Protocols of Transformation - When engaging any transforming process, if we know the transformation is under way, we can set up some protocols to avoid being overwhelmed by it all. Just keep in mind that protocols have value up to a boundary. If the boundary attempts to throttle or choke off the transformation, the protocols will eventually breach and become useless. If the protocols simply attempt to maintain an orderly progression, this can be very useful and instructive, and can provide an active substrate for knowledge transfer.

In our (Brightlight) framework deployment protocol, we roll things out in stages using a forward-education approach. This forward-education shows the users a glimpse or template of what-is-to-come so that when-it-comes, there are fewer surprises. When we display to them what we produced, their expression (or direct comments) are often, *So that's what you were talking about.*

Oh, I should say there is usually higher *anticipation* of the next-stage-of-things because they've been briefed and are ready for it. Is there any other technology that allows us to be this consistent, deterministic and predictive all at the same time?

This is one of the reasons why the Best Practice sessions at the Enzee Universe tend to resonate with the users. The machine is very predictable. Some things we don't do. Other things we never do. Still other things we always do. These things circumscribe our experience with the product so there's no mystery or gotcha's in play. We'll never have to exclaim -

"Now *there's* some fine print for ya!" - Shrek, *Shrek 2*

What are some of these protocols, if they are so well-known and blasted on the walls of the Underground catacombs for all passers-by to see and marvel?

Good question. It's covered a little later in a whole chapter on migration.

Realities of Transformation - As noted later, one of the most significant realities is that transformation is coming and we need to embrace it. Even today we may be on the other side of the "big" transformation and are happy with the initial outcome. Maybe we wanted more. Maybe we received more than we ever bargained for. Something has changed. It is obvious and tangible, perhaps larger than expected. A primary reality of transformation is that whatever we're doing now, today, in the workaday world, will not be the same this time next year. How soon this changes (it might be as early as next month) is not up to us. The reality is, we need to get into the raft, strap in and hold on tight. When the rush is over, we'll be glad to be downstream from it. But we won't be where we were (we'll be further along in *something*, we're sure of it). And we won't have any way to go back where we came from (it is an irreversible transformation). If we choose to step aside or forego the journey, we are perhaps no worse off than if we were working someplace that never had, and never will hear of Netezza. With one exception.

We *have* heard of it. This part is irreversible too. Once we taste the nectar of raw MPP adrenalin, it's a rush that cannot be matched, nor put down or ignored. Those who remove themselves from it are still transformed. And this is the Great Reality of encountering the machine. The encounter *itself* is a transforming experience. From this day forward, we will compare all other experiences to it. Something ran faster than Netezza. Or slower than Netezza. But the Netezza appliance will become our personal standard, the golden section, the Rosetta Stone.

Think I'm kidding? Practically everywhere I go where the Netezza machine was not selected in the proof of concept (rare I know) the people there still compare the winning technology with whether or not it still matches up (or ever matched up) with the appliance. At two of these sites, the sentiment is the same. Netezza won the Tournament but a poser was chosen instead. They pine for the appliance, wondering what their managers could possibly have been thinking.

This, however, is *unrequited* transform, and a sad state of affairs indeed.

There is an old adage that applies to dramatic encounters. Whether it's an encounter with a rock star, or a head of state, a celebrity or royalty, is that we can tell the difference between some-one who has *actually* met the celebrity and someone who has not. This is because "the encounter would have changed us." In the end, if there's no change, the encounter wasn't real.

This is why we can expect the encounter to change us, and frankly how we can tell whether a person has merely dabbled in an environment where Netezza was present, or if they have actually worked with the technology. It changes things.

The final reality of transformation, alluded to above and below, is that is never stops. The trans-formation train leaves the station like a locomotive. We're either on the train or we're not. Once on the train, the inertia of transformation is not as obvious, but one look outside the windows at the landscape rushing by and we know change is underway. We're going somewhere.

Risk of Transformation - There is an old adage that goes "There is risk in every stroke of the axe." Meaning of course, that the axe could slip and damage something important. While we could imagine that the risk of proceeding has built-in cautions, the risk of not proceeding usually has even more. The decision-maker finds themselves weighing the risk, or for that matter, weighing the readiness of the environment to accept the risk. As noted in the first chapter, being prepared to use the Netezza machine and being prepared for the transformation it will bring, are two different things.

Often the decision is less about whether the technology is right to solve the problem, and more about whether the technology *fits*. Does it fit the infrastructure, the people, the environment, the solution domain? To all of the above - yes and no. Yes it fits, we just have not realized the fit. And no, it might not fit *right now*. But this is the essence of transformation. If a person goes on a weight loss program, they might buy a number of clothing items that are too-small, as incentive to work toward fitting into them. Do they fit the person's tastes? Surely, but do they fit the person's body? Not *yet*.

Managers sometimes look at the fit of a technology in soft-skill ways. Does it appeal to my technologists? Will it appeal to my peers? The operators? Administrators? The conclusion to any of these is simply a measurement of risk. The manager who-really-needs-the-technology may choose to proceed forward (and usually does) but in context of managing expectations in order to minimize risk.

Case Study Short: One manager took on enormous personal and political risk in bringing the Netezza machines into an environment that was an ensconced and established enclave of a competitor technology. The proof-of-concept fell (wildly) in Netezza's favor, silencing those who had any technical objection. On that day, however, the objectors silently plotted the demise of the impertinent manager who dared buck their system. They starved him for resources and assistance, and generally made his life miserable from the inception of the project. Once the manager gathered a head of steam, however, the lack of assistance became visible, so the objectors reluctantly began to open up, just a bit at first. Nobody likes to be *seen* as a non-team player. Once the true benefits of the machine were out in the open, however, the objectors became jealous of the machine's simplicity of administration, ease-of-use and general good-vibe held by the team rolling it out. Before too long, the lay-sayers were behind it. What's not to love?

In short, the nay-sayers were transformed.

Case Study Short: The expectations were high and the spirits even higher as the managers signed off on the Netezza purchase and the technologists scurried back to their desks to prepare for it. Within a matter of days, they were notified that the installers would be at the front door of the data center ('cuz the Netezza guys waste no time). The modelers scrambled to put their initial data structures in place. The developers scrambled to get things set up on their Datastage instance so they could start talking to the machine. The infrastructure guys scrambled to prep for network connectivity and power. Then *whoosh*, the Netezza machines were installed and operational by the end of the day.

A manager looked onto this frenetic activity, and all the scrambling, and concluded that it was just *too* scrambled. He saw risk in all these people running about, clearly out of their minds with excitement. Clearly out of control and he was just the one to bring control. He ran into his office to start on a master project plan. With this would come a white paper on methodology expectations. After a week, he thought he had a good handle on it, but had to clear the project plan with his senior managers. He also had to clear his methodology plan with his Management Office folks. This would take weeks. In the meantime, the technologists were running around like chickens with no leader, and this frightened the daylights out of him.

By the time he received approval for his plans, three more weeks had passed. He called a meeting at the end of that week to roll it out, only to discover that his teams, without his direct intervention, were about to push their first implementation into user acceptance! In four *weeks?* How is this possible?

He called an all-hands-on-deck meeting to review the deliverables, but nobody accepted the meeting invitation. Five minutes before the meeting was supposed to begin, his assistant entered his office and closed the door. "We won't need a review, since all of the deliverables have been vetted by the principal technologists already."

"Oh really? And who authorized *that?*"

"You did," the assistant sat down, "All that stuff was delegated over a year ago."

"But they're about to put something into production!"

"It's under control," the assistant said quietly, "These are pretty smart people. They work together really well."

What the manager had not seen, is that in hiring the smartest people he could find, he had already mitigated the risk. Smart people do that.

Fallacies of Transformation - One of the most significant fallacies associated with transformation is the notion that options exist. Certainly some options exist to shape the transformation along a continuum, but there's no way to stop it. Another common fallacy is that we can completely control the transformation. Too many dynamic variables, many of them human and highly complex, are in play in any given moment of the transformation to presume we have control. Yet another common fallacy is that we will watch the transformation happen around us, leaving us somehow unchanged. This of course is no different than watching news programs about how someone has signed over our company to another parent company. How could we be exempt from such an event? Even if we choose to depart the situation, this too is a form of change, because we wouldn't have done it under other circumstances.

Too-high expectations, or the **False Wow**, is another fallacy. Often our proof-of-concept will show that we can do that particularly evil series of operations, that today take six hours, in six minutes, or even six seconds, and we mentally translate this to all of our operations. In one particular case, the proof of concept showed the most complex operations returning in less than five seconds. Ship it! Shouted the project lead, but when the reports were eventually rolled out, none of them were seeing this kind of turnaround. The culprit was in the architecture of the reports, because we could measure the queries on the machine. They were still coming back under five seconds. The rest of the time was spent in transit between the keyboard and the Netezza box. The reporting guys cried foul. To which we responded, Cry all you want, just make the reporting environment run faster!

Case Study Short: We did a proof where one of the queries was reduced from 25 minutes or more into a ten-second-or-less form. The principal on the project saw 2500x improvement. He then put this on a powerpoint slide and starting shopping it around. This eventually made it into a statement of work demanding 2500x improvement on all operations. We had to talk him off the ledge on this one, because half of his operations took thirty seconds or less already. Every query in Netezza has a finite cost, and no-way, no-how was he getting 2500x on any of those. If we had agreed to the condition however, this would have been a False Wow. The Wow that is propped up by the false expectation that all queries will experience the same boost across the board. This is not a reasonable expectation so we need to guard against it.

In all this, we find people wanting to engage the process and drawing on prior experience to shape the outcome. Calling upon prior knowledge, not having engaged the means and options facing the existing opportunity before us, is no different than "doing it the old fashioned way." in any other context. Not having encountered Netezza before, any prior experience, except in conceptual data modeling and warehousing, has specious value. I recall upon first encountering the Netezza machine, how many things that I had trusted as tried-and-true aspects of data warehousing, had to be rethought, refactored or simply set aside. The fallacy here is not the dependence upon prior knowledge, but the *projection* of prior knowledge as if it applies. We can experiment to validate assumptions, but we need to keep a very (and I say again - very) open mind.

Case Study Short: A colleague tells me that in his most recent client experience, one of their principals had just come from another environment where the data warehouse implementation had been a bumpy ride until he had fixed everything. In a prior setting, he had likewise been a turn-around artist, and now would bring this acumen to bear on this new Netezza migration.

However, his half-baked ideas about data modeling and relationships, and practically bipolar approach to dealing with multiple managers, kept everyone in a complete tailspin, including my colleague. He could not tell, from day to day, what the priorities were or even anticipate the elements of an approach he had long since mastered. He would say *zig*, but this principal would say *zag*, just because he wanted to investigate the outcome and see-what-happened. Before it was done, everyone around him wanted him to start experimenting on his own time and not use them all for lab rats. Nobody wanted to chase a known failed approach down a rat-hole just to placate this guy's curiosity.

So even the open-mind directive has its limits!

The Whew-fallacy, is the assumption that the transformation process will stop, the smoke will clear and we can step back to observe the wonders of what it wrought. No, once the transformation commences, it never stops. It may ebb and flow, but transformation is underway all-the-way. Hmm, all the way to what? Good question, did we ever assume it would have an end? At least now we can assume that our environment is braced for change because it is geared to embrace change as part of its core reason for existence.

The People-fallacy, alluded to above, is in failure to **trust our smartest** people to make it work. Even if we bring in special help like consultants or the like, our own brain trust should be trusted. The secondary fallacy to this, is in placing too much **trust in untested** individuals. It is common for someone to hire or conscript untested personnel and then listen to what those personnel have to say about the project direction or technical focus. If said individual is bringing bad practices from another site, we don't want those. If said person is projecting their inexperience into the workflow, we don't want that. If said person is the loudest in the room, this is probably the highest risk of all. Don't commit the fallacy of handing the keys to a person who has never driven a car, or for that matter, claims to have driven a car but we have no idea whether they can drive it well.

An additional fallacy, which should be obvious on the surface, is that we should regard the Netezza rollout as a green field. Not as "another" place where we plan to host the warehouse that's in the "current" place. Shoveling it out of one hole and into another is not the right approach. It's actually a missed opportunity. Failure to properly characterize the system from whence we are escaping, will invariably cause us to commit the **Final Fallacy** - that of migrating functionality that has no other role but artificially propping up an underpowered system.

Resistance to Transformation - One firm foresaw that the machine could possibly change many of the ways they operated, so they put things in place to brace themselves from this impact. The process of bracing for the change was itself a change, and created another layer of crushing red-tape overhead in their already over-fattened policy matrix. Not only did this extra layer brace for the change, it effectively created a stalemate effect so that nothing could get done. A senior manager learned of this situation and called for a moratorium (yet another change) on all the debilitating policies so that they could realize their investment. After a year of development and rolling out multiple mission-critical warehouse solutions, these operationally-adapted people had long-since forgotten what it was like to be asphyxiated by artificial constraints - *on a development project.*

Resistance to the transformation doesn't stop the transformation any more that trying to shore up our home against floodwaters will stop the flood. It might stop the flood from coming to us *personally*, for the time being. But if the flood isn't going away, we'll eventually be subsumed anyhow. Attempting to resist the irresistible, has its own risks.

One manager attempted to side-step the assimilation of the Netezza machine by nay-saying the providers that were rolling it out. On the eve of the primary production deployment where the machine would run side-by-side in production / parallel to the actual production systems, this manager made his way around to all of the satellite divisions making an impassioned speech as to why the implementation would utterly fail. In every watercooler conversation, even on email and social networking, he was on record as being the guy, first-in-line, to say I-told-you-so.

But it was not meant to be. The parallel production test completed its 30-days *without even a hiccup* and was assimilated on day-31 as the new production environment. The deployment of this environment was itself a game-changer for that corporation, only accelerating its ascension into a more successful realm of existence. This particular manager was given something else to do with his time. People still question his judgment even in small matters. It's so unfair.

Unknown of Transformation - In the theme of There Be Dragons, people feel that the Netezza technology is so uncharted that it needs special attention. Would we offer special attention to a new appliance in our home? Perhaps because it was new, but not necessarily because of its functionality. We bought it for a purpose and that purpose is upon us. We can either apply it toward that purpose or start doubting why we bought it.

Ahh, the great unknown. It comes upon the individual something like this: The hapless data warehouse manager is constantly swamped with work because his existing systems are so under-powered he will never get ahead of the churn. When we install the Netezza machine, suddenly the churn doesn't look so scary, Then one day we're in front of the churn, and then one day it's behind us, and soon we call it a wake, then a memory. In this transition, the workload factor is changing. We're getting ahead of the workload and even the backlog of stuff that's been deferred for so long. One day it's all under control and we're at the empty whiteboard, no longer staring at the work before us, because it's all behind us.

And the white board is blank. This realization is an anxious experience for some, because until now all of their creative juices have been pushed toward solving problems-at-hand, not actually seeking out more problems to solve. Not to worry, since many of our managers will see our additional capacity and start to send more work our way. In some circles, capacity flows downhill.

But the point is, the known is behind us. The unknown is before us, and we now have to deliberately transform into creative, proactive thinkers. We may never have considered this before. It remains an unknown because the opportunity never presented itself.

Pain of Transformation - Change is very stressful for some. In fact, some environments dislike change so much, they wrap numerous policies around it so that change cannot happen without approval! And then along comes this uppity appliance, a change-agent with a pretty face, and they are undone!

The pain of transformation arrives whether we want the transformation or not. It's like this: a childhood friend of mine was told by his father, just weeks before he was about to enter seventh grade, that he would have to start playing tackle-football. Now many of you know in Texas, football is a bit of a juggernaut, to say the least. This young man's father had played football in high school and by gosh his son would play it too! Just one problem, this kid was a geek (like me) and wasn't very good at sports. In fact, he avoided team sports because of his lack of athletic abilities, and now he faced the portent of being suited up in practice gear, a coach yelling in his ear and all of the good athletes standing around shaking their heads while he tried to be a good player. I felt bad for the guy, as this was very painful and scary transition for him.

He did what he could to deny the situation, including misbehaving so that he could get himself kicked off the team. Today that would probably work, but back then he had no other options. This only made it worse for him, because the coach would decide the punishment. More workout time.

Oddly, after the first year he'd grown to like it even though he wasn't any good at it. He'd found a groove and it had changed him. Then he signed up for another year, and another, four years total before it came time to try out for varsity and he did not make the cut. He wasn't really surprised. But the transformation he endured was one of character-construction more so than the game of football. Truth be told, coaches don't actually *teach* the game to the players, they simply coach the players to play it as the coach wants it played. He told me that he is still confused over this rule or that, or when it's okay to do this but not that. Who cares? Now he is a very successful manager over a data warehouse/IT operations shop. His kids are in soccer, but they *wanted* to play.

He related to me that something ticked over inside him that first year, that a situation had been placed before him and he would not back down from it. He would not quit, nor let the system or the situation get the best of him. He would put his best into *it,* so that nobody could say he didn't do his best. But it became his personal choice to be a victim or a volunteer, a person tossed about by bad fortune, or a person in charge of the situation, grasping it with gusto. He noted that even the star players of the football team, to a man, were all washouts in college. But he had found a center, and a skill that would last him all his life.

We may find some pain in the transition from our old technology to the Netezza machine, but the worst thing we can do is quit, fail to grasp the opportunity with gusto and be left in the shallows. Embracing the change might require a little faith, but with a machine this powerful, it's not a leap of faith on its behalf, but on our own. It's a chance to find out what we're made of. Because if we quit, fail to embrace and walk away from the opportunity to engage, another form of pain will sweep over us.

The pain of regret. And that, my friends, is much worse.

INDUSTRY TRANSFORMATION

WHEN I TELL PEOPLE THAT the industry will experience transformation, at first they think I'm talking about the latest data warehouse guru's pronouncement on changes in the various *new* technologies or approaches. However, in this context we're talking about a complete, complex and often protracted-duration shift in the business focus of the industry's major players, most particularly the ETL vendors. Dare I name-names? I dare, and will propose that the vendors of the world such as Ab Initio, Informatica, Expressor, DataStage (also an IBM company!) and the other toe-in-the-water SQL-transform players like SSIS and Oracle Data Integrator, will ultimately step up to the plate and embrace the future. I don't need to predict the future, because it's already here and the players who intend to play are already going there. It looks like this:

Netezza has all the power in-the-machine. The other appliances do too, but none of them are positioned to be data processing *machines* in the same manner as Ab Initio or Informatica are data processing *products*. What's that you say? A non-believer in the notion that the simplicity of an insert-select SQL statement riding on a substrate of hundreds if not thousands of processors, is a better and more scalable plan than the internal functionality of <your favorite ETL tool here>?

Well, now it's time to pick (and not nit-pick) on one or two of them because they have vocal proponents that sincerely believe that they are ready for the SQL-transform prime-time. First in the hot-box is a nameless open-source ETL tool, with Oracle Data Integrator on deck. The reason I don't want to name the ETL tool is that it's fairly recent on the scene and may not last long anyhow, so we'll discuss in terms of capabilities and weaknesses that we could apply as a yardstick to measure any technology.

I was in the presence of several champions for this ETL tool when I started asking simple questions about scalability. "All of it would depend on the size of the server they were running on." Which brings us back to - *Doh!* Why didn't *I* think of that? And what of the general functionalities associated with transformation? Oh, they said, you need to plug in a custom Java module for most transforms.

Java? *Really?*

Without belaboring a point, we've already noted that Java and bulk data processing are like oil and water. And now we'll embrace a tool that is *dependent* on Java? Methinks, well, methinks *not* but in this particular case the vendors were aggressive, believing that they could just point to the GUI and claim victory, as though it was all that mattered. Now don't get me wrong. I'm only picking on them because they have a built-in dependency on technology (Java) that is a proven non-starter for data warehousing. So point, click, drag, drop and we're done. Almost done, anyhow until we have to build that bolt-on Java module. But hey, we do the rest of the work - the work that we *thought* was important rather than the work we're actually *doing*. (For such is the way of open source).

What's that? We want to plug in a SQL statement for Netezza to run? The process to support this is to (a) Fill out this rather tediously formatted template, (b) spend more time debugging the template than the SQL itself, and (c) once completed, we have SQL-transforms! Really? What if I want several *hundred* of those? (you know, because I have several hundred *tables*)?

Blank stare.

Recall in Underground I described a similar Texas-Two-Step from Sybase IQ, their proponents at least had an answer. "Nobody does it that way." Yeah, thanks. That tells us that *you* don't do-it-that-way. But pretty soon, *everyone* will be doing-it-that-way and we'll visit the installation CDs for your technology in the Chicago Museum of Ancient History.

Then our team experienced the infrastructure wonders of the technology, an open source technology that behaves as we would expect from something designed and concocted by committee. We're treated to special events, like the server spontaneously rebooting, the overall flakiness of the interface, like something *so* not designed by an architect-in-charge. Oh, but it's an open-source tool, which is supposed to the best, richest environment within which to build a software product - right? Only if we know the domain-at-hand. A gaggle of Java developers who don't know beans (yes, Java-beans) about large scale data processing can still crank out a stellar *functional* product, but it will reflect the skill and experience of the collective whole. Or rather, it will (and does) reflect the *naivete* of the whole as it concerns scalability. *In Java.*

Now, the reason I'm picking on this approach (along with the product discussed in an earlier chapter) is that it showed up in a Tournament of Posers and is proponents started hawking the product like it was a real player. The only thing worse than listening to posers hawking their product, is talking a client off the ledge after they've drunk deeply from the vendor kool-aid.

Conversely, the most successful products (like Ab Initio) have an MIT-Brain-Trust that IMHO is second to none in their understanding *and* execution of large scale data processing capabilities on SMP hosts. It shows in the product (not an open-source). If we want a collection of handy features, say, for screen manipulation or user interaction, these are transactionally-driven aspects that open-source solutions can easily master. But when we're talking about leveraging the hardware assets for maximum power, that is, maximizing *physics*, the average programmer won't know what to do. Why is this? In the technical circles I run in, people I know shake their heads when I talk about some of the *simpler* problems I deal with, and start a sentence with something like, "Over there, the table had three billion rows and..."

Okay, I can stop right now, because I've already lost them. They cannot fathom a system with billions of rows. The Java guys can't either. (Oh sure, a transactional database, but not a bulk-processing data warehouse). What does it say of a software product for which such scales are not accounted for? No dots to connect here.

Moving right along, with the hybrid ETL-tool-SQL-Execution, we hear the same message from Informatica, Ab Initio et. al. who can help us execute the arbitrary SQL statement on that-machine-over-there, but they don't actually shepherd or harness the construction and maintenance of the SQL statement itself. It needs to work "as written" - you know, the already-hand-crafted, big fat insert clause and the equally monstrous select clause along with its pernicious filters and such. Supply a hand-crafted SQL statement and we will run it for you.

And now try a few *hundred* of those hand-crafted wonders. I'm getting to a point here, I promise.

Ah, the aficionado ascertains, if I'm really doing all this processing in the Netezza machine, and it has all the functionality I need, then why do I want to use this ETL tool at all?

Why indeed?

At such junctures, the customer looks me in the eye almost like they expect me to defend the ETL tool. Come up with some brilliantly formulated expository on why the ETL tool will save their tail under pressure, or is somehow useful because of that-thing-you-didn't-know-about. But no, my answer is:

Why Indeed?

This leaves a knot in the throat of the person who really wants to *believe*. Those who have been sold on the <fill in your product here> will not tolerate nay-sayers. It is heresy, you see.

I tried an experiment with a bunch of teenagers once (actually it was so much fun I've done it a lot). I hold up a book and ask "If I let this book go, will it hit the floor?" And as I was holding it, I would provoke a debate on why we can know the book will fall to the floor, whether we know something about gravity, the consistency of nature, or stuff that we consider the background-noise-of-life-kinda knowledge. After what is usually a lively exchange where everyone agrees that the book will indeed fall to the floor, I put it back in its place. Invariably, one of them will ask "Aren't you going to *drop* it?" To which I respond "Why do I need to?"

Why indeed?

The tension of the *obvious*, is just killing them.

Back to the story, the average customer or IT folk are used to hearing the almost knee-jerk defenses for their favorite drag-and-drop tool. If someone who is very experienced doesn't offer one up, it's a lot like the book not hitting the floor. It's *supposed* to, but it wasn't given the opportunity. The ETL tool was *supposed* to receive a resounding defense. It just didn't. Why is that?

The next generation of appliances, have so eclipsed these products in power and functionality, that the ETL products really don't know *how* to respond to it. Here's why:

The common ETL tool has been constructed and marketed as the data-processing-central for all our enterprise data. How can they abdicate such a hard-won position to an *appliance?* Moreover, they have spent countless millions in performance enhancements on their products, and along comes this uppity appliance that challenges it all, how could they *possibly* honor their stockholders by giving the nod to the appliance?

Then again, how *would* they do this? By providing an integrated means to interact transparently with the appliance as though it's part of the family? Hmm, does this mean that DataStage may step up to fill this slot? (Being another IBM product and all). This product is already used at many sites to harness a Netezza machine. With one drawback: It likewise can only execute the SQL-transform provided by the developer - a hand-crafted, ready-to-execute, shrink-wrapped and ready-for-inclusion in their SQL harness. Sure this *runs* the SQL statement. But it does not address the issue of constructing and maintaining the SQL statement. It does not respond nor is aware of changes in the catalog metadata. It does not validate data types nor tell us that our intermediate table distributions might not play well. It doesn't help us at all.

None of them do.

As such, they don't promote the best use of the Netezza machine.

What does *that* mean? I've stated elsewhere that the power of Netezza is actually realized by leveraging smaller, simpler SQL statements rather than the Oracle-style big-fat SQL statements. With high overhead to implement only one statement, this discourages the use of multiple smaller statements because they rapidly become too unwieldy to manage. The developer will fall back on the notion that a few "simple" SQL *components*, however complex their internal *statement* may be, is the best path. But it's actually the path of least resistance. By this measure, the SQL-Transform capability in ETL products "supports" the leveraging of "a few" SQL statements, but not the *hundreds* we will see necessary to support a high-performance SQL-transform flow model.

So think in these terms: We close our eyes and imagine a moderately complex ETL application. How many "drag-and-drop" components are on the canvas of this visual flow environment? Ten? Twenty? The most complex ETL applications I have seen literally have hundreds of components at various levels of functionality. In applications like those in Oracle Data Integrator, we'll see a spider-web of components surrounding a relatively simple function. Then we'll see dozens if not tens of dozens of these. They don't share their metadata and configuration mechanics all that well, because they were intended, by the tool vendor, to be "supported" but not "integrated". There is a huge difference in the two.

"Integrated" means that we simply put the rules into the component and it will manufacture the SQL statement for us. It is metadata/catalog-aware so can give us hints and clues to keep us away from known pitfalls. Are *any* ETL tools doing this?

"Support" for the SQL insert/select means that *we* can carefully hand-craft a SQL statement in our favorite SQL GUI like WinSQL or Toad, and when we are satisfied, we copy-and-paste that into the ETL mechanics, wrap some connecting logic around it and we're done. This creates a lot of overhead, programming, testing etc. If the same SQL statement is better served in broken-apart form, we are now signing up to build out a harness for each *additional* SQL statement. The portent of this work puts the kabash on the desire to do it, even if it's the best approach and the most efficient execution. It's just too much programming overhead.

Never mind that the SQL statement might be *better* served broken apart into smaller, faster and more nimble chunks. If we bite off the additional work we will have to use multiple ETL-tool SQL components to handle these broken-apart operations. They *look* nimble when they appear side-by-side in the SQL GUI tool. In the ETL tool, they are not *actually* side-by-side, but component-by-component, separately managed, executed and maintained. The ETL tool likewise thinks that *flow* components should be linked together by a "flow line", with the assumption that it actually represents the physical mechanism through which data flows. But there is no such concept in the ETL tool for a SQL component. Each one is standalone, regarded as shared-nothing, and all of them will execute at the same time unless we apply some pretty stiff phasing logic to make them sequence correctly. Over in Netezza, the data "flows" between tables, down on the hardware, and the only way the ETL tool can track it is to *assume* that the data is "flowing" between two SQL components because it is "sharing" the same intermediate table as data is passed along to the final target table.

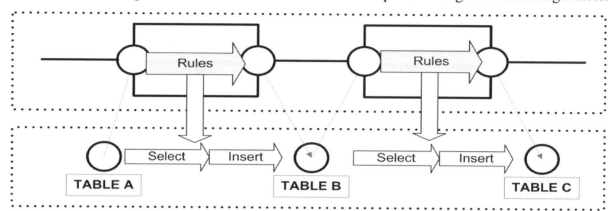

In the simplified depiction (above) we have two SQL-Transforms components as we would functionally expect them to be represented on an ETL tool design canvas (upper half of drawing) along with the expected behavior they would engage inside the machine (lower half of drawing).

In the upper half, control transitions to the first component and it will contain rules used to generate an intermediate table (Table B) and SQL statement (Select/Insert) to fill, where the Insert faces Table B and the Select will source Table A (in truth, the Select could source any arbitrary number of tables). Once completed, it transitions control to the next component.

This in turn manufactures an intermediate table (Table C), the target of the Insert, where Table B (among others) is the source for the select statement. The bottom half is what happens under the covers (we don't want to know anything about it or manage it). The upper half is what the developer actually sees and deals with, that is snapping together components and applying rules. The developer will not make a SQL statement or worry about the flow used to manage the data it produces.

So ETL tools don't represent this relationship, and in fact have a lot of issues with these concepts. Or rather, ETL tools don't represent these concepts *at all*.

If we embrace a SQL-transform-flow model, the issue that the (currently available) ETL tools have to deal with is its own relegation to the role of a data transport mechanism (with column-level transforms and scrubs) and to the role of workload orchestration in the Netezza machine. But all that other *high-end* functionality in the product, like transform mechanics and yes, performance, are set aside for these more rudimentary tasks. What ETL tool vendor signs up to be the data transport / workload orchestration platform while another, high-powered appliance gets all the glory?

And this is where the appliance's inflection point puts painful pressure on the ETL vendor. And why the ETL vendor will have to be dragged, kicking and screaming into the 21st century. This is the *transformation* we will see in the ETL vendors, or we will see another vendor rise from the mist who has heartily embraced this future. Will this new vendor eclipse or subsume the others? Probably not (likely it will get assimilated by one of them!)

But the point is: The transformation is afoot. The industry is moving toward appliance-based, centralized processing because technology has naturally moved this way. As the client-servers once moved off the mainframe to gain more power and agility when the data sizes and complexities were low, now that those same sizes and complexities have risen, the marketplace still needs the agility of the microprocessor but the power of the mainframe (without the doggone cost of the mainframe). Ahh, the appliance is the ticket.

And the transformation is just that: the movement of the industry to put its data back "under air", where it belongs.

So let's not just talk "pie" in the proverbial sky, but about the features and capabilities we'll need to make such a product viable and even, dare we say, *fun to use?*

Databases as resources, tables as data interfaces. This is a significant shift from common ETL-based thinking, that uses file streams as intermediate storage and a DML definition as the data interface to the file stream. Now we are using tables for intermediate storage, and the table definition as our DML.

Also unlike the ETL tool alone, our experience is far less self-contained. We need to use all these metadata assets locally, but activate them remotely. The Netezza machine is where the action is, and is the final arbiter of the quality of our work products. We'll likewise need the freedom to create/destroy tables the same way we would files. In a common ETL protocol, we would be required to install the tables as *officially* recognized resources. At least two ETL products would allow us to make a dynamic table to support multi-threaded loading. All of the others require us to set up a component to make the table, and another component to execute the SQL, yet another component to tear down the table. Each operation then has a tediously proliferating effect of SQL components executed in *phases* because they don't naturally transition control to each other in the tool (simulating a flow). Execute one, execute the next. Put them in their own phases so they don't happen all at once. Do it for hundreds of them. What a hairball.

Otherwise, set them up as processes in something like Autosys, where each operation is its own "job". Some folks are scratching their head on my objection to that one, because they architected one like it and thought it was (and is) brilliant, yet have never interacted with the people who operate and maintain it, who cannot stop complaining about it.

As an aside here, the primary groups of people who intersect and consume our work products are not just the end-users consuming data, but the operational users, administrator, maintenance and troubleshooters. All of them will have words about the efficiency or integrity of the operational run-time we deliver them. Want an eye-opener, go talk to your operation people about what will make their lives easier. Wonder no longer why they hate the non-optimized rollouts of marginal technologies.

No, the flow model needs to follow an easily managed, gated processing protocol that is easy to set up and maintain, and doesn't require the developer to maintain the actual SQL transforms (the application logic after all) as a bunch of spinning plates. Think about it, we *want* our developers focused on application logic, not juggling a canvas full of components that, while "visual" aren't connected with any kind of flow lines. Recall if we have a visual environment, we want the transforms connected with flow lines, we want the flow lines to represent intermediate tables, and we want the flow itself to represent the DDL of the table. This allows us to connect columns inside components, and if we need to set up several columns on the left with several on the right, we're actually defining the columns that the system will use to manufacture and toss an *intermediate table*. Hey, doesn't sound too complicated, does it? If we break it down to components, we have all kinds of options.

Now the component consuming the table from the left hand side will allow the developer to plug in all manner of rules as the data ultimately passes to the right hand side, and of course this will be reduced to a SQL statement, executed on the machine. The problem here, is that the existing tools purport to do this but only go halfway. What we need now is a way to measure the effectiveness of the SQL statement and the freedom to break it into multiple smaller SQL statements. In addition, to automatically analyze the statements and their attendant tables for the optimum distribution, so statements finish with the least possible overhead. Oh, and how about dynamic analysis so that we get some ongoing metrics out of it, you know, to report to a centralized metrics monitor so we can proactively keep the flows healthy. When was the last time our flows started running out of gas and we didn't know where to start looking?

How about gross metrics for performance, efficiency and information flow, like an Observation Deck? Hey, shameless plugs are okay because it's my book. But those who experience the benefit of these kinds of metrics know the value. One of the early implementations of an OD discovered that the majority of processes feeding the Netezza machine were performing singleton operations (a real no-no for those of you in-the-know) and what's more, over half of these were *updates*. Frankly the customer didn't have a clue that this problem was so pervasive and that it had so easily crept up on them.

As it turned out, the last "project" effort they had executed had expanded a bunch of the ETL components and flows to support an additional feed. This feed effectively doubled the bad flows into the machine and brought it to its knees. In point of fact, the original implementation had been marginally executed, and now this additional pressure had brought the marginal implementation into the light. Ongoing metrics would have found these products earlier, and would have no doubt given the customer a much better experience with the machine for a longer period. After all, once these issues were remediated, the machine that had for the longest time been "very busy", suddenly went quiet. Seems that it had been overloaded with *inefficiency*, not real workload.

Inefficiency in other technologies, Exadata for one, is found in the architecture itself. Exadata's dependence on shared disk storage is it's Achilles' heel. Considering that Oracle keeps pumping out new forms of this device, it's clear that they took seriously some lessons from the prior incarnations of the technology. They clearly listened to someone. But have you ever put your ear to a train track rail to listen for the train? We can literally hear it coming for many miles away. Oracle seems to have their ear on the wrong rail, and might even be looking in the wrong direction while they are listening, because the Netezza Freight Line is bearing down on them and they cannot hear it.

The shared disk storage architecture of Exadata means that it will always be enslaved to the marginal. Recall the story of the marginal country singer who became (and remained) a superstar overnight when she deliberately chose to fire her own family (who held various supporting positions in her entertainment realm) and hired professionals who knew what to do? Perhaps it's time for the Exadata product managers to go out into the marketplace and hire some folks who understand data warehousing, and who understand the marketplace they are competing in? Hey, they are really, really trying to transform to meet the appliance challenge. Theirs is a story, though, of being appliance-challenged more so that challenging the appliance. Oracle has changed and will continue to change. Their place in the market is likely waiting for them. Whether they get to secure that place seems entirely up to them, and not their competitors. Why then, the hesitation?

I had mentioned Oracle Data Integrator earlier, so now let's take a deeper look. This product is also tuned, configured and deployed as though it only knows how to support Oracle-facing queries. Those who point the product to a Netezza machine will scratch their heads and wonder. Then they realize how different the two architectures are, but remain unconvinced that it's something as simple as shared disk storage. After all, shared disk *seemed* like such a good idea.

We experience an interesting effect when the product is first encountered. It's all point-click/drag-drop and all is right with the world. We connect up our first SQL-Transform, and while it's a bit tedious, we learn a lot about the product. The second one is easier. As is the next. When we get to ten or so of these, we recognize a pattern and want to exploit it. Just one problem: We will have to revisit all ten and retrofit them. No worries, it's only ten, so we rip this work out in short order and continue with our progress. Along the way we note more opportunities to share, but we need to retrofit all those, too.

Then something unexpected-that-we-should-have-expected happens. The data model changes. Now we have to tediously retrofit the changes into all the work we've done. And re-test it before we can move on. This lack of metadata/catalog awareness, especially as it relates to assimilating SQL-Transform impacts, feels a lot like we're developing on a cushion of hot air that's about to deflate out from under us at any moment.

Case Study Short: At one site the ODI development project initially had a strong head of steam. Over time, the project simply stalled out. When we encountered it, nobody had made any progress on it for months, yet it still drove some portions of the solution. It had been rolled out in waves, and once the first several waves were in play they realized their need to retrofit. This was unfortunate in the sense that most of their production stuff had to be retrofitted and re-tested, and nobody wanted to sign up for that. So the project lurched.

The primary problem here is that ODI is set up largely to support smaller-scale flows. Not the hundreds-of-transform flows that are often elicited by a Netezza-centric rollout. On top of this, its propensity to use the Netezza catalog as an operational database turned out to adversely affect its performance in dramatic ways. So even if the Netezza SQL-Transforms were tuned to the max, the drag was now in the *product* shepherding them. It's sort of deflationary to find out that we *could* move faster if only those lead boots weren't around our ankles.

The last part of this discovery was that each time they opened up one of the SQL-Transforms for review, we found a relatively simple operation surrounded by a spider-web of complex activity. It's no wonder that each one of these was so tedious to roll out and why nobody wanted to go back to test them. I was breathless in a simple five-minute review!

The issue here is that the simplicity of Netezza was actually overshadowed by the complexity of he visual environment (ironic, I know). I can see that if we're using shell-scripts or program code that there's an aspect of documentation and due-diligence to keep the assets in the light-of-day so they don't seem so black-boxed or ambiguous. But in a visualized environment we expect the complexity to be removed from view, so to speak, because the visualization is supposed to simplify and clarify all that stuff.

But this is exactly the opposite of what we witnessed. We saw that the simple functionality of the SQL statement was being buried in a sea of functional lines between a dozen or more supporting components (*that could not be shared easily* with other SQL-Transforms). So not only was this difficult to understand, it invited *cut-and-paste* of one to make another. This of course will copy all the functionality we want to keep, but will also propagate all the bugs we haven't discovered yet. Hence the constant need to retrofit and re-retrofit.

"It seems like there's a lot of overhead to do simple things," someone noted. I agree with this.

One person asked the question, "If we already have ODI installed, is Netezza compatible with it?" And the answer was "Yes." Of course, this is true in no uncertain terms.

But that wasn't what we saw. The principals there had *chosen* ODI to roll out after Netezza was already well-established in the shop. This is not a case of *grandfathering* an existing implementation on top of Netezza. This was a case of building a new implementation, which proved to be incompatible with Netezza. This was true in no uncertain terms.

I have no expectation of course, that ODI will transform to step up to this plate. It had a prior existence as an enterprise product before being purchased by Oracle. Now that it's a satellite product of Oracle, it will no doubt maintain the same marginality as all of Oracle's other satellite products. Alas and forsooth.

FRAMEWORKS: RULES-BASED STUFF

WE NEED TO lay a *little* groundwork that some may be consummately familiar with, others not so much. We need to speak the same language and use the same concepts, so bear with me. I promise it will be pain-free.

One of our clients noted, "That term *framework*, it's a little overused, and little cloudy." I hear ya' and so as we move into this subject area, let's be clear. A framework is like the superstructure of a large building. It has shape and strength, but does not presuppose the details of how people will use the building. It only presupposes that it will in fact be a building with certain non-optional parts (like plumbing, electrical etc). Likewise a framework in our domain has to provide certain non-optional capabilities that presuppose the need for the capability without nailing down a specific implementation. This is a tall order, no doubt and not to be entered into with some deep experience in the solution domain for which we purport solve problems.

A framework drives high-reuse into the *core* so that leveraging it on the *edges* becomes a very consistent experience.

Over a decade ago I suffered through the malaise of installing a product that purported to be a data warehouse in-a-box. It would slice-and-dice metadata into a data *mart*, not a data warehouse, so lots of stuff was missing that our client did not expect to purchase. Not only that, but in their rush to market they "missed a few things" that make such endeavors successful. Whether they missed them by lack of experience or lack of product maturity is immaterial, because we felt the pain on day one.

This is why I approach the in-a-box offerings with some degree of skepticism. Our company promotes a framework as a set of solution accelerators. They accelerate *us*, not the folks who work for our client, in rolling out a Netezza-centric solution. No doubt our client counterparts could take over once the solution reaches a state of maturity, but not in between. This is because we don't expect the client to understand migration projects. Most of them will only execute one of them, and will not attempt to record their actions for posterity. Those of us who have done dozens and collectively hundreds of them, know all the pitfalls and opportunities and want as much automation and acceleration as possible. Things that our clients may see no value in, we see extraordinary value in.

And because these are accelerators, we arrive with the full intention of designing and implementing a custom *solution* with the accelerators providing wind at our back. It is therefore our *experience* that is standing up the environment, not an inflatable warehouse-in-a-box.

Which brings us to another sticky topic. When we arrive on site, we invariably meet those who have done it before (in a prior career life) or just have a "pretty good idea" as to what needs to happen and when. They may also have a "pretty good idea" of what kind of overall outcome to expect, and may have already sold this outcome internally to their principals. Lots of mixed messages floating around by the time we show up.

But without us ever showing up, the mixed messages continue and at some point the project must launch and it must be architected from a common mind. Whether this mind is an architectural committee or our resident super-guru, we have to decide how much rope to give them so that some accountability keeps everyone sane.

How does a warehouse-in-box fit into this model? Well, in committing to such a product we're by definition closing off all the arguments. Whatever the product can do, we can do. And whatever it can't, well, we'll have to work around it, won't we? In a framework/solution approach, the workarounds are minimized because customizations are right-sized into the core or into the implementation, but either way have a firm place in the solution, not a workaround, bolt-on or afterthought. Shrink-wrapped, warehouse-in-a-box offerings cannot do this, no matter what they claim.

In computer systems, everything is driven by a rule of some kind. We have network transportation rules, program execution rules, system management rules and this barely scratches the surface. The theme of all these rules is not completely obvious, so I will call it out here:

The theme of a rules-based system is to capture the expert knowledge of human minds, and reduce it to *mnemonics* (e.g. predefined, tokenized or parameterized metadata) such that a consuming process can act on the mnemonic to affect the same outcome as the human expert. We distill expert knowledge all the time. Even in small ways, if I ask someone to "open", this may not have enough context to provide a complete instruction. If I point to a door and say "open", the listener has enough context to act. Likewise in Texas, the word "touchdown" only has meaning in football and tornado warnings. In a military context, the word "tank" could mean an infantry attack vehicle or a container under an aircraft wing.

A framework is simply a formal, predefined *context*. Whether it's a framework for discussion, debate, litigation or athletic competition, the framework defines and encompasses concepts and presuppositions into a form that is mature enough to use simple, mnemonic tokens as a language base. In a framework, the *mnemonics are immersed in context already*. This allows us to issue simple collections of mnemonics (as rules), to affect wide, sweeping and complex operations with the expectation of consistent behavior and outcome.

The formal name for expert-systems comes from this very same concept, except that once one is steeped in expert systems for enough years, one realizes that expert systems are all around us, doing the work of the experts without their continuing presence.

How does this apply to us? In computer applications we will see repeating patterns, especially at the operational/infrastructure level, but also in how applications are tactically and internally managed and controlled. If we build an application that has start-to-finish monolithic functionality, we have not truly embraced the spirit of rules. But if we codify the operations into data-driven form, we have at least taken one step closer to a rules-driven application. We are then attempting to let the data (and metadata) steer the process and logical flow rather than doing it with hard-wired code. Is this simple to do? In fact, it is so simple to do that once we do it the first time, we will start basing everything on the same principles *and* we will start experiencing lift and productivity. We are on the way to building out a rules-driven framework, one that can adapt (or be easily adapted) to the shifting sands of business priorities.

However, while it is simple to do, it is not simple to test, extend and harden for production, nor is it easy to anticipate how developers and operators will want to interact with it. No one part is particularly difficult, and any given component is a simple part of a larger whole.

But it's not *easy*.

If it were easy, anyone could do it, and we'd be out of a job. So let's set some expectations here between what is simple, what is easy, and what is just too hard. It's counter-intuitive, so bear with me as we spot-check our nomenclature and definitions.

- **Simple**: Snapping parts together with minimal effort to control larger, more complex processes and the their outcomes
- **Simplification**: The development process of harnessing complexity and distilling into simpler interfaces
- **Simple-minded**: The notion that enterprise components do everything we need for them to do, even the most complex parts, without any effort on our part.
- **Engineering**: the process of bridging or working around an enterprise product's weaknesses to achieve desired outcomes.
- **Complexity**: the natural form of technology - if it's technical, it has complexity
- **Artificial complexity** - the unnatural form of technology - if a development process is out of control, or engineering and workarounds rule a solution, much of the attendant complexity is artificial. If we have lots of performance props that only exist because of the underpowered system, these would evaporate if we had more power.
- **Framework**: *Acknowledgement of the existence* of complexity, the need for simplicity, the danger of artificial complexity, and the focus of engineering into a deliberate, identifiable architecture that addresses all of it in manageable context.

In context of the above, these are inconsequential and perhaps even unidentifiable in smaller systems. Simple versus Complex - the distinction often washes away below certain size and volume thresholds. However, the larger and higher functioning the solution, the more these begin to matter, so much that ignoring them will lead toward debilitating inefficiency and the *lack* of controls we seek so desperately.

Case Study Short: On various forums where I am wont to virtually wander, a sentiment exists that people can pretty much solve any problem given the right this or that. But the naivete of these statements is clear when complexity rises or data volumes breach our system capacity. In fact, one could say that they built their systems with the inherent lack of scalability because they could never imagine needing the scale. Isn't this the same as someone building a road without anticipating that it would ever be overloaded with traffic? We would forgive the roadbuilder if it was twenty years prior to a large population influx. We would not tolerate such foolishness in the midst of growth and the ever-present need for more capacity.

Case Study Short: As an example of *simple*, an ETL developer had several flows pointing toward an Oracle database. He wanted to take a more systematic approach to the loading of the new Netezza machine, so chose to drive the ETL flows into flat files, which could easily be picked up by a more battle-hardened flat-file management system. It would then shepherd the files into the machine. His manager had other ideas, and told him to *keep it simple.*

So he pointed the ETL flows to the Netezza machine true point/click form. Once the load was finished, out of thirty million records only a hundred thousand of them loaded. *Where did the others go?* Investigating further, he found that the ETL tool considered itself as a separate, self-contained environment, likewise as it faced Netezza. If the Netezza machine had any special needs for loading data, it was Netezza's problem. So the developer acquired some additional ETL tool-supporting components to face the Netezza machine, but with no better outcome. Even after scrubbing the data with all his might, adding an additional layer of flow control, a larger portion of the data loaded. But the problem was inherently in the flaky interface between the ETL tool and the Netezza machine. If he simply dropped the files to disk and let the file manager pick them up, the files loaded (the file manager could be configured to use nzload) without any issues at all. No drips, errors or blunders. But when attempting to interface the ETL tool to the machine, the poorly implemented protocol controls were the ETL tool's undoing. It was attempting to use a simple ODBC interface, but wasn't harnessing it all that well.

Okay, so which one of these turned out to be the simplest approach? When workarounds and engineering are required to achieve a relatively simple result, we're not moving toward simplicity. We are adding artificial complexity. In short, "simply" pointing the ETL tool toward the Netezza machine with the assumption that the ETL tool could pull it off, sounded simple, but was really simple-*minded.* Some ETL tool harness databases correctly, other do not and for the most part don't really expect to have to answer as to *why* they don't. They are the vendor for one environment and the database is its own environment. Bridging the environment is an interface problem and nothing more. They will claim that they support the *interface*, but harnessing the *database itself* is not their problem.

Case Study Short: Upon arriving on site, the principals said that they had "a lot problems" with the Netezza machine, and "it wasn't doing" what they thought it would, or should. The loading is so slow, lamented one, and the box is tied up with the loading, said another, so it never comes up for air. Yet another said, we get a lot of data loss, the inserts and loads pile on top of each other and some of them never complete.

Upon closer examination, we found that the information architects had plugged continuous components into the Netezza machine, trickle-feeding it with data like they did all their other databases. After all, connecting it up only took a few days and data was flowing. Once the first flow was connected, they pointed another thirty or so towards it, eventually rising into the multiple hundreds of connections inserting data at every moment of the day. The machine was almost shaking with the influx of the information.

I've documented that the latest S-blade configuration (and Mustang predecessors) are not transactional machines. Loads of *one gigabyte or more* are optimal load sizes, because each load has a finite cost. Incurring the finite cost on *many* smaller loads is worse than incurring the finite cost less frequently for larger loads.

So we embraced a best practice (another example of one of these is in Underground) and throttled the load activity in to a collection mechanism. Did this increase the complexity of the solution? Actually the *complexity* was already in play with all these hundreds of load operations, because the principals could not see the forest for the trees, so to speak, and the root cause was obfuscated by the frenetic activity. Only an objective, deliberate harness could bring it under the necessary control. This is a common occurrence in systems of scale, so we need the extra layer of diligence to guard against such problems.

Case Study Short: As an example of artificial complexity, we migrated a system from an operational Teradata environment into the Netezza machine. About halfway through the project, a subtle effect in the data arose. The data arriving from the sources had disconnected primary/foreign keys that had never been corrected. Rather than correcting the keys in the faulty transactional records, or taking such records offline for remediation, the original architects had moved toward manufacturing dummy dimensional data so that the transactional data would have a place to join. Both approaches have a place, somewhat, but the simple fact was that over time, the owners of the Teradata machine had allowed these bad connections to continue unchecked and unchallenged, to the point that when we executed the migration, we discovered over thirty thousand missing keys, leading to over one billion disconnects in the data.

Regardless of whether we can manufacture fake data or correct faulty data, didn't it alarm *someone* that almost a third of their data store was artificially manufactured data? At some point, someone had to make a call to go clean all this up. What happens when half the data is manufactured, or when two-thirds of the data is manufactured? Where does the manufactured data end and the real data *begin?* I can tell you, and you probably won't like the answer.

In signal processing systems, noise is always a problem. Whether video, sound, infrared or any other kind of signal, noise-*reduction* makes the rest of the signal clearer. The common cell/wireless phone has built-in noise reduction to clarify the telephone experience. In all this, how much noise would be acceptable for a *text* message? One in three characters? One in ten? How many dropped calls are acceptable for a cell phone? One in three? One in ten? How about the voice signal on the phone? Is it okay if the signal is one-third static? One tenth?

We can see that noise in the data is not only unacceptable, most people have a much stricter tolerance threshold than we'd like to think. Perfection, for some, is the goal. Excellence, for others, is the only *achievable* goal. What is the difference? There is no such thing as a perfect computer system. However, excellence is a function of upward continuum, and is a series of achievable goals that never presume perfection. That's your free philosophy of the day!

Back to noise. When the noise level in any system reaches a certain threshold, the system can no longer distinguish between noise and the real signal. One could imagine that this threshold is reached at the fifty percent mark (if half the data is noise, *which* half is noise and which half is real?). But it's not that simple, There has to be enough real data in the signal to offset the noise, or to avoid attributing the label of noise to our real data. This signal-to-noise ratio is different for many analog systems, but for database environments, especially those that deal with money in one form or another, the tolerance is always the same.

Exactly zero.

Is this tolerance achievable? In many cases yes. In others we have a tolerable fuzziness because it is correctable data. In one internet advertising firm, the front-line servers spend a lot of time scrubbing for robot-generated signals, deliberately fraudulent signals and other noise before it ever entered the data processing domain. Eliminating the noise clarified and simplified the downstream processes.

The point is, kill the noise as close to the source as possible. Trying to fix it with data-rigging in the downstream, or even in the reports, invites engineering, workaround, artificial complexity and will eventually cause our precious environment to so functionally harden that we can never add any significant functions or capabilities anymore. But in the aforementioned environment, one could imagine that ten percent is at least three times better than *thirty* percent! With that level of noise in the data, nothing is trustworthy. All of it may as well be junk.

This is why a rules-driven tool or business model is effective in tamping down the brush fires and maintaining control of information at a high level - and detail data at the lowest level. A rules-driven model takes us way out and above the level of hard-coded application logic. We harness the noise on our own terms and push the information through with strength and clarity, not faith and hope.

But make no mistake: Simplification is not easy to implement. It is imperative to make things easier for downstream work activities, such as enhancement, troubleshooting, operations and administration. These things are rarely at the forefront of a developer's mind when putting together a solution. We can embrace this simple fact by separately harnessing these issues (e.g. a rules-driven model) and requiring the developers to interface to it with simple rules, because we have simplified their interface to the system. Is this easy to do? Of course not. Is it simple to implement? Surprisingly so. Will developers like it?

As a trainer for Ab Initio many years ago, I noticed an interesting, consistent trend among the students. The ones who knew and understood *data* could zip through the class and point-click their way to success. One ones who were more technical, like DBAs, spent more time analyzing the problem in terms of their own technical knowledge base, not in terms of a business application problem.

We have to get the developers out of the weeds of the technical implementation, and into the zone of solving the business problem. If we as architects embrace this approach, we will have some work cut out for us in simplifying, even over-simplifying the developer's interface to the environment. The natural fallout of this will be exactly what we want. The developer works out the rules and the architecture converts it to flows and generated SQL statements. Our developers are now officially out of the hand-coded SQL business and into the application problem solving business. And they won't trouble themselves for operational integrity, metadata capture, ease of troubleshooting or maintenance and administration, because we'll solve all that stuff in one place.

So see, it's not *easy* to simplify things for others. It's *easy* to do it the soft way, allow workarounds to rule the environment, artificial complexity to creep in, and generally allow mayhem to begin making our lives miserable.

This old adage attributes this sort of outcome to slothful people. Now, I know that the average tech folk work long hours and the word "slothful" is hardly a proper moniker. But in the case of the adage, it was addressing "soft" choices. If we continuously make-soft-choices for our development and architecture, the outcome is the same as if we let-it-go through deliberately foregoing the work at all. One is passive sloth, one is active sloth. But again, it is impossible for me to in good conscience label any technical person I know with something as provocative as "sloth" - but I do know a number of hard-working people that have occasionally allowed *soft* choices to creep into the mix. Those soft choices were simply compromises that ultimately blossomed into problems that, in systems of scale, became areas to remediate.

A number of years ago a business guru made the impassioned appeal for the pervasive use of rules-driven engines to capture expert knowledge from the Subject Matter Experts. The data warehousing industry stepped up to the plate with a compromise, that of putting some business rules and metadata around the problem. The business metadata then became the defacto rules through which code would be produced, but did not tie the code to the dynamics of the business metadata. If the metadata changed, the coders would be commissioned to realign the code with the metadata.

Then came the bifurcation between the "design time" metadata and the "as executed" metadata. The "as executed" metadata was merely intriguing to technologists, but analysts locked onto the value of it. They didn't have any problems with declaring that the "as designed" metadata was being derived from the as-executed metadata, but they still wanted their hands on the "as executed". Not only that, they wanted it *versioned* as well. All this is a little abstract, so I'll give an example.

Analyst A runs a report on Monday morning and sees that one of the numbers seems a bit off. As he examines further, nothing is adding up to be what it's *supposed* to be. He has the expert knowledge to know for sure. So he pops open his metadata browser to find the definition of the column in question. From here he wants to browse data *lineage*. That is go backwards in time to find the columns that fed this questionable data, including browsing the join and filtration logic. Sort of like having the target columns on the right hand side of a grid, the source columns (or rules) on the left hand side, and the join/filter logic displayed at the bottom. The Analyst now has the option to click on any given column to take him backwards to the prior transform, and prior still until he gets to a point where he observes that the transform has been recently modified. He now wants to see the prior version of the transform side-by-side with the current one, or in a fancier model, overlaid on each other with color coding so the differences are obvious.

He now sees that a column was not handled correctly in the most recent version, and somehow this escaped the sieve of regression testing applied to it.

Could as-designed metadata assist with such a mission if it was not at least directly tied to as-executed model? In the Ab Initio EME, the data lineage appears just this way, directly and intimately tying together the as-designed and as-executed models. Of course, that's Ab Initio, a self-contained purveyor of its own syntactical programming language and structural definitions (DML) and directly integrated to the graphical environment used by developers. In Ab Initio, the design and the development take place at the same time, so there is no loss of sync. I am not suggesting that Ab Initio is the only one doing this, but they do it so well that customers ask for their metadata engine without desiring the remainder of their offerings. So well-rounded and well-executed is their metadata approach.

But *we* don't have Ab Initio's language-base to construct our transform inside. We have to do it with SQL For best results, *generated* SQL rather than its pernicious hand-crafted form. Does Ab Initio generate SQL? No it does not. Does it *harness* SQL so we can perform lineage? In part, but not for the *hundreds* of Netezza-facing SQL-Transforms we need it to harness, and not in transition-control pipeline model so that we can manage it as a flow. Not a gaggle of standalone SQL components.

Rules, then, still have a critical role in our programming protocol, but the language around Business Rule is so tightly coupled to SQL that when we use the term Rule, people automatically think about the one-liner of SQL that lies between each source column(s) and their respective target column. Rules for our purposes, are those things which capture more than just business knowledge, but operational processes, design patterns, reusable constructs and more.

In a framework, *rules are a structured form of the framework's recognized mnemonics*. They are more than a glyph on the Underground catacomb walls. They simplify a description of behavior between structures and processes.

The more we use rules to drive the activation of our code, the more adaptive our code becomes. If our rules are interchangeable forms of data and metadata, we have the upward synergy for a system that can rapidly adapt to change with minimal impact to code. We call it a framework.

A framework organizes a common configuration based on known environmental rules and resources, coupled with known application needs and resources. That's a little bit abstract, so let's look at a few of the things that a healthy framework needs to support (in a data warehouse paradigm).

A Netezza machine is an input/processing/output machine. It is a simple and elegant model. Many people use the machine as a store-and-query / load-and-query device with no desire to perform any additional data processing on the inside. If we are one of those folks, this chapter is probably not for us. Otherwise, we are open to embracing an approach that will transform more than just our data. It will transform how we solve problems and the steps we take to solve them. It will simplify the complex.

But it will not be easy, in this sense: When standing up a new Netezza machine, people have a lot in mind, and a lot at stake, for moving their designated solutions onto it. Many times it's a new solution, but most of the time it's a migration. I delineated in Underground what to expect with a migration project. But the point is this: the process of standing up either one of them, is transformational for many facets of the environment, including the people, operations, development, testing, deployment and how the project is managed overall. And for the record, it's okay to make mistakes during this period, because the Netezza machine's power can make up for mistakes. What it cannot make up for, are glaring inconsistencies in project management, architectural approach and expectations on development and testing. With flaws in any of these, they are likely institutionalized flaws that must be overcome with time, and perhaps with some growing pains.

This transformational process and outcome runs on different tracks for different people.

Case Study Short: One of the speakers at the 2009 Enzee Roadshow Conferences said that she was very satisfied with the final outcome of the project and it had certainly met and exceeded all of her expectations. But her story was one of delivering in the midst of people who did not want to change. The transformation was underway even before the machines arrived. People thought they would not have a job if they did not accede to a future with Netezza. Some simply refused to participate or even assist, while others dusted off their resumes and hit the road. Undaunted, she muscled through these transformational pains, with the power and reliability of the Mustangs helping her through the valley, eventually to a mountaintop experience that was transformational to her career and the prospects of her company. Those who once nay-sayed her were buying her lunch rather than trying to eat it. Those who had written her off were now writing her in, to their appointment books and future projects. The world was now her oyster. She received a job offer from another firm and freely admitted that if it had been just six months prior, she would have taken the offer, probably for less money.

So time changes things, but Netezza over time is *transformational*.

What does all this have to do with Rules? In the bowels of our operational environments is a solution that wants to get out. It will probably be the one we choose to convert into Netezza. It was ensconced over time with care and feeding and probably not documented very well, and practically all of the *rules* for its operation and logic are tribal knowledge.

Now is the time to take that tribal knowledge, the Subject Matter Expert material, and reduce it to rules. Not just business metadata in a spreadsheet growing stale, but tangible, actionable rules that are part of the coded environment and serve to steer process and logic *at run-time*. Is this hard to do? After the fact, undoubtedly but not impossible. I have written elsewhere that the design patterns we see in a first implementation appear as wispy ghosts, or like a flashlight that gives us two seconds of light every ten seconds. The patterns *emerge from* the application, usually in latent form, so we refactor them into reusable components But we sometimes can't get a good picture of what's going on until the application is finished and all the cylinders are firing.

Or can we? In a data warehouse application, tons of stuff will be a common substrate. Acquiescing these aspects to hard-coding is just foolish. But what of something like, say, distribution key mapping? We might not be able to tell what the distribution keys will be when we first get started, but we can certainly drive their selection and maintenance with rules. Here's an example:

Let's say we accept a file that contains the data model in Create-DDL form. We could handcraft this model in a script, or we could receive the model from ERWin, ERStudio or any number of other modeling tools. All of the tables for the application are in the file. I mentioned elsewhere some assets we build from this table as part of analyzing it to make it ready for repeatable installation. One of the things I did not mention was how we deal with several particularly useful aspects of table creation. We expect the DBAs to keep up with application-related columns, but not always the following aspects:

- Operational/infrastructure columns - namely the audit_id, warehouse_id and current_ind, discussed elsewhere in this book.
- Distribution key - some tables will have one, some won't. The default model will always

use random. Rules can drive the other ones.

- Hash ID and Keys - a major benefit of the SQL toolkit (ask for it by name from your product engineer) is the Hash8() function, which we can directly leverage to create BIGINT identifiers. When we hash, we get the same value for the same string key, so we can use them as unique identifiers, for deduplication and yes, as distribution keys
- Applied constraints and metadata (primary/foreign keys, nullable columns, comments etc) and how we enforce these with the application (because Netezza does not)
- Data domain control (installing and un-installing data DDL by subject matter)
- Manufacture of transient intermediate assets, including tables, synonyms and views for the sole purpose of data processing
- Error processing (e.g. constraint violations) and error remediation

For legacy systems (where we may be migrating or sourcing *from*), we don't have access to anything akin to hashes, distributions or even a formal ERWin/ERStudio model. Many of the concepts we are about to implement are entirely foreign to those systems and sources. It is incumbent upon us therefore, to provide a minimal, rules-driven substrate so that we can apply consistent rules to those sources without directly addressing their shortcomings application-style (manually modifying their DDL).

Distribution rules

We keep a simple metadata file that we name for the target database, such as rep.config or rpt. config.

```
[DISTRIBUTION]
TABLE=vendor COLUMN=vendor_id
TABLE=customer COLUMN=customer_id
```

Note that in the above rules file, named for the database, can contains rules for all tables, all rule types. Our rules compiler scans this file once and produces the various assets. This way we can maintain the rules in one place, but deploy them for fast access later. We don't want to scan this rules file on-demand, so we compile it into fast-access files that we can easily execute to export and expose their contents. We'll produce a loadable file that has the following notations in it, and once loaded, are callable from anywhere in the runtime.

```
rep_customer_distribution() { echo customer_id }
rep_vendor_distribution() {echo vendor_id }
```

Note the "overloaded" nature of those function calls (looks a lot like an object-oriented interface. Now from anywhere in the runtime, wherever I have need to capture the distribution for the table I have in hand, I simply call:

```
mcall=$(s_tolower ${working_database}_${working_table}_distribution )
mdistkey=$( ${mcall} )
```

If my current working database is the REP, and the current table in hand is the CUSTOMER table, the value of `mdistkey` is now `customer_id`.

The rules file should support various predefined operations key=value pairs, which are in turn compiled to produce, in this case, a single distribution map for the database. Why would we keep this separate from the modeling tool? For many cases of adapting sources into the machine, and for development and adaptability, it is very difficult to maintain these in the data modeling to. And some data modeling tools don't recognize the distribution key at all. For example, we may be getting the DDL directly from the catalog (of an upstream source system that only exists in the catalog). If it's inside an Oracle or Teradata machine, we don't get the distribution key from the DDL. So installing it via rules is the most effective and manageable way.

This is more than a matter of convenience. The ability to immediately access the table's distribution key without accessing the Netezza catalog, will remove any drag such a catalog access would create. As the applications grow and the catalog assets increase, we really want to maintain our alignment with it, but not constantly hammer it with queries.

Hash Keys and Hash IDs

The NPS SQL Toolkit has a function called hash8() that will apply a hash algorithm to a string, and will return the same hash value (as a big integer) each time it's called. For clarity, if I were to call hash8('David Birmingham') today, I will get the same resulting value tomorrow and forever. It obviates the cross-reference tables we might use for the same purpose (e.g. surrogates from natural keys). I have seen the hash applied to very large strings with no collisions, so it makes for a consistent way to convert a natural key, even multi-column natural keys, to a single consistent surrogate value.

This effectively creates a data [2]fingerprint, something we can use to uniquely identify the information in a manner than will be consistent across entities. For example if three key columns appear in one table and the same three in another, we can hash8() the three values and this will create the same hash value for common keys. We can now join and aggregate on this ID rather than on the three keys. Imagine if we had ten keys, or more? Hashing these into an integer simplifies the data model and makes navigation much easier and obvious.

The hash keys and IDs are more interesting because they appear in pairs and are applied along a continuum. We define the hash keys in the rules file, and companion hash ids are automatically constructed when the DDL is applied.

Lets say we have an intake table from the customers database, but the customer's uniqueness is defined by the system ID (we have multiple customer systems), the customer identifier for that system, and an internal identifier prescribed by the upstream source, three keys in all. When customers arrive from their various locations, we need all three keys to keep them in sync.

So we will have a database called INTK_CUSTOMER_MASTER containing all the tables we will ever need to support upstream customer information sources. We'll have entries in the database rule file like so:

```
[HASH KEYS]
TABLE=customer  COLUMN=hash_key1  FUNCTION="a.system_id||'@'||a.customer_id||'@'||a.
internal_id"
TABLE=customer COLUMN=hash_key2 FUNCTION="a.system_id||'@'||a.customer_id"
```

When the compiler runs, we'll parse the above and drive the distribution key into a generalized rule repository file.

```
intk_customer_master_customer_hash_key()  ·
{
COLUMN=$1
if [ $COLUMN = "HASH_KEY1" ]
then
echo "a.system_id||'@'||a.customer_id||'@'||a.internal_id"
elif [ $COLUMN = HASH_KEY2 ]
then
echo "a.system_id||'@'||a.customer_id"
fi
}
```

The above rules will also be applied to create column names in the CUSTOMER table whenever the DDL converter is applied. It will make the following:

```
HASH_KEY1 varchar(1000),
HASH_ID1 BIGINT,
HASH_KEY2 varchar(1000),
HASH_ID2 varchar BIGINT
```

So we can see that the HASH_ID fields are also added as companions to the HASH_KEY fields, using the same identifier suffix values as those on the hash key field.

Now upon the finalization of any data into a given database, our framework's finalization logic will leverage a finalization script that reads data from the staging table (or intermediate table that was just loaded). It will formulate a SQL statement to support the finalization, and while doing so will access the rules file above. If it detects hash keys in the DDL, this will prompt it to ask the file for the hashing rule. The finalization script will then *manufacture* the insert/select in the following manner:

```
insert into $INTK_CUSTOMER_MASTER_CUSTOMERS (
...
HASH_KEY1,
HASH_ID1,
HASH_KEY2,
HASH_ID2,
...
...
)
select
...
a.system_id||'@'||a.customer_id||'@'||a.internal_id ,
```

```
hash8(a.system_id||'@'||a.customer_id||'@'||a.internal_id ) .
a.system_id||'@'||a.customer_id ,
hash8(a.system_id||'@'||a.customer_id )
...
from $TEMP_CUSTOMERS a;
```

We could optionally perform a pre-finalization update operation to accomplish the same thing. I have seen cases where these kinds of keys are peppered throughout SQL and become very unwieldy to manage and keep in sync. But by putting them in these hash key rules, we have a one-stop shop that all processes access for a common instruction set.

Likewise, if we really wanted to leverage one of these as the distribution key, we would simply name the given hash_id column in the distribution map for the table. The columns would be added, the distribution set, and then later at run time the distribution values would be applied. But can we see how these things must happen in a certain, predefined order? Can I define the HASH_ID1 above as the distribution key, but allow it to remain null until populated with an update? Clearly not. We have to populate the hash id value before we can use it for distribution, otherwise we risk putting the data all-on-one-spu, because the distribution keys are all the same value - NULL.

We had another rather interesting situation at a customer site. They wanted some non-key values scrubbed to a default value, because the data on the source system was not supposed to come over to the target system. They didn't want to remove the possibility of taking it later, they just didn't have permission to take it now. This was not a problem for the production system, only the development environment. Ahh, well, we have a way to do this don't we? We simply add another rule to our common rules repository and it will work same way as above (e.g. when working on a given database, load its rules file. When the designated table appears, watch for its columns and if they appear, simply apply the default into the select statement for that column).

We had another need at a customer site where the primary/foreign key were not matching and were creating a lot of records in the exception processing tables. As it turned out, many of the keys had mixed case, but the Netezza machine does not perform case-insensitive matching. The only way to reconcile this would be to either put an "upper()" function into the final result of each one of the transforms, and only for the specific keys in question, or we could do like above. Put all of the tables and keys into a rules file, in our case INTK_VENDOR_MASTER.xfr.sh. It will contain entries like:

```
[TRANSFORM]
TABLE=VENDORS COLUMN=VENDOR_ID FUNCTION=upper(vendor_id)
TABLE=VENDORS COLUMN=VENDOR_STATE FUNCTION=upper(vendor_state)
```

Hopefully the reader sees a pattern in all these rules - Table/Column /Function. We can pack a lot of power into those three little items. We can also extend for more patterns in other types of rules, but these are the core workhorses.

Thus when the finalization runs, it will wrap the entire pending result in the given transform. If no pending result has been applied (as in the case of the hash keys above), then its just a pass-through and it will be interpolated thusly:

```
insert into $REP_VENDORS
(
...
VENDOR_ID,
VENDOR_STATE,
...
) select
..
upper(VENDOR_ID),
upper(VENDOR_STATE),
..
from $TEMP_VENDORS ;
```

These are simple ways to apply rules almost like macros, but not really. A macro is executed as as substitutionary code or enrichment code. But here we are enriching the code itself (the SQL) as *metaprogramming*. Metaprogramming is only possible with rules. And it can only survive and thrive in a framework-based solution.

And we can also see how bash shell is perfectly suited to this kind of parameter substitution and metaprogramming without a lot of overhead or things getting lost in the mix.

I would continue to caution, however, to standardize the *types* of rules so that the DDL handlers can burst out a preliminary rules file with predefined sections and rule types. This allows us to jump right in, tweak it a bit to configure and customize it, then run our compiler to burst out the aforementioned assets. Does this sound like a lot of work?

Here's what we're trying to accomplish:

The data will flow from end to end in our system. But now we have another form of data, the metadata that flows from our modeling tool, into the catalog, and driving our control assets, columnar and table behavior, and generally supporting pattern-based activities that would be rather daunting without a means to plug in the automatic behaviors. We're still in the SQL zone, so rather than do it like the ETL tools do it (that is, require fully-formed SQL statements and then harness those) we will instead build rules from the catalog metadata that will in turn manufacture the SQL statements.

In this case, SQL statements flow *from* the metadata, not the other way around.

As noted in the beginning of the chapter, a framework provides a run-time context. Within this context we can load up rules which are simple mnemonics that only have run-time value in the framework's context. If the framework is set up to self-configure for its environment, the databases, the transforms and all the assets it will harness, then applying and activating these simplified mnemonics can deliver sweeping movements of application activity. We achieve the patterns of reuse that are otherwise elusive and we have a foundation upon which to build better, stronger applications over a longer duration.

CONSUMPTION POINT ARCHITECTURE

NOW WE SHALL FORAY into the heady realm of the reporting interfaces (and secondary operational interfaces). Do not fear, as I shall be your guide, and shall dissuade both beast and foul cur from impeding our voyage.

Here is our overarching consideration:

Don't let the tail wag the dog. The reporting (or consuming) system and its constraints or needs *should not dictate* the machine's internal implementation. Build the data model to align with the power-physics of the machine.

The consumers should be *adapted* to these data models, not the other way around.

A warehouse, most especially its ancillary consumption or reporting arteries, are requirements-driven, and the requirements drive *backwards* into the flows. We essentially have a number of requirements, the majority of them quite unfortunately unspoken. We have system, scaling, capacity, administrative, operational, performance and of course, data content requirements. We could even say that all the requirements *outside* of the data content requirements utterly eclipse data content by a factor of ten or more. If we ignore these, our system may be excellent at reporting, but it won't be as viable in operation.

The problem is, the report builders may sincerely believe that because the requirements are drivers, *so is the reporting tool*. This is entirely inaccurate.

Even though the reports are a driver, we have to think ahead. Sometimes *far* ahead. This is a journey that should be embarked upon by folks with updated maps. Those who have scratched out the *There be Dragons* scribble and replaced it with, *Been there, Done that*. We could elect to lurch along. However a robust reporting environment, especially at scales that will crush a mediocre implementation, requires a strong shepherd.

Anecdote: A friend tells me that one of his acquaintances had been driving on a wet road and slipped off into a ditch. Someone stopped to help him and advised that if he just gassed his car, it would ride down the ditch and up the other side, where he could drive on the grass until the next driveway some fifty feet away. It sounded like a plan, so he complied and drove his car deeper into the ditch. Nothing good comes of this story. He finally had to call a tow truck. If he'd been patient, the tow truck could have pulled him out with a common winch. But stuck deep in the ditch they needed bigger, more expensive equipment.

Case Study Short: Our team rolled out a system that had both operational and reporting re-

167

quirements. The original design called for an operational set of tables facing the demands of the operational back end. Then we rolled out a set of tables that took several of the largest tables and redeployed them on a different distribution key. The principals thought that these extra tables, comprising an additional several terabytes of space, were superfluous and a waste of space. We were told to back them out. Once the system arrived in a position where the reports could run, they were very slow. Unacceptably slow, in fact. Of course, if they had expressed their minimum time for a report turnaround prior to telling us to remove the additional tables, we would have had grounds to *defend the presence* of the tables.

Then something very predictable happened. Rather than go back to the original plan (back out of the ditch), people started driving deeper into the ditch, swarming around the machine to discover why it wasn't returning the reports in an acceptable time frame. We had run some tests with the reporting-table model with phenomenal results. It was more than ready for prime-time, but the "decision" to preserve those several terabytes (in a 100-terabyte system) was something they *fully intended to defend* while the engineers swarmed the machine.

So that was a lot of malaise that continued for many months after I had tied a bow on the operational back end and had moved to another client. This problem continued as they upgraded and shifted the data around in a futile attempt to make the machine do something other than what it was designed to do. The *operational* distribution was not suitable for the *reporting* usage, and did not allow the machine to leverage its full physics to support the reports.

Back to requirements - here is a clear case where an overarching requirement (minimum return time for a report) was unspoken. But once spoken, the focus of the project should have gotten behind the mission of making the reporting requirements the *driving* requirements. Instead, the project got behind the mission of defending a system-facing priority of *preserving storage space*, and swarming their internal engineers in an exercise of Sysiphean futility. One of the users rightly noted that they could buy a terabyte of space from Best Buy for a few hundred dollars. Whether this is the right way to regard it or not, the users saw that the whole database size was twenty terabytes on a system with one-hundred terabyte capacity.

Would *three more terabytes* kill ya?

Over a year later, they finally rolled out the reporting model in dimensional form, and solved all the reporting performance issues with a *single delivery*. If reporting *requirements* had been given the *proper weight*, the users would not have experienced the *actual wait,* in time to market.

Another requirement that is unspoken, is the need for the reporting environment to push things into the Netezza database, often for performance reasons but also for functional reasons like row/column management and complex windowing logic that the reporting system doesn't handle well, if at all. Another common request is a 'writeback' capability, that is the need of the user to run some reports, formulate some information and then write this back into the database as a query filter or other purpose. We don't want them writing data directly into the reporting database. Also that multiple user groups will have a need to share the reporting database but may have specific, user-centric needs for supporting data. What if we are soft-deleting data in the reporting database, tagging each deleted record with a special value? The reports would have to regard this value as a common filter in order to avoid accessing old data. Do we want to put these one-offs into the master database? No, we really don't, but what's the alternative?

Case Study Short: Upon implementing hundreds of SQL-transforms to affect a reporting outcome, the operational users informed us that their interfaces would no longer work. The data that had been backfilled from the prior system had been filled with null strings for many defaults, and their consumption environment had been programmed to depend on the presence of nulls in character-string fields. Unfortunately, our SQL-transforms, from intake all the way to the reporting hub, had been configured to rigorously zap null strings to empty strings. This was causing havoc in their consumption of the data. However, we could not convert these empty strings back to null strings or the SQL-transforms would break. Why is this?

In Netezza, whenever we concatenate strings with the double-pipe (a practice that was replete in our SQL-transform logic) if any of the values are null, it makes the whole string result null (this is ANSI-SQL behavior). Our alternative would be allow nulls into the strings, then to wrap a null-check on every single time we touched the data for SQL-transforms, meaning a wholesale rework and retest of all the existing logic. This seemed so untenable, and of course is anathema to the best practice of avoiding null values in the warehouse.

Existing (simple) transform logic: `Col1 || Col2 || Col3` (if any column is NULL, the entire result is null). Proposed: `nvl(Col1,'') || nvl(Col2,'') || nvl(Col3,'')` Do we *really* want to address hundreds of transforms, and countless thousands of columns, to re-wrap them with null checks? No, we didn't when we built them, we don't in the future, so we really need a better solution than this right now!

The solution was found in the simplicity of a consumption point. For this operational user, we formulated views that used special logic for each varchar field, converting empty strings to nulls on demand. This allowed the empty strings to remain in the database and keep the transforms intact, but also allowed their legacy interface to work as originally designed. Win-win.

The Consumption-Point, also called a proxy, is a separate database filled with views. It can have tables also, but even those tables will be accessed with views. Where do these views consume from? Largely the reporting database, but they could stretch out all over the machine if need be, to reference databases, our historical repository, even the intake databases. The point is to provide a one-stop-shop for the users to enter the system. This consolidates their specific needs and customizations into one place, provides a mechanism for security, and an abstraction of the reporting layer from the actual data. In short, we can expose as many or as few views as we like, not necessarily the whole world.

It also gives us the capacity to boost performance by tuning the views. We could also point any of them to a stored procedure for even more control and data power, transparent to the reporting layer. We can make wholesale changes to the underpinning logic and structures without destabilizing the structure seen by the report. These kinds of adaptations are simple and automatic when the reports never directly access the data.

We've seen cases where a product like Microstrategy was pointed to one consumption point while an operational system was pointed to another. The operational consumption point exposed only a handful of views, because this was all it needed.

Why do this? One of the most significant problems in reporting integration is the tight coupling of the reports to the data structures. Tightly coupling these will create several pernicious issues, namely that the data architects cannot be certain if any of the tables are being used, which ones and how often. They can check the query histories but this won't help them with stuff like annual, manual or intermittent access. Even for operational consumption, it is best to define a set of views that are the operational system's only point of contact with the database. This allows us to know exactly what operations are accessing which tables or assets, because they have been deliberately exposed. It then offers the architects the freedom to maintain, refactor and even redesign the underpinning data model without disrupting the consumer's experience.

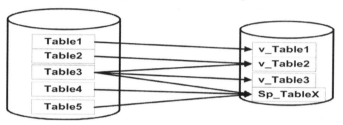

In the simplified depiction (above) the tables where data resides (left) are consumed by the various views, stored procedures and UDFs in the consumption point (right). The consumption point is a "proxy" database, containing only consumption structures. We may choose to consume one or more databases or storage types, as these are immaterial to the consumption point. We now have the freedom to alter the structure and behavior of the data model or the reporting model independently, without tightly coupling the two.

This allows the architects to create reporting *adaptations*, not the least of which are stored procedures or UDFs to support reporting data needs, but also to accept formulated views from the reporting team. Often the reporting team know exactly what they want and can create a view to make it happen. They submit this view to the architects, eventually becoming part of the standard DDL installation for the implementation. In addition, we may see needs for column-level or row-level security that are difficult to enforce in the reporting layer, and can be installed as part of the view logic for the given table(s) on a case-by-case. The flexibility of installation, maintenance and management are (at least) the goals.

Considering write-back or localized tables to support specific customizations for the consumption point, now we have a place for them and not just a placeholder in another master database. If many custom consumption points are in play, and each of them has direct access to the master reporting store, then we also have to put these localized custom tables into the master store. Once this happens, the clutter of these tables starts to rise, along with the tedium of their administration in context of all the other master tables. In addition, the users of the other consumption points may see and start to leverage those tables for their own use. It's hard to deny them access to an available table. Once they develop a dependency on it, a table that was originally designed and owned by one consumption point user group now no longer has the freedom to change it to meet their needs. They will then request another set of tables or another implementation, and this is probably not what we intended at all.

In another vein, in the consumption point we will have at least one proxy view for each table that performs a simple select-all. What if we have a soft-delete indicator that is used instead of actually deleting the records? No worries, the Select statement in the view can transparently regard this, or any other filter value to make these things transparent. But what if the default view doesn't do what we want? We just change the view with an override view. How does this work? The reporting developers formulate the view, and for that matter any other one-off views that they find useful, and provide them as DDL metadata. This is then merged into the implementation process for automatic installation.

The most interesting part of this approach in Netezza, is the ability to reformulate an existing table into yet another table of the identical structure, except on a *different* distribution key. If one consumption point uses the default distribution while two others each use a different distribution key, these are easily accommodated with the consumption point approach. We simply formulate additional tables and then each consumption point's view-definition consumes the table configured for it. Thus one consumer group does not have to settle for a poor experience simply because they require a different distribution model than the other consumers.

View Kung Fu - Reporting Adaptations

In keeping with the above discussion, our BI folks will invariably claim that a given default view is not good enough, and want to enhance it. Often this results in highly efficient hybrid view that gives us exactly what we want with minimal overhead. This activity is in the realm of a **reporting adaptation**. That is, the standard approach doesn't work for some scenarios so we need to accommodate an exceptional case. Of course, there's no guarantee that even a hybrid view will do the trick. We may need to leverage precalculated values in the table.

We also might need to use a UDX or a stored procedure. When Underground was published, stored procs were not available. Now we see them as very powerful reporting adaptations (more on this later). By using a stored procedure for the exceptional case, we get the best of all worlds.

Either way the views, underpinning tables and even the stored procedures should exist largely as select-and-consume interfaces.

If we treat views as *objects*, we will be tempted to *nest* them. We eventually run into a snag, primarily in the maintenance or update of the view. We will tweak it here or there and put it to bed. Then do this again, and again, and like good object-modeling folk we will see some reusability in that view logic. Rather than attempting to create each view from scratch, we will *nest* the views, and so begins the sad tale of performance malaise.

Netezza views should not be regarded as objects, at least not in the common sense. This is because a view can oversee access to billions of records, so "just including it" in another view or even as part of an inline join, can invite a world of hurt to our query performance. In addition, exposing such views to the BI tool gives it permission to nest or join them in any fashion they choose. This too is a bane of large-scale reporting. I cannot count how many of these nested-view scenarios I've had to tease apart and untangle, sometimes only to return and find they have implemented more! Where does it end?

For clarity, a view provides us with a single SQL statement and a join/where-clause. We can roll a lot of functionality into a view, so why *wouldn't* we want to mix-and-match views to get the right functional effect? Well, that's just the problem. *Functional* and *scalable* are feuding step-sisters who don't like each other very much. If we get something working just right but it cannot scale, we will curse the machine. If we can scale but cannot achieve the desired functionality, then what the heck good are ya?

Trust me, there is a balance here. In a prior chapter I noted the need for rules-based metadata. SQL-generation based on those rules is the best way to control and deploy correctly formed and properly scaled queries. The BI tools do it don't they? We point/click and add some salt here and there, and boom! SQL just drops in our lap, all a-glitter and ready for action.

Another factor is that we'll get to the point where the BI tool cannot formulate the right query. Perhaps it is RDBMS-aware and expects index structures. Netezza doesn't dance on that floor. A pernicious part of integrating BI tools is just that: expecting that it will know all it needs to know to interact with the Netezza MPP. As we may painfully discover, this a false expectation.

Case in point, we might have a very creative intersection table between two large fact tables, and we can formulate a query that will browse the information-we-want in mere seconds. Then we plug in our BI tool and ask it to manufacture a query to do the same thing, but it struggles. Now we have to make a call: do we deploy the BI tool in the hopes that later product releases will resolve this, or do we install a view or stored procedure that *adapts* the BI tool to our data model, and then wait for the BI tool to get better in a later product release? We can always toss the adaptation when our BI tool gets better, but we cannot allow our user-experience to languish until then.

Netezza views are great in that they project their metadata, and likewise only project the columns requested in a consuming query, not all of the columns named in the view. This takes the burden off the BI tool to know more than it has to, but also exposes our table to BI tool mayhem if the tool cannot leverage the view correctly.

Let's divide the types of views into two loosely defined buckets, selected largely based on scalability. The simple view accesses only one table. The complex view joins two or more tables to get the answer. Both of them, however can oversee a result that is potentially in the billions of records, so we have to exercise care in their deployment. It is harder to misuse a simple view, but the BI tools seem to find a way.

The problem with a complex view, is that one or more of the join tables could themselves be views. Under this, we might find even more tables or views in play. I've seen views nested more than ten levels deep, but whether deep or shallow they carry a very common problem with them: that is expecting the views to behave as objects. You know, just drop a view into the join, it already knows what to do. *Functionally.*

But all this will tend to confuse or at least set aside the Netezza optimizer as it attempts to slog through the view-chain to stabilize the query. Are we saying that a view can *only* join tables and not views? No, we're saying that a view *should* only join tables and not other views. The immediate objection to this assertion is that many queries share logic with other queries, so a view helps to encapsulate that logic.

Encapsulate eh? That's an object-oriented word, and *these* views are *not* objects. They are facades representing billions of rows of data, not reusable, inheritable objects. In essence, they are *select-and-consume* resources. No nesting, no joining, just select-and-consume, and this drives some folks crazy.

But let's cut to the chase. We *want* to leverage object-oriented principles of reuse, inheritance and encapsulation, but we absolutely *cannot* allow this to be implemented with nested views or views nested in a master join. The risk of a runaway query or simply blowing the optimizer's mind is ever-present and will ultimately cause grown men to cry like little girls when the queries just-won't-behave. Okay, maybe not like little girls, but cry nonetheless.

Our main enemy here is Transactional Thinking. That is, the notion that we can install nested (inherited) views because they handle transactions-at-a-time anyhow and any given instance of them will have a negligible performance problem - is completely washed away when dealing with multi-billion-row scales on a Netezza platform. It's not a transactional platform, so each view potentially initiates a *full* table scan. Multiply these nested upon nested views and we have nested tables scans - sometimes several separate scans on the same table. Which is more efficient, to look at a multi-billion row table once, or multiple times?

Case Study Short: One customer had a query that started running very slow one day. We went through a process of discovery to find out what had changed. Seems that a new version of an exist-ing view had been installed, and the bad query was consuming this view deep under the covers. The bad query and view were both accessing one of the largest tables in the database, the bad query was now scanning the big table *twice*, taking a double-hit on the master query itself. Even worse, the changed view did not leverage the big table's zone maps or its distribution key. So a change in one place dramatically affected unchanged functionality of a master query. These things can take weeks to peel back the layers to discover.

Because we are embracing solutions of extraordinary scale, dynamic objects have a propen-sity to lose performance integrity over time. What worked yesterday may not work today, so we have to tune it. Netezza is so efficient that this tuning necessity may not arise for years after the implementation. (In one case, *four* years afterward). By that time, the knowledge of the system's dependencies are not fresh on everyone's mind, so it is easy to make a spot-fix on the view and deploy it. In so doing, we may create a cascading effect for all the other places that consume the view (with the expectation of original behavior).

In short, the latent nested view architecture is a minefield. We should not implement it because it creates trouble from day one, even though nobody has stepped on mine just yet.

Case Study Short: At one customer site we had to sift through six levels of view logic to find the performance problem. The customer wanted to know what they should do to fix the problem, but "the problem" was in the overall implementation and the *nested views*, not the one bad view, or for that matter, the recent performance symptoms of a minefield implementation.

Views can behave as traditional objects if they are single-table views or they leverage addi-tional tables that are small and inconsequential to performance. We should not include a big-fat table in a view as part of a performance boosting strategy unless we can designate that the view is in fact a standalone entry point and not something that can arbitrarily participate in the JOIN clause of another master query. Why is this? Invariably we will forget the complexity of the view and then attempt to join it in another operation. For a BI tool, this could be highly problematic as well, because a view that was once simple could spontaneously go complex, and if it affects performance, we'll be pulling our hair out to find the problem - through what reduces to a scavenger hunt, or worse, a submarine hunt.

As an aside here, I am not decrying Netezza's inabilities, because these aspects pervade all non-traditional database systems. However, *BI tools* are specifically configured and optimized for traditional database interaction. It's their bread-and-butter marketplace position and they don't see a need to invest otherwise. This is why we need a consumption point, to adapt them to the machine rather than let the tool drive architectural decisions in the data model. I mentioned earlier that Microstrategy has an affinity for snowflakes. Good for them, but we'll need to adapt this affinity rather than architecturally align with it.

That said, many BI tools simply choke on automatically forming a "complex" Netezza query because there is an implicit assumption of indexes via primary keys, and if these don't exist, the BI tool does the best it can, which in many cases is the least-common-denominator of a query structure. This this doesn't play well on the SPUs for large-scale queries. I cannot count how many times I've seen a convoluted query that we just *de*-engineered and simplified, and ran an order-of-magnitude faster than the one conjured by the BI tool, yet nothing the tool folks could do seemed to make the BI tool form it the same way. To the rescue: a view that did the right thing - and that was that.

What's that? Putting together a canned view diminishes the flexibility of the query? Only marginally, and since we're dealing with billions of rows, we don't have much runway for "ultimate" flexibility anyhow. The larger the datasets, the more we need to make sure the queries are as efficiently formed as possible. And since this means as *simply* formed as possible, we're not talking about BI Tool query engineering, but query *de*-engineering[1].

To avoid pain and injury, don't treat all views the same. If we have a complex view, we should tune and designate it as standalone. No matter how much we like its results, it is better not to just arbitrarily include it in another join. The primary reason being: most views are not set up to regard a distribution. So when we include it with another join, the resolution of distribution might take the form of least-performing, lowest-denominator. We don't want that.

One alternative, oddly, is to CTAS/execute such a view in context and insert its data into a temporary table, then use the temporary table in the master join. This affords us the option to (a) leverage the view's normally small output (b) preserve the distribution, (c) align distribution to the next operation (d) simplify the implementation. Of course, the BI tool may not support this, or may support it in an inefficient fashion. Most of the major BI tools will accommodate advanced scenarios, so get your product support rep on the wire and have a heart-to-heart.

Yet another alternative is to use the view like an in-line view, except in the where-clause in correlated sub-query. This can often take the form of a where-not-exists clause or the like and can also be very efficient.

Another alternative is to break apart the view's logic and assimilate it into the larger view so that all logic is preserved. But we'll be maintaining that logic in two places, right? Not necessarily. We have a lot of view DDL executables that do not directly spawn from a modeling tool. Several of those being in BASH script, which provides for parameterization of logic through rules.

If we put the logic into a rule, then produce the views by including the rule-based logic, we will maintain the core logic in one place (the rule) but actually deploy two views that leverage it exactly the same. They are not sharing a view, but the *same rules* that create the view.

This is essentially what happens under the covers with many object-oriented environments anyhow. Multiple objects will consume another class and deploy an instance that *includes* that class (like a macro) rather than consumes that class (like another object), so this approach embraces that inheritance pattern. Not in the dynamic run-time of the view, but in the view's initial DDL-level deployment.

```
MYLOGIC="
a.limit1 between 50 and 60 and
a.limit2 between 1000 and 50000 and
a.tran_amt < 10000 and
b.employee_id <> 9999
"

 view1="create view view1 as select col1, col2, col3 from mytable a where $MYLOGIC ;"
 view2="create view view2 as select col1, col2, col4 from mytable a join yourtable b
on a.id = b.id where a.col1 = b.col1 and $MYLOGIC ;"
```

If our modeling tool supports this capability as part of its functionality, we should leverage it before simply bolting a view into a join. If our modeling tool does not support it, this scripted DDL scenario is easy enough to formulate and leverage without a lot of overhead. The objective: two views that both behave as optimized joins sharing *the same logical rules*, rather than one view that contains nested views.

Either way, there is a theme here. Simply including the complex view as part of another join's logic as though it was a table is risky and can, even at the outset, offer up such bad performance as to be a non-starter. So a plain-vanilla practice should be to make the complex view behave in a standalone *query-and-consume* fashion by default. Make no assumptions that it is okay to arbitrarily include it in a larger query's join clause.

The further downside is that a de-facto join-with-a-view can work really well at the outset, but the scale of the data can catch up to the even the most robust of implementations, and wiring up the complex view dependencies creates a problem that will not scale, but will only become obvious over time (a minefield).

Case Study Short: One group invoked a standard for view naming conventions. The simple views would have no prefix at all, so they would look like tables to the casual user. Fair game and all that. The complex views were labeled as v_<viewname> as a cue to a user or report builder: *don't use it in the join of a larger query.*

We might think that if there was an implicit rule to avoid using anything "v_" prefix that people would play nicely. But not so, since our reporting users may have come from a RDBMS background where it's perfectly okay to mix views into the master query. *Awareness* of the standard is one thing, but actually *embracing* it is another. We cannot protect our systems from people who either don't know the rules, don't understand them, or cannot map their experiences from an RDBMS to an MPP.

So a suggestion here would be to name the view in a manner that is a departure from common view nomenclature. Calling it an sp_(NAME) might draw the ire of our admins who want stored procs named for what they are, and not obfuscate their names. But if our views are not *really* common views, and have caveats on their usage, we need a safer naming convention, one that aligns with the goal we are trying to achieve: that of adapting the BI tool to the MPP.

One group used a naming convention of "bi_<name>", while another used "rpt_<name>", and still another used the common acronym for their given BI tool. The point is to adopt a convention that is somewhat *unconventional*, so that those with conventional thinking are able to *transform* their thinking without finding themselves in a minefield.

Stored Procedures

In a typical RDBMS model, the stored procedure is a poorly executed form of SQL-transform. It either does set-based bulk (and not very well, being SMP-bound) or it does a cursor-based-transaction-at-a-time model that is likewise unscalable everywhere it's tried.

So we apply a reporting adaptation, that is the use of a stored procedure (or even a view, UDF or precalculated table value) that serve to assist the BI tool in serving up data in a timely manner. As noted prior, not all BI tools generate the right query combination(s) for Netezza, so we might need to give the tool's SQL generator a little boost by installing a view or stored procedure. The stored procedure is especially handy for multi-stage or multi-pass queries where the BI tool can't seem to optimize things the way we need.

Case Study Short: I wrote up a Gather 'Round the Grill essay on a particular encounter where the BI tool was pre-summarizing a large table to around a million rows of summary data. Then it performed filters on this result, then it performed the final summary, a result of some four-hundred rows. Of the many instances of this scenario we had to remediate, they had a common pattern: the BI tool was unable to understand the table's mechanics well enough to optimize a query.

I rewrote this chain of events by reversing it. We would first filter all the data we did not care about, and this resulted in several tens of thousands of rows, not the original lightly summarized one-million rows. With filters applied, we then summarized this into the same result as the first version. But the difference in performance was a radical time reduction.

If this is a mission-critical series of queries, we need to consider moving it into a stored procedure to execute the sequence in the inverted form. We get the boost we want and a transparent reporting adaptation (that we can easily toss once the BI tool can handle our truth).

However, all that said, I would still adjure people to build these things around a rules-base rather than code each one from scratch. For example, if we know that we need to put certain query logic into a stored procedure, then the infrastructure for construction and deployment of the stored procedure should be canned. It should then dovetail our specific queries into it, perhaps even reconstructing or reshaping them to fit the stored procedure context. But we should not be in the stored-procedure-coding business any more than we should be in the SQL-coding business or the view-coding business. All of our application-facing SQL statements, views and stored procedures should be the *outcome* of a factory-oriented process, not the starting point from which the application springs. Factories are easy to fix and extend. Hand-crafted SQL and supporting operations are not. Factories align with the architecture-centric approach. *Hand*-crafted applications are ultimately a one-trick pony.

RETRO-ROCKETS

IT'S BEEN A WHILE since I've seen anything contrasting architecture and application, so bear with me while I state some obvious truths and then get into the less obvious nuances, that is separating the application from the architecture so that we can be more agile.

If I were to enter various customer processing domains, I would find several different approaches to problem solving, especially where it concerns standing up "system" stuff like supporting utilities, and where it concerns application stuff like SQL or business metadata. In some locations, this is a hodge-podge, where in others it is well organized and sophisticated. In yet other places, they are moving toward the sophisticated model, vestiges of the past remain that are still running, aren't breaking, and nobody really cares about retrofitting. In short, they are putting their efforts where the heat is highest, and there's nothing wrong with that.

A purely application driven model will look and sound like this description from a colleague.

We deployed the ETL tool and its supporting utilities. Then we started tying together the flow to get data from the sources into the machine. From there we put together some additional SQL statements we wanted to execute after the data was in the box. This flow is similar to most of our other flows, runs on a daily basis and we haven't had much of an issue with it. Last month our directors told us of an initiative that will change our upstream data model and will affect our target model, although we can't be sure of the scope of the impact. The last time we went through this, we had to overhaul all of the flows and about the only thing we kept around was the connection hooks between the ETL tool and the target machine. We really could not salvage the rest of it, and it was just easier to rewrite it than to try retrofitting it. The reports to the users became rigid a long time ago. We just don't have the staff to allow the reporting environment to experience upheaval each time they need a new data point. The senior managers hate it, but the middle managers would rather have stable data that works rather than new metrics that don't. We have half a dozen data sources upstream that they currently load into spreadsheets and cross-integrate to the reports on their desktops.

An architecture-driven model will look and sound like this description from a colleague.

We are constantly hammered with new data types and data points. Once a year our managers re-negotiate contracts with our data vendors to get more, less or swap them out entirely. Our internal reporting folks run ad-hoc queries on the data stores, giving ideas to the report jockeys, who in turn press on us for data processing capabilities. Our reporting environment is like a beehive, and they change the reporting features practically by the week. We must have thousands of custom reports, but all of them are built on the same templates. I have to incorporate a brand new data source next week. If it goes as normal, I will have the new data source integrated and data into the machine before the weekend.

Oh that the above tale could be told across the fruited plain, but alas, most folks still build out their warehouse as an *application* rather than a living environment. Even those who want the living environment, still see the warehouse almost like an Application Service Provider-styled offering. Some may even defend it this way! But it still puts the whole warehouse inside the same monolithic development lifecycle, and cannot break free.

In Underground (Configuration Stuff) I gave a rundown of the contrast and context of doing things the application-way versus the architectural-way. I received a lot of feedback on that chapter, mainly that it told the right tale but they wanted more detail. So here we are, in the next round of details and I hope that this hits the right spot, or more of the right spots, anyhow.

In an architectural focus we have to see the application as *along for the ride*. I know we'll put a lot of work into standing up the application. What I would rather avoid is to have all that work be essentially throwaway when the next great thing comes along. Surely we can preserve *some* of it? The ideas that make the environment great are not in the application, but in the architecture supporting the application. If the two are commingled, we have no choice but to throw out the good with the bad.

So let's draw a circle now around the stuff we want to keep. And then whatever falls outside of it is fair game for replacement. Doesn't sound fair, does it? There are things we won't care to preserve and other things we will wish we had tackled in a way that let us preserve it. It's time to put all those things on the page now. On the next round, we might refine the page a bit more, but one thing is for sure, if we don't start putting things on the page, it's *all* fair game for replacement.

System Facing

We now have a Netezza machine in your hot little hands, have tasted the nectar of uncharted adrenalin and our brain is buzzing like we've had ten shots of Five-Hour Energy. So many ideas, so little time, and - wait - so little plan in place. Take a breather, lest thy molecules vibrate so fast that you sink into the earth.

Everything about the machine's power-plant is system-facing. Not to put too fine a point on it, but now we need to understand how to adapt our business models and ideas into the power grid. This is not particularly difficult since Netezza designed the machine to accept our relatively unvarnished data models as a starting point. Perhaps a crude starting point, but it will serve us well as a learning platform and we will refactor as required.

What's that, the boss wants the data model in place, perfect and ready before loading even one byte of data? Hmm, well I would say *get a new boss* but they are not so easy to trade-in. Give the boss a copy of this book, point him to this section of the chapter and make him read it out loud. Oh, well, that might not work either. Alas and forsooth, if the boss is that inexperienced, he or she will change their tune shortly. Netezza is all about transformation. Do not be alarmed. These things take a natural course. Take a deep breath. Heat is rising. It's all good.

Back to the system. Anytime we deliver a data warehouse, we have two core capability sets.

One faces the systems, that is our data processing systems, data storage, networks - everything we are about to experience with the machine belongs firmly in the realm of physics. The second core capability is the reporting environment, itself a system with a different set of priorities, but needs the agility to do battle with the users without destabilizing the back end.

Within these two cores, the former moves like the spinning of the earth. Slow, plodding, deliberate and consistent. The second moves like a spinning tornado without the attendant bending of physics or velocity. We need separate lifecycle controls for each. The first deals with capability, while the second deals with features and functions. Don't get them confused. Features are consumers of capabilities. We might see certain core capabilities in the reporting zone, and may see this same delineation in the reporting systems, where part of it is architectural and capability-driven, and the other part is very volatile and user-driven. This pattern repeats itself all over our computing environment and we need to pay attention to harnessing things where they make the most sense.

Harness Capabilities

And let the features *emerge* from them. The capabilities we're interested in, all face the system. More importantly, they will face the Netezza system and will be intimately commingled with the capabilities of the machine. Once we harness these, features will automatically emerge. For example, we want to process things in a flow, but we have to do it with shared-nothing SQL statements. Both the SQL-statement generation and the flow model are capabilities that we want to fortify and extend to support applications (features). Once harnessed, the flow becomes our capability published to the application. We then express features through the flow, effectively leveraging all the capabilities. Does this sound hard to do? It's not particularly difficult at the component level, but as noted in another section, the flow simplifies things for the application. Simpli*fication* is much harder to promulgate than simpl*icity*. Netezza has simplified parallel processing so that we can embrace the simplicity exposed to us. Our users and developers will want this simplicity aggregated to something more useful. A single SQL statement is simple. Flowing hundreds of them is not. But this is what we are charged with simplifying.

In any system, regardless of the quality of the design, developers tend to capture certain things so they don't have to revisit them. These are usually found in the form of patterns, but they are often not realized until the application effort is complete. Walt Disney said of *Snow White*, that they had learned so much about how to do things, and the do's and don'ts of animation, that they could then approach something more advanced, and produced *Pinnochio*. Whether we've seen it recently (with our kids) or just a long time ago, an adult can become almost mesmerized with the quality of the artwork alone. In the opening scene with Jiminy Cricket sitting atop a book, one could freeze that frame and get lost in the shading, tones and infinitesimal attention to artistic detail. Each scene is a work of art, not just a cartoon. This is the level of quality we can expect to achieve when we harness what we have learned into reusable capabilities.

Input-Process-Output

The first thing we'll notice, perhaps even purchase the Netezza machine for, is the same thing we would purchase any of Netezza's competitors for. Fast loading of the data. High speed access of the stored information. All of the technologies that think they are nipping at Netezza's heels, are fooling themselves. By attempting to define Netezza in terms of their own short-sighted designs, every white paper they produce has a gaping hole in it, and that hole's name is Processing. The large-scale intake and large-scale analytic/reporting capabilities are frankly bookends when we pop the hood and look at the wide range of possibilities inside the machine, to transform the data after it first arrives. In fact, our teams coach other teams on how to bridge the gap between intake and outtake.

Architecturally speaking, this transforms the use of a table from a static storage mechanism into a dynamic storage *way-point*, an intermediate means to an end. This option isn't even open to us in the other competitor products, where the simple act of declaring a table requires administrative intervention to get the table's collateral correct (whether an index, table space, file system allocation or other supporting stuff). Not so with Netezza. We can manufacture tables on the fly, because each time a table is created, Netezza handles all the overhead for us, automatically.

Case Study Short: In one shop trying to pull off an internal data processing model (using one of Netezza's competitors), the application effort was one long and exasperating haul. The machine could handle the eighty-five (85) or so SQL transforms running end-to-end. But the database admins could *not* handle the notion of over eighty intermediate tables to support the effort. They mandated that these intermediate tables had to be predefined, the DDL submitted to them for review and optimization, and then operationally used-and-truncated on each run. With these constraints, the cleanup of the tables meant that developers and troubleshooters had no forensic evidence of the flow's progress (they were driving blind). Worse, the transform operations could not be multi-threaded. That is, the tables represented "the only leg" of the flow and there would be no more legs, certainly no branches of legs. Why is this important? If multiple developers are working on the flow, there is only one path in the machine. They have to stand in line to run their work (you know, like the old mainframe days with a stack of punch-cards).

This sort of artificial constraint was necessary for the admins to maintain their sanity, but also necessary because the competitor machine just could not support wildly and arbitrarily dynamic creation/drop of tables. So at both the system and administrative levels, the overhead was too expensive to make SQL transforms viable.

What the admins saw: If we let the developers have their own dynamic thread of tables, with five developers that's over four-hundred tables in-flight. Leaving them behind to create another four-hundred, and another for debugging and troubleshooting, and in a day we're talking about thousands, if not tens of thousands of tables. It all seemed *so* runaway.

Housekeeping

This is another non-optional aspect of SQL-transforms that the admins (above) would have appreciated more, but would not have removed their personal need to validate the optimization and instantiation of each intermediate table.

If we make a lot of intermediate assets, we have to clean them up. ETL tools won't do this automatically, so we'll have to add it to our programming when using them. For the ETL tool, this becomes part of the application, not part of the automatic processing substrate. So we'll likely require some customized, perhaps even non-portable housekeeping tasks per application. They are non-optional, so we need a way to make them part of an operational, automatic model. If we're really focusing on the application logic alone, such cleanup activities should not have to be *deliberate* at the application level. It just clutters the application and makes housekeeping error-prone.

Keep this in mind: If we wanted to make a temporary file, a simple approach would be to make the file, use it, then delete it. If we needed lots of these, we would make all the files, use them, and then at the end of the application have a routine that removed them. We'd have to do this for each application thread. An architectural approach, on the other hand, would expose a temporary-file factory. We would call the factory for a file and we would get one. Our factory can keep track of all the files we requested during the job's execution. At the end, we simply call a housekeeping function (or one is called automatically for us) and the factory cleans up all the files. Some C-language aficionados may see shadows of *malloc()*-harnesses in this approach, where we had to make memory-factories to provide us with snippets of storage for our in-memory operations, but also keep track of everything it allocated so that at the end of the program, it could release it all back into the wild.

Why is this necessary?

If the job fails or gets interrupted, we could end up with all those temporary assets sitting out there, without any reference to their existence. With a housekeeping function, we keep track of the assets *as they are created*, at two levels: One is the level of the current run-time. Second is the level outside of the run-time (for assets like run-time logs we may want to keep around after the job finishes up). If the run-time fails, the second level still has reference to the asset. The run-time is responsible for immediate cleanup. Periodically an automated process can take care of the outside-the-runtime files.

This works for intermediate tables as well, or any other intermediate asset. Tag it for housekeeping when first created, then we don't lose track of it later.

Flow-Based

I've seen several models for harnessing SQL-transforms. A prevalent one is the process-based approach. This is perfectly viable if we have process-driven activity. It basically means that we are tracking each activity or operation at a fairly detailed level. Ostensibly this is for the purposes of recovery or restart from failure.

Another form is the flow-based model, which stretches the activities of a single process across hundreds of operations in the flow. The only objection that people have to this model, is that it's not process driven and as such has no detailed recovery points. It performs checkpointing at strategic stopping points, but does not provide a recovery for the many hundreds of in-flight operations between these checkpoints.

Something to consider, talked about elsewhere in this book, is the actual function of checkpoints for purposes of recovery. Checkpoints exist so that we don't lose time, and we can recover from a failed flow without breaching the allotted time window for processing. For example, if a process takes two hours to complete, but we only have three hours in the window, a failed operation does not have time to start from the beginning. We need a way to checkpoint the work so that we can restart mid-stream.

However, in a SQL-transform scenario, especially inside Netezza, each operation takes mere *seconds*. Put them in an end-to-end sequence, and we can execute hundreds if not thousands of these operations in a matter of *minutes*. So even if we have a four-hour window, what of it? We could restart the same job a *hundred times* inside this window if we like.

So the point is, checkpoints at the individual operation level are meaningless and will actually slow the process down considerably. They will increase the overall complexity dramatically - but there will be no payback. Operationally recording hundreds of processing junctures in a matter of minutes, has no value *whatsoever*.

However, what does have significant value is a flow-based control that focuses on harnessing the many operations into something we can see, report on and manage. We don't need detailed process control for this,we need a flow controller.

A last word on the process control method. We arrived on site and were presented with the process model that the client had "decided upon" rather unilaterally, and would not hear our wisdom concerning a flow-based model. After much pain, they rolled out the process-based model only to discover that the operators didn't use it, the administrators hated it and it created a truckload of white-noise in the implementation that made debugging very difficult. They spent as much time debugging the process model as they did the application itself. Over time, it was noted that the process model actually delivered more defect reports against it than the whole of the application flows combined. So where was the real value? Nothing, it just made for an unstable platform that obfuscated the application logic.

Another bane of process-control scenarios that was discussed in Underground and noted in this context, is that many process-control *log-table* designs use an insert-update approach. That is, the initial job control record is inserted when the job launches, and then it is updated later when the job closes. If multiple jobs are in flight, their update operations will invariably collide. The Netezza storage system is not transactional, but such a model expects transactional behavior. The resolution of this is to use an insert-only model where the job startup is recorded in one insert and then its closure recorded with another insert. Two records instead of one. Some balk at this suggestion, believing that two records are a waste of space. Yeah, verily, if this were a transactional system, but the process control table, even with double the entries, will never even approach a substantial fraction of the size of our smallest solution data table, so such anxieties are misplaced.

Back to strategic checkpoints. The most manageable protocol is to use a finalization operation which requires all in-flight flows for a single job to synchronize just before they enter the target database. This allows us to record their entry but also gives us the most obvious juncture to check for any errors that may have arisen in one or more branches of the flow. Quite frankly, we could end up with dozens of parallel processing branches, each one finishing in relative seconds. Meaning that from the point they are released as a "thundering herd", they will all arrive at the finish line in relative moments. At this point we perform a set-based check for errors. If anything arises that is inacceptable, we can set aside the entire job, all the flows, with no penalty. The real penalty of course would be to allow all of these flows free-running-access to the target database, finalizing as they individually complete. Then if one of them fails, we would have to back out all of them. There is very little penalty in synchronizing the flows, managing their ingress to the target, then recording their arrival. There is a much higher penalty for failing to manage this operation and then get stuck with a target database in an unknown state.

What does this look like? In an intake scenario, we bring data into loosely defined intake tables, and then use a transform operation to copy this into the final intake table. Once all the data is in their final form, and all intake operations complete for a given intake session, we can then verify if all the data has arrived safely. It would be bad indeed if we were intaking eight reference tables and one transactional table, and the transactional table intake died for some reason, invalidating the context of the reference tables. Or for that matter, multiple large files arriving in any context, where the context itself has to be preserved or none of the data has any meaning. This scenario is a significant step up from the average data warehouse flow model, that pushes one table at a time in shared-nothing tradition. An ETL tool cannot of its own capability manage these contextually-sensitive shared-nothing operations. If it has eight dimensions to push and one of them dies, it has no power to back out the data that it has already sent to the machine. Nor will any number of pleas to the vendor be honored for such capabilities. Perhaps in the future, one can hope. But not as it stands today.

So the second place where we have a flow-juncture is similar to the intake, but faces our individual target databases such as the Repository or the Reporting database. When we perform any number of transform operations toward these, we would make a structural copy of the table we intend to populate, and put this table into a transform database. Then manipulate and fill the table with all the correct information, then push this to the target as an insert operation. When we do this with dozens of tables from many dozens of transform operations, it makes for a controlled entry of the data and something very easy to manage (and more importantly, very easy to roll back). Thus we have another error-control checkpoint. If all of the transform operations and their target tables do not complete without error, we now have the option to forego the finalization of the data. Or for that matter, if we're running development, testing or production, we could invoke levels of leniency depending on the region of operation. We have more options available to us in a harnessed approach like this.

Metadata, thy name is Kick Butt

Lots of folks say their product is "metadata driven", but what does this really mean? At a minimum we want to know that if the database's structural metadata should change, that the assets consuming it could also easily conform.

This is impossible with hand-crafted SQL statements. They are formed on the expectation of stable structural definitions (table names, column names etc). If any of these should change, the SQL statement is invalidated. Imagine the valiant attempt to apply such a change as part of an end-to-end flow with dozens if not hundreds of intermediate SQL statements? Do we have to pop open and tweak each one of them? Seriously? When one column change is in play, this seems rather tedious, but what if more than one column has been added, or even subtracted? How do we easily affect this change? In the plain-vanilla hand-crafted SQL model, we can't. In the aforementioned model where all intermediate tables had to be predefined before deployment, how would such changes affect the structures? It is not uncommon to hear stories about implementations with those technologies and constraints, to require many weeks or even months to affect even insignificant changes.

Metadata driven? Methinks not.

This is why SQL-*generation* is non-optional. We should employ structural transform templates that are coupled to the structural catalog metadata. If the catalog structures change, an automated process can quickly update the transform templates. If the SQL is always generated *from* the transform templates, we now have a metadata-driven model. Of course, simply adding/subtracting columns from these templates does not guarantee that they will be accurately handled in the SQL statement. Or does it?

It is true that when adding columns to the transform templates, there is an expectation that they will arrive somewhere, even if passed through onto the final target table. What we have found is that in mature models that require this kind of intermittent maintenance, over ninety percent of the added columns are *simply pass-through* quantities. The remainder serve to support a particular integration point (such as a critical join that needs a new attribute to steer its outcome) but even these are very low-impact, single-point-of-failure situations. So that if we have a model that supports automatically dovetailing metadata changes from the catalog to the template, this is often the most we'll ever have to do for the vast majority of column-level maintenance.

And since the SQL statements and intermediate assets are directly constructed from the templates, we are effectively metadata-driven.

Why is this important? As of this writing, the primary ETL tools on the market still require a hand-crafted SQL statement to be inserted by the developer and tailored into the component that will execute it. This model is far too hard-wired to be eligible for true SQL-transform. By that I mean, true SQL-transform is metadata-driven and easily supports hundreds of such SQL operations as a normal part of the design. ETL tools are not metadata-driven for these activities, and support incidental or tactical inclusion of such operations as part of a larger flow of work. Unfortunately for us, the transform operations *are* the flow of work, and every other part of the ETL tool is an incidental support.

But that's just the structural part of the transform. There's a whole lot more.

We would also like to leverage metadata-driven DDL, discussed elsewhere in this book, that is used at the point of DDL construction. It's one thing to accept the DDL structure from the DBA or modeler, and quite another to enrich it with operational columns and other supports that increase the value, speed or logical elegance of the processing model. We would derive such things from metadata that affects the metadata. For example, if we want to apply distribution keys but our modeling tool does not understand it, we need a way to define the distribution model in metadata rather than hand-crafting the DDL after the DBA sends it to us. We would then process the DDL to merge the separately defined distribution model into the deployed DDL. In so doing, we now have the option to manufacture other distribution-related assets that can assist at transform time, including transform warnings that tell the developer something like this:

```
Warning: source tables are using the distribution key [keyname] but this
key does not appear in the join statement.
```

Why would this be an important message on a Netezza machine? These metadata-level diagnostics are impossible to achieve with a standard ETL tool, so we must consider this as part of our architectural capability when building out a platform. The developers need to know this, as do troubleshooters. Many times have I arrived on site for an assessment and the first thing I look at is distribution. It is the source of power for the Netezza machine.

Case Study Short: In reviewing an environment for a telco, our team found that the customer had picked DataStage (already noted as one of the more robust choices for SQL-transform, and not because IBM owns it). But something was wrong. As their data had grown, and now they had just assimilated another telco, the machine was being crushed with the data load. But it didn't *seem* like all that much data. The general conclusion was that in all the updates, inserts and joins, nowhere did the distribution keys show up. In fact, one particularly prevalent key seemed like a better candidate than the one they had chosen, But it didn't matter. If they weren't using the keys in the actual queries, they may as well be using no distribution at all. I mentioned all this in their assessment, and the objection I received was very interesting. "It is as though David thinks we don't know anything about distribution keys, or principles of distribution." Of course, this was not the case at all. I lauded them on a very sophisticated and innovative implementation. My only observation was that the distribution keys weren't being used - anywhere. So it really doesn't matter how much one knows about the principles of distribution if they are not being applied.

Two of our consultants remained behind to work out an experimental performance model. One to use their existing distribution but to add the keys to the Join phrases. Another to pick the apparently more viable distribution key. Their default time for the average flow was around fifty minutes. Once the first change was applied, it reduced their runtime to around fifteen minutes. Once the alternative key was applied, it reduce them to less than five minutes. That's a 10x improvement for some simple tweaks to the *metadata*.

Which brings us back to dough. That is, the dough they were spending to have these guys sitting around for fifty minutes for each test run, when they could have been performing tests every five minutes.

We now see that the payback is not always in the reduced runtime. If our flows run ten times longer than they have to, our testing and development will take ten times longer than it has to. Our time to deployment will be ten time longer than it needs to be. Oh, correct that one. We will still have to deploy on time, but we will have tested the product *ten times less than we could have*. Something to think about.

Along the same lines as offering up warning as to lack of distribution key usage, is something a bit more subtle. If our target table has a different distribution than our source table(s), this will detract from the boost of a co-located *write*. Many Enzees are more than familiar with the principle of a co-located join, but this is largely in context of a reporting model where the data is on its way out. What of the data is moving from one set of tables into another (SQL transform insert/select)? If the target table has a different distribution than the source tables, it is guaranteed that the data will be redistributed as part of the operation. This is not particularly bad if it's the finalization portion and we really are just copying data. But if we're integrating multiple sources into a target, and the source all exist on one distribution key, it will be faster to insert into a target using the same key.

Why is this important? Many SQL-transform flows are the combination of multiple operations moving from multiple source tables into fewer or different tables, with many intermediate tables in between. The more efficient this intermediate process is, the faster the overall flow will be. So we must not think in terms of aligning the data to a particular target distribution until we have fully taken advantage of the source distribution. For example, what if our final target is distributed on key(a) and all of the sources are distributed on key(b)? It would be best to formulate a structural replica of the target, distributed on key(b), and then do all the data integration using the same co-located read *and* co-located write. Then as a final operation, copy the data from the resulting table into the final target, taking the redistribution penalty only once. I would *strongly* suggest experimenting with this approach for more complex flows.

In any case, we can now see the value of being able to detect distribution conflicts (or opportunities) and exploit them in our favor.

Let Rules Rule

The above metadata discussion is implicitly bounded in rules. I recall a rather oblique discussion with some technical engineers about the value of "business metadata", translated as such into a "source to target map". The technical engineers were accustomed to collaborating with the business analysts and testers across the cubicle walls and on IM/Chat. They could resolve the world's problems before bedtime - with one glaring problem: The resulting code did exactly what the users and testers wanted it to do, but nobody had written anything down.

Now, I understand the overall defects in most technical approaches, such as the need for an "as built" design model. Or an "as deployed" functional specification. We all know that the value of a formal functional specification starts to grow stale with each passing project day. Nobody updates the functional spec and by the time we're done, what we've built can potentially deviate, in significant ways, from the original design and functional description. Those documents are now stale and nobody plans to go back to review or update them.

Contrast this to a base of predefined, actionable rules that are formulated using the expert knowledge of the Subject Matter Experts and the technical wizards. This creates a best-of-breed scenario that sticks. The rules aren't going anywhere are they? And they represent a mind-mapping model of how the system should behave when the rule is in play. Will the rule's conditions be met and the rule "fire"? And if the rule fires, what will be the outcome? Will it be a programmable outcome or a canned, one-size-fits-all outcome? Both have value and both carry risk.

Let's say we have some canned intake patterns like Change-Data-Capture and Deduplication. What if we could use rules to deploy database/table functions like these:

```
intk_customers_customer_data_dedupe()
intk_customers_customer_data_cdc()
```

Now let's say we have a file that is dedicated to a source database, containing rules for each of the areas we want to apply a pattern to. In this case, we'll just use dedupe() and cdc().

```
[CDC]
TABLE=customers  <other rule info here>

[DEDUPE]
TABLE=customers <other rule info here>
```

Of course, we could do it the other way around:

```
[CUSTOMERS]
OPERATION=DEDUPE <other rule information here>
OPERATION=CDC <other rule information here>
```

However, since we want our environment to be flow-oriented, we will likely find that the first notation is most useful. Primarily because we will focus on operations rather than tables, and those operations have to arrive in particular order. For example, we may simply want to perform deduplication and change-data-capture. The question is, which one should come first? In deduplication, we want to compare an inbound data set to itself, and will usually result in the elimination of a minor number of records. In change-data-capture, we might need to load the same group of records every day, knowing that only a few have changed. In this case, change-data-capture will radically reduce the overall data content. Not only this, but the duplicates that were present yesterday are still there today. By carving out yesterday's data, we know have a true picture of duplicates and the deduplication process itself has less data to process.

But take a look at the prior notation. It leads the developer to believe that the DEDUPE will happen first because it is the first in the list. If we will never do it first, this is misleading. We could be just as misleading in the prior notation by placing the DEDUPE block before the CDC block. However, if we are rolling this out as a template, it is much easier to depict the flow of operation in the template (the dedupe will appear first, then cdc) so that there is less confusion. What we're trying to accomplish is to provide a means to have developers install and configure rules to affect pattern-based behaviors.

And then the notation prior to that, recall:

```
intk_customers_customer_data_dedupe()
intk_customers_customer_data_cdc()
```

We can now formulate these specific function calls and put pre-canned operations in them, tailored to the specific database, table/column/datatype and rule information as provided by the developer at design time. This allows us to boil-in how we would implement the rule as a best practice, including adding any special Netezza-centric hooks. Of course, if there is no rule for a particular table, there is no function call created. This allows us to setup rules for the tables we want to affect while all others follow default behavior. At the startup of the flow, we load these functions into memory (all of them)so that when we encounter databases or tables at run time, we "attempt to execute them". Their absence will not make the attempt-to-execute fail. But their presence will definitely execute the rule.

How does this work? When we are processing the data for intake, there are clear, known junctures when the data is ready for the above processes When we reach those junctures, for the given database and table currently in hand, we formulate the function call:

```
${database_name}_${tablename}_cdc()
```

Then we can test for the existence of this procedure call, for example in bash with the bash function:

```
declare
```

If our fabricated function exists, we call it immediately. The context is already exported to the environment and the timing is perfect, so we get the desired effect. What if a developer never installed a rule for the table we're currently processing? No rule got loaded, no action taken.

All brought to us by the magic of metadata.

Case Study Short: I had the privilege of working with some really sharp physicians and medical professionals in the creation of a rules-based engine for fraud detection in medical claims. The basic premise was that the standard Current Procedural Terminology (CPT) codes had agreed-upon billing standards. These are the codes that we see on the medical form as we exit the doctor's office, with the ones circled for what the doctor applied that day. The doctor has agreed to bill according to certain rules, and these rules had been codified in the system. Basically a claim would arrive and the expert system would apply only the rules pertinent to the given claim (using some fairly advanced lookup structures). It would then apply the rules to the claim and take action, like setting aside claim-lines in favor of others, effectively changing the claim into something that the doctor should have billed in the first place. Initially the system was designed to save money and deal with fraud. Eventually it could be used to profile doctors as to those who played well and those who did not. But it also created a "sentinel" effect, that if it was that good at detection, the doctors would naturally beef up their own diligence in order to avoid a violation.

The point being, a large number of people worked on the system, the rules and their behavior to the effect of baking their expert knowledge into it. We often hear about expert systems that perform wide, sweeping activities on the stock market, making the same decisions that a stock professional would, only with greater accuracy, speed and volume. The principle is the same. Take known rules, bake them into reusable metadata assets, and use them to deploy active components that will apply the rules on-demand. We'll look at an exception processing model later.

How does this apply to us? We have subtle requirements for what we should process or apply, and *when* we should apply it. For transform-related rules, these are found in the SQL statements themselves. But what about global issues like default values, primary/foreign-key checking, and other default (but global) behaviors that we want to make automatic? These cannot be effectively applied in a simple, one-shot transform or even in application-specific, hard-wired constructs, or we will constantly have to revisit them for tweaks. We'll end up having to revisit them across applications, since little of the logic is reusable at the application level.

The answer is in a rules-based approach, where we can generate components from rules, and then deploy those components into the application as a framework. They then behave as chameleons of sorts, quasi-objects that exist between the rules and the application, but affect the data correctly, globally and with predefined timing. Part of this is metaprogramming, part of it is not. We'll see some more examples later.

One of the most effective ways to manufacture these quasi-components is with a rules compiler We may get primary/foreign-key metadata from the modeling tool. We then take that and convert it to rules that our environment recognizes. We then activate the component builders that operate only from the rules. This allows us to manufacture all kinds of rules for all kinds of reasons, and then consistently (and automatically) build the run-time components from them. The rules compiler is a form of factory. It takes assets from the left-hand-side (rules) crunches them and produces cookie-cutter components on the right-hand side. The factory products are then deployed "as is". If we need an update to the factory products, we produce them in development, test them as normal, and then deploy them. The factories never leave the development zone. Only their work products do.

Now we're approaching a metadata-driven behavioral and run-time model, leading to a metadata-driven application.

Boil Your Brain

Into the architecture. (Boil your colleague's brain, too). And yes, leave the death's-head moths out of it.

Don't let the phrase "expert system" elicit thoughts (or practices!) of all kinds of formal mathematical rules, axioms and the like. We don't have to go there. The practical application of an expert system is to get the thoughts from our brains and into the technology, or more specifically into to the form of actionable instructions that will operate *just as we would*, if we were flipping the switches manually.

Getting our brains into the architecture is not only responsible, it allows our leaders to leverage our intellect vicariously, and at scales that we could never personally attain. I have installed systems that boiled the brainwaves of myself and my colleagues into some of the most sophisticated, well-tuned and screaming systems that have ever graced the silicon of a CPU, but it wasn't just because I was in the room. I may have been a facilitator or even the broker of the knowledge offered by one of the SMEs or another source. My responsibility was to activate it with the technology at hand. If we think of ourselves in this role, that is the orchestrator or the broker or the like, rather than the person responsible for *all* the creativity, it takes the pressure off so that we really *can* offer up some creative stuff. But unless we get all that stuff unpacked from our brains and into the technology, it's still stuck between our ears, with the only point of egress as our fingertips, on the keyboard, over and over and over and over.... You get the drift.

Rinse and Repeat, said the Raven, Nevermore

With the above sentiment, we know that certain things are repeatable. We keep coming back to them. Failing to automate them is a form of self-punishment that is unacceptable in the twenty-first century. Architectural excellence requires a foundation, and that foundation begins between our ears. We can always leverage the gray matter betwixt the temples of another, but they'll probably want credit for it. So best to just go to the source(s) and educate ourselves. This would be practically any major best-seller on Data Warehousing or flow-based development approaches.

But I have to offer a caution - the Netezza machine is specifically configured to harness all the core aspects of data warehousing. We'll study the core of the data warehousing practices and then pop the virtual hood of the appliance and see, hey, it's in there. I alluded to this in Underground, that the internals of the machine are set up to do data warehousing like everyone else has always done. That's why, when we see people being unsuccessful with the machine, it's because they have little foundation in the problem/solution domain of data warehousing, or even bulk data processing.

I also mentioned in Underground that bulk data processing is a lost art form, and is not considered glitzy or glamorous to speak of in mixed company. Even in technical circles where geek-speak is encouraged and honored, bulk data processing just doesn't move the needle.

But get it under our belt we must, because in the end anyone can bring a gun to a knife fight, but the Big Black Box is like a Howitzer - it trumps all other weapons and eclipses all other challengers. Let them yawn as we process libraries of congress at a time, and we put it to bed before turning into the sheets ourselves. Let them ruin their eyes on gooey! screens and cathode radiation. Transactional processing is now our fodder. It drives the interfaces to the customers and nibbles at the edge.

Bulk processing delivers to the decision makers. Analytics creates the nectar of kings.

To Refactor, or Not to Refactor, Is there a Question?

Or the other vernacular, *when in doubt, rewrite*. When using hand-crafted SQL-transforms, the ever-present fear is that the data model will so radically change that we will find ourselves swimming in a SQL-rewrite and will want to exit this model forsooth and forthwith. This is why the hand-crafted SQL-Transform model is so despised. Upon first release, all is well and the flows are humming. Secondary, incremental releases are a little work, but not particularly tedious. Then along comes larger-scale functionality, especially the kind we want dovetailed into conformed data. Now the changes in the data model will open up holes in the flows, peppered all over. Regression *testing* is always in the headlights on this kind of effort, but we don't want regressive *programming*. It's just too big a pill to swallow.

So refactoring is then stunted. We become limited in the application of new ideas or approaches because the impact-curve is too steep already. We can't keep our head above water with just the maintenance of all this hand-crafted stuff. This is exactly the model we were trying to escape when we migrated to Netezza, so why do we find ourselves stuck in it again?

This is precisely why SQL-generation and SQL-Transform factories are not only handy, they are non-optional gear. When (not if) we need to refactor, we can address the capabilities promulgated by the factory, regenerate the SQL-transforms from it and then re-execute. Whenever the data models must change, we perform a metadata-based differential-and-merge, not a hand-crafted submarine hunt. It's certainly a lot less to unit-test for the developers. But I would take it one step further.

The *testers* will also use SQL statements against the data model and its attendant catalog metadata. They will therefore have a need for generated SQL also. They will want to apply logic to the work products and likewise live without fear of a data model change. Their plight is no different from the developer's. If we really want an accelerated delivery chain, we have to address every link in the chain. This approach allows developers to leverage metadata-driven merge-and-purge of their SQL-Transform templates, which in turn drive the production of SQL statements. We'd like to provide testers with a merge-and-purge as well, so that the path to re-fortifying their tests is supported more easily. We'd also like something else from the testing staff: If our SQL-generation model provides SQL statements that can be visibly validated outside of the factory setting, it keeps the testing staff from getting *too creative* with their test scripts.

Case Study Short: The developers had just delivered the second-of-many releases to the testers, who were now running full bore regression tests on the work products. At the end of this cycle, the testers produced a wave of defects that stunned the developers. Upon review however, some fundamental flaws in the testing approach rose to the surface, effectively declaring void all but a few of the test case results. The problem with this outcome was not that the testers were particularly incompetent. They simply misunderstood how to use the Netezza platform to affect the testing process. Moreover, they had opted to use tightly-wound, single-shot queries for each test case. The developers would then have to unravel and tease-apart these queries to show where the flaw existed. This too-creative-test-implementation bogged down the developers, who had to take additional time to tease apart each test case and re-validate it. What we want are simplified test case execution, and a way to enforce this on the testers.

Had the testers been privy to a SQL-generation scenario the same as the developers, they could have leveraged it as a rules-driven test harness that manufactured SQL for *them*, in a manner that was highly visible, repeatable and yes, independently testable in case they were concerned that the SQL-generator itself was flawed. With everything out-in-the-open like this, the developers and testers are producing very different forms of SQL, but can experience the same metadata-driven safety net of rules-driven, not hand-coded-SQL-driven approach.

We will need to refactor. This is a mathematical certainty. We simply need to reduce the impact of the refactor so that we can maintain momentum.

RE-ENTRY SEQUENCE 11

LET'S TAKE A DEEP DIVE into the various elements of a data migration project. In the Case Studies chapter we'll see some in-context data migration issues, pertinent to those anecdotes, but here we'll boil up a bit more of the stew so we can see additional things in perspective. While this is not a comprehensive discussion, it will provide at least a bit of insight on what to expect and how to approach the problems.

In Underground we discussed the mechanics of execution. You know, functionally specify, port the stuff we want to keep, don't assume that just because something exists that it has a functional role, and be on guard for performance functions masquerading as business functions, or engineering that is propping up performance, because we won't be needing those, either.

But something else is afoot. A transformation is underway and we're standing in the epicenter. It might not seem obvious at first, owing to the whole "eye of the storm" effect. Let's not diminish or disregard the growing energy around us, but rather focus it for productive ends.

Data migration projects have very specific, one-time requirements that are difficult to dovetail into an existing operational environment. This is especially true as it engages the culture around the development lifecycle. Some caveats and known pitfalls are necessary to review.

The migration is a one-time initiative. It is special.

Migration projects by definition violate policies in every imaginable way. I recall a funny story about a bunch of parents sitting around talking while their children watched Disney's *Pinnochio* in the other room. In a conversational lull, they overheard the owner of Pleasure Island note that foolish boys will soon make "asses" of themselves. Later in the movie of course, the boys literally turn into donkeys in some pretty intense scenes (for young minds, anyhow). In any case, the parents were taken aback by the use of the word "asses" in the cartoon. A debate ensued as to whether they should allow their children to continue watching it, or allow their young minds to be exposed to such words.

The point is this: the sheer naivete of the parents in thinking that this word, used in cartoon, would have any significant influence on their children *in comparison to* the words they heard every hour of every day at school and on the streetcorner. Perhaps they had forgotten how foul a young child's mouth can be. Not their own child, of course, but when interacting within a pluralistic, public society, especially a school system, the language is driven by the lowest common denominators. The ruffians and curs that these parents would never allow their children to be friends with, much less invite into their homes, expose their little ears to much harsher words than "asses" on a regular basis. And certainly words in a much terser and (adult-oriented) context than the movie *Pinnochio*.

It is this naivete that comes to the fore in our project principals, managers and folks who feel they must align with existing policies *at all costs*. The migration project, by its very execution flies in the face of the vast majority of the etched-in-stone policies of the environment. Attempting to nit-pick (as with the parents above) misses the much larger picture. And in missing this larger picture, the portions of that picture that will ultimately crush or debilitate the migration project are constantly looming and must be addressed deliberately.

In no particular order, some immutable truths about the migration are worthy of note. These are not altogether particular to Netezza migrations, but directly apply to one just as they would apply to any migration project. They are discussed in detail following. We ignore them at our peril.

- One-time/first-time initiative - Many of the things encountered in the project will never be encountered or addressed again. So it's okay to disbelieve staffers when they say that they have "done this before" (migrate to Netezza) because so few have actually done it, and those who are on staff likely rode the wave and didn't take notes. Their memories will likely not intersect comprehensively with the reality imposing itself even now upon our environment.
- A project leading to an environment - the migration has to be treated as a project but it is all about standing up a living environment.
- The timeline will slip - so *many* unknowns and buried-things await us, the sheer naivete of attempting to "fix" the timeline will be painfully obvious, at least twice. I have often warned people that the timeline dates will slip *at least three times*. Where, how and for what duration, is as unknown as all the forgotten functionality under the floors we're about to rip up. Many years ago, a project principal *assured* me that he had been through migrations before, knew all the ropes and not-to-worry, and all that. The first time the project timeline slipped, because of undisclosed/undiscovered functionality, he went ballistic. Brace yourself.
- The project will lurch - we will see ebbs and flows in project acceleration. Developers and testers will need breathing room. Normal flows of life will affect the project's speed.
- It's a *testing* project, not a *development* project - development in a migration is often a nit, where the majority of work is in testing. Don't withhold testing resources (machine power or people) unless we want the timeline to slip even more.
- If tracking defects formally, be aware that early in the project, false-positives abound. The total count of invalid defects may regularly be *more than five times* the count of the valid defects. Testers need time to come up to speed. Give the developers a break.
- First-time movement of data will take many weeks - the data we're migrating is behind a physical and functional fortress. Nobody ever planned to move it out in quantity.
- Deliver when things are ready, not when they are due - the worst mistake someone can make on a migration project is to attempt a demo or even a pre-delivery of functionality that is not ready. The onlookers will remember everything they see.
- Let target-requirements rule - Intermediate databases, intake zones and various other func-

tional necessities are meaningless if the reports are wrong. Likewise if downstream consumers cannot capture the correctly formulated data. Get the outputs right and let them drive all the activities leading to their outcome.

- Flow is the overarching concept - many people think that the *storage* of the data is the most important concept, but know this: nothing is *happening* to the data when it's in storage. Only when it's *on-the-move* should we have a concern. When analysts look at the information on the screen, they will not question the storage techniques if the data itself is the wrong value.

So when the migration project launches, the principals should - and *must* - garner a wide range of guarantees and permissions from the folks that govern policy so that any mistakes made in the migration are not treated with the same draconian flair as the equivalent action in another, more mature and production-centric context.

Case Study Short: We put the master-stroke on the 6-month project and submitted it to our superiors. Within days we had a meeting where they asked us to divide all of our numbers by three. They said, Convert the six-month project into a two-month project, or it will never get approved. So we went about cutting down the timeframes to fit their needs, and resubmitted it. Keep in mind that on any project schedule, no matter the context, changing dates doesn't change the actual time to delivery, and reporting more aggressive target dates, especially abnormally aggressive target dates, only serves to seal the inevitable: we *will* miss the date. Oddly, when the project was roughly one month into the schedule, it became obvious that we'd only scratched the surface on the deliverables. Some of the managers were mildly alarmed, so called a pep-talk meeting where they looked at us sternly and said, "You committed to these dates. We expect you to hit them." All of us looked around at each other until one of our more vocal leaders said, "No, actually *you* committed *us* to these dates. We're just trying to help you hit them." At the end of the second month, when we were due to finish, we were roughly one-third into the tasks on the project plan. One of the planners, dismayed by our progress, lamented "At this rate, we won't be done for *another four months*." Imagine that.

Case Study Short: The Netezza appliances installed and humming, a project lead had to get data migrated from the source system into the target database. One evening he logged into the environment and using a simple series of "select * from table" operations, he pushed the data into the file system. This took several hours, but he was prepared to wait for it since the development team needed all of it the very next day. Four hours later, data in hand, he loaded it into the new target data warehouse machine without any problems or fanfare. He tested to make sure all of the data had made it, and all was well. He departed the office and got a good night's sleep.

The last night's sleep he would have as an employee of the company.

For the next day, he entered the building amidst a flurry of policy violations, all centered on him, and he was now public enemy number one. The charges? (a) He had downloaded data, in quantity, from a production system and placed it into a non-production system. (b) He had pulled data that was normally masked from developers, and fully exposed it without masking on the target machine. (c) He had dropped sensitive data into unencrypted files which had remained exposed for many hours on the disk drives, ripe for the taking by any savvy hacker. (d) Lastly, he had transmitted data in bulk from one data center to another, without permission of the data center managers, and such an action always required permission to avoid saturating the bandwidth between the buildings. Taken all together, these were grounds for termination, and without so much as asking him why all these things happened, the office security folks hovered over him as he packed up his office things and escorted him out the door.

In the meantime, on the other side of his office building, a project kickoff meeting was underway, for which he was supposed to be the leader. They sat for a half-hour awaiting his arrival before his boss finally took over the meeting and gave everyone their charge for tasks and project priorities. He left the meeting in a huff, wondering where his project lead had gotten off to, so stopped by his desk. The now-empty desk. He did not find out *for two days* what happened to the project lead, who by this time had found gainful employment, a better position and better pay - with his former employer's *competitor*.

A migration project has special needs and actions that by definition violate the policies of the environment. Mainly because the data was first placed into its current home where, by design and by policy, it became gradually encased in a cocoon of protection that we are about to utterly violate and set aside. We need the data out. *All* of it.

One leader asked me point blank: *Are you saying we just set aside policy to make this happen? They'll hang me from the highest tree just for suggesting it.* No doubt they would, and me along with him, so no, this isn't what I'm saying.

It's this simple: de-facto anti-migration policies are wrapped around mature environments. When a migration project comes along, those de-facto anti-migration policies are suddenly in the way. Will we just set aside those policies and *turn a blind eye* to the things we *obviously* need to do? (like moving data in quantity from point A to point B). What about all the other necessary things that are not so obvious?

Rather than turning-a-blind-eye-for-a-while or making exceptions, a better way to do this is to simply get permission. In many cases, the permission is granted forthwith. It is the *failure to ask* for permission, or even *giving ourselves* permission, that has policy folks up-in-arms. What's that? If we ask permission, it will take too long? Maybe so, but that's just another telltale sign that the environment is not ready for the transformation.

Case Study Short: This is a composite case study that pops up like a prairie dog on practically every new project whether app-dev, web-dev or data warehousing. I mentioned it prior in this book but it definitely deserves honorable mention again. Simply this: It is standard "policy" to purchase hardware and place the weaker of the machines in the development environment while the strongest of the machines arrive in the production environment. Considering that most migration projects will not enter production for as far out as six months, perhaps even twelve months, we might wonder why the initial project effort takes so long. After all, we have a *Netezza* machine, don't we? What's the problem? Chop-chop, snap-to-it and all that.

But this problem can be diminished or even mitigated if all of the available hardware is *made* available to the developers and testers for this first very-large-bubble of work. This one-time/first time workload that will require extraordinary testing efforts *will only be protracted* if our development and testing platforms are underpowered. If we have a production machine that is four times the size of the development environment, we can get *at least* four times more work accomplished on it than on the development machine. In addition, it will *definitely* take four times longer on the development machine than it would have on the production machine, because data warehouse projects are not about coding or development, but about *testing*. Each testing effort is not a query or two, but a battery of queries. If the battery requires one hour on the development machine, it will require fifteen minutes (or less) on the production machine. More capacity, more testing, higher-quality product. Even if we do less testing, we get to market sooner with the solution. Is either of these a bad thing?

But policy will sometimes stand in the way of such practicality. And this means that production machine will sit on the raised floor with nothing to do while our developers slave over the under-powered development machine. How is it underpowered? It is trying to muscle through the first-time/one-time bubble of work-that-will-never-exist-again. It is underpowered for the *bubble*. And as we pass the larger machine every day and see its lights blinking from behind the smoked glass, we can almost feel it mocking us. No, it is not mocking us. The policy that has *placed it there* is mocking us.

What's the worst that could happen? In many cases, because a migration project is underway, the principals and powers-that-be take on a "just this once" mentality. They will allow the team to "get away with stuff" because they need the unfettered freedom to build out the new system. The problem with this protocol is that as we mature the solution, the environment around it is still artificially relaxed. If this continues for too long, the solution will exist in policy vacuum, which is certainly not a desirable state of affairs. The most appropriate strategy is the "watchful eye", that is, while the policies may be relaxed for the sake of productivity, they are not being set aside. Here's an example: at one site the primary systems had a home-grown system watcher that tracked the usage by each developer and analyst. One day an analyst who normally executes the same canned queries each day was suddenly making queries deeper into the data. This alerted an operator who, rather than initiating a witch hunt, simply sent an email to the analyst for an explanation.

Oh, he realizes, *you're profiling data in preparation for a data migration.* Now he knows that not only are these deeper queries warranted, he will likely see many more of them coming from other project personnel. So does the operator turn a blind eye to the activity "just this once" or should there be other protocols or controls in place so that the activity, while allowed, will still have some boundaries around it? It clearly cannot be a free-for-all.

And these "additional boundaries" are usually a healthier way to approach the rollout for all involved. It keeps the data security staff from flashing-out when they see these deep queries, eventually becoming deep extractions. If they know it's part of the migration project, now it's a simple matter to capture each event (they were being captured anyhow) and send a weekly report to the project boss. Anything that appears out of the ordinary or an employee cannot explain, should elicit further scrutiny. But just keep in mind the level of scrutiny we're talking about.

At some point, we have to either embrace our employees with trust, or reject them altogether as disloyal. There really isn't any middle ground. Either we trust them, or we don't.

Anecdote: Each day a man left the factory with a wheelbarrow full of empty boxes. The guards stopped him each time, certified that the boxes were all empty, and let the man go his way, blissfully unaware that he was stealing *wheelbarrows*.

The point being, our employees *already* know how to steal from us. IT divisions hire smart people, the kind that can solve deep integration problems on a large scale. Any of us might have one or more of these gurus in-house. One leader told me that his expert on data analytics was summarily chastised for having violated an intellectual property policy while performing one of those many one-time actions. Rather than condemn him, they kept an eye on him. Over the course of time he never executed one of these again, so no action was taken. Later in the project, this same technologist performed the very same action. Only this time it was with mature, tested intellectual property about to move into production. Now the protocol had changed, and the security detail were somewhat less merciful on the second go-round. After all, the accused was about to exit the project for another client's site, who could be a competitor. The security detail is not required to second-guess or "err on the side of conservatism" or any such like. They can condemn or elevate a person based on criteria that doesn't even apply to a migration project.

So in all this, it is important that the security folks and the people overseeing firewalls and the like, be notified that some strange and anomalous activity will be rising from our ranks, and they should pay attention to the activity but not be so quick to draw conclusions.

Anecdote: A child came inside from playing and without any fanfare, went straight to the shower. She scrubbed herself clean, toweled off and changed clothes. Just one problem: She wasn't in her own home, but the home of a friend who was her age and her size, so the clothes fit her. The shower wasn't hers, nor was the soap or the towels.

She had visited the home numerous times, and on sleepovers her friend's mom had overseen their night-time routine to take showers and get into bed. And on occasion they had played together and she had needed a change of clothes, so her friend's mother had helped her find something to wear among her daughter's things. While none of this was particularly harmful, to both Moms it certainly felt out of place.

The reason being: the young girl had given *herself* permission to do something that her friend's parents had only considered reasonable as a *one-time thing*. Showering, changing clothes, all for one-time needs. The parents had not considered that their one-time generosity would lead this girl into thinking that she had permission to do it anytime she wanted.

Back to our problem. We have some one-time needs that are obvious. The fated project manager above actively engaged those needs, but the policy makers around him were not willing to make any exceptions. And this is where we are, to actively and deliberately make allowance and exceptions in a migration context and no other. It's a one-time thing, and we need breathing room. But we don't need permission to do it now and forever. We have a bubble of work and activity to get past. All of it will be scrutinized, but the level of scrutiny and the reasonableness of the actions, will determine whether we will have a healthy migration project or one that just lurches along without making any apparent progress.

So no, I am not suggesting that policies be set aside, I am suggested that they be extended, enhanced and adapted. For this one-time migration action, and then everyone can go back to business-as-usual.

We could liken this process to the construction of a building. First-time-only activities for the building include: prepare the ground, lay the foundation, set up the superstructure, run electrical wiring etc. We can see that we will never revisit any of these things again, but they are important, in fact critical to the health of the building, especially as it regards its architectural integrity. Imagine forgetting a floor, or an elevator shaft. We cannot revisit architectural flaws like this.

One building owner in New York wanted a separate elevator to his upper penthouse floors because he was tired of riding the elevator with the common folk. After much deliberation and the assessment of expense and effort, he realized that it would be cheaper to tear down and rebuild the entire building than attempt to retrofit it with an new elevator shaft. He also realized that the cost of a helicopter pad on the roof, along with a helicopter service was a far less expensive operation. So he opted for helicopter service. But he still has to ride the elevator in inclement weather. The new elevator shaft in the building would have been an architectural bolt-on. The helicopter option is a workaround. We would rather avoid both.

Back to the story, the migration project is a one-time initiative. We need to keep this in mind as we move forward with the effort, because we will encounter bumps and impasses along the way that seem like failure points, but they are actually waypoints. Times for us to fall back, regroup, reassess and initiate a new assault. This is because building out a warehouse is the act of standing up a living environment. It is not a project in the strictest sense.

But the one-time-migration has all the trappings of a project, with the portent that it will become and is becoming a living environment. So we need to pay attention to certain aspects while deferring others.

For example, in the construction of a building, would we hire security guards to screen tenants? Of course not, because the tenants aren't using the building yet. Imagine how ridiculous it would look to see tenant security guards checking the badges of the construction crews. No doubt another form of security is necessary, but not the same as we would see with tenants. Case in point, in the building where we work with a client, our badges are approved only for certain floors. We cannot make the elevator go to floors that aren't approved on the badge, nor could we piggy-back with another tenant because each floor has turnstiles requiring the badge for access. Would we need this level of security for a construction crew member? Certainly not at the outset of construction, which is where we are.

I know that what I'm describing sounds perfectly reasonable to many of you but trust me, it sounds like fanatical-cowboy-stuff to others. Bear with me as I make points along the way that will likely apply to most readers.

So the operational parts of the solution require scrutiny and higher attention, and we will certainly get to those as the solution matures (just as we would tighten things up as the building construction matures). But having them in place at the outset is a ridiculous form of micro-management. I have had to remediate environments where this level of micro-management had been in play, and it was nothing short of a crushing, almost suffocating effect on the project.

One example is invoking full-tilt, interdepartmental defect reporting at the same level of scrutiny as a mature environment. This is a common mistake, and the balancing act is simpler than it sounds. We can use formal defect tracking as long as it is self-contained within the project. A more mature environment may include reporting defects up through one or more levels of management. This would be necessary for a mature process, because such defects are not acceptable in a production solution. But for a migration, where even the subject-matter-experts are re-learning the long-since-buried logic in the old environment and attempting to map it into the shining, never-existed-before future state, we need to make some significant allowances to keep from crushing the effort altogether.

One project was subjected to defect reporting that rose several levels of management above them before they could affect any actions on the defects. In a migration project, where everything is new and churning, this is a lot of noise in a room that would better function with less of it. Managers were being alerted with defect reports and counts that they had never thought possible, all because their testers were learning the environment too, and many of the defects were themselves invalid. This elicited accusatory finger-pointing and unprofessional conversations. It need not be so.

Recall the notes at the front of the chapter: Early in the project the total count of invalid defects will eclipse the total count of valid defects by a factor of 5x or higher.

Breathing room, one might call it. Lighten up, says another.

One colleague related to me that in a recent migration project, the policy folks came out *en-force*. Formal defect resolution would be in full effect from day one. Any defect reported by the testers would be dealt with in the same manner as production-level defects. We'll see in a moment that this is not only inappropriate for the first stages of a migration project, it's downright toxic.

Some principles to embrace in a migration project include:

- Delineate between what is a first-time/one-time activity versus an operational one.
- In order to assure a productive testing approach, testers will gradually grow into a mature understanding of the technology and the new business model leveraging it. They may be required to change their testing approach altogether, so it is not safe to assume that they are firing on all cylinders on day one.
- In order to assure a productive development approach, developers will gradually grow into a mature understanding of the business and technology. They will be required to think about problems differently and implement their solutions in sometimes counter-intuitive ways. It is not safe to assume that they are firing on all cylinders on day one.
- The above conditions, between developers and testers, cannot be minimized. Their initial rollouts, both of the development work products and testing work products, will be flawed until they can mature their knowledge. This is why invoking formal, production-strength testing protocols is unfair to the tester (they receive reprimands for flawed test cases) and to the developer (who receives the brunt - and the reprimand - when a defect arises). So a developer produces stuff, the tester tests it. And in many cases the developer will have to point out to the tester where their testing protocol is flawed, producing a false defect. The tester fears the false defect as much as the developer fears the defect report. Both of

them are struggling to get on their feet so let's not continually *punish them for being on the learning curve.*

- Project managers who are accustomed to speaking one language and one terminology will find themselves in a more rarefied atmosphere. They will feel rushed, exasperated and sometimes like they are gasping for air. They, too are in a re-training mode and will have to rethink how they manage this migration project, because it has so few aspects of the operational projects they are accustomed to. In short, some activities must precede others, and will precede only once. Get things out of order because of expedience (such as the availability of certain personnel, or the lack of availability of technology) and the rest of the activities will lurch along, sputtering rather than smoothly gliding along.

Each of the above groups will make honest mistakes as they are standing up the new environment, so it is inappropriate to hold them accountable for such mistakes in the same way we would in a mature production environment, where the same mistakes may increase risk and cost.

The opposite is true for a migration project, where the cost and risk is not in the production environment (it does not yet exist) but in failure to put the new system into production.

Think for a moment about the differential in cost between full-time developers, testers, project manager and business analysts all focused intensely on the migration, versus the part-time operators, admins and troubleshooters in a production environment. Think also about the Netezza machines in the other room waiting for the new solution to be deployed. They are a sunk cost with no return-on-investment until the new solution is actually deployed. Risks and costs are directly inverted, and this is also a one-time condition. The policies that impede *deployment* are actually in the way, and are part of the problem rather than the solution.

Case Study Short: A colleague relates that his project managers were all accustomed to operational projects against a mature warehouse. When the migration project began, the well-paid consultant that they had hired simply mandated that the two key requirements for success would be (a) a reasonably mature data model and (b) an accompanying source-to-target-map. The project managers disagreed. They believed that valid test cases should be put in place prior to the commencement of any work.

After much argument over this topic, and some heated debates all through the day, one of the project managers called in the head of the testing group. This person said that not only would he *require* a source-to-target map and a mature data model *before* they could even construct test cases, he wanted all of the test cases built against the reporting environment, not the underpinning data structures. This is because, even if the data structures themselves are without defect, this is immaterial if they have to be changed or augmented to support reporting. So reporting priorities should be driving the conversation, not the data model.

The project managers *still* disagreed, and proceeded to put together a very strange project model indeed. What was the outcome? The predictable sputter of a project being operating by people who have never executed a migration project before, and likewise don't understand the technology or business model. They were in over their head.

The unknown. And here is the most significant issue affecting the developers, the testers and the timeline. The people who own the operational environment from whence we are moving, really believe that they understand all of the technical and business parts of the system.

They really, *really* do.

Believe that is. They really, really *believe* that they understand it all, and honestly, in their heart-of-hearts, think that they can get by with a minimalist view of functional specifications because they "know all the rest". Here's a short version of what they know, or think they know:

Workarounds added to make up for shortcomings - they forgot about those, or they have been assimilated into tribal memory.

Bad data - they fixed along the way with a variety of hooks, processes or sheer genius. We're about to pull all of it into the light again. These may include rigged-up data types or conversions, truncated/trimmed strings, magic numbers, embedded unprintable characters, malformed or mis-aligned data, hand-crafted data, information that was imported from another system and never scrubbed or reviewed (they swore they would get around to it!).

Performance enhancements that they believe are functionally necessary. We'll have to tease these things apart like trying to pull cotton seeds from cotton. There is a reason why the cotton gin became so popular, and we need scalable methods to tease apart these things so they don't bog us down. This amounts to de-engineering the original system, but we still only do it once.

Inter-technology interactions - while the Netezza machine is a fairly open and malleable system, don't expect other technologies to play well in the sandbox. See this book's chapter on Teradata as a prime example.

Data migration - the physical movement of data from the old system to the new, in quantities that will never, ever be experienced again.

Large-scale backfilling: the conversion of the original data structures into the new data structures through a series of one-time transforms and integration rules. The backfill can take a long time to test and deploy and will never execute again. It is destined for mothballs by its very design. It is a "maiden-voyage" operation. It only sets sail once, and never again.

Case Study Short: After many days of struggling with a particular report output, one of the analysts finally threw his hands up in exasperation. The data was there, the parameters were identical to the original report, but the numbers weren't matching. He called in one of the client's analysts to take a look over his shoulder. The client analyst took it aside and likewise struggled with it for hours. Then one of the senior analysts came alongside and told them, *You have to filter those records on that column, eliminating all the records with the value of "100"*. To which both the analysts stared at him, in shocked surprise. What does the "100" value mean? *Don't know,* said the senior analyst, *it's just what we use.* They plugged this filter into the query and the values tied-off on the very first execution.

Hidden and unknown tribal knowledge. They really, *really* believe they know where all of it is buried.

Case Study Short: One environment had an operational-styled data model in an Oracle machine. It had been used for both operations and reporting for many years, but now needed to be migrated into the Netezza machine. Twenty-five terabytes of uncompressed data had to move from the Oracle machine, across the network and into the Netezza machine. No network storage device available to them had this much space. No other option existed except to move the information in a pipeline directly across the network from the Oracle machine to the Netezza machine. This one-time backfill of information had to be flawless even though it would run only once, perhaps twice in production. This process had to be tested, re-tested and *uber*-tested to make sure it would cover every possible nuance of data as it moved from the old model to the new model. So a process that was only supposed to run once, would run over a thousand times as part of its testing protocol.

For three days of data, the entire execution ran in fifteen minutes on the development machine, and in five minutes on the production machine. Multiply this by three years of information, and the sheer wall-clock time of the physical migration had to be carefully managed. Running days-at-a-time of data was the most appropriate approach, since we could measure and check errors on each segment. It would be devastating to attempt running it end-to-end for all data, only to get partially through it and encounter a failure. This is exactly what happened, but only in isolation for a few of the segments. With all the other segments safely inside the machine, we fixed those spot-problems in the other segments and everything worked fine.

So this mass-data movement is something that takes everyone by surprise. They think in terms of the mechanics of data movement, but have not considered a wide range of non-scalable aspects of the environment that will impede their plans. The Netezza machine can pull the data inside with breathtaking scale. No doubt about it. But what about the other parts of the environment? Can we extract data easily from an environment that was specifically designed to host data without mass-extraction as a priority?

Case Study Short: Keep in mind that operational systems are geared to get data inside the machine using high-frequency, small-size transactions, but cannot get the data back out for report-ing, that is low-frequency, large-scale operations. It is, after all, why we are moving to Netezza. Somehow this aspect is forgotten when attempting to extract this data for migration. One Oracle shop had ten terabytes of operational data that would require three days of non-stop extraction activity simply because the tables were not indexed to support the extraction, so all tables had to be dumped out "as is". Mercifully, these were dropped onto network storage so we did not have to pipe them to Netezza across the network. The team thought they were home-free in that all they had to do to load history was to load these files, and then catch-up with the operational system. This would have been a great plan, except the source system *had no means to determine* change-data-capture so that we could pull only new-and-changed.

So in the end, we had to re-extract the entire thing just prior to going live. On top of this, the file system was set up on simple gigabit ethernet, which while fast enough for transactional pro-cessing, only offered a max of fifty megabytes per second on the transfer speed. With so many terabytes to move, we had to be very diligent in planning the point of cut-over so that we could meet the data transfer window and cut-over live without a hiccup. In this particular case, the sys-tem started the extract at the close of business on the prior Friday, with the expectation to finish the transfer into testable form by Sunday afternoon. With Monday a holiday, confidence was high that the we would go live well before the opening bell on Tuesday morning. But Wednesday came and went, as did Thursday and Friday, requiring almost ten calendar days to affect the total transfer.

Nobody expected this level of latency. In an after-action investigation, we discovered that the operations center had noted the high-level of traffic and were concerned that it would impede transactional processing, and had forgotten that Monday was a holiday, so sometime Sunday had dialed back the available bandwidth for the transfer to *one-tenth the max*. No wonder it took so long.

Keep in mind that we don't normally think about including additional people into the dialog for these kinds of things, which is what makes them one-of-a-kind, special, and in need of more visibility so that people don't inadvertently torpedo the activities.

Expedience is often the next curve in the road, to be guarded against deliberately, because just beyond the curve, the road gets dark, the skies get stormy, and all the bridges are out. In migration projects the temptation toward expedience is ever-present. A common joke is:

If you don't have time to do it right, when will you have time to do it over?

Gathering steam. For a migration project, the execution of the migration is only part of the problem. Once the development team gathers a head of steam, each time they roll out an incremental part of the solution, it will seem like a tsunami of stuff for the testers to take on. If their regression tests are not scalable, and their testing personnel not knowledgeable, the outcome is predictable. They *will* fall behind.

If the testers fall behind, the developers will have no place to deliver their goods into. And make no mistake, each delivery will have the same ever-increasing functional strength until the end, where the testers will feel the drinkin'-from-a-fire-hose effect at full throttle. Testers will not have enough time to review it if their testing processes are not scalable and flawlessly repeatable. More importantly, if their knowledge of the new system is still immature, it is more likely than not that their first testing implementation will be flawed and will deliver a large number of false defects. This will slow down the testers, but will also slow down the developers as they will have to fully investigate each defect to determine if it is real or not, and then fix the real ones. If a large number of them are false defects, the effect is to bog down the development team to remediate the products of the testing staff. Nobody is winning here.

Case Study Short: One development team seemed to be getting a large number of false defects in their queue, so finally had a discussion with the testing team lead to see if their testing processes could be shored up or assisted in order to avoid the malaise of the false defects. The answer was surprising: *Frankly, you guys produce so much stuff with that Netezza machine, that my testers are swamped all the time, so even if there's something slowing you down that shouldn't be, at least it's slowing you down a little bit. If you were running at full speed, I'd have to double my staff.*

Case Study Short: One environment leveraged testers for all sorts of mission-critical systems, and decided to use the same group for testing the migration project, just as if the migration project could be dovetailed into their mission-critical processes. No sooner had they gotten their first release than they started struggling with the testing approach and methods. They were required to communicate with the developers only through formal protocols, so for each "defect" they found, they first *had* to report it, then they could formally dialogue with the development team. Over ninety percent of these first defects were false, partly because they did not quite yet understand the new model, nor did they understand the new technology. And because the environment had mission-critical processes in place, the defect-count was raised to the attention of the senior managers, which in turn brought the heat on the development team. But when the development team reviewed the defects and found so many false ones, this blowback hit the testing team, rising up into their ranks of management, and people being called onto the carpet for having so many false defects. Those mission-critical systems were being overseen by the same testers, after all, and if they were this incompetent, it could represent a contractual breach.

Seriously?

This is why the migration project is special. It should not be subject to such draconian, high-process actions. Imagine when all the smoke cleared, how all these managers felt when they realized that their developers and testers had effectively been sequestered from each other, and all they had to go on were the tenuous specifications of some of the data modelers and aficionados of the existing system, themselves overworked and not always responsive to questions? On top of this, the testers had not been a part of the project from the inception, but had been considered a "resource pool" that could be turned-on-or-off like a switch. Many readers who are seasoned in these sorts of things, see how foolish this is. Data warehouses contain knowledge. Migration projects are deep, detailed knowledge transfer. Nobody is a plug-and-play resource.

Even more egregious, this large number of defects triggered certain automatic *policy* actions inside the company, not the least of which led to the scuttling of the development crew! Imagine their surprise after they had reported that over ninety percent of the defects were themselves false, and on the edge of this discovery were walked out the door? It sets up the unseemly notion that policy will be followed no matter how unreasonable, *even to the risk of deferring the deployment altogether*.

When the project team tried to get a new development team together, no skills were found in-house, so they advertised on the street. But the Enzee community is very small, and word does have a tendency to get out about such things. With so many new Netezza projects launching at sites that have no such issues, why would a seasoned Netezza expert deliberately walk into such a hornet's nest? Yes, they had trouble re-staffing the project. *Yawn*. What else is new?

More importantly, they had every intention of doing it the same way all over again. Some folks never learn.

Make no mistake - unreasonable, inflexible adherence to policy *automatically defers the project deadline.* It gives people permission to take longer because the risk of doing otherwise is too high.

Migration projects are a continuum of discovery and implementation. Invariably, subject matter experts with deep involvement in the current implementation will be completely surprised by what they find when the migration team "pops the hood" to begin fully characterizing the scope of the effort. Therefore several levels of scope are in play:

What is functionally known – these are the obvious parts that most managers can roll off the tip of their tongue, usually have some documentation around and may well be the centerpiece of the effort. The stakeholders will attempt to inventory the capabilities and features of this environment to the best of their knowledge.

What is functionally forgotten - these are "gotchas" that everyone in the room has forgotten until someone stumbles across a table, piece of code or a component that is not accounted for. We'll find a lot of these, because nobody can keep track of everything.

What it functionally assumed – these are the non-obvious parts but are gleaned through "tribal storytelling" usually through white board sessions and picking-the-brains of technologists. Detailed assumptions are usually not dangerous, but broad assumptions have to be brought to the fore to avoid primary impacts to the project.

Case Study Short - One subject matter expert offered up long series of operations that their data had to follow. Nobody had ever characterized this algorithm before so it seemed quite complex and daunting. But when one of our experts looked it over, this complex algorithm reduced to two simple steps. This is because the original experts had seen the problem *transactionally*, but our expert saw it as a *set-based* problem. The outcome was the same, but each used a different approach. Many functional assumptions are simply the attempt of a technologist to map the solution *from* the source technology rather than remap the solution to fit the target technology. When promulgated, the simpler algorithm often seems too good to be true.

Oh, it's true. And it's *good* to be true.

What is functionally unknown, but knowable – such as certain technical implementations, code bases, spreadsheets and other collateral that are supporting documents, products or processing artifacts, even code and implementation details that shed more light on the functional necessities of the implementation. Of course, any existing documents are usually stale beyond any usefulness, and any new forms of the document, especially those that have recently been produced to support the project, are usually so superficial that they demand much deeper analysis. *Make time for the analysis,* because accepting someone's word, or diagrams, as the final form without question, is rarely wise.

What is functionally unknown, unforeseen or actually forgotten – this is a black hole of knowledge that cannot be fully characterized and will be discovered along the way. It represents the highest risk to the timeline of the project. It is also the clearest and most important reason to embrace an adaptive approach to the migration. Absolutely nobody can be omniscient about the end-to-end functional needs and requirements, or how they were originally implemented. Flexibility and collaboration are in order here.

As in the above case study, if a more flexible approach had been embraced, the tester and developers could collaborate in harmony until the project's functionality could get on its feet. Of course, if the policy of the company requires that these things be in place from day one, why not embrace them and run with them? No worries, just don't do it on a fixed price or rigid timeline, because a migration project can easily blow both of them, big time.

This is especially daunting for hardcore project managers, who see the breach of a deadline as tantamount to a character flaw on the part of those making the promises. A project manager who is this inflexible has no business overseeing a migration project. Their rigidity will often be expressed in highly unprofessional terms. I've seen perfectly reasonable, even-tempered project managers start to smolder, glow, spark into flame and become a raging forest fire of anxiety. Perhaps migration projects require a special temperament, or perhaps this is yet another opportunity for the right person to grow and transform as a result of the experience.

Case Study Short: One project manager looked me in the eye and assured me deeply that his people were competent and knowledgeable. Several of them had come from product companies and had performed migration projects before. No, not with the Netezza platform, but they had been through a migration crucible and felt they were the best qualified to lead the migration. The project manager said to me, "I know you think it's hard for a migration project to stay on schedule. But we've done this enough times to have it down. So let's just agree to some deadlines and then we can get started." Sounded almost like an attorney. Almost.

My Dad (a former prosecutor (32 years) for the State of Texas) says this of attorneys. that they will sit across from you at a deposition, then will close their book of notes, set it aside and say "Let's just talk for a bit, just you and me." But make no mistake, you're still on record. It's just a ploy they use to get your guard down.

So my response to the above project manager was simply, "We'll put those *guidelines* into the project plan. But in a migration project, there is no *deadline*."

This was taken rather harshly by this project manager, who later admitted he really had been using manipulative language to get me to commit to a deadline. After all, the original date of the migration rollout actually slipped by three months. The slippage was nobody's fault in particular, but if we had committed to a deadline, fault would have been assigned, and it would have fallen in our lap. This project manager really had reported deadline-dates to his own managers, but had added enough slog in the schedule so that the final heat wasn't so bad. It's the responsible thing to do.

I mentioned elsewhere that my wife does large-scale facilities and occasionally encounters architectural issues like dry rot, termites and the like. Imagine a client taking one look at the termites and rallying the troops to blame her for it, or the contractor who discovered it. It's ridiculous on the surface, yet is very typical of some project-level discussions I've had or seen transpire in the past. Right down to "You're the experienced person. You should have anticipated this!".

Is it really that easy? *Really?* Wow, if I had that kind of clairvoyance, what the heck am I doing with my career? Just pick few winning lotto tickets, and some for my family, get bored with my millions and move to the coast.

What is functionally desired but not previously forthcoming – the migration project may be (and usually is) borne on the wings of complaints, that the existing system has run out of gas or the ability to continue to functionally mature, and many critical feature-requests have been delayed for too long, are piling up, and are (at least) one reason behind migrating to better technology. If these are not directly considered in the architecture and planning, they will have to be retrofitted later. Either case requires embracing an adaptive approach because it is effectively implementing new stuff while assimilating it into the old stuff, further increasing the "unknowns" for all involved. This especially impacts data modelers and testers, who may have to rethink everything they are doing.

Case Study Short: One business group was tired of the same-old "as is" reporting. So they wanted to have some "as was" reporting added in. This is not particularly hard to do, as long as the data model supports the as-is/as-was model, or perhaps in retail terms could be called "as-is/as-sold" model. But then something took a turn, and someone asked for "as of" reporting, meaning that they would pick a date for the main query, but designate certain dimensions to be clamped into a particular time frame, perhaps even a specific date. But wait, that's not all, they wanted some predictive power to be able to ask "as if", extrapolating certain items forward in time to determine where a trend might lead. The first two, the team could pull off with common modeling techniques, but the second two represented a challenge. First in that the existing model would have to be revisited for compatibility with such an approach, and second in supporting the testing phase. How does one say that a predicted trend is invalid? And just because it's a prediction, if it doesn't come true then does this represent a defect?

Quite unfortunately for the "as of" scenario here, some of the business folk overheard a watercooler conversation that the reporting team, and the reporting tool, *absolutely required* equi-joins for all the work. That is, while others could implement an as-of model fairly easily using date-range lookups, this team would have to figure out how to make it happen with equi-joins. Or would they? A casual conversation at the watercooler *does not a requirement make*. Yet, the integration and the modeling team struggled for many *weeks* to make this work, not realizing that they were chasing an artificial requirement and an artificial constraint. The reporting system had no such absolute equi-join requirement and the reporting team's plan all along, was to use date-ranges for the as-of queries. So where was the disconnect? First in attempting to solve a problem that did not exist, second in attempting to solve it the wrong way, and third in not knowing the difference.

Case Study Short: One group chased down the path of attempting to cascade keys through dimensions and into the fact table in a Quixotic attempt to support an as-of model using equi-joins only, similar to the model above. Once the dimensions were in place, we began to play around with this cascading keys model. Basically, each record would be outfitted with a Unique ID and a the same Unique ID plus the incremental slowly-changing-dimension index. This would then be captured in the parent table, and that record would be captured in its parent table etc. Of course, we considered it our honorable duty to show why such a model does not and cannot work, but it was the brainchild of a soul who had the client's ear (yet another contractor!) and so we had to perform some degree of due diligence before requiring the model to get on its knees so we could *cap*-it, Mafioso-execution style.

But lo, the client's own modeling team came to this conclusion and did the dirty work for us. In one eventful meeting, their lead designer held the model under the water and watched it flail until life ebbed from its soul. And in the middle of all this, the contractor who originally proposed the model went down kicking and screaming as well, defending its viability to the very end. Humorous to tell, one of the simple walkthroughs of the model showed that by the time the cascade had gotten five levels up (yes, it was also a snowflake) then it would have to go two levels down again, and then back up, porpoising through the data like a fish in the sea. Then we would have to use some iterations to boil these up, some estimating as many as eleven loops to make sure the keys all cascaded correctly. Our contention was that this could never be adequately *tested*, as the data was found in error, how would we know that it was a data error, a looping error, an index-to-the-looping-error - whew! For someone who likes to preach simplicity in the data model, this conversation was an anxious one indeed!

But as I say, we started out with the intention of heading full bore toward a coup-de-gras on this approach because we knew it could not work, and had failed every time it had been tried. The takeaway from all this is not the inexperience of the contractor in promulgating an already failed model (this carried its own punishment). Rather, this is yet another case of having what seems to be a good idea, watching it crumble before our eyes, and then being able to reset the direction *almost immediately* toward a model that would actually work. Netezza's power lets us perform such magical feats and remain aggressively adaptive because it has the sheer power to dig folks out of a clay pit. In fact, at the end of the meeting noted above, the conclusion was that with *a few minor* modeling changes, we could completely forego the cascading keys nonsense, push toward a healthy and maintainable model, and do it in a matter of *days*. Oddly, it took more time to analyze the model into failure than it would have taken to implement it correctly. Alas, some people need to see evidence of failure, as theory or conjecture are simply not enough.

Back to the subject of long-overdue functionality wanting to piggyback onto the migration project:

In essence, these new functionalities were not only new to implement, they were new concepts *entirely*. While the textbooks could have helped them (at least), the cross-communication between the teams would have helped more. Whenever people see a new project launching, or an initiative that is a retrofit or a migration to an existing system, they automatically see it as an opportunity to squeeze in the long overdue functionality that some folks may have already given up on. So expect this kind of stuff to jump right out of the woodwork onto the desk, complete with their vociferous champions. Just watch out for those who champion untested theory, not reality.

What is functionally expected (but unspoken) of the new implementation – The clearest example of this is the expectation that certain reports will return within "x-number-of-seconds" or that other unspoken expectations will be met de-facto. The Netezza platform is very powerful and in proof-of-concept can show certain complex queries returning in mind-blowing speed. Some people will want to see this nimble, mind-blowing speed from start to finish. However, if the specific expectations are not on the radar (for these and many others, such as back-end processing windows and such) we may face a performance tuning exercise late in the game that will elicit rework in the flows, and the attendant re-testing of those flows, but also rework and retesting in the reporting layer as well. Embracing an adaptive approach also braces for these kinds of surprises.

Case Study Short: The implementers had seen the incredible speed of Netezza and wanted it for their reports. Then they proceeded to design the reports in a manner that could not leverage Netezza's power. These base architectural flaws (in the reporting implementation) were later reviewed by architects who were masters with the reporting technology, and wondered out loud why anyone would want to implement the reports they way they had. Their answer: The templates had come from reports running in Excel, and had directed the reporting engineers to build the reports so they would operate identical to the Excel implementation. The disconnect: The users hated the Excel implementation because it did not align with their workflow model. They were *stunned* to see it reproduced in the new reporting implementation.

Scope - As a principal involved in scoping such an effort, we often find three forms of "scope" that have to remain on the table, in full view of everyone *for the course of the project*. We often observe that scope rarely creeps. It often perches on a starting block and waits for the pistol, and is in full-bore runaway when the pistol fires. Keeping the scope under control is no different than firefighting.

• *In Scope/Out of Scope* – Specifically defined in the contract or SLA, and will help to keep the project on track (for internal efforts) and keep a consulting/contractor effort from getting de-railed with unrelated issues.

• *Change in Scope* – unforeseen additional activities, or removal of activities (such as existing vestigial functions that are no longer in use) that may have impact on the timeline and level of effort. Some of these are easily absorbed by the project timeline and budget on an individual basis, but taken as a whole can have an impact along the continuum of the timeline that can and will delay deployment. Imagine adding an extra day here and there to an already tight project timeline? Or how about just an extra hour here and again? Those hours add up to days, and days to weeks.

• *Magnitude of Scope* - in this regard, for a function/capability that is already on the radar. We sometimes see that a particular process may have orders-of-magnitude more complexity than first realized. This will materially change the effort and impact the timeline. Even if we can keep the other basic forms of scope under control, this one is the bane of migration projects. We cannot always predict what form it will take, but we can predict that it will take form. It's important to bet on this probability as a certainty than just blindly hoping that *our* migration project, of *all* migration projects, will get an exemption.

Case Study Short: A project team had come on board to perform a preliminary analysis and design, but critical parts of the information were withheld from them. Rather a representative of the functionality "told them" what was in the box, but would not let them see it. Taking their word for it, they signed a contract and within days *discovered* that what was in-the-box was orders of *magnitude* more scope that the representative had - er- *represented*. Rather than calling a full stop, the team attempted to implement it but got bogged down. When the timeline slipped, they reminded the principals of the gross discrepancies in the provided collateral, but enough time had passed such that the project manager looked him in the eye and said "It's not my fault that you missed this during the design phase." These kinds of responses border on psycho-ceramics, er, *crackpottery*.

Fixed Price v Time-and-Materials - I've noted elsewhere that for a migration project where the contract group wants to make money or at least break even (I can't imagine) then a fixed price is not the ticket. At *all*. However, if the group wants to accept the risk and presume some degree of loss in exchange for a higher goal (like more projects over the long term) then this could be do-able. With the clear understanding that the risk is real, the loss is real, and the loss could be permanent if there is no follow-on work.

For consultant and contractor groups, migration projects have enough high-risk unknowns that it is impractical to execute one on a fixed price. Perhaps a not-to-exceed basis may be appropriate, provided that the scope can by circumscribed and characterized in a manner that reduces risk for all involved. Migration projects are *not common development projects* specifically because of their one-time nature and the inability to determine the deeper levels of the unknowns without further assessment. Even a formal assessment and design phase may not reveal the hidden scope issues at a detailed enough depth to properly characterize the level of effort. This increases the risk of the project, and may require a proposing consulting firm to pad contingency into the contract to buffer against this risk.

Approaches

For the vast majority of operational or warehouse migrations, the eventual rollout will consist of a one-time backfill to catch-up the history into the new model(s). It will then move toward a daily or incremental process that will be the ongoing operational protocol. The implementations of these two models are in flux for the duration of the project's development and testing. The backfill may require extensive deduplication, where the incremental may require change-data-capture. The objective is to have the data "lay down" in the tables as if the incremental model were in play from day-one of operation. Some groups even attempt to backfill the information this way, running a day-at-a-time in repetition for as many days as they want to preserve.

The nature of these operations requires a lot of knowledge transfer. From the outset, it is important to treat the project's functional knowledge base as lacking maturity both in the technical assets and components, and in the knowledge level of testers and developers. Testers usually lack the necessary knowledge of the target technology and developers lack necessary knowledge of business cases.

The best approach is to use adaptive, collaborative methods to converge, intersect and mature these knowledge bases over time without invoking the more formal production protocols better suited for mature, installed assets. Migration projects exist on a continuum of understanding and maturity. As such, defects introduced in one collaboration session may evaporate in the next. Software built for one part of the flow may have to be re-addressed when a downstream inadequacy is discovered. These are natural and healthy discoveries, but play unchecked havoc on an environment that needs lockstep compliance to policies and controls better fitted for a production environment.

There is an ever-present necessity to find opportunities to pre-process information in upstream transform parts of the flow, so that downstream transform operations are optimized. *This keeps the complete length of the flow in flux.* Only active collaboration of the developers and testers can close the gap. Formal, interdepartmental defect reporting only creates noise, and should be set aside until all flows have been reviewed by the reporting users. If formal defect reporting tools are used, these should remain self-contained inside the team's structure until the entire product is approaching production maturity. If this means that the back-end portions must enter UAT in states of partial construction, this is acceptable as long as the functional end-points (reporting information) have passed all integration testing.

Case Study Short: When describing the above to a seasoned testing crew, many of them breathed a sigh of relief. They knew that the incoming functionality would be difficult to navigate and that they would need time to get their arms around it. The testing leader, however, would hear none of it. He invoked even steeper protocols than those required in the production environment under the pretense that if this new incoming functionality could cross over such a high wall, it would indeed be worthy of production. Within weeks of this announcement, two developers and three testers, one of whom had already been through a migration project, cast their vote with their feet and walked off the project. Contractors were hired to fill in the gaps, but something odd kept popping up, that is these contractors were one after another just plain losers. No sooner would they put a test in play, report the defect and cross their fingers, than a developer would decompose the test case and show where the defect was invalid. The testers, it seemed, could not penetrate the teflon of the development team. The functionality was coming at them so fast and furiously that in sheer quantity alone, the team would need to hire ten more bodies just to meet primary deadlines.

The testing leader would not relent. Hiding behind policy, he ran the project into the ground. One of the managers above him finally decided, after numerous reports from the rank-and-file, that the testing leader should be replaced, and so he was. The new leader was a member of the existing team, fully understood the needs and priorities, and initiated something amazing. Active, formal collaboration, complete with scribes and digital photos of the whiteboards (sometimes those camera phones have 1001 uses!). The overall knowledge transfer within just two weeks of this new direction got the testers back on track. Moreover, it completely removed the adversarial tension between the developers and testers.

Of course, we realize that *some* tension has to exist between testers and developers, but when the testers feel like they are being tied to a post and then struck repeatedly with rubber truncheons, one must wonder why a job in housekeeping or food service would not be a better career choice. In the new model, the testers were able to embrace their value, not feel as though they were constantly at risk for things they could not control.

Case Study Short: One of our managers took one of our testers for a walk-around-the-pond outside the main building. She wanted to have an open discussion as to why this tester was so completely uptight all the time. As it turned out, most of the functionality passing through his office was never *officially* tested. With a development staff of fifteen people and only two testers, he felt the crushing pressure of responsibility. The manager poked him in the shoulder to get him to open up. When he was dismissive, she whacked him on the shoulder to emphasize her request. When he was once again dismissive, she positioned herself in front of him and forcefully shoved him in the chest with both arms, catching him off-guard and almost causing him to fall down the embankment, where the pond water waited to claim him. A military veteran, until now he had decided to keep his fears and anxieties to himself, but this really set him off, so he got back in her face and said *"Stuff comes at me ninety miles an hour and who knows if it works or not. My title says that I'm supposed to know, but I cannot know. I don't even have the time or staff to know. And if something goes wrong, they'll be at my door demanding of me. What will I tell them?"*

And this was for a common app-dev project. Wait until we get a Netezza machine in house and it ramps up head of steam. The resulting work products will come in such a tidal wave as to *crush* the best testers and make them wonder if they will have a job tomorrow. Active collaboration and formal interaction keep the environment healthy while maintaining the proper functional boundaries. Everybody knows what to expect because they're all *in on it*.

"I'm leaving the project," said the PM to her boss.

"Oh," he replied, "Not sure how you're doing that. I'm in charge of all the projects and I haven't approved anything like this."

"Be that as it may," she swallowed, "Today is my last day on the project."

"Like I said, that would be a neat trick."

"It's interesting that you only care about how I intend to pull this off, but not why."

He leaned forward on his elbows and in his richest condescending tone, asked, "Okay, humor me."

"You've noticed that of the last ten people we've hired in two months, only three of them are still here."

"All seven of those people violated policy and had to be let go," he leaned back in his chair, "That's out of my hands."

"I realize that," she said, "But I can see that the things we need to do to stand up this reporting environment will never happen. Policy will never relax and it will never get on its feet."

"That's a bit of a dark assessment," he said, "We'll get through this."

"I know I will," she smiled sweetly, "I was just notified three weeks ago that because these people were let go, and the circumstances of their exit, that it will be a negative mark on *my* salary assessment."

"That's true," he agreed, "The policies are meant to provide incentive for us to be more diligent in our hiring."

"More diligent," she smiled again, "*When we can't find any of these people* no matter how many places we look, and when one comes available we keep them for a few weeks and fire them. It's not like there's a big ol' pond of people out there to choose from. It's not like we get to choose when there's no choice. We take what we can get."

"Doesn't change anything," he said, "It's just how we operate."

"It's not workable," she said, "And by the policy, I won't be eligible for a raise this year, maybe not even next year. That's not what I signed up for. This is hard work and it's not unreasonable to expect a reward at the end of it."

"Not in the budget anyhow," he said, "We don't operate that way."

"I know," she grinned, "but I found a way to get back together with all of the people we hired and let go. It's a new project and I'm excited about it."

"First I've heard," he said, "That would be another neat trick. All those folks were put on a non-re-hireable list, and that's something not even you can overcome."

"But I have," she said, "And I'll be working with all of them on Monday morning. Our number one competitor picked all of them up, they need a project manager, and most of the people over there already know me. It's a win-win."

She rose, produced a flat envelope and laid it on his desk," That's my resignation. Today is my last day with the company."

"Wait a second, you can't leave without two week's notice."

"Is that the *policy*?" she smirked, "And what are the consequences if I don't give you the two weeks?"

"You won't be re-hirable."

She laughed, "I'm okay with that. What else?"

Unnerved by her laughter, he said, "They can withhold your last paycheck indefinitely."

"That's a myth. It would be against the law. Any other straws you want to grasp before I go?"

He stood, his anger rising, "Listen to me young lady. You have to follow the rules like all the rest of us!"

"I am following them," she said, "and if you have any doubts about it, check in with the guys over in Human Resources. And according to policy," she turned for a parting shot, "A termination like this requires the company to give me a payout based on my number of years of service."

He swallowed.

"And so I get a pay increase for leaving, and a bonus *too*."

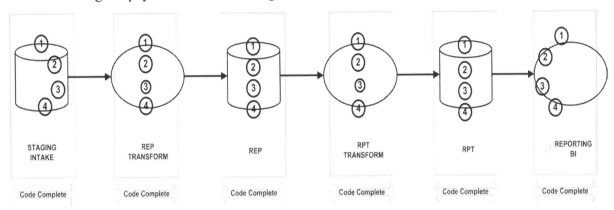

The depiction (above) is a representation of a waterfall or stovepipe model. Each portion from Intake, Repository Transform, Repository Functionality, Reporting Transform, Reporting Functionality is developed in a stovepipe,, and must be built, approved, code-complete and fully debugged as a standalone functionality. Even though we could stand these up alongside one another, if the constraint is that one has to be ready before the next, building them in parallel can be an unstable experience.

Its primary Achilles Heel is the reporting data model. No sooner will we get to the reports than we will find that we need special structures and additional flows we did not account for. Now we have to go back and *refactor* the flows that people thought had been signed-sealed-delivered. The problem here is in regarding the parts of the flow as *applications*, and the databases as standalone functionality, when they are simply legs and waypoints of a flow. Enforcing a stovepipe model will be a bumpy ride.

But we see how the data *flows* from end to end, following a *horizontal, flow-based form*, not a stovepiped functional model. Attempting to shoe-horn a migration project, most especially a flow-based model, into this stovepiped deployment approach will artificially protract the project timeline, increase cost and rework and is anathema to data warehouse development. In fact, it is *adversarial* to the mission of development and testing the flow model.

Some people, especially testers, roll their eyes when I suggest that the adversarial nature of the developers and testers is a bad thing. But look carefully at what I said. Not that the developers and testers are adversarial to each other, but that both groups are adversarial *to the mission of the project*. Developers and testers both will start engaging in behaviors that are more in line with self-preservation than the quality of the outcome.

Case Study Short: My (very young) nephew was visiting and wanted to play Jump Start Typing on the computer. It's a fun game to learn typing, but in order to beat the clock or the game, one has to *actually* type and not try to hunt-and-peck. Only real typists can beat the game, so the player has to learn to type for real. He made it past several levels before he finally shouted to me across the room, "Uncle David, you need to come over here and type along with me so I can get more points!" Ahh, he had the right idea. *Beat the game.* But he was doing it with methods that were adversarial to the mission of the game: *to make a good typist.*

So as we connect the dots, we should not encourage our developers or testers to "play the game" of policy conformance if the outcome will be adversarial to the mission of the project: *high quality, stable and durable deliverables.*

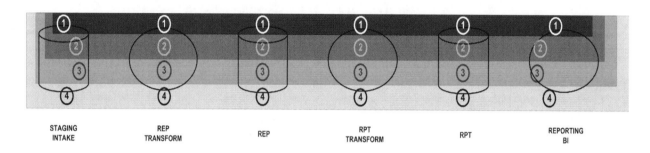

In the depiction (above) is an iterative, adaptive model for deploying a migration project. To explain the graphic, the Iteration (1) of work (dark gray) is spread out across all the resources up to the reporting environment. The second wave of work (Iteration 2) is also spread across the resources, but includes the functionalities of Iteration (1). The Iteration (3) includes both (1) and (2), while Iteration (4) includes its own functionality plus all that came before it. This builds repetition and strength into the flow foundation and shakes out all assumptions very early in the project timeline. The project manager who thinks-in-stovepipes cannot conceptualize the above, because there is no regard for the assets as a flow. For a stovepipe thinker, they are databases, and by definition endpoints, not *waypoints* as in the flow model. Of course, the flow model sees the Intake and the Reports as endpoints. This is also a challenge to the stovepipe-thinker.

Some of the highlights of this approach include:
- Subject matter areas are identified and designated on the far right (1-4), in the reports, and these are driven backward into the flow.
- Subject areas face user groups or functional groupings of user workflow and have nothing whatsoever to do with a report's frequency of use.
- This solidifies the requirement-driven nature of the flows. They will now possess the parts that are necessary to support their reports and no more.
- Requirements-driven approaches are the most successful in data warehousing in general and migration projects in particular.

- If additional parts are necessary that are outside of the reports, these represent another subject area
- Each subject area flow is matured alongside the others as an integrated whole, but the deliverables are deployed in these testable subject area groupings horizontally, not vertically.
- The Repository database, Reporting database and their supporting transforms *will exist in transient states of partial completion* as the individual subject areas are deployed horizontally and not vertically (as stovepipes).
- It is normal for the databases and their transform flows to enter UAT in this partial state, because they are supporting a given set of **reports in a UAT-ready state**.
- Likewise, the only valid test of the reporting flows and database content, is the UAT testing at the reporting subject area level. Testing the data along the flow path is useful, but not the final arbiter. Focus the testers where it counts.
- Measure performance of the backfill and incremental flow models separately. A thirty-minute run for the history backfill is not an arbiter of the duration of the daily incremental. The two are not related.
- Preserve/reuse flow logic and business logic wherever possible. Build the history and incremental flows as dovetailed operations. This will allow us to execute the backfill once, flip a switch, and then start the incremental flows knowing that they are using the same flow logic. Using separate, non-reusable flow logic in a migration project is not desirable and can significantly protract the project timeline (and the count of defects) while attempting to coordinate and synchronize the logic between them.

Migrations are first-time events, first-time development projects, first-time installations. Everything about a migration project is a first-time, one-time event, so does not easily dovetail into an environment that is already geared to manage mature, repeating production assets. The migration project's assets won't be mature until very near the time when it is ready for UAT or even thereafter (eliciting first-time feedback from the reporting users), so certain allowances should be made for adaptive approaches in modeling, collaboration, defect reporting and the like.

Some Tips

- Using automated scripts, expand the data model's columns (especially numeric columns) so that the flow of information is not constrained by sizing mismatches. Toward the end of the project, re-profile the columns and convert the ones that are necessary, re-shrinking the remainder to their original sizes (I noted how to do this elsewhere, it's easy with NPS 6.0).
- Migrate functionality within identified subject areas starting from the reporting system backwards, not the source-systems forwards.
- Identify and designate subject areas of reporting functionality (regardless of frequency-of use, these are functional subject areas)
- Select the subject area that represents a centerpiece of functionality. Build-out this centerpiece from end-to-end, source to eventual target. Build remaining features on this foundation.

- Build out the data requirements, information flows that support this subject area only
- Validate assumptions early. It is critical that the reporting environment be given priority in standing up its first subject area. It is sometimes advantageous to stand up the first entry-point presentations so that we can validate the reporting tool's interaction with the database. This can serve to polarize and solidify the reporting assumptions. Likewise, the source-to-target maps for a single subject area should be rolled all the way out to the reporting database as quickly as possible, even if all the data isn't ready yet. We are simply validating architectural and implementation assumptions at this point.
- Take on the next subject areas one at a time, and finally in parallel as the flows stabilize
- Subject areas are not found in the databases, but the *reports*. Attempting to mature database functionality without the reports will ultimately lead to mass rework in the database flows once the reports start consuming the data, and invariably reveal unforeseen discrepancies. Report functionality must be considered and integrated as early as possible, and this means selecting limited, subject-centric reports and quickly maturing the flows associated with them.
- Do not attempt to scatter-shot functionality across these subject area boundaries (e.g. based on frequency-of-use), because it will cause the reporting subject areas to be artificially stunted in their maturity.
- The databases upstream to the reports (e.g. the operational repository and marts) will exist in *states of partial functionality* until very near the time for UAT deployment, perhaps even thereafter if the UAT reporting user feedback will affect rework in the flows.
- Deploy into UAT at the subject-area *reporting* level, not the flow-code-complete level. Get the user's feedback from the reporting environment while the centerpiece is still malleable, as it will solidify over time. Initial user feedback is often very different from ongoing user feedback, so allow for this first-time/one-time transition also.
- Backfill of history, while in production may be a one-time event, will be tested and executed hundreds if not thousands of times during the development and testing phases The entire workflow environment should be adaptive to changes in the full length of the flow from source to reporting. Spend some time focusing on the performance of the backfill flow, since this will buy us back enormous amounts of time over the backfill's existence. Keep in mind that we may run the backfill over one thousand times before deployment. Saving one minute means saving one-thousand-minutes (2 days). What if we shrink an inefficient twenty minutes down to ten minutes? We've just saved two *weeks* of project time.
- Prior to the first-time UAT deployment, use formal face-to-face collaboration for system integration testing rather than impersonal production-level defect reporting protocols. The new project is an infant in production environment and cannot be expected to behave with production maturity. Formal collaboration protects the testing process from watercooler agreements, but provides for a rich, knowledge-transfer interaction between the developers and testers so that their knowledge of the technology and business subjects grow in an integrated manner. Data subject experts are then leveraged in one place/one context for common understanding rather than hopping across the aisle each time a developer or tester

has a question or clarification. This matures the business logic and increases the testing quality. Production defect reporting protocols are applied as the project's assets approach the production zone.

- Build the environment with the *anticipation/expectation of change* rather than artificial rigidity. Non-adaptive approaches will require the developers and testers to take steps that are in fact adversarial and combative to their own mission and to the mission of the project as a whole. Telltale symptoms of this adversarial model include the need to freeze certain assets like data models or system configurations, the need to formally report defects on things like relaxed data type constraints or the presence of vestigial assets that may eventually be cleaned up prior to deployment. It is a work in progress, and the workroom may be cluttered while the project is underway. There is no need to formally regard the drop clothes, half-empty paint cans or other one-time/first-time artifacts that may be cluttering the virtual landscape –for now – because it is a one-time/first time condition of the development project.

Avoid Re-Entry Burns

The purpose of this chapter is to provide some guidance and protection against some very common pitfalls in organizations attempting to adopt new or different technologies. However, one can see from the tenor of the chapter that a number of overarching factors can make the migration project an exciting and promising time, no differently than what an astronaut experiences upon re-entry, or what a pilot experiences when engaging descent.

After a long adventure, we're coming *home*.

De-Engineering - We're not re-engineering, we're *de*-engineering. Taking away all the chaff and trappings to simplify and clarify the original functional mission of the solution. Everyone involved will be excited about this prospect, and will learn more about their systems and data than they thought possible. Transformation is underway.

Knowledge transfer - of the corporate information stores, of how Netezza works, of the original designers of the source systems. We're making stronger professionals with this project. They are transforming.

Corporate hope - of the project principals, the management and in many cases as high as the CEO. They look forward to more capacity, so they can take on more business, grow, become wildly successful. Transformation of our *corporation* is in the future. Some folks might be counting on it. For others, available capacity will be an unexpected but welcome boost.

Strong foundation - for other applications or struggling solutions that need a new home. We have forged and pioneered a path for assimilating them. They might be stunned at how quickly their stuff is assimilated and activated, now that a core strength is available. Subsequent migrations will seem more like adding family members to the house rather than the initial construction of it. But make no mistake, those struggling solutions have seen the transformation and want to be a part of it.

Don't let the artificial complexity of the existing sources and solutions dissuade from the goal. Success is a lot closer than we imagine, and as this chapter notes, many of the things in our way are entirely artificial. Human assumptions. Human policy. Human process. Human protocol. If we can realign and right-size these human factors for the migration, the outcome will be a transformed platform not only in technology, but in all the human factors as well.

SET-BASED STUFF

THE NETEZZA PLATFORM doesn't do transactions. We could shoe-horn a transactional interaction into the machine, but it would start shuddering in rejection no differently than a patient's body rejecting a poorly transplanted organ. It just doesn't belong. More importantly, if we *want* it to belong, we simply misunderstand large-scale data warehousing. Not meaning to pop any bubbles or come off as provocative (okay, maybe a little) but the fact remains that we must stay firmly in bulk/batch processing space, and anything we do in onesy-twosy form is not compatible with it. I may rinse and repeat this mantra if necessary.

People ask me a lot about this whole set-based-thinking protocol, because they really want to think in terms of sets and not singleton or smaller transactions. Bulk processing, baby, is doing things wholesale, not retail, so think about how a physical warehouse works. Things arrive on palettes and are stored in crates. Customers don't ask the warehouse to break-a-box for a single item, because that's not how wholesale works. In fact, it's the polar opposite. Rather than asking for parts-of-a-crate, we're asking for how-many-crates.

So we'll look at some pervasive set-based topics here, the first of which is exception processing. I occasionally enter rather animated, hopefully not heated conversations about referential integrity in the Netezza machine. After all, it doesn't enforce integrity (we don't want it to, trust me) and there is no concept of actively forced-values (apart from nullable fields). Honestly, this kind of stuff is so application-driven that I would *rather* it be governed by externalized metadata anyhow. But in this conversation, the person wanted to know *why* Netezza doesn't enforce referential integrity. I walked through this scenario briefly in Underground, but here we'll look at an actual solution (complete with DDL!) and hopefully the concepts will become a bit more concrete.

I noted that [1]Rule #10 is a cruel arbiter of our fate. It mandates that we should not involve an SMP-based RDBMS in bulk-processing. This is because such an engine is ultimately transaction-oriented, and this is its Achilles' Heel. But nowhere is this more evident than how it processes referential exceptions.

If we have exceptions turned on while we are loading a table, the RDBMS will carefully triage each record as it arrives, slowing the loader to a crawl. Our DBAs get around this by turning off the exception checking during the load, and then back on again when the load completes. The engine will then effectively sweep through the constraints to make sure nothing has been violated, and will provide a pass-or-fail either way. If it fails, be mindful of this: *the database cannot fix the problem.* It can only report the problem. If the database cannot fix it, then where is the integrity of the data ultimately applied? *In the processes that produced the data.*

So to answer my colleague's question above, why doesn't Netezza enforce referential integrity? Is not the right question. Since we know that the <data processing application name here> is responsible for making the data ready for the database, including guaranteeing that the constraints won't fail. So how does Netezza handle this? *Why is Netezza even part of the question*, if the constraints have to be formulated and controlled in the *application producing the data anyhow*?

And if Netezza did perchance "enforce" the constraints the same way that the SMP RDBMS does, what would Netezza's role be in the process? The same as the RDBMS - a gateway, or rather a troll, to tell the data that it cannot *pass*. But it *cannot fix the problem*, only the application producing the data can do that.

So now let's say we've loaded up all the data into our Netezza-based data store, and let's also say we have a target form of the same data. An Enterprise Data Store Repository (REP), representing the business (like an ODS, but so *not*). The DDL provided to construct this, we will assume, arrived with primary/referential constraint metadata.

As a note, some readers may well have databases on site with the same names or acronyms as I use for working examples in this book, but I am using an industry-termed database acronym here, and likely so are others. Don't imagine, then, that I am talking about *any* database in particular, any more than I am taking about a particular database when I use the industry term "database". 'Nuff said.

Enter the referential integrity problem. What happens when data arrives in the REP and it doesn't have the correct key values, or missing key values, such that the processes accessing it can re-create the data relationships (like to create reports or even a downstream reporting mart)?

More specifically, a transaction arrives carrying a value in a key field that is not represented in the referential/dimensional data. This value came from *somewhere*, we are certain of it, but we have no reference to it for the time being. Is the value trash? Does it represent a reference record that somehow failed to make it into the machine? Is it missing altogether?

We have a several options (not all are listed, just the most popular)

- Isolate the problem transaction records and report them to the upstream sources so that they can correct the erroneous data
- Isolate the problem transactions and do nothing with them. They will not participate in the data model but may never get corrected either.
- Upstream sources could make us whole with a fixed transaction or enriched referential information to satisfy these key values.
- Simply manufacture "faux" or placeholder/default referential records in the database that allow us to leverage clean inner-joins as we reconstruct the relationships.
- We can forego the default records and use left-outer-joins to affect the correct outcome.

Fixing upstream data: Uh, good luck with that. Most of the time this is legacy stuff, or in many of my situations, another data warehouse system we're migrating away from in part because this problem already exists and is uncorrectable. So there's nobody upstream to regard our woes. It never hurts to try, however, as in some rare cases there's someone who *can* actually fix the stuff and the problem is killed at the root. Invariably however, they cannot fix all of the referential problems, so we'll have to deal with them another way anyhow.

Manufacturing default records: Some may simply cringe at this notion, because it means officially embracing "false" information in the database. Or does it? If an incoming transaction carries a key value that does not exist in the reference/dimensions tables, is the transaction false or is the referential table incomplete? What we have is a disconnected relationship, and we need to rectify it somehow. Hold that thought.

Left-outer-joins: will pull the data together and cover the fact that the relationship isn't real. It will *still* manufacture data in the database, because this is what a left-outer-join is *intended* to do. I know a lot of folks who leverage left-outer-joins as the option of first resort, in part because they don't have the permission to *officially* create dummy records in the first place. Oh, but they *are* creating dummy records, you see, they're just hidden under the covers by the natural outcome of the left-outer-join.

So in both cases, we are creating data. In the first case, the data is created deliberately, out-in-the-open with high traceability. In the second case, the data is created passively, under-the-covers with practically no traceability. If we have to manufacture data anyhow, take a guess at which one developers prefer? Or rather, which one *appears* the most?

But wait, David I have hundreds of tables in the REP that have some smattering of missing information. Are you telling me that I have to specifically and deliberately install a default record for *each* of the missing relationships in all the other records that reference it? Seriously?

Uh, no. I am not a fan of manufacturing whole records in the database. After all, and think carefully about this: Will manufacturing the referential / dimensional data actually *solve* the problem? Let's say we have a case where one transactional record has four keys that are supposed to be in a dimensional record, but none of them are. Now, do we make *one* dimensional record to hold all keys, or do we make *four* dimensional records? This is a non-trivial decision, since it can affect counts, amounts averages, summaries- *whew*.

In commonly applied data warehousing principles, there is the overarching pursuit of "valid values". If we have a null, it should be replaced with an approved default. If the data is in error, it should be corrected. The users have a say, of course, since they need to know how to find the information. Changing the data changes downstream behavior. Leaving the data broken means it is lost forever. So the choice isn't hard, that we need to correct it. But correct it to *what?* A set of user covenants must be garnered and applied.

This is not a dissertation on the value or application of defaults, or the practices either way. Whole shelves of books are available on this subject. The following is simply one (perhaps two) approaches to harnessing the problem in set-based form. For discussion we'll align with one approach. If the reader likes another, the concepts are quickly portable. Appliances make it easy.

We'll go with the correct-the-transaction model because it's the simplest to prototype. It also makes sense because it has the highest volatility and contains the broken value, so why allow a broken value in one record drive the manufacture of more useless information? Let's face it, fake data. The reason why this is a bad idea, is because if the data is broken we are failing to *recognize* it. We're just letting it pass and even giving it a home.

In one particular case, the fact table had some ten thousand transactions that had a malformed account number. This value, as recorded by the transaction, did not exist as a key in any of the dimensions. But by looking at the data, we can easily see the issue, can't we?

Dimension	Transaction
23	0023
41	0041
351	0351
457	0457
298	0298
98	0098

We observe that the above keys have leading zeroes that are not present in the dimensions. Are we to simply forego snipping the leading zero from the value? If the dimensions carry some values without the leading zero, and some with it, we clearly need to fix the data *somewhere*. Converting the data type to integer might make all of it go away, right? The principals of this environment decided to add more dimensional rows to account for the missing data, when all they really had to do was fix the existing dimensions, by fixing the leading zeroes.

The conversations around the application of this problem reached some rather shrill and unprofessional proportions. We even suggested that they perform a test to see which one would be easiest to manage, update, enhance, etc. But they would hear none of it. The manufacturing of dummy dimensional records to account for this problem was already an ever-present thorn in their side. A running joke on the reporting team was that these were "*de*mentional" records, poking fun at the dementia exhibited by those who supported the approach. It is now several years later, and while some of their reports have weathered the storm, many of them still provide false or skewed answers because of the inconsistency with which the dummy records have been applied. One report team member recalled that the current reports do indeed *work* like the old reports did, but then again, those reports were never accurate either.

So the objective is to collaborate with users, set up covenants to determine which types of correction rules and values to apply, then set up simple replacement-value lookups or algorithms that deal with the issue out in the open. This means three things: (1) we won't be operationally manufacturing any new records in the database, (2) we won't be arbitrarily changing data that doesn't fit, (3) we get to keep all the records that showed up, without throwing any of them away.

Win-win-win, I tell you.

So this applies to all primary-foreign key relationships across the databases, right? Who the heck has time to keep up with all those keys, write SQL to specifically deal with them and keep it all in sync? I mean, come *on*.

I'm not suggesting that it be a manual process, or even a process borne on rudimentary logic. Rather, in using some set-based magic we can easily affect this outcome, do it in a metadata-driven form, and it will be consistent for all tables. More importantly, we can apply the same logic to all databases independently for the best possible effect.

In leveraging metadata to pull this off, we want a couple of themes, one is that the process should be model-driven, and second it should follow a rules-driven approach rather than a simple series of software commands. The rules-driven approach is more adaptive, since we can add rules of different kinds and grow this over time as a powerful asset. Likewise we want to treat it as a *compiled* work rather than a dynamic one. In set-based processing, anything we can do to "can" a process as reusable, we should run, not walk toward. The basic flow of the process is as follows:

- Capture the primary/foreign key map for the database (we get this from the model-driven DDL)
- Compile rules based on the map
- Compile canned script(s) based on the rules
- Install the script(s) as the canned run-time executable.
- Only revisit the capture/compile cycle if the data model should change.

The first and foremost asset we will need is the primary/foreign key DDL. These are usually produced by the modeling tool expressed as a structured query to affect the database. Something akin to "ALTER TABLE" commands, or the *actual* ALTER TABLE commands are the best starting point.

This in hand, we can now construct some rules. Why do this? If we have formal rules, we can manufacture them as entities on the database, complete with rule identifiers. If these identifiers are attached to the exception records, we then have context (later) as to why a given exception exists.

We will need several tables now:

Exception types - oh yeah, we have referential rules, but also domain violations, malformed data, lots of reasons to have an exception called out

Exception rules - a static data set, described by the exception type, that represents all of the rules that may be executed on the database for the given exception type. While we may manufacture rules from the PK/FK metadata, we can also enrich the rules with such things as default value behavior and check constraints. A rule after all is something we fire when we find a problem, but now that we know what the problem is, why can't the rule give us more info on whether the problem has a predefined user covenant, and just apply it? Oh, yes we will.

Exception fact - When a rule fires, we get a record in this table, carrying the detail of the exception itself, including referential/transaction table names and columns, and the expected values, even a reference to the offending row.

The process follows thus to get the referential check off the ground:

- Consume the primary/foreign key map and manufacture a rules file (a simple shell script can produce this).
- Upload this rules file content (for reference purposes) into the Exception Rules table. (format of this to follow)
- Take the rules file and likewise manufacture a series of specific SQL-Transform queries that target the tables and keys named in the rule.
- Use the given rule's ID as part of the query result so that we can tie the exception to the

rule that fired.

- In the rule, we will have a reference table, a transactional table, and one or more key column names.
- We will create a series of instructions that, when executed on the database, will capture the exceptions for the tables and keys in question.
- The instruction sets are designated only for tables for which PK/FK information exists.
- Each time the system runs, we will encounter one or more of the tables in question.
- We fire the rule for that table on demand.

I would suggest that even this be regulated, because if we really plan to (later) correct the data in the upstream, or in previous transform operations, the quality of the data will rise and the exception count will fall. But we can only track this if we run the exception processing often, and use its exception-fact results *in a truncate-load*. Otherwise we may have exceptions in the system that have long since been fixed but remain as vestiges in the exception fact table. It is important to keep in mind that the exception table is a *fact* table, with the additional constraint that it is remanufactured with each run to report the health of the database since the last time it ran.

So all of that is very abstract. Let's pop the hood and look deeper.

Here are the pseudocode DDLs for the structures we'll use, first is an Exception_Type, which could be considered superfluous by some, since the types of exceptions will be rule-driven anyhow:

Exception_Type:

```
ET_ID integer,
ET_Description varchar(300)
```

Now we get to the Exception_Rule, which will be manufactured from the DDL into a file and will be uploaded to the database for reference purposes.

Exception_Rule

```
ET_ID integer,
ER_ID integer,
ER_IDX integer,
ER_TABNAME varchar(300),
ER_COL_NAME varchar(300),
ER_COL_IDX integer,
ER_DEFAULT varchar(300)
```

Now for the exceptions, which will be the result of the firing of rules above.

Exception Fact

```
EX_ID bigint,
ET_ID integer,
```

```
ER_ID integer,
EX_PK_TABNAME varchar(300),
EX_PK_COLNAME varchar(300),
EX_PK_ROW_REF bigint,
EX_FK_TABNAME varchar(300),
EX_FK_COLNAME varchar(300),
EX_FK_ROW_REF bigint,
EX_VALUE varchar(300),
EX_VALUE_TYPE varchar(200)
```

That's about the size of it. I only added the Exception Type table for completeness, but the core of the set-based process will be the Rules and the Exceptions.

Now we'll go to our ERWin or other modeling tool and command it to dump the DDL for the primary and foreign key map. It will produce a text file containing Netezza-facing notations similar to:

```
Alter Table <Tablename> Add Constraint <Constraint Name> Primary Key <Column List>
Alter Table <Tablename> Add Constraint <Constraint Name> Foreign Key <Column List>
                References <Tablename> <Column List>
```

It's easy enough to parse out these entries, find the PK's, the PK/FK combinations and now we have a rules-base for capturing (a) unique constraint violations for the PKs and (b) referential constraint violations in PK/FKs. Incidentally, this is exactly what the common RDBMS would do, except its engine (being transactional) is too slow to be useful and also cannot do anything to help us find-fix-or-filter. Bash shell can handily pull this off with simple parsing, so we'll keep it that way. I will once again encourage you to use the str_get_word() and str_get_word_delim() bash functions (found in the Appendix) to get a feel for how easy this is to do.

First things first, let's tokenize the file by adding some useful white space:

```
SRC_FILE=$MY_PK_FK_DDL_FILE
TFILE_A=$(create_temp_file)
TFILE_B=$(create_temp_file)
cat $SRC_FILE > $TFILE_B
cat $TFILE_B | sed -e 's/)/ ) /g' > $TFILE_A ; cat $TFILE_A > $TFILE_B
cat $TFILE_B | sed -e 's/(/ ( /g' > $TFILE_A ; cat $TFILE_A > $TFILE_B
cat $TFILE_B | sed -e 's/,/ /g' > $TFILE_A ; cat $TFILE_A > $TFILE_B
SRC_FILE=$TFILE_B
```

What does all this do? It simply puts white space around any occurrence of a right or left parenthesis, and removes all commas. This allows us to see the values in the file as parseable tokens without any intermediate noise. The "comma" character will only show up if the PK/FK relationship contains two keys. This will be an annoyance, so we will remove it. Likewise if either of the parenthesis characters is "touching" a column name, a simple parser will see the column names as "(col)" or even "(col1" and "col2)", again an annoyance. We can also remove all other extraneous text like "ON DELETE CASCADE" etc so that all we have are the pure textual tokens for rapid browsing and rule creation. Even on large databases and marts, this parsing scenario will only take a few moments, but we want it to be efficient in the script for purposes of maintenance.

So now we'll set up a simple loop that reads the file and presents one line at a time. Most Enzees can do this in their sleep:

```
while read line
do
<body of the loop>
done < $SRC_FILE
```

Now for the body of work inside the loop itself. We will have four primary variables:
- PTABLENAME - the primary key table, or in our case, a reference or dimension table
- FTABLENAME - the transaction table (or fact table) containing the foreign key of the primary.
- PK - contains one or more columns on the primary (reference) table, separated by a space
- FK - contains one or more columns on the foreign (transaction) table, separated by a space

Once we capture the above, we can make the rules on them. In the loop below, we will examine each token and keep track of the current token (tok) and the prior token (ptok). If we see a keyword in the $tok variable, it means that the value we want actually precedes it. Likewise if $ptok has a keyword in it, the value we want succeeds it.

```
ptok=""
RULE_IDX=0
for tok in $line      #this will present each token in the individual line
do

#get the F and P tablenames based on the text of the line
if [ "x${tok}" = "xADD" ] ; then FTABLENAME=$ptok; fi
if [ "x${ptok}" = "xREFERENCES" ] ; then PTABLENAME=$tok; fi

ptok=$tok             #capture the previous token
done                  #end of loop inside the read-line loop
```

Now we'll just use the string functions to wrap up the PK and FK values. Recall that in the DDL for PK and FK, the PK appears last and the FK appears first:

```
FK1=$(str_get_word_delim 2 "(" "$line" )
FK=$(str_get_word_delim 1 ")" "$FK1")
```

The above will simply chop the line into sections based on the "(" character. For our purposes, the text after the "(" is what counts so it is the second token, hence the "2". From this second half, we want the first section, based on the ")" as a terminus. And *voila*, we have effectively parsed the foreign key from the string. Now let's go get the primary key

```
PK1=$(str_get_word_delim 3 "(" "$line" )
```

The above will capture the third section of the string delimited by the "(" character, in our case the beginning of the PK definition.

```
PK=$(str_get_word_delim 1 ")" "$PK1")
```

And the above will capture the text up to the next ")" as a terminus, effectively parsing the foreign key from the line Now all of our information is complete.

The next concern is simpler, in that we have to regard the presence of multiple keys in the PK/ FK mix. No matter, since the value in the PK is one or more column names separated by a space, and the FK likewise.

We can make short work of this, and I don't want to sound too remedial, but when on site with the client, we have to run before we can walk, right? Er, well, anyhow, we need to get the basics in place before we can drive the data in set-based processes.

Now we want a rule for each of the keys encountered (one rule for the primary, and one for the foreign). If we have two keys for each table, that's four rules. Most of our relationships will have two rules since the tables only have one primary and one foreign key. Why not boil it into one rule and be done with it? Partly because we *can* have multiple keys per relationship, but *usually* won't, and mostly because we want to reuse the Exception_Rule table for all kinds of other rules, like domain ranges, invalid data checks, etc. A whole gamut of potential rule types and configurations await us, so it's best to keep the rule as adaptive as possible. But keep it simple too.

Moving on, we'll need two small loops, one each for the PK and FK. Let's do the PK first:

```
SP_P="|"
RULE_IDX=$(expr $RULE_IDX + 1 )
colidx=0
for pk in $PK
colidx=$(expr $colidx + 1)
  echo "500 $SP_P $RULE_IDX $SP_P 1 $SP_P $PTABLENAME $SP_P $pk $SP_P $colidx " >>
$RULE_FILE
  done

colidx=0
for fk in $FK
colidx=$(expr $colidx + 1)
  echo "500 $SP_P $RULE_IDX $SP_P 2 $SP_P $FTABLENAME $SP_P $fk $SP_P $colidx " >>
$RULE_FILE
  done
```

Note in the above two rules, the $SP_P serves as a pipe delimiter so we don't confuse bash. The first parameter is the Type identifier, which I have stubbed here as the value "500" as an exception type. (We will have lots of other exception types.) The third parameter (1 and 2 respectively,) will become the ER_IDX. So that an ER_IDX of "1" will always represent the primary key information, and "2" will always represent the foreign key information. Likewise the $colidx will represent the order of the columns so we don't get lost when trying to reconstruct the order of things. Even though these are written to the file in order, and will be read back in the same order to produce the final exception processing scripts, we will *also* be loading this file into a table to support analysis, and the ER_IDX / COL_IDX are important to keep things collated in their original order. Databases don't do that for us, and the only reason we want them in the database is to support downstream analysis and review, not for utility.

Now that we have the rules in the can, we have the option of setting up the rule to be loaded into the database in a separate stream, but for now we need to pop open the rules file and take the next more dramatic step - manufacturing queries in a formulaic manner that will hit their respective tables and keys, formulate the exceptions and load them into the Exceptions table. Keep in mind the order of things:

We just received the new PK/FK DDL map from the DBA. We just ran it through our rules compiler. We won't need to run it through the rules compiler again unless the DBA ships us another update to the PK/FK map. So now our source-of-record will be the rules file. If we follow this theme throughout our exception mapping process, we can formulate custom metadata, glean manufactured metadata (like DDL) or simply hand-craft the rules. One way or another, the *rules* become the source of record and will drive the exception processing.

Why do this? In an exception processing protocol, we need for *rules* to be the primary driver. While we could say de-facto that the PK/FK DDL is a set of rules, it is not adaptive to other kinds of exception processing, such as invalid values and the like.

We have one client who has designated that if a noted column's value shows up in mixed case, to apply the rule in another way. For them, rather than mark the exception in the table, just upper-case the column's value and let it pass. We may mark the exception in the Exception table as having fired, for the sake of traceability, but hey, maybe not. After all, if it has to fire for every processing cycle, the information is redundant. We already know the problem exists and we're even correcting it. Overall, however, this is how we apply sweeping, set-based operations to obtain consistent results across a wide range of data quality problems.

Now for the next stage, producing the canned operations that actually examine the information, and record the exceptions in the Exceptions table. But even here, we will generate a series of SQL statements based on the rules. These will in turn be deployed as an asset to execute at whatever processing moment is appropriate. The important factor here is that we've gone from DDL, to rules, to deployed script, which itself will not change unless there is a change in the metadata itself. If the DBA supplies another DDL file, or we need to enhance the rules, no matter. We simply remanufacture the rules, then these SQL statements and redeploy them, in factory-fashion.

So the first process is to read the rules and reconstruct their position as PTABLEBAME, FTABLENAME, PK and PK strings, just as they were before we made the rules. Hey, I know it looks superfluous, but recall we're using the rules for a reason. And even if the DBA cannot supply us with a valid PK/FK DDL, we can still make the rules, can't we? (Also keep in mind that for many legacy systems, there is no PK/FK DDL).

Here is a simple means to read and re-parse the rules file, in case anyone is interested:

```
SP_P="|" ;   P_ER_ID="" ;   FK="" ; PK="" ;
while read line
do
```

```
ET_ID=$(str_get_word_delim 1 "$SP_P" "$line" )

ER_ID=$(str_get_word_delim 2 "$SP_P" "$line" )
ER_IDX=$(str_get_word_delim 3 "$SP_P" "$line" )
ER_TABNAME=$(str_get_word_delim 4 "$SP_P" "$line" )
ER_COL_NAME=$(str_get_word_delim 5 "$SP_P" "$line" )
ER_COL_IDX=$(str_get_word_delim 6 "$SP_P" "$line" )

#check to see if rule ID has changed
if [ "x${P_ER_ID}" = "x" ] && [ "x${P_ER_ID}" != "x${ER_ID}" ]
then
mret=$( build_rule_script $PTABLENAME $FTABLENAME "$PK" "$FK" "$P_ER_ID" )
PTABLENAME="" ; FTABLENAME="" ;   PK="" ;   FK="" ;

fi

#do this for all rules
if  [ "x${ER_IDX}" = "x1" ]
then
PTABLENAME=$ER_TABNAME
PK="$PK  $ER_COL_NAME"

elif  [ "x${ER_IDX}" = "x2" ]
then
FTABLENAME=$ER_TABNAME
FK="$FK  $ER_COL_NAME"
fi
done < $rules_file
```

Armed with this data for each rule, we can now call build_rule_script to process the rule's complete information. We'll use P_ER_ID to mark the rule transitions in the file, so we'll know when to take a pause, process the rule's information, and continue with the next rule.

The build_rule_script is also a simple function, but it has some subtle characteristics that we need to make sure are covered. Firstly, what if the columns and tables given to us in the DDL file are inaccurate? What if they don't exist at all? Now is the time to check on this, because it's a bad time to find this out when the final script is actually running.

We'll now use PTABLE and FTABLE as shorthand for the respective table names.

```
mcols=$PK ;  mselcols="" ;  mcom="" ;
for mcol in $mcols
do
mselcols="$mselcols $mcom $mcol" ; mcom="," ;
done
nzsql -q -d $TARGET_DB -A -t  -c "select $mselcols from $PTABLE limit 0 ;"
mretp=$?

if [ $mretp -ne 0 ]
then
echo "Could not find columns [$mselcols] on table $PTABLE"
fi

mcols=$FK ;  mselcols="" ;  mcom="" ;
```

```
for mcol in $mcols
do
mselcols="$mselcols $mcom $mcol" ; mcom="," ;
done
nzsql -q -d $TARGET_DB -A -t  -c "select $mselcols from $FTABLENAME limit 0 ;"
mretf=$?
if [ $mretf -ne 0 ]
then
echo "Could not find columns [$mselcols] on table $FTABLE"
fi
```

Otherwise, we are ready to proceed and wrap some simple SQL statements. But first, we need to match up the names of the PK columns with the FK columns, which in most cases are the same column name, but this isn't true for the others and we need a generalized way to handle it. Below we will capture the FKs first, with a placeholder for the PKs, then fill in the PKs with a string-replace function, and off we go.

```
mcols=$FK ; colidx=0 ; FK_WHERE="" ; mand="" ; FK_SEL_COLS=""

for mcol in $mcols
do
FK_WHERE="$FK_WHERE $mand a.$mcol = b.xxxPKCOL_${colidx}_xxx "
FK_SEL_COLS="$FK_SEL_COLS $mcom a.$mcol "
colidx=$(expr $colidx + 1 ) ;  mand="and" ;   mcom="," ;
done
```

And now for the PK columns:

```
mcols=$PK ; colidx=0 ;
for mcol in $mcols
do
FK_WHERE=$( echo "$FK_WHERE   | sed -e "s/xxxPKCOL_${colidx}_xxx/$mcol/g" )
colidx=$(expr $colidx + 1 )
done
```

Notice how in the above notations, we are using the PK columns as replacement values to the placeholders we installed in the prior FK loop. This will match the PK keys to the FK keys one-for-one to make a valid query. Note below that the use of $TGT_DB is the primary location of all the tables to be examined.

```
SP_D="$"
SP_Q="'"
MSQL=$(cat <<!
create temp table fk_check as select warehouse_id, rowid row_id, $FK_SEL_COLS from
${SP_D}${TGT_DB}..${FTABLE} a
where not exists
(select 1 from ${SP_D}${TGT_DB}..${PTABLE} b where $FK_WHERE ) ;
```

```
insert into ${SP_D}${TGT_DB}..EXCEPTIONS (
EX_ID , ET_ID , ER_ID , EX_PK_TABNAME , EX_PK_COLNAME ,
EX_PK_ROW_REF ,   EX_FK_TABNAME , EX_FK_COLNAME ,
EX_FK_ROW_REF ,   EX_VALUE )
select row_id, 500, $ER_ID ,
${SP_Q}${PTABLE}${SP_Q} ,
${SP_Q}${mcolp}${SP_Q} ,
${SP_Q}${FTABLE}${SP_Q} ,
${SP_Q}${mcolf}${SP_Q} ,
warehouse_id, ${mcolf}
from fk_check a;
!
)
```

Now let's echo the value of $MSQL, which contains all of the queries above, into the deployed script file:

```
echo $MSQL >> $DEPLOYED_SCRIPT_FILE
```

and now this file will contain an entry that looks like the following, after all the symbols have been interpolated in the "echo".

```
create temp table fk_check as
select warehouse_id, rowid row_id, fk_col1, fk_col2 from
$TGT_mytranstable a
where not exists
(select 1 from $TGT..myreferencetable b where a.fk_col1 = b.pk_col1  ) ;

insert into $TGT..EXCEPTIONS (

EX_ID , ET_ID , ER_ID , EX_PK_TABNAME , EX_PK_COLNAME ,
EX_PK_ROW_REF ,   EX_FK_TABNAME , EX_FK_COLNAME ,
EX_FK_ROW_REF ,   EX_VALUE )

select row_id, 500, 1 ,
'myreferencetable'  ,
'pk_col1' ,
'mytranstable' ,
'fk_col1' ,
warehouse_id, fk_col1
from fk_check a;
```

So the objective is to put the actual run-time queries into the deployed script file, such that any $ vars appearing in this file are the same one actually available at run-time to all other scripts running in the same instance of processing. But clearly these would be very tedious to code and maintain by hand. All we have to do now is execute the deployed script and it will fire the rules, capture the exceptions and now we have a record for all to review.

Typically the first time we run these, the results are kind of scary. At one client site, we received over three-hundred and forty *million* exceptions. However, when diving deeper, we found that several of the larger tables had an intermittent empty key value. These tables being in the billions of rows, it's not hard to imagine racking up hundreds of millions of exceptions. However, upon remediating even one of these tables, we saw the exception counts take a nose dive until we remediated them down to zero. They still pop up occasionally like the proverbial prairie dog, but it's under control now.

Now, I am certain that you can glean other set-based ideas from the principles above, and apply them in creative ways for other kinds of problems. Just keep in mind the overarching objectives and principles, regardless of whether we apply them to exceptions or other issues:

- Rows are affected in scale, with multiple, sweeping movements
- Use intermediate tables to remove join/rollup pressure from otherwise monolithic operations - breaking apart a large complex query into multiple smaller ones exposes the business logic, simplifies maintenance, and has an overall shorter duration. All good things.
- Intermediate tables are effective placeholders for precalculated data - don't calculate and recalculate information (using math, for example, in the where-clause). Simplify the downstream joins by performing precalculations up front.
- Intermediate tables are effective filters for rooting out data we want to either keep or dismiss - it is often far more effective to build a simple intermediate table with filtration values, then use this in join or where-not-exists, that it is to perform the full-blown join/filter on the larger table.
- The outcome, as the net of all operations, both in the data product and the *overall* duration spent to process it, is a productive goal.
- One ultimate goal, however, is to break the problem apart into achievable, maintainable steps. This preserves the scalability of the labor required to maintain it. The more reusability and rule-based operation, the more we push the knowledge of our experts into the application rather than having it outside, locked inside their brains.

Set based windowing.

Now let's take a look at some set-based windowing functions. These allow us to manage groups of records. The most likely candidate algorithm for this is a slowly-changing dimension. I'm using these not as comprehensive solutions, although the reader might find some value in using them for a springboard (and feel free to do so). Just keep in mind that we're diving into windowing examples, not examples of slowly-changing dimensions *per se*.

So we have a scenario where several of the dimensions are considered slowly-changing. Two of them use a start/end date scenario and one of them uses an incremental counter to version a record based on duplicated keys. We'll take a look at the first scenario now.

Our record is described as follows, and for simplicity we'll keep the table names and column names the same.

Intake table (in the intake database):

```
Create Table Test ( T1 Integer,  T2 Integer, Start_dt Date ) distribute on random;
```

Target table (in the target database):

```
Create Table Test ( T1 Integer, T2 Integer, Start_dt Date, End_dt Date,
SCD_Idx integer, Warehouse_id Bigint ) distribute on random;
```

Note above that I am adding the End_dt and the SCD_Idx at the same time just to simplify the example. Normally we would use one or the other, but usually not both. The warehouse ID is something I like to use to uniquely identify a record out of a sea of records. This is really non-optional when it comes to large-scale databases. I know of folks who get along without them, but having them simplifies operations like the one we're about to do.

The scenario is this: For a start/end-date managed SCD, when a record is added to the target, the first version of the record is given an end-date of a maximum value, like 2099-12-31.

When new records arrive that share the same values for the T1 and T2 keys, we will set the currently oldest record's end_dt to the youngest incoming record's start_dt, minus one. For those cases where the start date and end date start out equal, it is possible that this approach will accidentally set an end-date to the day prior to the start-date, so we'll fix that, too.

Conversely, for an integer-version form of the SCD, the SCD_idx will start at zero and move up. Each time a new record arrives that shares the same values with the T1 and T2 keys, we will take the current maximum SCI_idx, add one to it, and use this as a basis to set up the correct SCD_Idx values for the incoming records.

Case 1, inbound records:

T1	T2	Start_dt
100	11	2010-01-01
100	11	2010-02-01
100	11	2010-03-01
100	12	2010-01-01

Expected outcome:

T1	T2	Start_dt	End_dt
100	11	2010-01-01	2010-01-31
100	11	2010-02-01	2010-01-28
100	11	2010-03-01	2099-12-31
100	12	2010-01-01	2099-12-31

Now we'll intake some more data:

Netezza Transformation

T1	T2	Start_dt
100	11	2010-04-01
100	12	2010-02-01

For the total results:

T1	T2	Start_dt	End_dt
100	11	2010-01-01	2010-01-31
100	11	2010-02-01	2010-01-28
100	11	2010-03-01	**2099-03-31**
100	12	2010-01-01	**2010-01-31**
100	11	2010-04-01	2099-12-31
100	12	2010-02-01	2099-12-31

So the new records are arriving and getting reset, but we're doing it in groups. Let's take a look at what we'll need to make this happen.

First, let's assume that we have in place a local replica table that looks like the target. We've just filled it with the data from the source so now we need to set its date sequences correctly. The first thing we need to do is pull over the rows that represent the max-row of their respective key-based groups, but only for the keys that we currently have in our hand. We don't want all of them. Along with these record will come their Warehouse_id, so I have a way to get back to them.

```
insert into $replica_table select a.*
from ${tgt_db}..TEST a , $replica_table b
where    a.T1 = b.T1  and a.T2 = b.T2   and a.end_dt = date('20991231')
```

The next thing we'll do is the windowing function, so that all of the records for a given group are lined up in sequence, but only based on the existing maximum record of the sequence.

```
create temp table t_scd as select a.rowid row_id,    a.T1 , a.T2 , a.start_dt ,
nvl( lead(a.start_dt) over
  ( partition by    a.T1 , a.T2   order by a.start_dt ),
    date('20991231') ) end_dt
from $replica_table a
```

Sequences in hand, now update the replica's records with their new values:

```
update $replica_table a   set
a.end_dt = case when b.end_dt=date('20991231') then b.end_dt
else b.end_dt -1 end from t_scd b where a.rowid = b.row_id
```

And of course we need to repair in case the end_dt accidentally precedes the start_dt.

```
update $replica_table a  set
a.end_dt = a.start_dt where a.end_dt < a.start_dt
```

So now we have a minor dilemma. We need to perform an update of the target to set the max-date for the original records we pulled over to start things off. Now, I'm a big fan of using designated unique identifiers to get an absolute, hard-lock on the original record in question. This is one of those cases, since the business keys are duplicated and there's no other way to naturally re-identify the original record from whence it came. Since we copied over the warehouse_id, this is now very easy to do. Rather than update the old record, however, we'll just delete it.

```
Delete from TEST a where exists (select 1 from $replica_table b where a.warehouse_id
= b.warehouse_id)
```

Of course, in the above delete, we would want to parameterize the distribution keys also, because as the table grows larger the delete will become slower without including the distribution keys in the where-clause.

Now we finalize the entire body of records to the target, inserting all of the records in the replica table while applying new warehouse ids to the rows that need them. In deleting the original records and performing inserts with new records, we have thereby simplified our update-record protocol. It also gives us the option to use official soft-delete indicators, namely that we would update the original record's soft-delete indicators and still perform a complete insert of the body of work.

In the above, we only need a few parameterized quantities:

- Tablename (Test)
- Partition keys (T1, T2)
- Order-by keys (Start Date)
- Index key (End Date)

Armed with the above as rules-driven parameters, we can now enable SCD for as many tables as we want.

So in just a few simple steps, we have a repeatable SCD algorithm we can apply to all of our tables that would use the same method. Also note above that I highlighted the portions that can become parameter-driven, showing that while the several SQL statements are exactly the same for all application of these algorithm the particular details of the table can be parameter-driven.

Now let's take a look at the second scenario.

First, we will not use the same tactic as we did with the dates. All we really need are the max SCI_IDX values corresponding to the keys we have in hand, and a temp table will work just fine.

```
create temp table t_scdmax as
```

```
select max(a.scd_idx) scd_idx ,   a.T1 , a.T2
from ${tgt_db}..TEST a , $replica_table b
where    a.T1 = b.T1  and a.T2 = b.T2
group by   a.T1 , a.T2
```

Armed with these max values, we then create a temp table and perform a rank() window function that will provide us with an incremental rank for all records in the inbound replica.

```
create temp table t_scd as select a.rowid row_id,   a.T1 , a.T2 ,
a.start_dt , a.scd_idx ,
 rank() over ( partition by   a.T1 , a.T2 order by a.start_dt   ) scd_idx2
from  $replica_table a
```

Now we update the table by adding the maximum value to the increments, and we end up with the incremental pattern for all. At this point, we don't have any updates do to. We just insert these records into the target and they take their places as incremental replacements.

```
update t_scd a  set
a.scd_idx = b.scd_idx + a.scd_idx2
from t_scdmax b where    a.T1 = b.T1  and a.T2 = b.T2
```

And for those with no existing max, just use the assigned index because these are all new.

```
update t_scd a  set
a.scd_idx = a.scd_idx2 where a.scd_idx = 0
```

But the above just affects the temp tables, so now we need to apply these new index values to the actual data table. Note the use of the rowid to get the hard-lock on the original record.

```
update $replica_table a  set
a.scd_idx = b.SCD_IDX
from t_scd b where a.rowid = b.row_id
```

In the above, we only have need to parameterize a few things:

- Tablename (Test)
- Key columns (T1, T2)
- Partition Columns (T1, T2)
- Order-by columns (Start Date)
- Index column (SCD_IDX)

From the above, we can formulate rules and then leverage the same SCD for multiple tables using the rules for parameters.

So that's set-based SCDs in a nutshell. How many operations did we perform? Only a handful, and these had sweeping, set-based effects on the tables at hand. And while for many of the readers of the above, the concepts are remedial and simplistic (you implemented them a long time ago) they provide excellent mental fodder for the incoming brood of new Netezza users.

The takeaway here is to avoid the use of transactional thinking when performing these kinds of operations. I have seen the above SCDs, and many other forms, require ginormous amounts of code, operation, timed execution and the attendant headaches and maintenance of such artificially complex solutions. I've also watched heroes ensconce themselves as the go-to experts for those same complex solutions, building their empires around them.

Case-insensitive collation

Not to put too fine a point on it, but case-insensitive collation isn't particularly welcome in large-scale data processing. Primarily because *any* form of on-demand conversion in the from/ where-clause is not scalable. Teradata and SQLServer both support case-insensitive collation. In migrating from either of these environments, we find that the mixed-case nature of the columns has been something that the database has allowed but is not particularly useful nor desirable. Especially when it comes to a large-scale query. Consider the following values:

Us	US
uK	UK

We can tell from sight that the above country-codes match up with each other, but the database cannot. Netezza has no case-insensitive feature, [1]nor do we *want* it to have one. A case-insensitive collation means the case is being converted invisibly on-demand. It is also a source of *invisible drag* (on-demand conversion in the where-clause). In Underground I noted that one of the strengths of Netezza is the ability to precalculate data in one query to use it in the next. Upstream precalculation of complex values is usually a single-pass operation and results in optimizing the downstream operations that leverage its outcome. So if it's a best practice to precalculate complex values, what of simple ones, like upper/lower case?

The principle is no different. We should embrace formulating data quantities in the upstream that take pressure off the downstream. Considering that the upper/lower case issue will be used widely in the downstream, anything we can do to optimize it in the upstream will buy back an enormous amount of processing time, removing the on-demand invisible drag.

Why is it invisible drag? So let's take a look at the visible-version of this drag. What would be required if we forced the collation effect into our on-demand model?

```
select * from table1 a join table2 b on upper(a.mycol) = upper(b.mycol)
select * from table1 a order by upper(a.mycol);
```

Are either of the above viable in a large-scale setting? Clearly not, since we will perform the *upper()* conversion over-and-over again, on-*demand*, regardless of how many times it is fetched. I know of folks who have models that use mixed-case for search and collation, but they follow a fairly rigorous protocol to avoid accidental hamstring of the processing environment and more importantly the reporting environment. Solutions to this include:

- Simply convert the value to upper or lower when first encountered. As the data is loaded into the machine (as part of intake-triage) zap the column to a predefined case. We will never encounter the problem again, guaranteed.
- If a mixed-case *presentation* is desired, such as for reporting/display purposes, maintain a reference table containing the valid-values for the column.

In the reference-table solution, expose the valid-value table as a lookup to the reporting environment so that it can be leveraged for drop-down selection and the like. When data first enters the machine, use a one-time, forced-case-insensitive comparison to the lookup to find the right replacement value - e.g.:

```
update table1 a set a.col = upper(b.col)
```

See how it looks oddly like the one I said we should not use? This is because the one we should not use is *on-demand*. The above is a one-shot operation we will never revisit. By converting it once we take enormous pressure off every downstream operation that touches it, effectively leveraging the upstream-precalculation model even for simple values.

Check-Constraints

The non-nullable column is the only form of constraint the Netezza machine will actively push back on. Declare a column this way and attempt to insert a null, and it will fail. Other types of constraints like valid-values or domain violations, Netezza will store the metadata for them but not actively do anything about them.

Once again, that's okay because we don't want the host or the MPP involved in row-by-row checks. A comprehensive approach to this will yield a scalable and reusable set of components. Without diving directly into code or script, let's look at concept and principal.

Noted in the prior section, we now have a mechanism to take a record offline. We can fire a constraint rule based on a discovered violation, and this rule can either take an action to correct it (with a default) based on a user covenant, or we can remove the record from the flow.

Just as above, we will define a simple rule to capture the constraint. Then we can decide how this rule will be captured. Should we simply type the rule into a flat file? Should we glean the rule from a DDL file? If we are to remain firmly in the model-driven zone, then the ideal way to do this is as we saw above. Take the DDL and compile it into a more useful form. Consider the following, a notation that is easily gleaned from the create-table DDL:

```
TABLE=CUSTOMERS   COLUMN=CUSTOMER_ID FUNCTION=NOT_NULL
```

So why would we formulate the above if we could just let the database pushback on the insert/ select statement's action? We have several reasons for this. Firstly, when a Netezza SQL statement fails, it gives us little actionable information. We don't know which column failed, or if multiple columns failed. We don't know which row failed or if multiple rows failed. The only way we can deal with the problem comprehensively is to do so proactively. The rule format above gives us enough information to apply a pattern to all the table's rows in an effort to shake out the potential problem. It is fast and it is set-based. We can learn everything we need to know on a single pass of the data. We can apply just about as many rules to as many columns as desired during this pass, and it won't cost us nearly as much pain as the alternative - hand-held table investigation as a forensic exercise. Any takers on that one? Hmm, me neither.

Let's not stop at null values. What about an applied default?

```
TABLE=CUSTOMERS  COLUMN=CUSTOMER_ID FUNCTION=NOT_NULL DEFAULT=0
```

Now when a rule fires for the noted column, we don't take the row offline or report the exception. Like the aforementioned exception model, we just apply the default and move on.

```
TABLE=CUSTOMERS COLUMN=READY_FLG VALUE=Y,N DEFAULT=N
TABLE=CUSTOMERS COLUMN=TXN_CNT MIN=0 MAX=455 DEFAULT=0
```

Aren't these the kind of rules that we'd expect some automated pattern to apply for us? If the default exists, put it in. If the value is out of range, clamp it. If we don't have a default for it, add it to the exception fact table. When the time comes to consume the table itself, we perform the SQL-transform in context of where-not-exists in the exception fact. This guarantees that our exception process will guard against errors creeping into the data. After all, the null-check on the Netezza database itself can only keep data from entering.

It cannot fix the problem.

So now we have the opportunity to line these up like cookie-cutter updates to the intermediate table holding the information that we want inside the target table. Again, even an insert-only model can allow such updates, because they are not updates to the actual target. They are updates to the *local* data we *intend* for the actual target.

From the rules, we can then manufacture the correct update logic to affect the application of defaults:

```
    update Temp_Customers set READY_FLG = case when READY_FLG is null then 'N' when
READY_FLG in ('Y','N') then READY_FLG else 'N' end READY_FLG ,
    TXN_CNT = case when TXN_CNT is null then 0 when TXN_CNT < 0 then 0 when TXN_CNT > 455
then 0 else TXN_CNT end TXN_CNT
    ;
```

In the case of a null-check with a default, we simply apply and move on. If we need to capture the exception, we follow a similar protocol as outlined earlier in the chapter. But the pattern remains: we have one exception fact serving the entire database, and centralized rule-centric control of the exception behavior. To change the behavior, we change the rule. To enhance the behavior (extend the functionality of a rule) we need to enhance the rules component, but this will rapidly mature and stabilize.

Hopefully the above discussion shows the ease of the deployment of patterns to achieve the set-based power we're looking for. In many cases, the set-based power is simple to implement and then extensible as we go. The above examples all originally started from very simple prototypes and then we extended them in short order. The grand total time to develop and install the above ideas was minor compared to the lift and functionality received from them over the long haul. And since the problem domains are easy to characterize, the solutions for them are likewise consistent.

FINAL DESCENT 13

THE CASE STUDIES SECTION in Underground generated a lot of feedback. This one hopefully the same. But don't imagine that the case studies in this section are simply descriptions of derring-do since the last book was published. Oh, no - I'll still go back into history for some nuggets this time, compare them to recent adventures (maybe) and draw a conclusion that is simply astounding: things haven't changed much. Brace yourself, because my adventures might sound a lot like your adventures, not because they really are the same adventure. But because the continuum of *faux pas* in Data Warehousing are so consistent, it's almost like *deja-vu* all over again. A*hem*!

For this excursion, I had already received a number of anecdotes via email, and some via collaboration. Rather than assume these were "fair game", I engaged the individual on the phone, vetted the entire story and allowed them to edit it for content and accuracy. Some I used, and some I did not, and all agreed to forego any fee and any connection to the story itself. This, of course, protects the innocent while we dive into the stories. So if a reader thinks they may see shadows of themselves in the following pages, the reader can only know that the story might be about them if they actually engaged in a dialogue with me. Otherwise, it's guaranteed that "it's not about you" no matter how close to the mark the storyline might appear.

So in terms of Transformation, I'll offer up some case studies of folks who either embraced the transformation, went into the transformation kicking and screaming, were in denial of the transformation, or - what's that you say? *What* transformation?

As a note, Netezza's recent eBook *Simple is Better* highlights customers who rolled the machine onto the raised floor, flipped the power switch and were productive in *hours*, if not days. Many customers, however will not move so quickly. They have mature environments and Netezza has to be deliberately assimilated to avoid overall disruption to an existing user base. Wrapped around these environments are high walls of protocol *purposefully designed to inhibit a too-fast deployment*. How "ready" we are to receive the appliance, is largely based on the existence of such protocols, their maturity and our ability to adapt or even transform those protocols.

When the Netezza machine enters the shop, a transformation of some kind is underway. Our leaders want a change, and see Netezza as a change-agent. Of course, it *really is* a change-agent in lots of ways, so this expectation is firmly grounded in reality. What is not grounded in reality is that sometimes, just sometimes, the people who are embracing change intend the change for *someone else*. They *personally* intend to do things by status quo in a comfort zone. For example, the leaders may pick Netezza because their current stuff is running out of gas, and Netezza's power could take them to new heights. Problem is, they forgot to buy breathing apparatus with the machine, and now those new heights are rarefied air, and they are gasping for it. Netezza can take us into the stratosphere. It will transform how we do practically everything, and will open options that never existed before.

The real question is, *are we ready for it?*

Some are smiling about now, reminiscing about a first Netezza gig. Or perhaps hip deep in a Netezza gig and are wondering about running down the hall and pointing out these facts to a superior. After all, *they* bought the box.

I noted in Underground that companies will search high and low to find eagles in the marketplace, hire them, induct them and then promptly begin the process of converting them into ducks. The managers own a duck pond, it seems, and converting eagles to ducks is far easier than the opposite direction. As the Netezza machine enters the environment, the gravity of the duck pond is strong. Did they buy an eagle with the intention of converting it into a duck? Or is this purchase a turning point? Perhaps a desire to get out of the duck-management business? Will they take all their duck-management techniques and attempt to shoe-horn the eagle, and the eagle-drivers, into the duck mold? Eagles don't suffer such foolishness. The Netezza machine even less so. Its transforming power will show the ducks who's boss.

This can hit some folks between the eyes, so these first few case studies are from colleagues-in-the-fray who are either in the middle of the transformation or as consultants have been through it a few times.

Sometime after the publication of Underground, I caught up with a colleague who had just wrapped a particularly grueling project. But his lament was more about how his own people had comported themselves. In short, he just wanted to grouse a little, but I wanted root causes. He claimed that his leaders had actually sold the business by showing off their white papers, industry articles, you know, *written* expertise. My colleague also observed that about two weeks into the project, he learned that as a condition of selling the business, his leaders had promised that the first reports would be presented four weeks after project initiation. Now many of us know how dangerous this is. We often don't even have data *into the machine* inside of four weeks, much less have it in shape to develop reports. I mean, it would likely take that long to develop the reports *even if the data were available day-one*. So how did this happen? Simply speaking, the people making the promises were trying to get ink on a contract, absent the irritations of that pesky thing called reality.

After about the tenth week of the project, and his folks having stepped into as many tar-pits as he could stand in a lifetime, he finally asked one of the leaders, "Did you ever read those white papers?" To which he said "No." To which my colleague responded, "Have you ever read *any* literature or white papers on data warehousing or even functional migration of a application?" The leader firmly admitted, "No," with a chuckle, as if this was somehow beneath him. Then said, "Why do you ask?" My colleague said something bold and daring, "Well, all this time I thought you somehow had another master plan in play, and that you had set aside all the best practices because you had a higher prize in mind. Now I realize that you were just torturing us with your own ignorance."

Data warehouse projects never "fail" *per se*, they just reach moments of operational pause.

If deploying a traditional - er *underpowered* technology, the project will typically follow a very predictable path. As a worst case, from the inception an already overworked technology staff will build it on their own. It will be the product of many hit-and-miss events, touched upon in snippets of effort as they can pull themselves away from other duties, eventually resulting in a marginal implementation. While functional, it is destined for overhaul simply because it was the first of its kind. It still contains so many mistakes and faults that the builders would rather, in hindsight, have done differently. They learned a lot along the way and we should not diminish this education. Such technologists should not be disparaged for this kind of outcome, because all of them have functionally merged their technical knowledge with the business knowledge, and the next round will be phenomenally better than anything the principals and stakeholders could have expected.

Unless of course, the stakeholders commissioned tactical contractors to implement the first round and all of them are gone. Likewise with consultants. Of course I am a consultant so this might sound like I'm cutting my own throat, but we all know that consultants are transients. We arrive, deliver knowledge and expertise to the tactical technologist and the management staff. If the tacticians and managers are *themselves* transient, the knowledge transfer won't stick, will it?

However, assuming some stickiness and continuity, we will begin the next phase of development. The next phase could appear in two forms - (a) refactoring of the environment or (b) propping up of the environment with tuning, tweaking and engineering. Both will lead to another commitment to overhaul it or even replace it. Very often by this time, the leaders have lost faith in the original technology, no matter what it may be. They will allow the technologists a lot of rope, but will not have infinite patience.

Another issue is that, especially in high-process or high-regulation environments, the longer the original solution stays in place, the more it is circumscribed with protective processes and language, to the point of becoming ridiculous. We've probably heard about the fill-this-form-in-triplicate sort of Dilbertesque situations where we roll our eyes as if it's barely believable, and count our lucky stars that we've never encountered it. A case in point for one enterprise, the user lamented that he sent his change request a birthday card when it turned a year old. Another complained that it took six weeks to six months to add a simple column to one report. Still another complained that he had to start making "SQL ability" one of the pre-requisites for his *customer service advisors*. Seems the IT folks had exposed the data tables for anyone to use but had not bothered to make them especially usable.

One colleague spent an enormous amount of time scrubbing junk from the source data systems. From malformed data to unprintable garbage, the process was tedious and painful. Once completed, he reporting his findings and was told in a rather unprofessional, nay screeching litany of spitting epithets that *the production data was being used for critical reports. The production data is the system-of-record for over two hundred downstream systems. The production data is clean, one-hundred percent with no errors, MSG, fillers, preservatives etc.* After listening for over fifteen minutes to a barrage of defenses of the production data, he waited for the firestorm to cease, then simply said, "Spin it all you want. It doesn't change anything. Putting your head in the sand will not get rid of the junk." To which another responded, "I guess we just disagree on the definition of *junk*." To which my colleague said, "Hey, I will defer to TDWI and even to the owners and champions of your <formerly-favorite-ensconced-technology,> who have already told me that *it should not be there*. The evidence is clear, all of us have the same definition of junk. Just not all of us have the same level of *denial*."

Ouch, I said. I would have been a bit more congenial with the wording, but whether the words are terse or buffered, the fact remains that the junk is still in the database and isn't going anywhere. Spinning the situation doesn't get rid of the junk. In fact, *it gives people permission to leave the junk in the database* for fear of a particular syndrome in data management, loosely described as the Emperor's Clothes. Recall the old fable of the Emperor who commissioned some people to make him the best clothes ever, and they convinced him that the clothes were made of a fabric he could not see. He was too embarrassed to admit he could not see it. So he donned his invisible clothes and went out to show the townspeople, all of whom were too shocked to say anything about the Emperor's clothes. Except for a little kid, who asked innocently, "Why is the Emperor naked?"

Why indeed?

In context of our storyline, my colleague could see that the principals were *claiming* that the data had high quality, yet it did not. Claiming that data has quality, in the face of all evidence, becomes the first problem to overcome before tackling the data itself. But the situation got even more weird. The denial continued even after he was able to cordon off the offending records for a review. But the principals refused to examine the evidence. Now, it's a little-known, dirty little secret of the story of Galileo Galilei, famously decried by religious leaders for defying the belief that the celestial bodies were perfect, and that the Sun did not revolve around the Earth - that the *Aristotelian* academicians of his time, who dominated thought in the universities, were *also* staunch supporters of the geocentric theory. So between his faith and his colleagues, he could not catch a break. Yet his only words were consistently, "Just look in the telescope and see for yourself!" Ahh, this was my colleague's herald cry, *just look in he database and see for yourself!* and when he brought it up rather casually in a meeting, he was once again met with the screeching defense that the data is used for this and that and -

Almost like prefixing the defense with "How *dare* you?"

The point is, what they weren't saying in so many words, was simply "We have a lot of people depending on that data to be accurate. People who spent a lot of money, and we were on the last project *and that data is the result of our* efforts. Its ongoing presence and quality validates *our* promises to the users. If we agree that there's junk in it, this invalidates *our* promises to the users, we all get egg on our faces, and the political fallout of this could be quite real, tangible and result in some people losing their jobs. Not wanting to be on the chopping block, *they had better sing the praises of the data*.

In another setting some ten years ago, I was brought in to deal with a restaurant chain's inability to manage their point-of-sale software releases. They might roll out a new release to all restaurant stores once a quarter. But if a new restaurant came online, it would get the *latest* version of the software, not the one everyone else had just installed. This created a lot of disconnects in field maintenance and in cross-restaurant compatibility.

So we got together with the CIO, a business user and the head of the development division. When everything was carefully explained the CIO looked directly at the division head and asked

"Is our software at risk?"

Wow, what a loaded question. If the division head agrees and says yes, it gives the CIO permission to lop off his head for allowing the software to go into a state of risk. If he disagrees and says no, he is giving the answer the CIO *wants to hear* and the software will remain at risk. So in many ways, a CIO who does and says such draconian things is training his people to lie to him, or at least spin the truth to avoid repercussion.

"You can't *handle* the truth!" Jack Nicholson. *A Few Good Technical Guys*

And this, my friends, is the lot of the objective consultant. If I am in a place of consultancy and I see a similar problem and fail to point it out, the people who follow behind me may reasonably ask, "David was just here, and he *missed* this?" So you see, the folks like me could step up, point out the problem (and the solution) and work towards its remediation, or we could just remain silent and draw a paycheck, but there's no value in that, is there? My role is always transient no matter where I go, and often the principals and stakeholders will tell me directly, often within the first hour of my presence on site, *don't hold back anything*. But sometimes, what they're really saying is don't hold back anything *about those other departments. Leave mine alone.*

But even after all this, my colleague relates, it got *even weirder*. The principals at the client site got wind that he had not only identified the records containing the malformed data, but had *removed* the junk characters as they were being migrated into the Netezza machine. And lo, upon this revelation, the skies parted and the client's legal departments stepped into place, saying "Yeah, verily, thou hast *removed information* from the systems of production, and thou hast violated the covenant with thine client, and shall now be banished to the wilderness of ideas."

My jaw dropped, "Seriously?" To which he replied, "Yep. I was basically sidelined to watch it all unravel. They let me attend meetings, but I couldn't participate."

At one client, we had put some algorithms in play but did not remain for the final production rollout. We later learned that the end-users were very nervous that the reports they were now getting were quite a bit smaller in content than before. They carried all the same data, it seemed, but in streamlined form. What's more, vestigial records had been removed from the display, so there was a lot less data to slog through to find what they wanted. However, they were so *accustomed* to the vestigial information, they wanted our team to *put it back in place*. That's right, put the dirt back, essentially so they would have a baseline of reference. After reviewing this for a few weeks, they agreed that it was best for all to remove the vestigial artifacts, as they had no value. What they had not considered, is *how much the original bad data had wasted their time with clutter*. We found out later that their original morning exercises of slogging through the reports had taken up the first two hours of their day. Now they had their answers in relative minutes. Ecstasy ensued. Now, what to do with two extra hours in the day? Hmm, we'll think about that.

Author's note: Some ten years ago, consulting firms (such as the Big-Five firm I worked for) had a stated policy that went something like this:

It is easier to ask forgiveness than to ask permission.

This phrase assumes a lot of things, not the least of which is that is *presumes upon the mercy and forgiveness* of the person whom we may intend to cross. Today, some companies are so heavily regulated and scrutinized, that to embrace such a philosophy is not only counterproductive, in some circles it is suicide. Never underestimate the power of a policy enforcer to treat a "resource" with casual indifference. They will very impersonally flip the switch on our presence and go back to their daily routine, and never return our phone calls.

In the spirit of transformation, here are several cases where businesses installing or migrating data warehouses, found it to be at odds with their enterprise, which was simply unable to assimilate the product.

Exit stage, right?

A colleague tells a tale: In 2009 he arrived on the client site and heard several messages loud and clear. They were trusting his leadership and wanted his team to lead. They were savvy with data warehousing, but not this Netezza technology. They had people who were ready to help. They wanted to set up an aggressive, iterative model and break free from their existing procedural chains. Hey, all of that sounded good, so they wrote up a contract and got to work.

My colleague said that no sooner had they gotten the first release into play, when they realized a very serious disconnect in the way they had written the contract versus the way the company actually operated. The contract was written for a typical data warehouse, where subject-areas would be matured across a flow from back-end to front-end. But when it came time to turn over the initial subject-area products to their testing team, the testers suddenly wanted to see each database in its *complete* form, with all subject areas fully mature. In short, a stovepipe model. At first he thought they were confused, so went about having chalk-talks over several days to orient everyone one how they (his team) intended to roll things out, so everyone could prepare for the approach.

The leaders held a meeting that he naively thought was a kickoff, but only he and the client's project principals were in attendance. They told him that they didn't know what he was talking about, this whole "iterative thing". They hadn't understood it when he had first explained it, and now that they fully understood it, they didn't want to talk about it anymore. It seemed so strange and oblique, they never would have signed up for it if they had completely understood the concept.

My colleague did something pretty gutsy. He listened to their desires as to how they intended to run the project, a method and approach that was a known failure every time it was tried. He listened patiently, reflecting their words back to them so they knew he fully understood what they meant. Upon leaving this meeting, he held another meeting with his project team members (six of them) and asked them to come in the next day with their gear. Make sure all of it was scratched, because they were leaving it behind. The next morning they brought it to the office and arrayed it ritualistically on a conference room table. By noon the following day, he had another watercooler meeting with two of the project principals.

"I have to leave now."

"Where are you going?"

"I have another project waiting for me, and I start this afternoon. I just thought it best to give you a heads up."

"What about," he hesitated, "*our* project?"

"Well, you laid out a project approach that I cannot participate in. I have three other clients waiting for me to do it right. I do wish you the best."

"Wait a second, we have a contract."

"And you are in breach. Staying one more minute compromises my defense."

"Defense?" one huffed, "of *what*?"

"Look, I'm running late, stay in touch."

"Wait a second," said one, "What will we tell your team?"

"They're coming with me."

Hey, we test too

One colleague relates that he stood up a Netezza machine using a basic internal processing model. It used an ETL tool to harness and orchestrate the SQL-transforms to the machine. In this implementation, they used ten SQL-transforms that were essentially chained to run one after another. The deployment was stable and required little maintenance for almost six months.

Then the parent company purchased a sister competitor. The project-at-hand became an assimilation of the sister company's business data into the existing model. Unfortunately, part of the merger agreement included the import of the other company's business information and context, for which the existing implementation was not geared to receive.

My colleague was able to assess the total impact and found that this would only increase the functionality of the SQL-transforms by three additional transform operations on the front of the flow to integrate the incoming data into a common flow. The Achilles' Heel of the entire approach rested in the lack of capacity for testing. Not by the machine, but by the testing staff.

They came up with an interesting compromise, in that the SQL-transforms inside the ETL tool would be drawn out into a pseudo-generator that would both manufacture the SQL-transforms and the baseline queries for the testers. It would not dictate the test cases or approaches, but would provide an additional series of queries to cross-test the SQL-transforms in an external tool (like Toad) to support the work of the testers. This would allow them to close the distance on the total SQL statements they would have to produce to effectively test the data.

He told me, "I know it seems that fifteen or so transform operations should not need all that many test cases or supporting queries. Most people don't realize that the testing queries often outnumber the core operations by a factor of ten or more. They required over one-hundred-fifty queries to support the fifteen." Manufacturing all of this by hand not only seemed daunting, it wasn't scalable. This test-support approach offered a good balance without a lot of additional overhead.

This group was ready to receive the new data load and came up with a strategy to help the testers with their workload as well. This keeps the entire swimlane of work operational and running at highest efficiency.

Rendezvous

Another colleague wrote to me, and because I happened to be in New York City during those same weeks, we met a number of times for coffee. He related that in their current environment the client had deployed a 10400 for the production environment and a 10100 for the development environment. I knew where he was going with this (see my Enzee Community Blog entry "First Bubble Blues"). But his lament exceeded my expectations. He explained that on a typical 10100, which is a development machine designed for *one* small team, that the client had deployed their team, another development team, a testing team, a user-acceptance testing team and yet another non-related project had been given accounts on the machine as well. With all of this crushing work, the 10100 had not skipped a beat in its performance or reliability. His complaint, however, was that "just too many" people are on the machine to get any work done. Running at max performance is immaterial if there's too much workload.

Author's note: recall that any data warehouse project is minimally eighty-percent testing unless we have some kind of magic testing potion. Overloading a machine with this burden slows everyone down. It seems in his case, the client principals were agreeable to playing nicely on the same machine even if it would take longer to complete the mission.

He continued: So we worked hard with the other integration team who has a big Java engine they were interfacing to our back-end application. Basically the Java engine pulls data, crunches it on a big grid, and puts the answers back into the Netezza box where our transforms would process it and take it home. This happened on a daily basis, so there was time to work out a daily schedule and get things squared away.

Our side of the equation had been loaded up with history data and had been running this basic cycle for a number of weeks, but without having been hooked into this giant grid. The grid team had been doing manual simulations because the grid was too large to keep more than one of them around. I wish we had known this. One day they said they were promoting their code into the production zone to integrate with ours. I thought this was the first of many iterations of these integrations, because we had a number of things to do with the data model before we would be ready for prime time. I guess the other team disagreed. The first day they integrated with us on the primary platform was the *first day of production for them*. Yes, they were live in production, on the *first day* that the two fully-complete environments had ever been executed on the same platform together.

I was shocked and alarmed, he told me, and lost a lot of sleep over the next several days worrying about hiccups in the system. The problem was, that on the first day of production was the first day that the organization also had to report its data to major United States Federal Departments, official organizations under the Presidential Cabinet with "Department Of" in front of their names. Seems like they could have braced us for what they were about to do. But we had collaborated so hard, and our various counterparts had worked so diligently together that all of us eventually, collectively could breathe a sigh of relief. After all, the back-end was now in production, a target that we thought was at least two months down the road. We still had plenty of work to do, but the production deployment was smooth and without incident. The rollout approach was just a surprise.

Author's note: Some organizations are committed to collaboration and rapid, iterative integration because they know it's the path to success. I had been hearing how they were integrating the system, architected from the top-down but built from the bottom-up. Released in incremental stages of planned functionality so that the features were layered along the continuum of data flow. Integrating a subject at a time, burning the foundation into place as a rock-solid resource.

It was no wonder that on the first day of integration, the two systems played so well together, because they *really had been playing well together*, in different layers and parts, for many months. One of principals on my colleague's project said that he'd never seen anything like it in his life. It went so well, that the project was being spoken of as a flagship of project management and successful deployment strategies. Kudos to all.

The show must go on

Way back in high school I became enamored with stage performance and had my own traveling magic show. Part of the allure was in watching people's eyebrows raise when they saw a particularly well-executed illusion or sleight-of-hand, so I sat in front of a mirror for hours practicing these things. Even while watching television, eating or doing homework, I always had a deck of cards in my hand, shuffling, riffling, single-hand-cutting, all the usual stuff. In setting up the stage show, however, a lot of secondary logistics were in play. Organizing stage hands, finding pretty assistants who would work practically for free, training, blocking and ultimately executing the show.

I also learned in this process, through a professional stage manager, that complex projects like this require *compartmentalization* and *deferred integration*. He said, take a closer look at any television show you watch, and count how many scenes that all of the actors are in the *same* scene, versus how many scenes are just head-shots. Or for that matter, over-the-shoulder of one actor to another. That shoulder belongs to a stand-in who has the same haircut and clothing of the other actor, but he's not really there. What this means is that the actors can come to work one day, do all of their single shots, then meet up with all the actors on days more convenient for them all, and do the combined scenes. This translates to *live* stage production how, exactly? I cannot ask the audience to come back on different days to watch the show, right?

He laughed and said, No, but it's in how you *practice* the play. I know lots of haggard high school drama teachers who will get their entire cast together for blowout rehearsals. These take hours, so they tell the kids to bring snack and homework. The whole process makes the kids hate to get into high school plays. On the other hand, the smart drama teachers will divide the rehearsals up into compartmentalized segments. Say three people are in four scenes, so he will schedule only those four scenes for one evening of rehearsal. They complete all four scenes in say, ten minutes. Now they have the remainder of the hour to do blocking, entrance, body language and a host of other issues, effectively *"burning in"* the scene with lots of rehearsals in one shot. They can literally repeat the same scene a dozen times and get it spot-on. That option is not available with the blowout rehearsal model, because they are rushing from scene to scene and can't take much additional time for any of them. That's the compartmentalization part.

The deferred integration part is when the pieces are brought together. The scenes are set up as segments, still without the entire cast and crew. Toward the end of the cycle, full rehearsals are needed, but we can see how this model is a good steward of time in the aggregate, but also respects the time of the individual talent. It also does something else - it radically increases the quality of the presentation and it teaches the kids important lessons on complex projects.

Back to the story, where does *waterfall* fit into this equation? It is the blowout-rehearsal model that tends to stunt quality, reduce available testing time and generally feels rushed. Everyone is overworked, wishes they had not signed up, and will not have time to properly test the final product. It will feel like it was executed with expedience, not deliberate design. I have watched people hang their head in shame over what they produced, knowing it was not their best work.

But with the iterative model, we have time to test, validate approaches, toss out old and keep new, with the product getting better, tougher and more adaptive with each release. We're *actually* getting stronger and more capable, not just throwing feature-points over the wall.

We're burning-in the solution from the foundation up. Each delivery is stronger than the last, and the final delivery will be our strongest delivery ever.

Showtime.

But can we test it?

I've had numerous colleagues lament about both the accuracy and scalability of testing and the test staff. The functionality starts to rise and the testers are overwhelmed. They need a scalable means to test and respond to increasingly stronger functionality. Automated regression, metadata-driven test cases and queries, in short, the same things that the developers are using (a SQL-generation platform) is the ticket for scaling the work of testers.

As a consultant scoping a project, especially a very large one with lots of people and risk, ask direct questions about the testing process. If the testing group is not ready to receive our work products, we are already at risk. More to the point, if the testers come to us and start asking remedial questions, this should be a red flag. These are the people who will stand in the gap and judge the quality of our work products. The business will hear their voice and not ours. Don't let this happen *after* we have signed the contract. Get all of this out in the open up front, and have honest discussions about it. More importantly, be prepared to walk away. A big, challenging project is meaningless if we lose our shirt trying to meet Sysiphean goals. (a little Greek mythology lingo, there). Of course, this doesn't mean we *have* to walk away. If the client is willing to negotiate these things (and give us a time-and-materials contract) then we can minimize the risk and still be successful. Working a fixed-price gig with a testing team that is unable to receive our work products, is a lot like slitting our own throat, without the blood and all.

We are also a boutique firm with a lot of, in my humble opinion, very sharp and competent architects and developers. When we enter the fray with a Netezza-centric solution, our interface is largely the IT professionals. If the work products also produce data, then these are tested downstream with a separate reporting team. If the reporting team happens to be our group, they still straddle the IT shop and the business users. However it is a known quantity with all boutique firms, that we rely on our clients' Subject Matter Experts for business logic and they rely on our Subject Matter Experts for all things Netezza. This requires collaboration.

Train them up...

A number of years ago I was architect on a project that seemed to have a lot of training issues with the client's personnel and managers. I was not directly involved in the knowledge transfer and training activities, but I regularly attended our internal leadership meetings and every week was one tale after another of hiccups and failures in the training process. The lead trainer looked like he'd been run over with freight truck - several times. We reconnected at the '09 Netezza trade show in California and he'd just transitioned into a company that was using Netezza. I later followed up to pick his brain about his latest experiences and the conversation quickly gravitated back to his days in the training trenches. He thought it was pertinent because it had repeated itself several times with other companies, and seemed to have a pattern. Here is his tale.

Some companies are great to work with. Their people are competent and dedicated, with a co-operative attitude for success. On the other extreme are toxic workplaces that pride themselves in getting people to work (good internal infrastructure) but cannot see the forest for the trees when it comes to productivity or even technical competence in their staff. Invariably this leads to a training opportunity for me. Rather than replace their marginally competent people, in-house training should bring them up to speed. The problem is often systemic. It has less to do with the competency of the staff, or lack thereof, than the broken system holding them together. Sort of like *The Matrix* horror, if the system itself is the problem, how do you re-characterize the system so that the overall environment is healthier?

It's like people standing around leaning on shovels, overseeing a work project. Some of the workers were clearly carrying the weight of the team. In this case, however, all of the workers were standing knee-deep in a pool of waste. Some of the workers are trying to shovel out the waste while the remainder, rather than using their shovels toward productive end, use their shovels to whack others on the head (usually for spattering waste on them while doing the cleanup work). After a while, they realize how futile the effort is, stop trying and ultimate lean on their own shovels, or find different uses for the shovel, while others with more energy carry on the work.

I would conscript our architects to take deep dives into their existing technologies as part of initiating the migration knowledge-transfer. Many of them were knowledgeable about what the systems functionally supported, but few of them knew why or how the systems operated as they did. The ones assigned to the project seemed the least able to deal with the deep details of the migration, and their managers had been working operationally for so long that they fell back into the only model they knew from the last "project" they were on. Meaning that they were dusting off their playbooks for methods and approaches that used to work for them, ten years ago or more. The technology and workplace landscape has changed and continues to change so rapidly that all those approaches and methodologies have since been replaced or revamped, many times over, into concepts and terms that are completely foreign to them. In fact, it appears as though we are upsetting the applecart by bringing in something radically *new*, when they are the ones radically *behind*.

Another side effect of this, is that the competent people find a way out. They either move into a division of the company that is less toxic, or exit altogether. The end result is that the less competent people remain behind, further institutionalizing the systemic problems in the division. The incompetent people cannot find a job elsewhere and they are not paid enough to represent a risk to the company. There's just so many of them that it becomes a mind-numbing exercise to imagine how we would train them to be more effective. They are about as effective as they are going to get. Theirs is a system-imposed ceiling on the competency level of the environment.

This is a case where the Netezza transformation will be an even more significant shock to the system. That transformation is underway, is an immutable certainty. It does not regard whether the people are able to transform. What it may reveal however, is the nature and agenda of those who resist the transformation, or who don't appear to be transforming at all. Whether they are willing is sometimes immaterial, because change is afoot. Decision-makers see the appliance as the solution, and bringing in the Netezza machine is a game-changing event. If the people, however, are not competent enough to participate, how is this any different from the scene in *2001: A Space Odyssey* where the Monolith appears among the monkeys, and they throw bones at it but otherwise don't know what to do with it? The Big Black Box is suddenly playing the role of the Monolith and the workers around it are flummoxed as to what it means, how it applies, or what they should do with it.

Enter the consultant or new-hire who is savvy about all the necessary things, but all around him are people who don't understand him/her. Their ability to communicate is stunted by terminology, approach and methodology barriers that are systemic, not something we could have a meeting about, get everyone on the same page and move on. Everyone is already on the same *page*, but they are reading from different *books*.

We have capacity

One colleague relates: Our client wanted to dabble in the whole notion of in-the-box transformations. Once they tasted the power, more and more transforms started migrating into the machine. More disparate data sources followed, initiating more transform work. The architects had the presence of mind to harness the transforms early on. They felt it might grow out of control without some deliberate constraints, and this proved a wise decision.

Later that year, the principals announced that they had just signed a new, very large customer that would be larger (alone) than the rest of their customers combined. The Netezza appliance, configured as it was to scale on the inside, did so beautifully. Rather than crush the ETL environment, the core heavy-lifting transforms had already been assimilated into the machine. This opened up enormous amounts of latent capacity. When the new customer was assimilated, it produced nary a hiccup in the processing times of existing operations. Moreover, three new customers of equal or greater volume were added by the end of the year. Some openly wondered if their implementation would ever run out of capacity.

But does it scale?

Many years ago I worked as a product/sales consultant for Ab Initio Software and they used a very simple policy about their software product. It has proven itself out over the years and has protected their product and their company from the ills associated with the user-product-support. Ab Initio wants all of their customers to have an over-the-top experience with their product and their people. They accomplish this by deliberately screening potential customers for a product fit. If the potential customer does not pass certain criteria, they are not eligible to own the product and Ab Initio won't sell them a license. Now while this seems odd, think about the model itself. Companies buy the product to solve hard problems, and Ab Initio is there to assist. But if the client's problem is not really a hard problem in the industry sense, the outcome is predictable. They will swamp the vendor's support hotline for remedial activities. Things they should already be competent and experienced enough to solve on their own. If their environment was already mature enough, this foundation would already be in place. They would qualify for product ownership.

Case in point, a potential customer had serious data processing problems and was falling behind on all their deadlines. Heat was coming down on them from their own customer base, regulators and auditors, third party suppliers, in short, they were about to implode. They had gaggles of people on virtual roller skates running all over their digital frontier putting out fires and making things go with the binary equivalent of duct tape and bailing wire. When they told their tale of woe, some questions were in order.

How many transactions do you process daily? How big is your largest database? Do you have a reporting system in place? Who are the users? These are the equivalent of getting-acquainted "smalltalk" questions before we get to the deeper conversations. In this particular case, he was running a small database system and simply had foregone the expense of a larger system. He was running out of power for a reason: he had not taken the problem seriously enough. Anyone who buys and keeps underpowered equipment and believes that it can do the work just because they have faith in it, has not fully embraced the problem at hand.

This is one case were Ab Initio declined to take things further, to the stunned surprise of this customer-wannabee. What could justify such an outcome, and *who do you people think you are*? It works like this: A man has a large house and automobiles for all his family members. They go to the best schools, eat the finest food and often have catered parties at their home for select friends and family members. Their next door neighbor on the other hand, has been downsized at work, no longer has the financial wherewithal he once possessed when the markets were better. He likes the idea of catered food and calls up the caterer to bring some stuff to the house. He knows it is more cost effective to go to the supermarket, but he really likes the idea of catered food. The caterer shows up, lays out the various steaming buffets of meat, vegetables, sauces and drinks. His family fares sumptuously for over an hour, before they realize that they haven't even put a dent in the overall quantity of the food supplied by the caterer, who still has more food outside in his truck.

The point is, some products are intended for environments that need to scale and are *ready* to scale. If the environment isn't ready to scale, and has no particular need to scale, giving them overkill capacity doesn't help them solve their problems because they are not ready to receive the product.

Now we are back to the same point in the circle The environment's *readiness-to-receive*. Some environments already have a product similar to the one in question (e.g. Netezza) but Netezza is different. It *will* change things. If the environment is not ready for this impact, and cannot over time deal with the change in an effective manner, it may have an initially marginal experience with the product. A company may have wanted the transformation. The leaders may have bought it expecting the transformation. But plainly speaking, if we have an Oracle aficionado or Teradata guru in the house, what is the expectation that those folks will happily trot across the aisle and undergo transformation into a Netezza-centric future? Hey, it happens sometimes, but I am asking what would we *expect?* Some would not be surprised if various of these folks dusted off their resumes and moved on to a shop that fit their skills. But again, this is part of the environmental transformation embraced when Netezza first shows up. Was this part expected or planned for? If the environment is systemically *unable* to transform, expectations will be stunted and they may even wonder if their purchase of the product was wise.

Oh, it was wise. Don't second-guess that part. But this is where one must realistically evaluate the landscape. If the transformation isn't visible or is happening too slowly, we cannot rest the blame on technology or inanimate objects. Nor can we claim that those pesky fly-by-night consultants messed things up. Systemic problems don't go away without deliberate, actively applied *leadership*.

Before I get a nosebleed from standing on this soapbox, let's move on.

Speak your mind, or mind your speech

A West Coast colleague tells me: We were on a fixed-price contract to deliver a series of design artifacts. They liked our initial design so we contracted with them on time-and-materials to assist in the development and rollout. Honestly my role in the affair was to be more like a cheerleader than an architect, because the folks working there needed an organizer. Maybe a tour-bus guide could describe it better. Look over there, ladies and gentlemen, to our right is the fabled engineering burial ground, and you can see through the mist, the zombies of technology who refuse to cross over to the other side.

The appliances had already arrived and carried a mystique with them that was downright heady. Our offices were right down the hall from the glass windows on the production raised floor. In the first months there was never a day I walked past it or looked down in that direction and did not see one or more people standing still, staring at the machines. They are interesting to look at to be sure, but it made me (almost) wonder if the person was personally musing to the machine as to whether or not it would be kind to their career, almost like a totem. Maybe that's a little weird, but here in this part of California we have what my aged Floridian grandfather calls a "granola" culture. With granola, anything that's not a fruit or a nut, is a flake. That's his take on it, anyhow.

This machine-mystique bode well for me, and gave me passage to the netherworld of the company as well as access to its more lofty perches. I could speak to techie or C-level manager alike, all I had to do was make an appointment. This first-month honeymoon was fun, but it would not last. Alas the approvals had come down for the project to commence.

At the project kickoff meeting, one of the managers announced that the purpose of the project was to prove that the Netezza appliance could carry its weight in their environment. We have a lot of demanding deadlines and customers, and failure is not an option, and all that. Then he pointed back to me and said, If something goes wrong, we only have one person to blame. Everyone looked at me, as though I was tomorrow's roadkill.

From that point forward, the wind completely shifted against me. Everything I said was second

-guessed, even practices they knew were tried-and-true for data warehousing had to be revalidated in their minds, just because I had suggested it. One day I attended a meeting where some people were gathered to talk about the project. I entered the darkened conference room quietly just a little early and a number of people were basking in the glow of the projector. But what was on the screen sent chills up my spine.

It was a record of every suggestion I had ever made, with dates, times, people present who heard the suggestion, etc. In short, it was a running record of my time with the company and they were marking down every one of my statements. And it could only be used against me. I was partly stunned and partly relieved. Stunned that they had been taking notes on my every word, but relieved that everything I had already said, without exception, remained spot-on. I must say, however, the initial visceral shock of anxiety had me a bit numb. Then they shut down the projector, turned up the lights and waited for the meeting to start. People started filing in, some of them nodding to me, most of them smiling. I wondered if they were taking notes on my mannerisms and body language, too.

So at this point something swelled within me. A strange boldness that I cannot describe. These people were recording everything I was saying. They either intended to use it against me, or use it as a running mental dump of everything inside my head in case, you know, I got hit by a truck. No matter, they were in my head for sure and I felt like I needed to do something to turn this around, or at least get a handle on it. Something.

When the meeting started, several of their folks began to offer their architectural ideas for database layouts, flows and the like. Between you and me, David, we know there are only a few best ways to do this, and for whatever reason, everyone in the room was firing blanks. After half an hour of this, I said May I ask a question? All eyes went to me and I said Has anyone here done this before? Which elicited rumblings and tentative affirmations, some of them indignant. I stood, went to the white board and erased everything on it, talking ninety miles an hour the whole time, and for the next hour I held their rapt attention as I laid out a working model that answered all of their questions and concerns, and generally shined a light on the whole subject. People were very open and asserting and I thought the whole thing went very well.

The next day the project boss called me into his office and said, Today will be your last day with us. I really appreciate all the work you've done, but now we must part.

This was yet another shocking surprise, but coming on the heels of the prior meeting, I wondered that I might have offended someone, or been presumptuous in taking over the meeting, but like I said, I thought it had gone well. When I pressed for an answer, the project boss simply said that they appreciated all the work I had done.

Yeah, you said that. But where does it fit and where do I stand?

Outside the building, if you want a straight answer, he said flippantly, as if my inquiry was impertinent. Ooookay, I can deal with that.

Over the following months, I would periodically hear about their progress through some acquaintances in the building, and learned that they had launched the project with one of the architectures suggested by the know-nothings in the conference room that day. In this architecture, all of the databases would be rolled into one Big-Kahooonah style database. The data would converge to one place and be reported from one place. Not only that, all of the tables would be prefixed with a pseudo schema-name, so that they could be managed in groups. To me, this is no different than foregoing the directory system of my laptop and putting all my files into one directory, but naming the files in a way that helps me find them. In any case, the reason I had learned about this was that they had never gotten the enterprise backup system to work for the Netezza machine. The reason being that for their system, backups have to be taken of whole databases, not just designated tables. And this Big Kahuna database had all of the development, testing and user acceptance data for four separate projects, all rolled into one. Hey, you really can't pay money for incompetence like this. It's one thing for a know-nothing to propose it. Yet another for trusting managers to approve it. But for everyone on all projects to embrace it without a whisper of protest tells us more about the culture than we want to know.

One night an operator kicked off the wrong job and it dropped the main database. And in one fell swoop, no fanfare or applause, almost six months of data vanished into thin air. Now procedurally *and* operationally, they could eventually restore it all in a few days' time. But the final word was they intended to go another direction.

They want me to come back next month for the project kickoff.

Hunt for Red October, November, December...

One of my acquaintances in Chicago told me a familiar tale, which dovetails with several others here.

In their system, the operational data had to be managed with an extreme intraday model that is probably not like anything many have encountered. Jobs would arrive with data on arbitrary boundaries, some all at once, some several minutes apart, sometimes hours would go by with no activity. The operational systems formed a ring around the Netezza machine, but they had built all this stuff the right way. The problem is that they were trying to write reports against the operational model rather than a reporting model. Or rather, they had not taken the step to physically isolate additional tables on separate distributions, so that the reports could run at the highest possible speed.

I was called in along with a number of other consultants as engineer more than a guide. The objective was to find a way to make the box run faster "as is". They had us plumbing the query histories, collating timings, finding and fixing the "long running queries". But honestly, we could not find a smoking gun. Their largest fact table was over a hundred billion rows. On a 10400 machine, it would require over ten minutes to scan this table end to end. However, we found that over ninety percent of the queries were returning in five seconds or less. Of the remaining ten percent, less than one percent of them ever breached twenty seconds and these were not for the mainstream user reports. This kind of stuff is a bread-and-butter analysis anyone could get from a Netezza product engineer, but we thought we had roughly reconstructed the same results from the ground up. It essentially validated the findings that the Netezza engineer had provided to them over two months prior, but because their reports ran so slowly, they dismissed the engineer's finding as inaccurate and went about their own independent analysis.

When each of us separately reported our findings, and they validated the Netezza findings within a few percentage point of slog, the principals at the site were furious. I don't think I have ever seen anyone react so harshly. When my powerpoint slide hit the screen showing the metrics, the chief principal stood to his feet, leaned over the table and started shouting at me. I won't repeat the words but suffice to say, he did not accept my findings. I learned from the others who they had called that they had received a similar response. Essentially that they did not believe our metrics, since the proof is in the *reports*, and they were taking several minutes to return with results, some of them twenty minutes or more. In short, the metrics did not intersect with reality.

Well, we had only been on site a few days and still had some time to recover from this. We decided to take another track. If the database was not having any issues, then we needed to check the flow paths of the data, and now this included the round-trip from the user's desktop. So we gathered around one of the designated users and asked him to take us through some of the reports that he normally worked with. True to the tales, the reports were slow. We asked the report architect if there was any possibility we could get a copy of the reporting logs. We wanted to see what SQL statements were being executed in which order, to get more context to the problem. Also the round-trip of the report as it was consumed with multiple users.

One interesting artifact was that the reports were being *queued*. The reporting server was throttling the report execution rather than letting them all fly. For busy portions of the day, a report might sit in the queue for five to twenty minutes, but only require a few seconds to finally execute. No matter, the user experienced the full twenty minutes for the turnaround. We asked the architect why the throttle was in place and his answer was "best practice". We then asked him to think counter-intuitively and remove the throttle. Just trust the Netezza machine to do the work. He turned off the throttle and this took away the problem of the twenty-minute queries. But any given report was still taking over a minute, sometime as much as three minutes to return. While we had a significant win and high-fives all around, something else was afoot.

We then received the query log from the architect and this told us everything else we needed to know. The reports had been set up in sections, with several frames of activity. Each frame used one or more queries to fill out its portion of the information. As each of these carried queries that could take two to five seconds, with over twenty queries on any given report, this quickly added up to a net duration of over a minute. I asked the obvious question as to why these had been formulated this way, and the answer was interesting: *They match our old Excel reports*.

I then asked an impertinent question of the users, that is, were these reports useful like this? *Useful to someone*, I'm sure, was a common response, or something like it. Oddly (and this happens a lot, unfortunately) the report developers had assumed that the original Excel form of the reports were the gold-standard for how they should build out the environment, without asking any of the report users if this was even a useful format. Not even one of them thought it was. All of them thought that the format was being driven by *another* department. This imaginary department never materialized.

I also asked them if this sort of arrangement represented actual use cases, because the data arriving on the report form did not seem to be cohesive or flow in a use-case or user-consumption form. The answer to this was interesting, in that the report "frames" were just Excel pivot tables. They had not bothered to determine if the Excel workbook layout actually represented a user workflow.

Follow-on interviews with the users elicited the expected lament that the report architects had missed an opportunity to design the reports the way the users would actually use them, instead using the Excel form of the report as the baseline, and also expecting the Excel turnaround even though Excel wasn't hosting a hundred billion rows of data.

Back to the problem at hand. I asked if the reporting system could asynchronously stream these frames to the desktop so they would arrive independently. This way the user would start receiving data on the screen practically right away. Most of the queries would return in seconds anyhow. The stragglers would eventually arrive but the user experience would start its fulfillment immediately. This would give the appearance of faster report turnaround and the only delay would be the longest frame.

This analysis in hand, we formed hard evidentiary metrics around our notes and observations and made a follow-up report to the principals on our query findings, user interview quotes and the problem with the report queuing. Their answer was not nearly as harsh this time, but was even more interesting than their initial reaction.

They said, You don't know enough about our business to tell us how to architect our reports. *And the users don't either.*

Just a little more...

As alluded in a prior chapter, what if the way we think about modeling is actually constrained by the capacity of the technology? I've seen various types of architects and engineers do-things-differently, from concept to implementation based on the driving force of their machinery. Some concepts don't change, however, they just become a richer, crisper experience.

We had deployed an operational model that would circulate the business information through the Netezza machine every several minutes or so. No downtime for batch windows, this aggressive intraday scenario leaned heavily on micro-batch.

The reporting environment had been laid out as a quasi-dimensional model. The operational tables were laid out on a distribution facing the source systems and operational consumers. The reporting users, however had a different entry point and consumed the data in a different form (from a different angle, if you will). This would require a spin-off of three of the largest tables in the model, effectively replicating their content but recharacterizing the distribution. Of a twenty-terabyte implementation, this would add some four terabytes to the model on a machine that could hold over a hundred terabytes. This all seemed reasonable and sound, until the project principals made the unilateral assumption that these additional tables were a superfluous waste of space.

Not so, we argued. It may be redundant, but it's not a waste. We described how these tables would boost the user experience. But they could not see it, and required us to remove them. The reason why these tables were most interesting, is that they did not distribute nor join on a commonly understood normalized or dimensional model. Nor were they organized in a measurable if oblique form, or even an object-relational form. Some of the concepts of each applied, but nobody could really lay down an example of what particular theory or concept it aligned with.

But it aligned with how the users intended to navigate the reports. Whether they wanted jump-points here, drill-downs there, cross-references over yonder - the model had been crafted to harness the use-cases and workflow.

Without the model in place, the reports would still use the same workflow, only now they would have to leverage the operational model, its distribution and other factors. In essence, every report written was an on-demand shoe-horning of the reports and data model so that none of it worked very well. The principals blamed the machine. The developers blamed the reports. The downtrodden blamed the economy. Malaise ensued.

The report users were downright frosted when they heard about the removal of the tables that would have supported them. What the principals had forgotten, and is an object lesson for us, is that some concepts are valid regardless of whether we have the power to discard them.

Case in point, if this had been traditional technology, the architects would have put the operational model in one machine and the reporting model in another, connecting them with an ETL tool. This physical isolation would by definition provide functional isolation.

But somehow when we get into a power-house machine, the creativity takes an odd turn and we head down the wrong path. We have time to change this path, but it's best just to stay off the path entirely, as nothing good comes of it. In this case, the principals had set aside the primary benefits of functional isolation (the user facing distribution keys) in favor of a lower-performing, consolidated model that required less disk space. Let's not forget the priorities in play here. The principals set aside a major, beneficial concept for the sake of preserving hard-drive real-estate in a machine that had (and still has) more capacity than they would ever need.

The report performance suffered significantly. The principals refused to accept that blowing out the additional tables would make any difference and weren't even willing to experiment with it. Moreover, the only machine where this level of data actually existed was the production machine, so we could not make any form of convincing argument-from-evidence using the smaller machines. In the meantime, the users could not stop complaining.

One day the system admin and I were working on some basic backup mechanics and he began asking me about the model. While it was not completely my brainchild, I knew enough to walk him through it. While we waited for the backups to finish, he captured the DDL for the model, installed the tables in a temporary database and proceeded to copy all twenty terabytes of the production data into these tables. After all, they were basically one-for-one except for the distribution key. This would take a while even on the larger machine, so with my part done, I made a hasty exit but remained excited and anxious about the experiment the admin was about to perform.

At four-AM the next morning, my cell phone went off, woke me up and I thought I was just hearing things. It was the admin on the voice mail, so excited he was about to pop-a-gasket. I called him back and he related that all of the long-running queries that had so beset the reporting staff, he had manually executed them and they had returned in seconds. They had come back so fast that he had thought at first he had made a mistake.

Armed with this evidentiary data, together we made a case to have the reporting structures built and re-aligned to the new model. The only question that the principals had for the admin, and for the answer-to-their-problems, was completely unexpected. "Let me get this straight. You built a database on the production machine and copied production data into it? On a *production* machine? A production *database*? How much space did this take up? Who authorized this?"

Blah, blah, blah.

The principals weren't interested in being right, only in being political. The end of this story is a good one, because after enough complaints and sour user sentiment, the environment was eventually turned over to another division. The division head studied the notes, the results, the solution and the stand of the principals. He commissioned the build-out of the reporting tables on the secondary distribution key and from day-one of instantiating this model, the reports started returning in record speed. Users were satisfied, the birds were singing, all was well.

Unexpected reversal

When I have downtime, I try to catch up with friends and colleagues in town. One of them I once worked with in another part of my career and we still keep up. Although not a Netezza user, he is hip-deep in warehousing, decision support and reporting systems that span the globe. He also knows what technologies I have an affinity for. On this occasion, he related:

We're in the process of acquiring another company that we always thought was one of our most aggressive competitors. We're talking about a company that's been a constant source of anguish to our leadership for years. We would zig, they would zag, and sometimes they would capture major accounts before we even knew the opportunity was available. Remember when you were at our pool party three years ago and I had to disappear for an hour to deal with something? Damage control from something *they* did.

At some point our leaders got together, struck a deal and now they are part of our family. I'm leading the assimilation team and we're just coming down from two weeks with them. We walked in fully expecting whole days immersed with their teams and leadership, working up the data and strategizing with their analysts. We had decided that we would take with us the best of their staff and work on transitioning the remainder into new jobs with generous severance packages. But when we arrived, we found a small office space without even enough extra room for our team. Half of us had to work from the hotel. There were a total of twenty people in the office. They made sure that all of them came to work that day, because over half of them work from home. I was just shocked that the office and staff were no larger than our entire transition team. We really didn't know where to start, because we had been prepared to divide and conquer. Their leadership team met with us for the first part of the day and we went with the original plan, but now we would require their folks to visit ours in the hotel lobby and work with them there. We didn't have enough space in the office for forty people.

What became clear on that first day was that they had heavily relied on analytics and data, rather than sheer muscle, to compete with us all those years. They had been one step ahead of us because they had mastered the marketplace. Standing in the back of the office in what could only be called a makeshift data center, two big black Netezza machines sat their humming, mocking us. The next days were spent learning how they had used them to beat the pants off us.

Our problem was, we had thought that their team was ready to be assimilated into our company, so that they could learn how *we* do business, and they could help us become better by just adding their business savvy and intellect. But that they had leveraged high powered technology and analytics to accomplish what we could not, and that we had paid such a high price to acquire them, seemed both ironic and in some ways, downright unfair. I had worked hard and sacrificed to get our company in place the old fashioned way. They came in and let the machines do the hard work by an adaptive analytical formula. How could we assimilate this into our company without transforming *us* from the inside out?

At the end of these two weeks, I am concerned that our original transition mechanics were completely wrong. We had intended to take the best of their staff and let the rest of them go. Now I wondered if this would apply to our company, keep the best and let the rest of *us* go. Maybe even find myself on the outside looking in. We intended to transform them, but now they are transforming *us*.

He was concerned for the downsizing of his division, perhaps even the elimination of his own role. The better part of this story is once again borne on the available capacity of the environment. By assimilating the new machines and the analytics staff, the CEO and his sales folks were able to go after three of the largest sales targets they had approached over the past several years. In times past, each of those three targets had been concerned about their lack of technical firepower. On the flip side, they had not given the business to the smaller company because of a lack of management firepower. With the two merged, all three sales went-to-ink before the end of the year. My colleague's division *doubled* in size.

Yes, he finally admitted. It's transforming *us*.

How do we test all this?

I have received two separate stories concerning formal data warehouse testing scenarios, both for a migration project. I am a bit of an expert with migrations, so these were especially interesting to me. Methodology and process can make or break the effort. Both of these scenarios used the same defect reporting system, a web-based environment that allows multiple teams to enter defects for project, assign work and keep the responsibilities and workflows moving.

Both cases had a similar scenario for testing mature, operational systems. They had discovered over time that developers and testers would collaborate on their test cases, and this had slowly eroded the quality of the testing activity. Mandates had come down that when a tester built the test case, it had to be visible and properly vetted. If the test case failed, the tester was *required* to report it into the system. If the tester walked it across the aisle to check on his methods with a developer, this was perceived as tainting the testing process. If it turned out that the test case was invalid or an inaccurate way to test the functionality, this would fall back on the tester. If the test case was valid, it would fall back on the developer. Once reported, the defect had to be triaged through a formal managerial process. For mature, operational systems, this approach can keep the participants from becoming complacent about quality. For new systems or migrations, it can sometimes lead to unreasonable actions and conversations.

Scenario One, Adaptive Testing

The developers on the client-side team had rightly recognized that the rules and protocols for testing a mature, operational system were different for a new project like a migration. Because there are many dips, valleys, pitfalls and retrofits, essentially part of the learning phases of new technology and what it can do, they did not want to be unfairly punished for defects resulting in these simple disconnects. Otherwise the environment would be immersed in defect remediation before it could even get on its feet. One simple data error in a new system could cascade into many downstream errors, and reporting all those as defects was not only incorrect, it was irresponsible.

So they took the formal system into a more adaptive one. Testers were allowed to discuss their test cases with developers as long as they were doing it formally (in scheduled meetings for this purpose) and not at the watercooler or over the shoulder. Developers and architects were likewise allowed to collaborate with testing staff to make sure they were all looking at the right things in the right way. In addition, the defects were centered directly on the downstream reports, with the implicit assumption that if the reports were accurate, the upstream processes were also accurate. In a system where the ultimate rule of quality is whether the reports are accurate, this is the *only* valid arbiter of whether the processing flows are doing their jobs. In the next scenario we will see why this is true.

In this adaptive approach, the defects were reported within the team and not to management until the entire environment moved into the User-Acceptance-Testing (UAT) zone. This meant that the development and system-integration-testing (SIT) would be a fully-functional, humming engine by the time they entered UAT, and the managers would not be inundated with the unnecessary clutter of the pre-release defect reporting-and-remediation process.

What did this accomplish? The testers were nervous about testing new data systems on new technology and wanted more time to learn the environment before being held accountable for it. The problem was, they needed more collaboration from the architects and developers who were clearly coming up to speed on in orders of magnitude faster than they were. Likewise the developers did not want to take hits from defects that were simply misunderstandings on the part of the testers. Add to this that the source-to-target map from the old systems to new were in flux, as were the data models and the reports, there seemed to be too many opportunities for errors to creep in that needed to be more judicious than formal in their reporting.

The point is, for the vast majority of the development cycle, the environment is in radical flux and is unstable as a whole. Stability will come gradually, not all-at-once. This dovetails with the developers' and testers' gradually increasing understanding of the business data. If rigidity is invoked during this time of high flux, it is like attempting to pour a cup of coffee in an earthquake.

This was a very wise decision on their part, because a migration project *requires* an adaptive approach in the development and the testing. Any other approach is either inadequate or adversarial to the project's success.

Scenario Two, Stovepipe Testing

In this approach, the principals simply dismissed the idea that a different testing protocol was in order. They rather embraced the *production* testing infrastructure and processes already in place, without even considering the impact of this decision on the success of the *development* project or the quality of its execution. What we're talking about now is the *perception* of the senior managers on how the project is progressing, and premature reporting of early defects is the surest way to taint their perception. It is tantamount to offering up *false* reports on the quality of the products in-flight. Some of the readers are automatically dismissing this assertion, but early in a migration project the total count of invalid defects often outnumbers valid defects by a factor of two to one. As I noted above, this project has now embraced an approach that is *adversarial* to the project's success.

To illustrate the mental state of the project managers, the architects requested collaboration with the testers to make sure they were setting up the proper test cases. The testers were enthusiastically amenable to this suggestion, but the manager said no way, as this would taint the testing process, per policy, not reason. In this same conversation, the lead tester described the process and what happens with an "invalid defect". This same manager openly laughed and shook his head, saying Invalid Defect, now that's an oxymoron. How can there be such a thing? To which the lead tester simply responded, When we report a defect that is not really a defect, but is our misunderstanding of the business case. The manager stopped smiling, and for the first time had to consider the possibility that the testers could do something *wrong*.

And this was a foreign reality to him. Rather than reconsider his directive, he put his head in the sand and hoped for the best. It never arrived, because his decision already precluded the *best* from being part of the outcome. Now he was simply committing to the lesser of evils. It need not be so. All of these things are human decisions. Myopic adherence to rigid, impersonal policies when they are inappropriate for solving the problem at hand, is not leadership. Compliance perhaps, but not leadership. Words like this make me sound like a "cowboy" to some. It's the twenty-first century. Not the wild West. We'll get to that story later.

In a migration project, this is a primal fear of the testers, especially if they have no direct understanding of the deep internal workings of the system they are migrating from. Assigning testers because they are testers but not subject matter experts, carries a significant risk for the *proliferation* of invalid defects. This means we would expect the defects to rise rapidly, so the adaptive approach, keeping the defects between the teams and not under formal, production-level management scrutiny, is the right level of management to be the most successful.

Here are some of the symptoms that the project is already in trouble.

Defects are reported, but in following the formal, non-collaborative system, the defects rise several level of management before the development team is even aware of them. Once aware, the development team is told that there are ticking clocks on defects and they will be rated on how fast the defect is remediated. For the first one-hundred defects reported on the system, eighty of them were due to the misunderstanding of the testers on what they were testing. This eighty-twenty rule is repeatable and predictable when pressure is high and knowledge is low. *Early in the project, Invalid defects will outnumber valid defects by five to one.*

What's more, their test cases had also been formed as very tightly constructed, one-shot SQL statements that had to be teased apart and analyzed by the developers to determine what the query was actually doing, and then determine if the test itself was inaccurate. This could have been avoided with formal collaboration. The collaboration took place anyhow, but only as the developers were correcting the testing scripts (under the ticking clock) after the defect was already reported. This put the development team under enormous pressure to cure defects, do the work of the testers (fixing their scripts), as well as meet their own development deadlines. Project strength is being drained, and this *will* irreversibly affect the time line.

This put the testing team under enormous pressure, but it also put the managers into an adversarial position to the development team. What this process was immediately revealing, was the lack of preparation of the testing team. Not because they were incompetent, but because they really had not had the time to fully assimilate what they were testing or how to test it on the Netezza machine. The source of the adversarial position was simple: This testing team was responsible for testing all of the company's mission-critical systems, and the project effort was showing them in a less than positive light. This was intolerable. In fact, one of the principals directed the development team members be "very careful" in their wording of reporting the remediation of the test scripts. All of this could have been avoided if the managers had taken the adaptive approach and removed the walls and formal defect reporting for purposes of the migration project, and then turn them back on before entering UAT. This would have been the most productive approach and would have increased knowledge transfer, accelerating the project to success rather than standing up these artificial roadblocks.

By the time the flows were ready to move into UAT, a data modeler made a critical discovery. Their originally-promulgated source-to-target map (supplied by the client team to contractor and consultant alike), that had been used for all the development flows, was found to have serious flaws starting at the source systems. This would require redirecting the intake processes to now assimilate *ninety* new intake tables from the source. Now the team would be required to assimilate these new sources and debug the flows all the way to the end of the downstream chain, and regression-test over two *thousand* test cases. This discovery effectively invalidated over half the testing team's test scripts. Keep in mind that all of this is very visible to a level of management three levels above the team, so the scrutiny on these mistakes was crushing the project into the ground.

But such things are common *faux pas* in migration projects as the developers, testers and data analysts try to find their center and get a head of steam on the project. Micromanaged scrutiny derails this objective and keeps it derailed. The project will *never* get on its feet.

In all this, the data model had to undergo revisions as the development progressed. This is also common in migration projects, and easily assimilated by an adaptive approach, With a rigid stovepiped approach, the data model *must* be frozen so that the testers and developers are formally reporting defects against the same model and the same data. Usually for an artificially protracted period of time. If the tests were *centered on the reports and not the data model*, then changes to the model would be non-issues entirely.

Versioning the model is fine, but **freezing** *the model is the kiss of death.*

It is common to add operational columns to tables in support of transform flows. The Brightlight Accelerator Framework(C) likewise uses such operational columns, some of which are openly discussed in this book and in Underground. We use them because they are good ideas and always have been. Should the business include these columns in the formal business ERWin/ERStudio model? This is certainly their choice, and perhaps may be policy. But in a formal stovepipe model, invites scrutiny.

For this case, the testing team decided to run through the formal ERWin model and noted that each of the tables had several additional operational columns that had been added post-design. It had also included several hash keys to support some portions of referential integrity. The testing team had no choice but to follow protocol, and this was to report a defect for *each* additional column, for two separate data models. At least this time the testing team's manager gave a head's up to expect over *four hundred defects* to arrive on the development team's doorstep by the following morning. In an adaptive model, this action would have simply been deferred until the additional columns could be backfilled into the ERWin model, any time before arriving in UAT. With this action, the debilitating nature of the stovepipe model just rose into the stratosphere of the ridiculous.

Another aspect of post-design model management that is very common, is that the modelers typically size and type the data columns according to their best understanding of the data. But when trying to get data to move as a flow, developers often encounter mismatches in data types that are not foreseen or even predictable. These include too-large integers to too-small integers, likewise for strings and other data types, and are often perniciously peppered throughout the data model. A developer can literally spend days of his life daunted by these simple sizing errors. Fixing the errors as they arise feels a lot like playing the game of whack-a-mole, where the little moles pop up out of the hole and the player has to whack them with a mallet before they disappear again. What a total waste of time.

It is therefore another best practice of migration to adapt these models *so that the data can flow*. It places higher priority on *flow* than on storage. This means expanding numerics and integers to the largest data size, among other expansions. The adaptive model also calls for post-profiling to re-shrink these columns to more appropriate sizes once all of the flows have been completed and data *is in its proper functional place.* This may also require deferring the profile-and-shrinkage prior to moving into the UAT zone. Or it may be better executed afterward. Adaptability, recall, is doing what's right along a continuum, not necessarily at an artificial lifecycle juncture.

However, the stovepipe testing team saw such deviations as serious, reportable violations, and in their myopic adherence to policy, were steeling themselves for a fight to get these columns re-shrunken before entering SIT. This would mean profiling over two *thousand* columns and refitting them while the assets were still under development and the flows were still in functional flux. If the team did not shrink the columns, they would report all two thousand as defects. Now we can really see how the stovepipe model has gone sub-orbital into the something-out-of-a-Stanley-Kubrick-movie-level of surreal. Muted fluorescent lights appear behind the heads of each manager speaking to the team. Dr. Strangelove would have been proud.

The theme is clear. If the stovepipe model is invoked prior to entering UAT, the micro-management of the work products takes on debilitating proportions. It becomes *adversarial* to the development process and utterly obfuscates the purpose-at-hand - validation of *business functionality.*

It will, by definition, slow the project down and *jeopardize every target date* on the project plan.

I have noted elsewhere in this book that the adaptive model requires focusing on a centerpiece of end-to-end functionality, maturing this centerpiece until the downstream reports are properly operating. Invariably when the reports first run, the reporting team discovers data needs that were unforeseen. This now have to be brought forward through the flows and re-tested against the reports, maturing these aspects in a limited and controlled flow of work. If the flow passes through a source, then to an operational repository, and then to the reporting model, there is no way these two databases (repository and reporting) will be in a 100-percent state of readiness during this process. We *expect* them to be in growing states of maturity and partial states of readiness for the majority of the project's duration (because we are driving toward the reports, the *final* arbiter of the information's accuracy). Subject areas in the reporting environment are then developed on separate priorities and swimlanes of effort.

Contrast this to the stovepipe model, which requires the Repository to be one hundred percent code-complete before it can be approved, and this must happen early in the cycle because it feeds the Reporting mart. Oh, and the Reporting mart must be one-hundred-percent code-complete prior to proceeding to report building. Then when we get to the Report building, something happens.

As noted above, the reports will need things we could not foresee. But now, the code is complete for the two models prior to the reporting zone, and we must accommodate these data needs right away. We may have to add data structures, flows, etc to the existing system in order to support all these things.

It is invariable that unforeseen needs of the reporting environment will impose themselves on the data model. This happens at a frenetic pace during development, but will continue thereafter, ad-infinitum.

So which is easier, to add these things as part of an early discovery exercise, or afterwards when the flows and models have been declared code-complete, *requiring full regression tests of potentially thousands of unrelated feature points?* We don't have to regression-test stuff that doesn't exist, which is why it is more important to get these functional discoveries out of the way earlier than later. Waiting until the majority of flows are complete is too late.

Another effect this elicits from the development team, is the need to embrace an engineering approach to the development activities. This of itself creates additional workload to perform extreme regression testing of every deliverable. Some suggest that this might actually increase the quality of the work products, *but it does not.* In an adaptive model, the real objective is to get data to the reports in the most cohesive manner, not bench-checking unrelated code for execution errors. I have known of flow-based models that have errors in their execution for parts that are unrelated to the flow/functionality about to be tested. Asking developers to make these unrelated areas complete and ready, when they are not going to be tested, is debilitating and unnecessary.

In fact, I am not the first to say that when we encounter a need to use engineering principles to produce business data flows, *especially* with a Netezza machine, something has gone seriously wrong. The engineering has already been done, *in the machine.* Our focus should be on business flows and functionality. The testers should have a discrete set of flows and functions to examine, not an all-or-nothing testing protocol.

Some readers are shaking their heads about now, not believing that any group of people could possibly be so rigid and unreasonable in the face of these debilitating effects. But rest assured that the people immersed in the system are committed to the process, the policy and the rather draconian actions it may elicit. They know nothing else.

Keep in mind the nature of a migration project, especially toward a new and relatively misunderstood technology, using people who have never migrated anything before. In the stovepipe case, the managers considered themselves very effective and competent, perhaps even receiving accolades for their acumen in managing the "change management" process in a mature, operational production system. They initiate developers, set their goals, involve the testers, and sit back expecting an outcome. The outcome has always been the same for them.

In the migration project, they are stunned, taken aback and even fearful when the outcomes do not comply to their expectations. People start looking to them for response or reaction, and they don't like the scrutiny. They don't begin to doubt their own abilities or understanding, but immediately question the competence of the development team performing the migration. They are out of their element and defensive at every turn. Meetings with the developers become adversarial. Activities of the developers become indictments. Managers and testers stand accused. Finger-pointing, tail-covering, and unprofessional conversations ensue.

All *because* of embracing the wrong model to produce the work products. Using an adaptive approach is still hard work, but it's the only model that is *most* successful for a migration project.

If you or someone you know is about to start a migration project, carefully consider the process you are about to embrace. It can be a fun, rewarding and game-changing experience for everyone involved. In fact, it will be a just that. For *someone*. Why not you?

Cowboy Way

I mentioned earlier the "cowboy" perception people have of folks who *apparently* defy their compliance protocols for development and testing. But keep in mind what the compliance protocols are meant to do - protect the quality of the outcome and preserve the professionalism of the environment. I mean, these are the *minimum* expected effects of the compliance protocols.

When the deliverables first leave the development environment, we can expect at a minimum, first-time configuration errors. Something unforeseen in the new home has to be accounted for. This could be a database name, an undocumented convention. It exists and people know about it, it's just slipped their minds. We already provide an adaptable set of tools that can be tweaked in-place to determine if the problem is in fact a configuration problem or something else. A stovepipe model mentioned earlier, would prohibit such tweaks. Rather it would require us to identify the issue, solve it in the location (development) where the issue does not exist, and blindly redeploy the deliverables with fingers crossed. This is nonsense. But as a "cowboy" suggesting that they make and validate these configuration tweaks in their *own* location (even as a one-time-first-time transitional issue), am I bucking the system or just integrating the code into a new environment? What is the most reasonable thing to do for the *first time installation?*

Way back in 1992, I was working on a system that had not left the development environment. We packaged up everything and then deployed it in the testing zone. The code immediately failed because of a significant discrepancy in a naming convention. I asked the tester if I could tweak the configuration and retry, and she said sure. We found two additional problems that were environmentally related, so I took notes and added these as adaptations to the configuration. Then we redeployed the code and lo, it worked the first time. During this exercise, one of the managers came by my cubicle and asked a direct question: *I hear you changed some code in the testing area today. That won't be allowed in the future.* To which I said, It won't be *necessary* in the future. This was just the first-time installation. I explained that the configuration, not the code, is what we had to change. He could not see a difference. It was all the same to him. Making any change in the testing zone invalidated the delivery. I totally agreed with him, and then asked him how I would have affected the fix any other way. He had no answer.

Policy versus Reason. Some call this the Cowboy Way. When we are doing something for the first time, or initiating a lot of First Times, like a *migration project,* policy needs to be balanced with reason in order to properly harness and stabilize the environment. And by the way, I was building adaptive models even before 1992. The configuration change that I made in that case, if the code had been hard-wired, really would have constituted a coding change, and my approach would have been undone. That this serious environmental difference could be affected and resolved with a simple configuration tweak should have been to my credit. Instead we're having another policy discussion as though this first-time/one-time transitional problem would be an ongoing issue forever.

At another site, we deployed a first-time installation for a client and upon reception the testers told us: *Oh, in our environment we put an extension on all the database names. For Development and Production for example, the database name might be Customers, but in our testing environment the database name is Customers_TST.*

We let them know exactly where to make the configuration change, and this may as well have been the entire project's undoing. They reported my suggestion three manager levels above us to let them know that the environment we had just deployed was *flawed*, would *require* the testers to change it after arrival and in so doing had violated a half-dozen policy issues. Of course, this characterization of a one-time situation into an operational violation was just a ranting over-reaction. But by the time this cat was out of the bag, the entire environment had become a whirlwind of confusion. Rather than attempt to educate them on the difference between code and configuration, we instead were required to play the same game.

So we quickly learned the red-tape protocols. With the request-for-fix in hand, we filed something called a delivery extension request that would buy us time to make the change. Seems that since they did not tell us that all of their databases were differently named, and this never came up in a discussion, we were privy to a reprieve on the timeline. Never mind that in our adaptable model they could have affected the change in a matter of moments and been underway. Unfortunately for them, the process of filing and approving the delivery extension would take at least a week to produce and a week to approve. The project sort of floated in the water for awhile. We were getting other things accomplished but could not make another functional delivery just yet.

Once approved, the clock started ticking on the amount of time requested for the change. Our team huddled and asked each other a simple question: If this database naming problem had come up with hard-wired software using it, how would it have affected the time line? Because this was the metric the client was using to both protect themselves from spontaneous change, and to protect the developers from unspoken requirements. Our team agreed that a minimum of a week would be required to affect the change and unit test it, then another week to integration-test it to all the various source databases (there were a total of nine). And on top of this, to make it flexible so that we could transparently switch from dev to test to prod without any changes in at all. Of course, all of this *was already built into our adaptive offering,* but the client actually wanted to be treated as if *none of it existed at all.* So we shared all of these numbers with the project team leads and they were devastated. This seemingly minor oversight on the part of the testers (in not telling us about the database naming issue) was about to cost six weeks of project time and there was nothing they could do about it.

Except, of course, *accept* the idea that tweaking the configuration *in place* is the most adaptive, accelerated approach, and because it's a *one-time transition issue*, does not constitute a breach in the *operational* standards of the lifecycle. The question now is: What would you do? Accept the six-week hit in the schedule, following all policies to the letter, or accept that this project is replete with first-time/one-time issues that will have to be resolved as-encountered if we want to keep the project on track and underway?

In fact, now I coach the first-time recipients of the deliverables to make sure that they understand and recognize that first-time environmental transition is a *very* high concern for me. Invariably they tell me that we will deal with such things when the time comes. *But* - I get their prior approvals, and their management's commitment that these first time transitions will be resolved with *in-situ* configuration tweaks, and carefully explain what it means. And then when we install the system for the first time and *invariably* encounter the transitional difference that everyone-knew-about but didn't-think-was-an-issue, I direct them to change the configuration and we don't have to engage a conversation as to why.

It is important not to make any assumptions about the reasonableness of what we intend to do, if we are surrounded by people immersed in policy and fearful of anything approaching non-compliance.

Speaking of the Old West, people seem to think that the times back then somehow had self-destructive people who bucked the system, saved the day but rode off into the sunset leaving everyone else to pick up the pieces of the things he broke while he was fixing things. That's a romantic view of the Old West. What was it *really* like? How about following a stricter set of rules because your survival depended on it? How about engaging a stronger, rigorous discipline in daily life because the agrarian lifestyle (still) operates on an immutable, uncompromising clock of planting and harvest that does not suffer creative indifference? Cowboys make the ranch *work*.

Mechanisms, automation, technology and communication have *reduced* the need for human discipline in every area of life. We expect and rely on automated, computerized systems to do for us the things that we'd rather no longer do for ourselves. In point of fact, a cowboy these days is someone who brings a reasonable, battle-hardened, disciplined wisdom to the table that is rare. Those who buck the system aren't cowboys. They're *outlaws*.

The Old Fashioned Way

"Antiquated methods," complained a senior Enzee while we waited to board our respective aircrafts. Both of us were on a delay in Chicago O'Hare. Enzees always have something to talk about.

"When we onboarded the project," he continued, "we were given high-end laptops, smart-badges, integrated VPN (the kind without the little FOB key) and generally initiated into their technology-fold within twenty-four hours of our arrival. All this set up a false illusion that they were both technically savvy and ready to embrace the future with savage indifference to the fetters of the past. Ahh, it was a glorious beginning."

"Then we began to notice telltale signs that something was amiss. Senior managers delegated enormous power to their underlings, dilettantes who did not understand what we were doing, or even why we were doing it. And they weren't completely certain why their superiors had assigned them to the project. At one point, a principal in their group openly admitted that he was working against us *because it was his job.*"

A colleague from a sister "boutique" firm relates that his firm was hired specifically because they used adaptive approaches while the other firms were rigid and stodgy.

"From day one we reviewed their assets. Their source-to-target map was weak, so we worked with them on it. Their data models were incomplete so we worked with them on it. Their data was dirty so we worked with them on it. Their specifications weren't solid at all, so we worked with them on it. Then one day they unloaded on us a big pile of unforeseen scope changes, so we worked with them on it. Even as their requirements were changing, and their business model was moving, we were adapting these things into the process as a portent of what their life would be like after deployment. After all, like you say a lot, David, the environment has to exist with the expectation of change, right?

"After we started producing work products, this started to crush their ability to receive them. We tried to work with them on it, but the project timeline was closing and we needed to get all of it out. Honestly we had burned enough extra cycles because of their lack of readiness anyhow. Then one day, some weeks before the final deployment, they told us that *our approach didn't fit their environment,* and they replaced us. If that's not bizarre, their project went into a tailspin as the replacement crew began to push back on the things we were willing to adapt. In other words, all of the things we were willing to work with them on, the new crew wasn't. Of course, they worked with the client to create all those assets but would not budge on the actual development until those things were completed and approved. This meant that the project, which we were almost done with, sat in the water for over six months.

"Then they took another six months to produce the functionality, now fully one year from the time that we were ready to deploy. During this timeframe however, they had to apply very aggressive project management to keep everything in sync. Unfortunately, by the time they went into production, they were already six months behind on the features that had been frozen out of the model six months prior. This new crew said it would take three months to assess these new functionalities, create an impact analysis and then begin work. No, not assimilate the new features now, but analyze them for impact for three months before doing anything. So much for being able to assimilate change.

"In the end, our model was the one that they had really wanted. The rapid time-to-market and agile response to change. The model that "fit their environment" was the one they received. Our desire to work with them *adaptively* appeared too much like a chaotic process. We worked with them but they were unwilling to work with us. Seems like everything we put in place challenged the status quo."

Author's note: This colleague points out something pervasive in many environments, that the policy, process and organization tends to dictate how all projects and environments will operate, even if they don't serve the business needs at all. Projects that are a shining hope to change the current malaise, are simply assimilated into the broken environment, and those who tried-hard to make it work another way, are seen as outlaws, or even outcasts.

Controlled chaos. Like the backstage of a play. Everyone knows where they need to be, what they need to do and when they need to do it. People are depending on them to hit their cues. Nobody is micro-managing the actors. There has to be some degree of delegation or the show cannot go on. For the above, they finished functionally, but buried the opportunity.

The Wild, Wild West

"Ever been to a wild west show?" Asked one of my friends as we were having lunch. A principal in a mid-sized consulting firm, He relates:

We had something of honeymoon experience when we first engaged. They had acquired several Netezza machines and we were anxious to help. Once the ball was rolling, I mean really rolling, we started seeing strange behaviors in their less experienced staff. They would challenge our leadership openly. Require us to repeat ourselves or answer the same question in multiple ways, or the same question presented as different questions. In essence, this was like meeting gunslingers at high noon.

But as I looked around, we had every element from an old television western. From the robber-baron Colonel to the corrupt sheriff. The town drunk to the house-of-ill-repute, a town blacksmith, school-marms, heroes with love-interests and even cattle rustlers. Good grief, it was surreal.

I openly joked about them behaving as gunslingers and they ran with it. We started seeing screensavers of Shane, John Wayne, Jimmy Stewart and James Arnett. Managers began speaking in terms of "notches in the gun", riding the horses, watering holes, corrals, broncos and trail rides. At first we thought it was cute until it became evident that they were mocking us.

Well, you can't win them all, and clearly their gunslingers (or should I say, hired-guns since all of them were independent contractors anyhow) seem to have everything under control. We did not renew the contract with them because the environment had become so weird and unpredictable. We just needed a place that contained a bit more sanity.

The principals of the project had been after us for over a month to get a new contract into their hands, and with the final week approaching, we hadn't done so. In each instance, we told them that we were not renewing the contract. All of us had another appointment with another client or two (hey, we stay busy too).

One of them finally asked if the contract would make it to them by the end of our current gig. We simply said no, but they were in denial. On the last day of our gig we turned in all of our laptops and badges, signed the necessary releases and made our respective exits.

On the way out of the building, one of the project principals happened to meet me in the elevator atrium and we made small-talk and chatted about this-and-that. I did not feel comfortable riding down the elevator with him, and as luck would have it, my phone rang just as the elevator chime heralded the elevator's arrival. I answered the phone and offered him a courteous gesture as he punched the button on the elevator panel. Before the doors could close, he said to me, "See you Monday."

One would think in all this disconnection that we would have heard from them the following Monday when we did not return for the next phase. But I did not hear from any of them for almost three weeks until one of them called me and rather sheepishly asked, "We've been piling up a bunch of stuff for your review and just wondered, you know, when you're coming back?"

I told him that our contract had expired and we had not renewed. He exclaimed, "Oh, no! We can fix that. Who did you give the contract to?" To which I said, "No, you misunderstand. I did not say that we *weren't* renewed. I said that *we did not* renew. We have concluded our business with you."

After a very long silence he finally said, "No kidding. Well, you could have given us a little head's up!"

I kept tabs on the progress of the gunslingers who had made our lives so miserable. In their rather unprofessional behavior towards us, the principals had assumed that the gunslingers had it together and could easily take up where we had left off. Upon this notification, the gunslingers got really quiet, spent their days hiding out in spare cubes where nobody could find them, and took down all of their wild-west paraphernalia. Seems their little party had gone a little too far and had been taken a little too seriously by the decision-makers. The project boss spent the next several months trying to find another team to help them wrap up the rollout.

With the gunslingers noticeably absent, they were not included on the short list of project participants in the follow-on work. But when the new team members showed up, these gunslingers also insinuated themselves into the kickoff meetings and all the initial onboarding meetings. The project boss took them aside and told them in no uncertain terms, "You will perform knowledge transfer of what you know about the prior effort. Answer any questions that they may have. But keep in mind, you will not be allowed to ask questions of them."

The gunslingers were shocked. One of them finally said, "You mean, *we won't be allowed to do our job?*"

Too-Small Tables

As an aside, I was engaged in a conversation with a colleague about the difference between small tables and large tables. I asked what the difference was, and he seemed to think we could nail down a definition. Small vs. Large. But it only seems this way. I asserted, "There are no small tables." Essentially inviting him to prove me wrong. He attempted to use some metrics, applying something to say when a table is "definitely" large and any other could be considered small. So now that we're in the Wild, Wild West, here's a story:

My Dad is a retired Texas prosecutor. He spent over thirty years as a Criminal District Attorney. He was also a marksman with a pistol, with trophies and everything. When I was young, he taught me how to shoot pistols. My brother actually competed, but both of us are adept. One day Dad emptied the rounds in the six-shooter, closed the weapon and slid it over to me. He asked very soberly,"Is the weapon loaded?" And since I had just seen him empty the weapon, I replied, "Yes." To which he very seriously asked, "Are you *sure?*"

Now this is one of those moments for a young man where we feel a rite of passage coming on. Without looking at the weapon, I counted the rounds on the table and said, "Yes, the weapon is empty."

Dad said, "Okay then, open it."

At this point I thought *Great, he sneaked a round into the chamber, right?* But when I opened the weapon it was indeed empty. I closed it, put it down and said, "Yes, it's empty."

"Are you *sure?*" he asked again, leaning toward me with eyes so serious that they bored a hole right into my forehead. I could feel something sinking into my stomach. He was trying to teach me something, but I was either missing it or he wasn't doing a very good job.

"The weapon is *always* loaded, David," he said to me, and let it hang in the air. Before I could object, he said it again, "The weapon is *always* loaded."

Clearly this made an impression on me, as I am sharing it now I can still see his eyes. Never would I see him more serious and focused than in that moment. I could now imagine all the bad guys he'd put away, wondering if they had been on the receiving end of that stare.

The lesson was simply this: We don't have the freedom to *ever* treat a weapon as if it is empty. The risk of being wrong, is just too high.

Now that's probably a little more serious than the matter of too-large tables, or too-small tables. But the complimentary lesson is this: Just because a table is "small" today, does not mean it will always be so. We need to treat all tables as if they can outgrow us, and model the environment and the tables accordingly. It never hurts to treat a small table as though it will grow too large, but it's really bad to treat a table (or design it) as though it's small even after it's exceeded the definition.

I recall one group that had set up their postal codes for the United States, but by the time our team had arrived, it had metastasized into a wide array of countries, each with a wild range of options on their postal codes. Their original solution was no longer scalable. We retro-fitted their model into a metadata-driven form, allowing them to scale in both managing the countries, and in actually processing data with them.

Small tables? *Is* there such a thing?

Unexpected Outcomes

A colleague relates: So one day I was told by my bosses to report to a bank in Boston, one that essentially did banking-for-banks rather than for retail customers. This was earlier in my career, so I had no clue as to what the status or nature of this institution was. So I arrived for the consulting interview, essentially a way for them to measure my brainpower before our consulting firm was given the nod. So I walked through each individual interview, bored out of my mind with the trivia that seemed to jump from the woodwork. Surely they didn't need *me*, a guru of very-large-scale databases. Couldn't just about *anyone* take this gig? I don't really know why, after sort of walking disinterested and disconnected through these chats, that they picked me for the job, but afterward I started receiving emails from all over the company. Congratulations for landing this client-of-clients, the be-all-end-all of client engagements, bagging the elephant and all that.

Really?

David, I had a chat with a friend outside of my company and mentioned the client name. Well, it seems that my ignorance had the very best of me, because this client really was the be-all-end-all of clients to bag, and I had loped through the interviews - I could not have been more disinterested without watching television while their folks talked to me. Hey, I'm not a bad person, but I didn't run in those circles, and someone could have *briefed* me, right?

This environment was especially memorable because they had such a significantly high policy-and-process curve that we didn't think anything would shake them from it. However, our project champion had apparently been given a very long leash to pull this project off and get things into the hands of the most vocal of their user base. With him pushing and them pulling, this was an unstoppable juggernaut.

We rolled the system out much faster than they expected, the principals were awed and the overall tenor of all our conversations was that the world would be our oyster within the walls of this corporation. Our project champion thought so too, and that the success of this project would see him into promotions and raises in the near term.

But on the eve of all this success, the CIO had different ideas about who should be in charge of what. Our project champion was passed over for the promotion he thought he deserved, and for weeks we barely had any conversation with him until one day he announced he was leaving. His replacement also favored us, but he was well behind the curve on what we were doing, where we were going, and all that. It so overwhelmed him that he asked for a transfer out of that corporate office and into an operational environment. His successor would be someone from the main office, who himself had come from another consulting firm that wasn't ours, and liked to give *them* the nod on practically every new project under his umbrella. His directive was not that we should bring him up to speed on the environment, but that we should bring his *designates* up to speed on the environment. Our replacements.

So we went from zero to hero in a matter of months, and in another matter of months we were no more than a memory, if that. Of interest here is that this was many years ago, and our replacements *still* struggle with the solution we had developed, but not because it was hard to manage or deploy with. All of their other projects, on "traditional" hardware platforms, were "stodgy", high-process, lots of management, protracted delivery schedules, perfect fodder for time-and-materials consulting. But what we'd built them was a rapid-release model for nearly interactive turnaround on requirements, coupled with an adaptive back-end implementation that left them with no excuses for slow delivery. The irony is that they made all their money in environments where they *depended* on the lethargy of the environment and the inefficiency of the solution to give them breathing room, where this solution left no breathing space and sucked all the remaining oxygen out of the room. Clearly this firm was not ready to take on such a task, as exemplified by the revolving door on their own employees who had been hired into stress-free, low-frequency jobs and now were drinking from the firehose - of *functionality*, not technology.

Shrinkage

I mentioned in Underground that one of my conversations with a project boss was, "What if I could make your six-month project turn into a three-month project with fewer people?" To which the initial response was "That would be fantastic" but on further reflection, commented "I think I'll pass, because it will mean I have to forego three months of billable hours." Don't you just love a consultant with the right priorities? (For the consulting firm, of course).

It this what the appliance does? Make it so our environment is so productive and so rapid-fire in feature deployment that our head is always spinning? Wait - isn't that what we *wanted?*

Some might read the above dissertation and conclude, "What you're saying David is that if we have a stodgy environment we should not call you, because you won't fit here." Ah, but that would have entirely missed the point. (For such is the way of stodgy thinking). I have learned to be consummately *adaptive* to most any environment I enter, and most if not all of my clients will attest that I will work with you where you *are*, to get you where you're going. Of course, the "where you're going" part is in your hands.

So the real question is not, "can your consultants adapt to your environment?", because that's not the nature of *transformation*. Nor is it whether a Netezza appliance fits into *your* working model, because most likely it does not.

The real question is, are *you* ready for the change? The appliance is bringing change, and change *is* underway. So are we in denial, resistance, or embracing and running with it?

My so-called Netezza

Mentioned briefly elsewhere in this book, we were invited to convert a retail data warehouse from Oracle to Netezza. They wanted to use DataStage as the ETL tool to pull data from the various retails sources and send them over to the Netezza machine.

Just one problem. There was no Netezza machine.

"We want you to design it as if the target was a Netezza machine," they said, "And then when Netezza gets here, we'll just swap them out and run with it."

"What will the target be in the meantime?"

"Another Oracle machine."

"Better be a really big Oracle machine."

Blank stare.

The naivete of this approach was stunning, especially when we tried to talk them off the ledge. One of the problems for resolution: the point-of-sale information would arrive in a single file with mixed record types. No worries, I assured them, because we can snip that stuff apart once its inside the machine.

We can snip it apart with DataStage, too, they blustered. We should let one technology do its job and let Netezza do its job.

"Funny," I kept repeating, almost like it was a joke, but s*o not,* "Netezza isn't really here to do its job."

"That'll change," they asserted. "In time that'll change."

At this point I reminded myself that this wasn't really a Netezza project, but an *Oracle* project. No, not an Exadata project, but a plain vanilla copy-from-Oracle-into-Oracle-lift-and-shift project. Pretending that it was a Netezza project or doing anything differently than a common Oracle project likely meant we would be teetering on a precipice for the near term, perhaps much longer.

Another problem, in that snipping apart this incoming file would produce ever smaller files, some of which only had a few rows of data. Since these would be arriving on a rapid-fire intraday model, we were concerned about the too-small-data-file issue I mentioned in Underground. Netezza requires larger files to be most efficient. The smaller and more frequent the intake, the more it's being treated like a transactional system.

When I explained to them that Netezza doesn't play as a transactional system, they didn't seem to clearly understand this. After much whiteboarding and general deep-dive discussions on the architecture, they still didn't get it. Without a machine to actually demonstrate it, we were constantly at odds with them on this and other subject areas.

At some point the project came to a head with the principals upset that the flow from DataStage did not seem like something Netezza could support. This from people who had never worked with the machine. We had assumed that they were going through this functional exercise because the Netezza machine was on the way any-day-now and we could eventually stop the argumentation. What we did not realize was that the Netezza machine had not been purchased nor even approved, and the process for either of these was sixty days minimum.

I rolled off the project before they had things rolling into UAT, but the integration testing team had missed the memo about it being a Netezza-targeted project and proceeded to re-question the entire design. Even while working for a new client, I found myself spending hours on the phone every day trying to bring the testing team up to speed on how to test on an Oracle platform while pretending to be a Netezza machine. It became more bizarre by the moment.

"The scanning queries you asked us to build run too slow," said one.

"But they won't run slow at all on a Netezza machine," I objected.

"The <fill in the blank> practice you asked us to put together won't operate unless we heavily index the target tables."

"You won't need indexes at all on the Netezza machine."

But at some point I had to "call it". This wasn't a Netezza project and pretending differently wasn't doing any of us any good. I finally told them, look, do what you need to do. If you need additional stuff, add it in and perhaps later when the Netezza machine gets here, we can just remove it and it will all work the same.

The team was elated and scurried off to make it so. The next phone call I had with them, they were happy as clams and they were finally getting work done. Just one problem: They were getting work done because they had completely revamped everything into an Oracle-centric testing model. By this time, however, I had already grown weary of fighting this uphill/upstream battle. Who were we kidding? If they wanted to complete the project within an acceptable time frame, they would have to set aside the Netezza pretense.

As of this writing, three years later, they still have not purchased a Netezza machine. Not for lack of desire. For lack of money. This tells us that the company can't afford a Netezza machine because they really don't have all that much invested in IT anyhow, or they really don't understand where Netezza can help them solve analytical problems. Or that they don't have any analytical problems to solve. They are a national company that is, as of today, more well-known for their closure of stores than their penetration in their market share.

Jung-L Luv

The principals told us that their plan was to take the rather subjective aspects of standing up a data warehouse and categorize them for study. The warehouse wasn't their particular goal, but the *process* of putting one together. If they ended up with a functional warehouse, fine and dandy. But they wanted to focus on the human element. How it affected the people who were actually building it.

To what value, was my innocent question.

So that we can learn, came the more-than-obvious answer.

But what will the learning be applied to? You won't go into the business of building data warehouses. You will only need *one* - for your enterprise.

They had not thought of that. Seems this team had been running around all over the company to characterize these factors in the software projects and other initiatives. The warehouse is not a project, I reminded them, but an *environment*. The rules are different here.

But what would you say is the most difficult obstacle to overcome? they pressed. Honestly, I wanted to answer, "Artificial studies like yours." Mainly because nothing they could glean from the study would be applicable anywhere else. Projects like this are borne on knowledge, personality and technology, a very heady brew. Repeating the same combination anywhere on the planet would be a false expectation.

A positive expectation would be that the greatest obstacle is underpowered hardware. Because this wasn't a problem with a Netezza machine in-house, we went down a laundry-list of other types of problems normally encountered on software projects, but this wasn't a software project. Still, the lifecycle questions and other inquiries around warehousing began to have a similar ring to them, so I thought I would mention it here.

As many pitfalls, drawbacks, challenges and the like that they threw at me, I did not disagree with any of them as potentially pressing on this or any other project. But what I also knew in my deepest soul was that all of their listed issues would wash away or turn into something else if only we had enough technical firepower at our fingertips. And this is a significant realization indeed. With a Netezza machine in hand, the vast majority of challenges are no longer. They are replaced with a different set of challenges, but these are not particularly difficult to overcome either.

One way or another, I didn't like having these guys "inside my head" so I asked them a question: Isn't it true that if your prior efforts had enough firepower, that they would all have been wildly successful? There would be no need for a team such as yours to go running around asking questions.

Firepower washes away a lot of bad vibe, baby.

Clear the decks

In early '09 our team began the work of migrating a highly active on-demand model from its home on Oracle into the Netezza machine. Essentially this solution had a number of disparate touchpoints from the local environment. The principals recognized the need to tease-apart and de-engineer the solution as we migrated into Netezza. These challenges included:

- Sybase extracts for statistics
- Ab Initio ETL jobs for loading data from the enterprise warehouse
- Large-scale analytics grid running on-demand operations
- Web-service download for interest rate information
- Oracle extract to capture additional reference information
- Excel spreadsheets submitted by the end-users
- Two large Oracle sources, one the enterprise warehouse and one the former Oracle environment.
- Microbatch analytics feedback on-demand

Three teams had preceded us. What they could not accomplish inside of three years, we put into a UAT zone within *two months.*

In the first place, each of the above integration sources and touchpoints had some degree of data processing utility wrapped around them. One of our predecessors had recommended WisdomForce to use for fast-extract from the Oracle machine. When it was learned that, because of our "overloaded" development servers (that is they contained forty-plus CPUs each) our purchase price for WisdomForce was simply too high, we had to seek other options. The folks at Wisdom-Force were none too happy about our rather vocal objection to their pricing model. Our principals did not disagree with the product's necessity, if only they could have come to an agreement on the pricing. Alas, we had to go another direction. As a note, however, I could see no issue with the pricing model *in comparison to how much work we had to do* to offset its absence. Our principals simply chose to incur the cost in another, less tangible form. *Sweat.*

Our mission was to re-integrate all of the information sources (with varying frequency and duration), bring their content into the machine, send it through various SQL transforms and then place it into the Repository as a resting place. Until the data had to move to the downstream.

So one by one we eliminated the utility running each of the integration points and replaced them with a simple extract / capture scenario directly into the nzload utility. This effectively integrated and flowed each of those data streams into the machine without need of the utility, and yes, this includes Ab Initio.

At first, the 10100 machine we were using for integration was overloaded and panting to keep up with the workload. Not because of what we were doing, but the *four other teams* that were burning the machine into the ground. Actually, the machine was a trooper and didn't have to prove itself more than the time someone kicked off a runaway query on it and it manufactured eight *trillion* rows before it died. Yes, these are the kinds of scales, accidental or otherwise, common on this kind of platform.

In moving the intake environments away from their former utility home, we had many degrees of freedom to leverage metadata for the intake. As alluded to in Underground, we manufactured our SQL assets, including the loosely-typed varchar-only table based on the target table, and the pre-fab SQL statement to transfer the data from this table to the final target. Also as noted on the Gather -Round the Grill blog in Honor The Host, we don't want to use an external table in place of these components. Use nzload to the varchar-only table, SQL-transform into the target table. If we use an external table, the SQL-transform happens in the host, not on the MPP.

Since this gave us many degrees of freedom with the data, we initiated multi-threaded loading. That is, rather than just generate a varchar-only table, we also created a transient version of the target table and used the AUDIT_ID in its table name. With this simple tactic, we were able to perform multi-threaded loading so that the on-demand processing could happen in multiples of operations at a time without having to thread through a single set of tables.

From this point we could perform business-level SQL-transforms into the target repository and were able to track everything in a load tracking table. We could also use this to perform surgical rollback.

The loader was interesting in that since it leveraged metadata and a SQL transform in the middle, we could also handle out-of-order columns and even business-name columns. The SQL-transform could handle and remap / align both.

Something arose in this fray that we wanted to harness better, since the SQL-transform was highly overloaded with functions to scrub data as it left the varchar table into the final target. We needed some additional power over the stages of data intake. The intake-table/transform/target-table combination was very powerful, but we needed more. I noted this in a prior chapter. As the data arrived we need to perform type-level validation (e.g. is_date() or is_numeric()). From there, we needed to screen or capture exceptions. This would guarantee that no invalid data entered the SQL-transform. Once inserted, we then had the option to perform any other kind of transform, create hash keys and ids, deduplicate and change-data-capture. None of these were trivial but they follow common, easily-prescribed patterns that would make things consummately simpler for the next downstream operation.

The back-end processing entered production within five months of inception, due in large part to the machine's undying resilience, the cooperative nature of the client and their commitment to agile methods and aggressive collaboration. The back end is still running as of this writing with no particular need for rewrite or overhaul, also due largely to the team's deep and thorough dive into the required business functionality.

The micro-batch model had some challenges that required some direct forethought and resolution.

Guarding against duplication - at any given time a microbatch would contain highly verbose error messages. These messages were canned and repeatable. We did not want to place them directly into the fact table because of their size. We instead used the SQL Toolkit's hash8() function to hash the error message into an integer key, then used this key in the fact table.

While there were no collisions in the hash key itself, it was possible and regular that multiple micro-batches could contain common error messages. The means to put the error message into the target database was to use an insert-into-select-from-where-not-exists so that it would never load a duplicate. Of course, this could not guard against two shared-nothing microbatches carrying similar information from loading their data simultaneously. The where-not-exists is not effective if two separate inserts are happening simultaneously. They are carrying common data but cannot see the data in the other thread. The solution to this was to simply synchronize the shared-nothing execution of these threads. They would essentially wait-in-line if another thread was in the middle of its finalization. Considering that finalization would take anywhere from ten to twenty seconds for any given operation, the wait would only come if necessary and would never be a significant delay.

Note that this process could not be harnessed with a simple synchronization unless we were directly harnessing the flow and deliberately performing a checkpointed finalization rather than allowing the tables to finalize separately and arbitrarily.

Guarding against nzload overload - As many know, the Mustang has an upper limit for how many nzload instances can be live at the same time. In a multi-threaded, on-demand loading model, each of the loading sessions can load multiple files in parallel. With multiples of these in place, we could easily see a breach of the total nzload threads. As with the aforementioned synchronization scenario, we also applied this to the intake module in a more surgical manner. It would simply check the Unix process queue for nzload instances. If these were at or near a predefined threshold, it would pause and wait. This guaranteed that no more than the threshold were running at the same time, regardless of how many on-demand sessions were underway. This also allowed the loading operations to self-regulate.

As a note, nzload can now self-regulate in this regard with common settings, so that it does not exceed a total count of load sessions. Is there *anything* that NPS 6.0 can't do?

Manifest-file loading - As noted in Underground, we took manifest-loading to a higher level. In this paradigm, the manifest file serves as a trigger file, containing the metadata describing multiple files to load into multiple tables. Each line in the file contains the full URL/filename and the target table to load. The loader uses this to shepherd the data into the machine. Several major, proven benefits were derived from this approach.

- Trigger and re-trigger - we could use the manifest file for repeatable testing of the same data.
- Special-use - we could leverage the manifest format for other uses such as dynamic derivation of the source and target. One particular example was of an Excel file with multiple record types in it. By using one manifest to receive the file, we could chop it into its constituent files, wrap them in a temporary manifest file and then submit this for loading, all in a decoupled, self-contained manner
- Automation - we could define pre-fab manifests for performing scheduled extraction
- Database extraction - not for loading files only, we could define an extraction as a file stream and load data database-to-database
- Flow-handoff - when executing a load, we may naturally want to handoff to a transform as the next downstream operation
- Upstream publication - sources that produce the data could easily manufacture and present

a manifest file because of its simplicity and straightforward format

- Ease of integration - in its trigger-file role, we could also (internally) formulate download-ed file streams from disparate sources, wrap them in a manifest file as a self-contained operation, then present them to the trigger directory. This would send all file streams through a common loading protocol, but also alleviated the headache of attempting to perform an nzload another way.

- Decoupled extract-and-load - we could formulate an extraction from a primary database, send each of its table contents to their respective files, formulate a manifest around them and then present the manifest as a trigger, all in decoupled form. We could also instantiate an instance of an ETL tool no differently than an extract from a database The ETL tool would then extract, formulate the data files, wrap them with a manifest file and present it to the trigger directory, all under central orchestration.

Intake data scrubbing, finalization data scrubbing - we were able to apply, via metadata, standard defaults (at the type-level) and specific DDL defaults at the table/column level. This kept dirt and nulls from entering the machine, and ultimately from entering the master data stores.

Metadata-awareness - In this implementation, we did not have the option to make the SQL-transform templates metadata-aware. That is, should the data model change, we would be able to merge the changes into the SQL-transforms, adding new columns and deprecating old ones. Or at a minimum, provide an impact analysis of the changes. We were, however, able to implement a wide range of metadata-aware capabilities that ultimately stabilized and fortified the long-term resilience of the solution.

One of the pitfalls, noted in another section of this book, was the inability to deploy formulated reporting tables to support the users (as a matter of policy, not technology). The reports were pointed to the operational model and suffered for it. As of this writing, the originally proposed reporting model has been deployed and the users are very happy with the response times.

Another note, a movement was afoot to attempt to get the operational model to work with the reports, in a Quixotic ploy to avoid purchasing more Netezza hardware. The client had needed more hardware even before the problem with the reports arose, so attempting to derail this transaction was counterproductive. They did in fact deploy more hardware, but this provided additional impetus to roll out the reporting model, not keep it out.

In addition, the principals involved in the project required a significant education in how to build and deploy these kinds of solutions. The technologists on the project were consummately professional in their patience while waiting for the principals to come up to speed. Once this was squared away, the entire team became more productive.

BI Tool Malaise - We experienced some malaise in the implementation of the BI tool, but this was in part because of the reluctance of the principals to embrace a reporting-centric data model. It was also borne on the lack of architectural skill of the principals as they wrangled with the chief reports architect, who really knew his stuff but did not have a voice. This was eventually overcome when all efforts to remediate report performance failed and the principals acquiesced to installing the dimensional reporting model. Only then did we see lift in the reports. However, it required the reports architect to rip out a significant amount of engineering he had put in place trying to make up for the weak performance of the data model. This is a clear example of how a failure to follow simple, easy-to-implement best practices (a simple reporting model) led to malaise and over-engineering in the consumption layer.

This is a universal truth of all data integration problems. They rise from the system layer, into the data layer and finally the application layer. Disconnected systems create instability and over-coding in the data and application layers, Likewise a stable system but a disconnected data layer creates over-coding in the application layer. Finally, an integrated system and data layer could still lead to over-coding in the application layer if the other two layers are unstable or dirty.

Over-engineering in one layer, or rather in a downstream component is usually the result of an upstream component not-taking-care-of-business. If we see over-coding in the reporting layer, it is time to refactor the data and system layers so that we can simplify the reporting layer. There is no benefit in an overcoded reporting layer. It is too hard to maintain and becomes brittle over time. Our reports architect was wise in ripping out all the extra trappings once the data layer was squared away.

But the significant takeaway here: the Netezza platform is packaged so the system and data layer are delivered with a bow tied on them. We can simplify because the majority of the effort is already complete when we install the machine and power-up.

14 CLOSING ARGUMENTS

This concludes the broadcast of this message. You may now return to your regularly scheduled programming, or shell-scripting or alas, hand-coding those SQL-Transforms. (Call me)

As we've seen in the prior pages, there's a better way. Set-based, generated transform logic, derived from the Netezza catalog and fully metadata-aware. It's just metadata programming after all. It's doable, and you're just the one to do it.

Or hey, give me a shout and I'll show you how to do it in person. Our firm happily helps En-zees realize their goals, objectives and sometimes even their dreams. We're not a dream-factory, though. We leave the dreaming up to you. We're more like, hmmm, dream *brokers*.

Transformation carries a lot of different meanings for different people, but hopefully in our short time together, we received at least a glimpse of the possibilities in our own work. Perhaps these pages helped us get past a bump in the road. Perhaps we handed it off to a lackey with the directive "make it so." Hey, I'm just here to help you get there.

Catch up with me on the Netezza community or as chance would have it, IBM developer-Works, where another blog is now gathering steam. I have officially wrested the rights for the *Netezza Underground* name from its prior enslavement, and now I can use it any way I choose. So for now, also find me on the Netezza Underground blog, generously provided by the kind folks at developerWorks.

Is there another publication underway? Let's just say I have enough material to write several more, and hopefully it won't take a year or two to make it happen. Not to worry, in that time I'll be working alongside some of you, stoking the fires of the locomotive.

We are living through a historical pivot in the technology industry as a whole. Some would say these kind of things happen every several years anyhow, so what's the big deal? No, this one is different. In almost twenty-five years of direct application of large-scale solutions, I've never seen a technology affect so many, so profoundly in so many ways, and in such *scale*. This book only provides a glimpse of the transformation. Our opportunity is but to get on the wave and ride it.

And it's a good ride, indeed.

SPLASHDOWN

THE FOLLOWING CONTENT serves as a an Appendix of sorts, containing code snippets, handy functions and stuff that can make metadata-parsing quick and painless. Some say that metadata belongs only in the database, but this entire book shows that the most effective approach is to activate the metadata by redirecting it to a more useful purpose. Metadata can provide information and it can be the impetus for action.

I'll start out here with some code snippets for the parts that I used in the examples. You can probably find similar snippets on various web sites on bash. This stuff is fairly common.

The bash functions below are to parse simple strings. I will give the snippet and then some examples.

```
#===================================
str_get_word()      #Returns the word at position in list
#===================================
# Arg_1 = position
# Arg_n = list
{
    echo $@ | cut -f2- -d\ | cut -f$1 -d\

}
```

Be careful if you copy the the one above, as there can be no space value after the last -d\ because the "\" character must be the last character in the line or the function won't work.

Let's say we have a string with the values:

```
str1="The quick brown fox"
```

And we execute to find values:
```
mret=$(str_get_word 2 "$str1")
```
The value of mret is now "quick"

```
mret=$(str_get_word 4 "$str1")
```
the value of mret is now "fox"

```
#===================================
str_get_word_delim()     #Returns the word at position in list
```

```
#========================================================
# Arg_1 = position
# Arg_2 = delim
# Arg_n = list
{
    VAR1=$(echo $@ | cut -f2- -d$2  | cut -f$1 -d$2 )
    echo $VAR1

}
```

In the above function, we can use it to parse for tokens that exist between the given delimeter character. In most cases, the delimiter can be put inside quotes, but in others you might need to assign it to a variable and then pass it inside.

```
str1="this@is@a@delimited string"
```

```
f1=$(str_get_word_delim 2 "@" "$str1" )
```
f1 is now equal to "is"

```
f1=$(str_get_word_delim 4 "@" "$str1" )
```
f1 is now equal to "delimited string"

That was simple, now let's put some structured text through a chop-shop. We want the values inside the first two parenthesis.

```
str1="primary(pk1, pk2) foreign(fk1, fk2)"
f1=$(str_get_word_delim 2 "(" "$str1" )      #chop between the two "("
f2=$(str_get_word_delim 1 ")" "$f1" )        #chop before the first ")"
k1=$(str_get_word_delim 1 "," "$f2" )        #snip before the first ","
k2=$(str_get_word_delim 2 "," "$f2" )        #snip after the first ","
```

f1 is now equal to "pk1, pk2) foreign"
f2 is now equal to "pk1, pk2"
k1 is now equal to "pk1"
k2 is now equal to "pk2"

```
#================================================
str_toupper() #Finds / replaces all occurrences of match in source
#================================================
# Arg_1 = source string

{
VAR1=$( echo $1 | awk {'print toupper($_)'} )
echo $VAR1
}

str1="This is a string"
```

285

```
str1=$(str_toupper  "$str1" )
str1 is now "THIS IS A STRING"
```

Sendmail for notification purposes.

The sendmail utility for linux is functional but a little clunky to operate, so here is a standard way to send a message body along with attachment (like a log file).

What we'll do is take make a separately executable file, roll all the statements we want to execute into it as a single structured command, and then execute the file. This sounds a bit like overkill, I know, but sendmail has some nuances that are not easily accommodated with a plain flat command stream.

First, make a file:

```
mailcall=$(create_temp_file)    #create a unique file for local use

SP_LT="<"
SP_B="!"
SP_P="|"
#===================================
mailcall=$(create_temp_file mailcall txt )
echo "(cat ${SP_LT}${SP_LT}${SP_B}; uuencode \"${LOGFILE}\" \"logfile.txt\" ) $SP_P
${SENDMAIL_FACILITY} -t -oi " > $mailcall
echo "To: $RECIPIENT " >> $mailcall
echo "Subject: [${APP_DIR}] Job Notification for AUDIT_ID=$AUDIT_ID " >> $mailcall
echo "" >> $mailcall
echo "---------------------------------------------------" >> $mailcall
cat $MAIL_FILE >> $mailcall
echo $SP_P >> $mailcall
chmod 777 $mailcall


#now execute the mail to send it out
$mailcall
```

If the data in $MAIL_FILE is as follows:

Job Completed
Status was Normal
Errors follow:
############
None found
############

And the Recipient is say, me dbirmingham@mymail.com

We can expect the contents of $mailfile to look like this:

```
(cat <<!; uuencode \"/logfileurl/logfilename.log\" \"logfile.txt\" ) | /bin/sendmail -t -oi "
To: dbirmingham@mymail,net
Subject: [ my application directory ] Job Notification for AUDIT_ID=21545


-------------------------------------------------
Job Completed
Status was Normal
Errors follow:
############
None found
############
```

Create a temporary file for local use. This function allows me to create a temporary file that is completely unique, and will place the file into housekeeping automatically so I don't have to worry about it later.

```
#=======================================================
create_temp_file()  #creates temp file and housekeeps it
#=======================================================
{
#   $1 = calling module - eg loader, mapper, backfill, etc
#   $2 = function - eg ins, del, sql, txt, etc

#   $3 = "PIPE" makes a pipe not a file
#   $3 = "NAME" makes nothing and gives the file name only
#   $3 = "" make the file normally
#   $3 = "KEEP" housekeep in archive rather than immediately after run
#   $3 = "EXTRACT" place file in separate extract dir, not local TMP dir

MODULE=$1
if [  "x${MODULE}" = "x" ] ; then MODULE=temp ; fi
FN=$2
if [  "x${FN}" = "x" ] ; then FN=tmp ; fi


#Now make it unique to the thread and to the job, and in time to the nano
mc=$(date '+%Y%m%d%H%M%S%5N' )
mpid=$$
mpid=${mpid}_${AUDIT_ID}

#now based on type, make the asset and return the full name
FTYPE=$3

if [ "x${FTYPE}" = "xNAME" ]
```

```
then
mfile=$TMP_DIR/${MODULE}_${mc}_${WORKFILE}_${mpid}_${FN}_temp
mret=$(housekeep_add $mfile )


elif [ "x${FTYPE}" = "x" ]
then
mfile=$TMP_DIR/${MODULE}_${mc}_${WORKFILE}_${mpid}_${FN}_temp
touch $mfile
chmod 777 $mfile
mret=$(housekeep_add $mfile )


elif [ "x${FTYPE}" = "xKEEP" ]
then
mfile=$TMP_DIR/${MODULE}_${mc}_${WORKFILE}_${mpid}_${FN}_temp
touch $mfile
chmod 777 $mfile
mret=$(housekeep_archive_add $mfile )


elif [ "x${FTYPE}" = "xTMPKEEP" ]
then
mfile=/tmp/${MODULE}_${mc}_${WORKFILE}_${mpid}_${FN}_temp
touch $mfile
chmod 777 $mfile
mret=$(housekeep_archive_add $mfile )



elif [ "x${FTYPE}" = "xEXTRACT" ]
then
mfile=$EXTRACT_FILE_MOUNT/${MODULE}_${mc}_${WORKFILE}_${mpid}_${FN}.dat
touch $mfile
chmod 777 $mfile
mret=$(housekeep_archive_add $mfile )

elif [ "x${FTYPE}" = "xPIPE" ]
then
mfile=$PIPE_DIR/${MODULE}_${mc}_${WORKFILE}_${mpid}_${FN}_temp
mkfifo $mfile -m 777
chmod 777 $mfile
mret=$(housekeep_add $mfile )


elif [ "x${FTYPE}" = "xTMPPIPE" ]
then
mfile=/tmp/${MODULE}_${mc}_${WORKFILE}_${mpid}_${FN}_temp
mkfifo $mfile -m 777
chmod 777 $mfile
mret=$(housekeep_add $mfile )


fi

echo $mfile
}
```

Rather than show examples of the actual SQL executed to manufacture stuff, let's walk through a simple control model for activating all this. Bear with me, because my intent here is to virtualize the framework as part code, part metacode, and part rules that make metacode from code.

So here are several workhorse functions and what they mean.

The first is a way to take the current working database (the context of the current operations) and the current working table, converting them to a function-call prefix. When we compile rules, we will formulate these functions and simply load them into memory. The framework will then call the functions at the appropriate processing point, and discover that the information exists, or it does not. If not, we will do something else at that juncture in the code. If it exists, we'll incorporate the results and keep moving. Either way, the metadata-driven metafunctions have been preformulated so that we don't have to calculate and recalculate.

For example, lets say in our database for Sales Intake, we have a table called Vendors. This table has a distribution key. We will define this parameter in our rules file, and then use a simple rules compiler to make a function call out of it:

```
[DISTRIBUTION]
TABLE=VENDORS COLUMN=Vendor_id, Vendor_Date
```

We would want to access the distribution key one way, that is to call a function associated with that database and table, to retrieve the distribution key. In a language like C++, this is done with overloading and other object-relational techniques. In our case, we just want the overloaded function name, would convert the above notation into the following:

```
intk_sales_vendors_distribution()
{
echo "Vendor_id, Vendor_date"
fi
```

and now we can simply call it:

```
mkey=$(intk_sales_vendors_distribution)
```

So the rules compiler looks for the rules around distribution, then manufactures these function calls with their instructions, purely to return the distribution keys for the table.

We would have a definition like the above for each table with a distribution, otherwise we'll just assume it's RANDOM.

If we have a single file where this and other such definitions are placed:

```
auto.intk_sales.config
```

Then all we have to do is load this file and all those predefined function calls, including the distribution key calls, are now in memory and waiting for us to access. How do we do this? The following function call helps us formulate the prefix for these function calls based on our current runtime context:

```
#=====================
function_exec_prep()
#=====================
{
MDB=$(nz_db_suffix $1 )      # get the portable database name (e.g. REP)
MDB=$(s_tolower $MDB )       # lower-case it
MTB=$(s_tolower $2 )         # get the table name, and lower-case it
MTX="${MDB}_$MTB"            #now concat the two, for a prefix to our work
echo $MTX                    #send me the result
}
```

So if my Working Database happens to be BL_JS_DEV1_INTK_SALES, and my table happens to be Vendors:

```
fnprefix=$( function_exec_prep $WORKING_DB $TARGET_TAB )
#fnprefix is now equal to "intk_sales_vendors"
```

Now in order to execute it, I need a way to first verify that it has been loaded in memory. After all, if a given table has never been given distribution keys, it won't have a definition for this function call (our rules compiler would not have made one). This notation uses the declare command to determine if the given function call actually exists or not.

```
#=======================
function_exec()
#=======================
{
declare -f ${1} > /dev/null    #try to locate the bash function in memory
mret=$?                         #capture return statis
if [ $mret -eq 0 ]              #did we find it?
then                            #yes, it's in memory all right
mval=$(${1} "$2" "$3" "$4" )   #then execute it with the additional parameters
fi
echo "$mval"
return $mret
}
```

Now we will execute the following:

```
dist_keys=$( function_exec ${fnprefix}_distribution )
```

Note how the above dovetails into the predefined function call, and will execute it if present, otherwise not. Either way the result is driven from the rules rather than cumbersome defaults or command-line parameters. While some look at this scenario and say that it is inflexible, it carries the right level of flexibility to support the following critical areas of SQL-based transforms, flow control and content control:

- It can't be easily hacked with command line or default overrides. If the function call exists in memory, it is the arbiter of the rule. The rule is predefined and the rules file/functions are precompiled.
- It is metadata-driven, and is just as stable and flexible as the existing DDL definitions
- It is dovetailed into the DDL definitions. After all, I can also derive distribution keys for a table at the time of the table's construction, then leverage them elsewhere in the transform model for key-based validations, cross-referencing or referential checks etc.
- The auto-load version of the file is packaged with the run-time, not the rules file that created it. This will make it even more difficult to justify a change to the file's content since it is the product of a factory, not hand-crafted SQL.

Lastly we have another handy function call that allows us to name a given parameter along with its default. If the function call is found, we get the value for the key. If the key is not found, or the function is not found, we get the default value:

```
#========================
function_val()
#========================
{
declare -f ${1} > /dev/null     #try to find the function in memory
mret=$?                          #capture the status
if [ $mret -eq 0 ]               #if found?
then                             # then execute with paramters
mval=$(${1} "$2" "$3" )
else                             #otherwise
mval=$3                          #default it to the second parameter
fi
echo "$mval"                     #and send it back to me
return $mret                     #also give me the status
}
```

As an example, if we wanted to set up the skiprows parameter of the nzload utility as something configured with a rule:

```
[LOADER PARMS]
TABLE=Vendors VALUE=1 FUNCTION=SKIP_ROWS
```

Now when we call the above, function_val, we would use three values, one for function_val, one for the name of the variable, and one for the default (or current) value.

```
SKIP_ROWS=$( function_val ${fnprefix}_loader_parms SKIP_ROWS ${SKIP_ROWS} )
```

We will need to manufacture a script at the larger, database level, to include the rules for all the tables it deals with. Since it is dynamically selected at run-time from a post-deployment location, we need to prepare beforehand.

So what's the secret-sauce in each one of these scripts? I'm glad you asked, because they will all be the product of a centralized factory, so all of them will behave the same even though they have the subtle nuances of different table names, keys and so forth, the solution for each is thematic and pattern-based. Now, we could set up a bash function that accepts table names and manufactures these queries on-the-fly. But I think what you will find (as I did) that the process of SQL generation has significant overhead, and if we can take this overhead once through a compiler function, deploy a canned script and then execute it, we get the benefits of precompilation as well as operational consistency. Win-win.

ABOUT THE AUTHOR

DAVID BIRMINGHAM is an enterprise solution architect who jaunts about in both the Overground and the Underground, as it were. He drives the Best Practices sessions at the Enzee Universe conferences and generally keeps abreast of the technology in a massively parallel way. If you're reading this, you may have already met him. If not, you might meet him soon, but it's all good.

He is a Senior Principal Consultant with Brightlight Consulting, a firm that has wrangled more large-scale dragons with Netezza than any other firm. The views expressed by Mr. Birmingham are not necessarily those of Brightlight Consulting, but he's okay with that.

Mr. Birmingham graduated in 1985 with a degree in Computer Science from Stephen F. Austin State University in Nacogdoches, Texas, still the best computer science school on the planet.

Since that time, Mr. Birmingham's 26 years of derring-do are comprised of adventures in military software engineering, high-speed optical processing, neural networks, artificial intelligence and expert systems, financial services, health care, pharmaceuticals, retail and various adventures with disparate enterprise technologies, spanning a wide range of problem domains, all of them large-scale and high-stakes.

But *yours* is a large-scale and high-stakes problem domain, too, isn't it? You won't hear anything else here but *Welcome to the Club!* Pull up a chair and let's talk war stories. Anyone in this domain is more than welcome and will always find a smile, a coffee, a danish (or two) and we don't turn anyone away!

In keeping with the spirit of the Underground, what happens in the Underground, *stays* in the Underground. Likewise if you discover any errata in the book, forward it on. We like to be accurate more than we like to be first.

References

[1]*Netezza Underground*, Copyright (c) 2008 VMII. All Rights Reserved. Referenced by permission. The context of the reference *definitely* reflects the views of the author(s).

[2]*Advanced Dimensional Modeling*, Copyright (c) 2007 EWSolutions, All Rights Reserved. Referenced by permission. The context of the reference and the content of this book do not necessarily reflect the views of EWSolutions.

About the cover

This is a Monarch butterfly emerging from its chrysalis. Think about the butterfly's prior existence, It was a caterpillar for quite some time, bound to the forces of gravity, doomed to walk the earth at its lowest levels, fodder for predators of all kinds, a grub moving among the twigs, fallen leaves and rotten forest floor detritus, with speeds that would make even a snail shudder in awe.

Then one day it secretes a chrysalis shell around itself. Inside this shell, the organism doesn't just sprout new body parts. It *liquefies*, literally self-digesting in its own juices through a process call hystolisys. Then from this soup arises a form that is so utterly different from its prior existence, the two would not know each other even if they met on the street.

Now the butterfly defies gravity, has a glorious existence as companion to the wind, the Sun and the most beautiful flowers on the planet. Whence came this transformation, and how would the butterfly explain its new form to another caterpillar? I'm just sayin'....

The butterfly epitomizes transformation in the *metamorphic* sense, where old and new are not remotely similar.

On the back over, there is mention of the Truth v4.2, which is an allusion to *The Hitchhiker's Guide to the Galaxy*, where the `Answer to the Ultimate Question of Life, the Universe and Everything` was analytically derived to be the value "42". I simply divided it by ten, and it seemed to fit.

Other Acknowledgements

The following corporations and groups reserve all copyrights and other rights to their registered trademarks and marketing. All descriptions of their respective technologies are likewise registered.

Netezza is a registered trademark of Netezza Corporation, an IBM Company

"It's what's for dinner" is a registered trademark of the Cattlemen's Beef Board and National Cattlemen's Beef Association.

- The **Butterfly** photo is part of Wikimedia Commons, courtesy Captain-Tucker.
- **Disney** and all its wonders are registered trademarks of Walt Disney Corporation.
- **Microsoft**, .NET and SQLServer are registered trademarks of Microsoft Corporation.
- **Teradata** is a registered trademark of NCR and Teradata Corporations.
- **Sybase** and **IQ** are registered trademarks of Sybase Corporation.
- **Ab Initio** is a registered trademark of Ab Initio Software Corporation.
- **Chevrolet, Chevy** and **Nova** are all registered trademarks of General Motors Corporation.
- **Oracle/Exadata** are a registered trademarks of Oracle Corporation.
- **Jurassic Park** is copyrighted by Michael Crichton.
- **"Great Scott!"** - Emmet Brown quote (back cover) from Spielberg's *Back to the Future*

Architecture-centric modeling concepts are copyrighted by VMII, the author and Apress / Expert's Voice.

This book claims no rights or ownership to any registered trademark or copyright, whether used or implied in this work, that at the time of this publication is not already owned or registered by any entity other than Virtual Machine Intelligence Inc.

The views and opinions of Mr. Birmingham are his own. They do not necessarily reflect the opinions of any of the aforementioned entities, current or past employers, clients, vendor partners or any other entity acknowledged or mentioned in this work.

The "Case Studies" and "Case Study Shorts", as well as mention of "RDBMS" have either been generalized or scrubbed to appropriately hide the identity of the actors and institutions, such that any claims to specificity are coincidental, inappropriate and unwarranted. For those who would complain otherwise, our standard answer is, "It's not about you."

INDEX